PETER BOHRMANN

bartender's
the
guide

PETER BOHRMANN

the bartender's guide

COOMBE BOOKS

5140 The Bartender's Guide
This edition published in 1999 by Coombe Books

ISBN 1-84100-301-8

Printed in Singapore

FALKEN Verlag wish to thank BORCO-MARKEN-IMPORT
MATTHIESEN & CO. KG for kindly providing the liquor and liqueurs
used in the photographs: De Kuyper Jonge Jenever, Oude Jenever; Van
Gogh (advocaat), Blue Curaçao, Red Curaçao, Triple Sec Orange
Liqueur, Green Curaçao, Crème de Menthe (green), Melon Liqueur,
Crème de Cacao (white), and Crème de Cacao (brown); Old Pascas
Light and Dark Rum; Sierra Silver, Gold, and Antiguo Tequila; Nassau
(orange liqueur); Gran Duque d'Alba (brandy); McGuinness Old
Canada (whisky); Finsbury Dry Gin; Pennypacker (Kentucky whiskey);
Nêga Fulô (cachaça); and Pisco Control Gran Pisco

German edition
Editor: Birgit Wenderoth
Photography: TLC-Foto-Studio GmbH, Velen-Ramsdorf
Illustrations and layout: AS-Design—Ilse Stockmann-Sauer, Offenbach
Design: FALKEN Verlag, D-65527 Niedernhausen/Taunus

English edition
Translation: Karen Green
in association with First Edition Translations Ltd, Cambridge, UK
Cover design: Philip Chidlow
Editor: Joseph F Ryan

TABLE OF CONTENTS

INTRODUCTION

RECIPES

APPENDICES

FOREWORD

If you like welcoming guests into your home and particularly enjoy being a good, imaginative host, be sure to include the contents of your bar or drinks cupboard in your hospitality arrangements. Why not offer guests an aperitif, for example, which turns anticipation of a good meal into a pleasure? Or, try offering an after-dinner cocktail instead of the more usual brandies or liqueurs.

The recipes in this book will help you to satisfy your guests' every desire, because you will find something for every occasion, from short to long drinks, from the traditional, classic cocktails through to fancy cocktails. Armed with this book, you will be equipped for your next party—after all, it has been written by an expert who is a master of his trade.

Jürgen E. Falcke

Foreword

Wherever merry, sociable people meet, they enjoy having a drink. Attractive drinks are always popular and recipes are becoming ever more imaginative. But mixing drinks can be just as pleasurable as drinking them when you see how easily delicious, beautifully decorated cocktails can be prepared with just a few ingredients.

It, therefore, gives me great pleasure to set you on the path to becoming a successful amateur cocktail mixer with the help of my knowledge and my professional tips. This book is intended to make mixing cocktails easy and a lasting pleasure, and to provide you with a good reference book to help make your next cocktail party, summer barbecue, Caribbean evening, or birthday party as enjoyable as possible.

I hope this book gives you an insight into the colorful world of drinks, and I wish you every success in mixing—and consuming—them!

Peter Bohrmann
Master bartender

BAR EQUIPMENT

You really do not have to be a professional bartender to be able to mix original drinks, providing you use the appropriate tools for the job. You will certainly find some of the utensils listed below already in your home, and you can always improvise with everyday kitchen gadgets. If, however, you go shopping to stock up on bar equipment, the important feature to remember is that the utensils should be easy to clean, which is why stainless-steel items and glass are particularly suitable.

A **cocktail shaker** is an absolute must for your home bar. It is primarily used to mix drinks with ingredients that are difficult to combine smoothly, such as egg yolks, liqueurs, fruit juices, and cream. Any good bar-supply store will stock a variety of shakers and you are certain to find one to fit your budget and needs. One standard version is a three-part shaker, which consists of a beaker, a lid, and a built-in strainer, to hold back pieces of ice and fruit pits or seeds when pouring the cocktail. Its disadvantage is that the strainer is very difficult to clean and the liquid pours out slowly. The two-part Boston shaker consists of a large stainless-steel beaker and a smaller one made of lead crystal, which fits inside and has the advantage that the glass beaker is also suitable for use as a mixing glass. I find professionals usually favor a two-part stainless-steel or silver shaker because it is easier to close than the Boston shaker.

When you use a two-part shaker or a mixing glass, you will need a round, stainless-steel **bar strainer**. This features an edge like a coiled spring, and it should fit exactly into the top of the shaker or mixing glass, making it indispensable when straining cocktails so ice and pieces of fruit or pits do not fall into the glass. If necessary, you can use a new tea strainer instead.

You will also need a mixing glass, sometimes called a shaker glass, for every drink which is stirred, not shaken, such as clear drinks and those made from easily blended ingredients. When shopping for a mixing glass, look for one with a capacity of about 1 quart (enough for 3 or 4 drinks).

A long-handled **bar spoon** is a versatile tool used by bartenders to stir the ingredients in the mixing glass, as a measuring spoon to add the correct amount of ingredients to many cocktails, and to crush flavoring ingredients. Most bar-spoon handles are 10 inches long and made of stainless steel or silver. At the top of the handle there is

Bar Equipment

usually a disc called a muddler used to "muddle," or crush, pieces of fruit, herbs, or sugar cubes. The spoon on the opposite end holds ⅙ ounce of liquid, or the same amount as a standard kitchen teaspoon. The rounded back of the spoon is also useful for slowly pouring layers of liqueurs into a glass when you do not want the layers to mix (see, for example, the Pousse-Café recipes). A bar whisk is also useful for stirring and mixing.

A truly indispensable item for your bar is a double-ended **bar measure**, because exact quantities of ingredients are needed for every drink. Also called a pony-jigger measure, these are usually made of stainless steel with a 1-ounce cup at one end, called a pony, and a 1½- to 2-ounce measure at the other end, called a jigger. When you go shopping, look for a measure with easy-to-read ¼-ounce and ½-ounce markings inside the jigger end. Alternatively, you can use a standard shot glass with markings on it. If you do not have either measure, use a standard set of kitchen measuring spoons—3 teaspoons, or 1 tablespoon, equal ½ ounce, 4 teaspoons equal ¾ ounce, and 2 tablespoons equal 1 ounce.

An **electric blender** is useful, especially for drinks like frozen daiquiris and those with ingredients that are not easily combined, but it is not essential. To purée fruit, whip cream, or prepare frozen drinks, frappés, and milk shakes, you need a blender with continuous speed adjustment, or you can use an everyday food processor. If drinks with

1 Bar spoon
2 Bar whisk
3 Bar strainer
4 Bar measure
5 Blender
6 Shaker
7 Mixing glass

crushed ice become a regular request at your bar or you host many cocktail parties, consider investing in an electric ice shaver.

Use a standard **ice bucket**, widely available in various sizes and materials, to keep frozen ice cubes conveniently at hand for the duration of any party or cocktail session. Ice tongs or an ice shovel are ideal to remove the ice from the bucket (do not use your fingers), but if you do not have either, use a large spoon.

Fresh fruit juices can be prepared using a lemon squeezer or juicer. (Electric juicers are not recommended because they squash the peel and seeds, too.) Many long drinks contain soda water, which is best added to the glass using a siphon. To use one, you simply fill the siphon with water from the faucet or use still mineral water. A carbon dioxide cartridge will make sure the water is always carbonated when you want it.

Another very useful tool is a pair of **bar tongs**, which can be used to loosen tight corks in champagne and other sparkling wines. A bitters or dash bottle has a doser cap and is good for storing ingredients that are only used in small dashes.

The other pieces of equipment that help to make your job behind the bar enjoyable are standard in most kitchens. These include a lemon squeezer and a nutmeg grater. No doubt your kitchen also

Juice press 1
Ice shovel 2
Siphon 3
Ice bucket 4
Dash bottle 5
Ice tongs 6
Spoon 7
Bar tongs 8

10

Bar Equipment

contains a chopping board (preferably with a drainage channel), a finely serrated knife, similar to a cheese knife, with two points for spearing pieces of fruit, and a citrus zester, also called a cannelle knife, for removing fine strips of citrus peel that make attractive garnishes. Small dishes for holding pieces of fruit and garnishes are also useful, as is a cork with a pouring spout, which can be inserted into any bottle to make pouring out measures easier.

Of course you also need a can opener, a bottle opener, and a corkscrew. A champagne or bottle cooler is indispensable. Toothpicks are an absolute must for spearing olives, cherries, and pearl onions, as well as for creating other garnishes. You might also want to stock up on brightly colored drinking straws in varying lengths if you plan to serve some of the more exotic cocktails. (Be sure to avoid straws which are too thin, otherwise pieces of ice or fruit can block them.) Different colored and shaped stirrers also make attractive decorations for long drinks.

 1 Small dish
 2 Chopping board
 3 Lemon squeezer
 4 Nutmeg grater
 5 Bottle cooler
 6 Drinking straws
 7 Toothpicks
 8 Stirrers
 9 Bottle opener
10 Bar knife
11 Cork with pourer
12 Corkscrew
13 Can opener
14 Citrus zester

THE ART OF GLASSWARE

Appearance is as important as taste when you are serving cocktails. Imaginative mixed drinks demand the appropriate glasses to enhance the flavor of the contents visually. Do not worry, though. You do not have to go out and buy all the glasses shown here. I suggest you start out with the glasses you already have and then slowly build up your stock as you discover which style of cocktail you make the most often. As a rule of thumb, six to eight different types of glass are adequate for a small home bar.

But first, a word about caring for your glassware. Always wash your glasses immediately after use, especially if you have used cream, milk, or eggs in the drinks. Also, take the time to wash your glasses separately from dishes and pots and pans in warm, soapy water. Then rinse them in clean, hot running water, so all traces of grease are removed. Gently dry the glasses with a clean linen dishtowel.

Here is a summary of the most common bar glasses. As you will see, your requirements will be determined by the cocktails you and your friends enjoy the most.

Glassware

Traditional **cocktail glasses** have sloping sides and a stem, making them ideal for drinks served without ice or large, elaborate fruit garnishes. But you may also find ones with a rounded cup, reminiscent of the popular style in the twenties and thirties and similar to **champagne glasses**. These come in a variety of sizes, with capacity ranging from 3 to 6 ounces. The large ones are most suited to drinks made with cream or fruit juice, and the smaller ones are perfect for dry aperitifs, other cocktails, and very alcoholic after-dinner drinks. By the way, the thinner a cocktail glass is, the quicker it will chill in the refrigerator.

Rocks glasses are short, with thick bottoms, and are also known as lowball glasses. They are so named because they are most commonly used for serving measures of straight liquor poured "on the rocks."
Old-fashioned glasses, another type of short glass with a bump in the bottom, are used for the eponymous classic blended whiskey and sweet vermouth drink. Both these glasses are interchangeable and come in a range of sizes, holding 4 to 10 ounces, while a double old-fashioned glass has a capacity of about 16 ounces.

Tall, straight **highball glasses**, holding about 8 ounces, are the ones to use for a spirit plus a mixer, such as scotch and soda or bourbon and water. **Collins glasses** are similar but larger and often frosted, and used for the sweetened gin and soda drink called a Tom Collins.

1 *Champagne glass*
2 *Small cocktail glass*
3 *Large cocktail glass*
4 *Collins glass*
5 *Rocks glass*
6 *Highball glass*
7 *Water glass*
8 *Old-fashioned glass*

Balloon-shaped **brandy snifters** range in size from 5 ounces, small enough to cradle in the palm of one hand, to ones for holding up to 3 cups of liquid. Whatever size you choose, however, the most important feature is the narrow opening. This allows the drinker to sniff the drink's concentrated aroma easily. Always remember only to pour a thin layer of brandy in the bottom of the glass—it should never be filled above one-quarter full.

An American-style **champagne glass**, also called a champagne saucer or a coupe, or a tall, European-style **champagne flute**, is the natural choice for serving any sparkling wine or aperitifs prepared with champagne or sparkling wine, such as Kir Royale.

Perhaps the most useful glasses to have behind the bar are wine glasses. The ideal **white wine glass** is thin with a tall stem and is tulip shaped, which bellies at the bottom and narrows at the top. The **red wine glass** has a shorter stem and is also slightly tulip shaped. The burgundy glass is the most versatile of the red wine glasses. It can, in fact, be used to serve beer and red aperitifs, too. A useful, inexpensive, everyday wine glass, with a balloon shape, which is suitable for serving either red or white wine and numerous cocktails, is called the **Paris goblet**. Note that when pouring wine, a big glass should be filled only half full, and a small glass only two-thirds full.

Dessert wines or brandies are served in a small, tulip-shaped **liqueur**

Brandy snifter 1
Red wine glass 2
Champagne flute 3
Champagne flute 4
Paris goblet 5
White wine glass 6
Liqueur glass 7
Liqueur saucer 8
Champagne glass 9

Glassware

or sherry glass, or in a liqueur saucer. You can also use the liqueur glass to serve fruit spirits and fruit eaux-de-vie. Dessert wine glasses are also appropriate for serving fortified wines, as well as flips, aperitifs, and other short drinks.

Alcoholic and nonalcoholic punches are popular for celebratory gatherings and other large parties. **Punch glasses** are squat glasses characterized by having a handle and wide opening, but not a stem. If you are serving a hot punch, grog, or mulled wine be sure to use a heatproof glass with a handle that will not become too hot to hold. In addition to the above classic types of glassware, there is also a plethora of special glasses, such as the **pousse-café glass** for the famous layered cocktail, the **flip glass**, the sour glass, and novelty glasses for just about every occasion. But, as already mentioned, it is only worth acquiring all these glasses in the rarest of cases, because most drinks can be served in glasses you already own, even if the style is not quite right. If, for example, you already have white wine glasses, use them for fizzes and crustas. If your champagne flutes are not too narrow, then you can also serve flips, frappés, and daisies in them. All kinds of tall glass or Collins glasses have versatile uses and, for example, are ideal for highballs, fizzes, and milkshakes.

Carafes or pitchers also have a place in your home bar. They are suitable for pouring fruit and vegetable juices, cream, and milk.

1 Flip glass or water glass
2 Pousse-café glass
3 Punch glass
4 Punch or fruit bowl
   glass

THE SECRET OF INGREDIENTS

DISTILLATIONS FROM WINE

Distillation is the centuries-old process used to produce alcohol. Heat is used to separate the components of a liquid, or mash, and as vaporization takes place the vapors are cooled so they condense into neutral spirits with little color, aroma, or flavor. The distiller then blends this neutral spirit with other alcohol or flavorings and may or may not leave it to mature, or age, until the desired flavor and aroma is achieved before bottling. Brandy and clear, colorless grappa are two examples of spirits distilled from wine, which you will find in most standard bar stocks. The following are the best-known distillations from wine produced in countries around the world.

Armagnac
Armagnac is a pale golden, fiery, dry-tasting French brandy. Under French law, only white grapes from the Haut-Armagnac, Tenareze, and Bas-Armagnac regions of Gascony, in southwest France, may be distilled for Armagnac. The distillation takes place after the grape harvest, which occurs between October and April. Unlike cognac, its younger cousin, Armagnac has traditionally been made with only one distillation, but a recent change in legislation means double distillation is now allowed, speeding up the maturation process, which takes place in oak barrels. Three stars on the label mean it has had at least two years' maturation; V.S.O.P., at least five years; Napoléon and X.O., at least six years; and Hors d'Age at least 10 years in the barrel. A vintage year on the label indicates the year of the harvest. A vintage Armagnac is never blended.

Brandy
First discovered in the middle of the thirteenth century in France as an attempt to produce a medicinal drink, brandy is now made around the world wherever grapes are grown. After two distillations, the clear, colorless alcohol is given its distinctive nutty brown color and flavor by aging in wood, often oak, barrels. The longer a brandy ages, the more refined its flavor is judged to be. In the United States,

domestic brandies are primarily from California, but there are many imports, some of which are highlighted here. Spanish brandies, which are light and taste slightly sweet, are among the best in the world, if not the best known. Italian vecchia Romagna and Portuguese single-distilled aguardente are also excellent brandies.

Cognac

Perhaps the best-known brandy in the world, cognac comes from a specific area in western France centered around the town of Cognac in the Charente region. To be labeled as "cognac," French legislation specifies the brandy can only be made from specific white grapes which are grown and later distilled within a strictly defined geographical area. Cognac production is governed by old traditions as well as the laws, so all the brandy is distilled at least twice and then matured in oak barrels for at least two years, during which time it develops its rich, brown color. The end result is 80 proof. Information on the label, also governed by law, explains the maturity of the cognac. Three stars or V.S. means the cognac has been matured in the barrel for at least two years; V.S.O.P., Vieux, V.O., and Réserve indicate at least four years; V.V.S.O.P. and Grande Réserve are cognacs matured for at least five years; Extra, Napoléon, X.O., Très Vieux, and Vieille Réserve are stored for six to 10 years in oak barrels.

Grappa

This clear, Italian spirit, about 80 proof, is distilled from the remains of the grapes used in wine production, the stems, skins, and pits. Grappa made from white wine is dry and fiery, while that from red wine has a powerful flavor. Although grappa is best known as an Italian spirit, versions of it are made in other countries, such as marc in France.

Marc

This French pomace spirit is distilled from the press residue resulting from wine production. Depending on the variety, it either tastes powerful and full flavored (marc de bourgogne) or light, dry, and very soft (marc de champagne). The alcohol content is between 80 and 90 proof. There is a flavor difference between marc made from red-wine and white-wine residues. A small glass of marc, served neat, is a perfect digestive.

Metaxa

The best-known Greek spirit, metaxa is distilled from black grapes. The alcohol content is about 80 proof. Stars on the label tell you how long the liquor was aged. Three stars means three years; five stars, five years; and seven stars, seven years. Bottles labeled as Private Reserve have been matured for at least 20 years, and have the smoothest flavor.

Pisco

This very tangy, colorless brandy is the national drink of Chile, and is the main ingredient in the refreshing cocktail Pisco Sour. Produced from black grapes with a high proportion of muscatel grapes, it is matured in clay casks.

Weinbrand

This German grape brandy, whose name translates as "burned wine," is distilled using some wines from neighboring countries, but legislation requires up to 85 percent of the final product to be German. It must then be matured for six months in oak casks holding a maximum of 1,000 liters (about 2,600 gallons) each. Old weinbrand must be cellared for a minimum of 12 months. If it is then at least 76 proof, it will receive an official reference number and can be sold. Like cognac, weinbrand is double distilled. Weinbrand should be served no warmer than room temperature, and is best served in a brandy snifter. If it is a little on the cool side, however, it does not matter because it will quickly attain the correct temperature through heat transferred from the hands.

DISTILLATIONS FROM GRAIN

Aquavit, genever, gin, and whiskey (or whisky as the Canadians and Scots spell it), as well as vodka and the unflavored German schnapps called korn, are all part of the extended family of grain-based spirits. Except for whiskey and korn, whose compositions are strictly controlled by legislation, these potent drinks can also contain so-called agricultural alcohol made from molasses, potatoes, and other ingredients.

Ingredients

Aquavit

The name of this strong Scandinavian spirit is derived from the Latin aqua vitae (water of life), and was once the designation for all liquor. The basis of the pale or golden-yellow aquavit is very pure, almost tasteless alcohol distilled from grain or potatoes with 96 percent alcohol by volume, or almost 200 proof. It is distilled with water and a variety of flavorings, such as caraway (the most traditional), cinnamon, cloves, coriander, dill, fennel, lemon peel, and star anise, along with a number of "secret" ingredients. The heart of the distillate is then mixed with neutral alcohol and softened water, and left to mature in the producer's cellars or warehouse. The alcohol content of Danish aquavit is 80 to 84 proof; German aquavit is 76 to 80 proof. Serve aquavit very cold in a short glass, similar to a shot glass; this is how its full, round, and distinctive taste develops. It acts as a stimulant on the stomach wall and is very easily digestible, so it is ideal to offer your guests after a meal as a digestive.

Genever

Genever is the Dutch national drink, and what is considered to be the first gin. The word genever developed from the French word genièvre (juniper), which is not surprising because genever, like some varieties of gin, has a juniper aroma. First-class genever is matured for several years in oak casks and is golden yellow. The alcohol content is 76 to 86 proof. The Dutch drink their genever neat and very cold in small, tulip-shaped glasses as an aperitif. Fruit-flavored genevers are also available.

Gin

This clear spirit is one of the drinks without which a bar would be lost. The alcohol is based on barley and rye, to which a mixture of selected herbs and spices, called botanicals, is added, such as angelica, aniseed, cardamom, coriander, juniper, and lemon and orange zests. After distillation, the gin is diluted to the customary drinking strength of 76 to 90 proof. "Dry gin," for example, is 80 proof. Gins, produced in England, Holland, and the United States, have different taste qualities. The most requested gins are those labeled as "dry gin" and "London dry gin." The dry designations developed to discriminate the contents from that which was labeled as "Old Tom gin" and "Plymouth Gin," both of which used to be much sweeter than they are today. Sloe gin is, in fact, a liqueur, not a gin, made by macerating crushed sloes in gin.

Klarer

This colorless, weak, and often flavorless spirit is made from potatoes, corn, and millet. The minimum alcohol content is 32 percent by volume, or 64 proof.

Korn schnapps

When a German orders a "schnapps," the chances are that it is this clear, grain-based spirit that is required, not the flavored, often creamy drinks called "schnapps" in the United States. Korn is the most popular drink in Germany, where it is traditionally drunk neat or as a chaser to beer. Produced from wheat, rye, barley, oats, or buckwheat, it has an alcoholic content of between 32 and 38 percent by volume, or 64 to 76 proof. If the designation Alt or Alter is on the label, the product has been matured for at least six months. Pure korn just tastes of grain, nothing else. If it is distilled from wheat, it is very mild; but if it is based on rye, it is powerful and spicy. Some varieties, called Kornbrand, contain a minimal addition of flavorings such as aniseed, cinnamon, cloves, or coriander. Apel Korn has been made with apples.

Vodka

In Russian, the meaning of the word vodka is "little stream." Vodka is a colorless, clear, smooth, and pure spirit with a neutral taste. It is distilled from mixtures of grains or potatoes. The top brands, however, consist only of grain (primarily barley and wheat, and occasionally rye). Its strength is usually at least 80 proof, with some brands being far more potent. Flavored vodkas have become popular and the range is constantly expanding. Widely available flavors include lemon, lime, pepper, and other fruits. In the United States, vodka is perhaps best known as the main alcoholic ingredient in Blood Marys and Screwdrivers, but in many countries it is drunk neat as a straight shot. When you serve neat vodka, make sure it is as near ice cold as possible. If you store your bottle in the freezer, the high alcohol content prevents the liquid turning to ice and it will always be ready to enjoy.

Whiskey

"Whiskey" may be the generic term for the most widely drunk liquor in the world, but you will find great variety, not least of all determined by where it is produced. Canada, Ireland, Scotland, and the United States are the great whiskey producers. Each country produces a different product, and within each country there is great diversity. Even the spelling of the word is not the same: the Americans and the Irish spell it "whiskey"; the Scots and the Canadians spell it "whisky."

Scottish whisky, or scotch as it is commonly known, is produced from malted barley or a mixture of grains, which can include malted and unmalted barley and the whole grains of cereals, such as corn or wheat. It is aged for at least three years in oak casks (traditionally secondhand sherry casks) before bottling. You will also see on the label if the scotch is blended or a single malt. Blended scotch, as the term implies, contains scotch from several distilleries and will contain malt and grain whiskies married together. Single malts, on the other hand, are produced from only malted barley. If the label on a blended whiskey also contains an age, that is how long the "youngest" whiskey in the blend was aged in the cask. One distinctive characteristic of some scotch, especially some single malts, is a smoky aroma. This occurs if the barley malt grains are dried over burning peat taken from the moorlands.

Irish whiskey, produced from barley, wheat, rye, or oats, is blended, with only one significant single malt produced. (The Irish use the term "vatting," not "blending.") After distillation, clear water is added to give the whiskey its final alcoholic content of about 80 proof. Irish whiskey is matured in wooden casks (for at least three years) that previously stored sherry, rum, or bourbon. As a general rule, Irish whiskey has a mellower flavor than scotch, and you will never find any with the smoky, peaty aroma of some scotches because the grains are not dried over peat-fueled fires. In the United States, Irish whiskey is best known as a component in Irish coffee or rich, creamy after-dinner drinks.

Of the American whiskeys, corn-based bourbon is king. Produced from at least 51 percent and up to a maximum of 80 percent corn mash, it also contains rye and a small proportion of barley malt. The greater the percentage of corn, the milder tasting is the whiskey. When bourbon contains 51 percent corn, it is called a straight whiskey; when it has 80 percent, it becomes a straight corn whiskey. After distillation, bourbon is matured for at least two years in new white-oak casks, which have been charred on the inside; this accelerates coloration of the whiskey and lends it a subtle sweetness and a faint vanilla flavor. (These casks are only used once for bourbon, which is why they are then sold to other whiskey producers, primarily in Ireland and sometimes in Scotland, where the character of their product relies on using bourbon-impregnated casks.) Good bourbon is aged for four to six years, but some is left much longer in the cask. Like scotch, bourbon is also available either blended or straight, the latter meaning that it has been distilled from a single grain and all the whiskey comes from a single distiller.

Rye whiskey, also popular with Americans and often simply referred to as rye, is distilled from a mash with at least 51 percent rye and matured for about four years. The taste is generally spicier than that of bourbon, and it also comes in blended and straight varieties.

Tennessee whiskey, which must be produced in the state to be labeled as such, is filtered through wood charcoal and is therefore very mild. Some of the best-known brands also have a distinct flavor, easily recognizable as different from bourbon because they are produced from a sour mash containing some previously fermented yeast (similar to the starter used to make sourdough bread; fresh yeast produces a sweet mash). This is the whiskey someone wants if they ask for a "sour mash whiskey."

American blended whiskey is a mixture of bourbon, rye whiskey, and corn whiskeys.

Canadian whisky is blended from straight grain whiskies and practically flavorless neutral alcohol, resulting in drink that is paler and lighter in flavor than most American whiskeys. This is why Canadian whisky is often used in drinks with soft-drink mixers, such as ginger ale.

DISTILLATIONS FROM FRUIT

There is practically no variety of fruit that cannot be enjoyed in alcoholic form, from cactus fruits from the desert or berries from the Arctic. But not all varieties of fruit are equally suitable for producing spirits. It depends greatly on the fruit's sugar content.

Eau-de-vie
This term is French for "water of life," and includes a wide range of colorless fruit brandies. Stone fruit, such as cherries, plums, apricots, and peaches, are most frequently used, but berries also flavor some of the best-known eau-de-vie. The fruits generally have so much natural sugar that the mash reaches 40 percent alcohol content by

Ingredients

volume, or 80 proof, during fermentation, so extra sugar is needed. One of the best-known examples is kirsch, or French cherry eau-de-vie, also called Kirschwasser in Germany. It is produced from fully ripe or fermenting cherries or from their juice, without any additional sugar and alcohol.

Plums are another popular ingredient for flavoring eau-de-vie across Europe. In Alsace, for example, blue plum eau-de-vie is called quetsch. In Germany, Zwetschgenwasser and Pflaumenwasser respectively are produced from ripe or fermenting blue or red plums. Mirabellenwasser is a spirit distilled from ripe yellow plums in Germany without the addition of extra sugar and alcohol. Eaux-de-vie made from quinces and apricots are also enjoyed.

Low-sugar fruits, such as raspberries, blackberries, and black currants, are at the heart of some equally popular eaux-de-vie. Their low-sugar content, however, means alcohol must be added to them before distillation, otherwise fermentation will not take place. Framboise, from France, has a mild, sweetish taste. Cassis, made from black currants, is combined with white wine to make Kir, the popular aperitif originally from Burgundy.

Poire William is an aromatic eau-de-vie, distilled from Williams pears. It has a soft flavor and a sweetish scent.

Tropical fruit eaux-de-vie are produced from bananas, mandarins, mangoes, passion fruit, and papayas.

Other fruit spirits

Another well-known fruit spirit is Calvados, an apple brandy made from the cider produced in Normandy in France. Under French law, the name "Calvados" can only be applied to distillations of cider which come from 11 specific areas. After distillation, Calvados is stored in oak or chestnut barrels and matured for at least two years. The older Calvados is, the more velvety and aromatic its taste. The color is amber to cognac brown. Calvados is a perfect digestive.

Calvados producers use a labeling system, similar to those on cognac and Armagnac, to indicate how long the spirit has aged in oak barrels. Three stars means at least two years; Vieux, Réserve, at least 3 years; V.O., Vieille Réserve, or V. S. O. P., at least 4 years; Extra or X. O., Napoléon, Hor's d'Age, and Age Inconnu, at least 6 years.

Other apple spirits, which can not be labeled as Calvados, are known as eau-de-vie de pomme, apple brandy, or aquardiente di sidre in Spain. In the United States, applejack is a domestic example of an apple brandy.

From Austria and Germany, Obstler is made from freshly fermented apples or pears, or a combination of both. The fruit variety must be listed on the label, and most brands are between 80 and 100 proof.

DISTILLATIONS FROM PLANTS AND ROOTS

Aniseed-flavored spirits
Some 1,500 years before Christ, these licorice-flavored spirits were valued as healing agents by the Egyptians. In the nineteenth century, absinthe, a potent aniseed aperitif distilled from wormwood, became a highly fashionable drink on both sides of the Atlantic, but intemperate enjoyment of it proved dangerous because it often led to madness or death. Consequently, early in the twentieth century, it was banned in many countries.

In the meanwhile, however, a plethora of "benign" successors developed; aniseed drinks which, in France, are known as pastis. They are based on star anise, with the essential oils being distilled and then mixed with sugar, pure alcohol, and various flavorings, such as mint, lemon balm, herbes de Provence, and licorice. Pernod and Ricard are among the well-known brands from France (now also available as an alcohol-free drink), and anisette is a spiced liqueur.

Greek ouzo and Turkish raki are also members of this big family of aniseed-flavored spirits. Ouzo is a sweet aniseed drink at 80 to 90 proof. Raki tastes dry and spicy, is not as sweet as ouzo, and is available at 80 to 100 proof.

Arrak
Similar to rum, this Asian spirit is distilled from sugarcane molasses with the addition of Indonesian red rice. Arrak is aged in oak barrels before it is bottled. The most respected variety comes from Batavia, in Indonesia, but similar drinks using a variety of ingredients, such as dates, also come from Goa in India, Sri Lanka, and Thailand.

Cachaça
This is a Brazilian spirit distilled directly from the juice of the sugarcane. The best-known cachaça is the straw-colored, clear Pitú. It has a soft, mild aroma and is 82 proof.

Ingredients

Rum

Formerly the drink of bootleggers, pirates, smugglers, and slave traders, rum was for centuries the most commonly traded contraband. The home of rum is in the Caribbean islands of Jamaica, Martinique, Puerto Rico, and Cuba. Here, as in the past—and among the Atlantic coastal countries of Central and South America—rum and sugar are important exports. Yet, the varieties of rum produced on the different islands differ from each other as much in terms of aroma, taste, and bouquet as do the wines of California's Napa Valley, or bourbon does from Tennessee sour mash. The exact recipe for rum production is always the distiller's secret. What all types of rum have in common, however, is their raw material—the brown, viscous molasses by-product of sugarcane refining.

After distillation, rum is clear and colorless. For light rum to remain clear, it is first matured in pale ash-wood barrels for only one year and is then transferred to stainless-steel tanks for additional aging. Dark rum, on the other hand, is left to mature for years in dark, wooden casks for five to seven years, where it develops its golden or brownish color and a full-flavored body. Caramel is also added to some brands to intensify the color. In between light and dark rum is a grade called gold, or amber, which is aged for three years.

Light rum not only looks lighter than dark rum, it also has a much more delicate taste than the latter. For this reason, light rum blends superbly with other ingredients such as fruit juices, liqueurs, and lemonades in cocktails, without concealing its own taste. Its slight flavor evaporates very quickly though, so light rum is not so well suited to hot punches and grogs.

Sake

Many people would not consider a Japanese meal complete without a bottle of this clear, usually straw-colored, fermented-rice spirit. Even though sake, which is the Japanese national drink, is often referred to as wine, its production process is more like that of beer. Sake tastes similar to sherry and has an alcohol content of only 16 to 17 percent by volume, or about 35 proof.

Tequila

Mexico's number-one spirit, drunk since the time of the Aztecs, is distilled from the blue agave cactus. Clear, white tequila, also called silver tequila, is bottled immediately after distillation. Gold tequila, or tequila anejo, gets its golden-brown color from several years' storage in oak barrels, during which time the flavor also mellows and becomes smoother. Most brands of tequila are about 90 proof. Mexican laws specify that only tequila produced in a specific geographical area around the town of the same name can be labeled as such. Mezcal is a similar drink distilled from a different variety of the agave cactus, but it does not have the same labeling regulations. Contrary to popular belief, mezcal is the Mexican drink that traditionally contained a worm in the bottom of the bottle, not tequila.

BITTERS

This generic term applies to all bitter liqueurs and bitters. Bitters are produced from herb and root extracts, from the narcotic components of (primarily) tropical and subtropical plants, and from spices. They are usually dark in color and valued for their appetite-promoting and digestion-aiding qualities.

Angostura bitters
Produced in Trinidad, this is probably the best-know bitters in the world and is indispensable to every bartender for flavoring drinks. It is one of the essential ingredients in classic Old-fashioned Bourbon Cocktail and what gives the pale pink color to a bubbling Champagne Cocktail. The exact recipe is a closely guarded secret, but the flavor is produced from extracts of Seville orange peel, angelica roots, cardamom, cinnamon, cloves, galangan (*Alpinia officinarum*), gentian roots, and quinine.

Aperol
Italian bitters, sometimes called Campari's "younger brother," with an alcohol content of just 22 proof.

Boonekamp
This aromatic bitter, at least 80 proof, contains a wealth of exotic ingredients, such as aniseed, fennel, licorice, bitter clover, poplar buds, valerian root, and wormwood, to name but a few.

Ingredients

Campari

This world-renowned Italian bitters has a heavily guarded secret mixture of herbs and Seville orange peel to thank for its typical flavor. This ruby-red drink was created in Milan in 1861 by the distiller Caspare Davide Campari, and has today become a classic aperitif. It is very good for mixing.

Cynar

This bitter Italian aperitif contains artichoke juice and herbs, and has an alcohol content of 16.5 percent by volume, or 33 proof.

Orange bitters

This is a combination of extract of bitter-tasting Seville orange peel and gin. It is only used to flavor a host of cocktails.

Tropical bitters

A bitter based on tropical fruits.

Other bitters

Other brands of European bitters include Amer Picon, flavored with orange and gentian; Branca Menta, which tastes of peppermint; Fernet-Branca, an Italian herbal-tasting bitter; golden, sweetish Karlsbader Becher Bitter (nowadays called Karlovarska Becherovka); bittersweet Punt e Mès from Italy, which is usually enjoyed while eating chocolate; golden-colored Suze from France; and herbal Underberg, which has been brewed to a secret family recipe in Germany since 1846 and is claimed to be a hangover cure.

LIQUEURS

It was doctors and monks several hundreds of years ago, in the search for medicines, who produced the first liqueurs when they used honey or sugar to sweeten the bitter herb elixirs for their patients. Today, liqueurs are defined as spirits which have been infused with flavorings, such as extracts (or distillates) of plants and fruits, fruit juices, or essential oils. They may also be sweetened with honey or glucose. Depending on the ingredients, it is possible to differentiate between herb, spice, and bitter liqueurs. Fruit liqueurs are made from fruit juice, fruit-flavor liqueurs are produced from whole fruits or parts of fruit, emulsion liqueurs are viscous and rich, and there are cream and whiskey liqueurs.

Liqueurs also differ in their alcohol content. Milk-, chocolate-, and egg-based liqueurs are at least 40 proof; fruit juice-, cocoa-, coffee-, and tea-based liqueurs are at least 50 proof; fruit brandies and vanilla-flavored liqueurs are at least 60 proof; and honey liqueurs and fruit liqueurs blended with triple sec, a white, orange-scented curaçao, are at least 70 proof, so an innocent-seeming liqueur can, in fact, be very strong. Liqueurs are indispensable for mixing drinks, whether to add color, or sweetness, or to enhance the taste.

Advocaat
This Dutch liqueur is an example of an emulsion liqueur, produced from egg yolks, sugar, and alcohol (usually brandy). It is at least 40 proof.

Amaretto
Amaretto is an amber-colored liqueur from Italy produced from sweet and bitter almonds, apricot kernels, and vanilla and other spices. Its alcohol content is 28 percent by volume, or 56 proof. The prussic acid contained in both almonds and apricot kernels is separated out during distillation.

Amaro Averna
This liqueur, which is also known as Amara Siciliano, from Italy is strong tasting and bitter.

Ingredients

Anisette
From France, this bitter liqueur is predominantly manufactured from star anise blended with flavorings, such as fennel, cloves, coriander, orrisroot, and other spices. It is at least 60 proof.

Apricot brandy
Apricot juice, apricot spirit, sugar and corn syrups, pure alcohol, and water are combined to make this brandy, which is at least 60 proof. If, instead of the aromatic fruit spirit, just a pure alcohol is used, any products produced in Europe can only be labeled as "apricot liqueur." Apricot brandy is popular as a mixer because it combines well with most spirits and juices.

B & B
This amber-colored liqueur is a mixture of Benedictine and cognac, and was introduced to the market in 1938. It is 80 proof, and is usually served over ice cubes.

Benedictine
This amber-colored, French herbal liqueur owes its name to the Benedictine monks who first produced the liqueur in 1510.

Cassis
This dark-red liqueur is produced from the juice of black currants, cassis being the French word for this berry fruit. The alcohol content is at least 20 percent by volume, or 40 proof. Cassis can only be called *crème de cassis* if it has a minimum alcohol content of 15 percent by volume and a specified minimum sugar content. Cassis is drunk neat as a liqueur, and also as an aperitif. It is combined with white wine to make a Kir, and with champagne or other sparkling wine to make Kir Royale.

Chartreuse
This French herbal liqueur was invented by an unknown alchemist as the elixir of life. Monks at the monastery of La Grande Chartreuse, near Grenoble, improved upon the alchemist's secret formula and developed yellow Chartreuse, the king of liqueurs, in addition to the original green version. Chartreuse, which has brandy as its base liquid, contains some 130 different herbs and extracts. Yellow Chartreuse is very mild and is 86 proof. Green Chartreuse is spicier and more powerful, and is 110 proof.

Cherry brandy
This cherry liqueur is produced from cherry juice. It is about 50 proof.

Cherry liqueur
One of the large group of fruit-juice-based liqueurs that are at least 50 proof, popular cherry liqueurs include Danish Cherry Heering, Italian Luxardo, and maraschino, an Italian drink made from sour cherries.

Cocoa liqueur
Produced from distilled cocoa beans or cocoa powder, cherry eau-de-vie is added to some brands for extra flavor.

Coconut liqueur
Made with coconut milk, this spirit is found in several forms, such as in Batida de Coco, Cocosala, or the generic crème de coco. It is also produced crystal clear in the form of Coco Ribe and Malibu.

Coffee liqueur
This liqueur, which is often also called "mocha," is produced from freshly roasted, ground coffee beans or from powdered coffee without artificial flavorings, and the result is at least 50 proof. Liqueurs called "coffee with cream" or "mocha with cream" contain at least 10 percent cream. Some of the most familiar brands of coffee liqueur are Kahlúa, a Mexican coffee liqueur with herbs and vanilla; Tia Maria, a Jamaican coffee liqueur with rum; and Batida de Café.

Cointreau
This liqueur is obtained from ripe Seville oranges and lemons, and is at least 80 proof. It is best drunk neat or over ice, and is used in cocktails. It is also used for mixing with other ingredients in cocktails, as well as flavoring cakes, pastries, and sweet desserts.

Crèmes
Many fine, viscous, and sugary liqueurs are marketed under the name "crème de ..." and are at least 50 proof. They mostly consist of cognac or brandy, and get their characteristic flavor from fruit distillates.
Crème de banane is a banana liqueur produced from ripe, aromatic bananas.

Ingredients

Crème de cacao is a pale to dark brown cocoa liqueur made from roasted and shelled cocoa beans and a touch of vanilla. Pale cocoa liqueur is sweeter than the dark version.

Crème de café is a coffee liqueur made from freshly roasted and ground coffee (see also "Coffee liqueur").

Crème de cassis is a tangy liqueur from black currants (see also "Cassis").

Crème de coco is a liqueur produced from coconuts (see also "Coconut liqueur").

Crème de fraises is a perfumed, delicate pink-colored strawberry liqueur.

Crème de framboise is based on raspberries and is a little sweeter than strawberry liqueur.

Crème de mandarine is produced from mandarin juice.

Crème de menthe smells and tastes like peppermint. It is available in white and green (see also "Peppermint liqueur").

Crème de noyaux is a nut liqueur made from ground hazelnuts and walnuts, almonds, cherry pits, and cognac or brandy.

Crème de prunelle is produced from plum extracts and brandy.

Crème de violette is a blue violet liqueur.

Curaçao

This is the generic term for orange liqueurs produced from the peel of a bitter variety of Seville orange. This variety of orange once grew predominantly off the coast of Venezuela on the West Indian island of Curaçao, hence the name. Nowadays, the dried peel of this variety of Seville orange almost always comes from Haiti. To extract the essential oil from the peel, the latter is treated with spirits, cognac, or Armagnac. Spices and herbs are added. Curaçao is produced in many colors, in clear (triple sec), in orange (Red Orange), green, and blue (blue curaçao). Nonalcoholic blue curaçao is available from specialty stores and suppliers.

Standard curaçao is at least 60 proof. Dry varieties with the additional designation sec (dry), or triple sec (extra dry), on the label are 70 proof. "Triple sec" is used throughout this book at the generic term for a clear curaçao.

Drambuie

The Scottish whisky-honey liqueur consists of 15-year-old scotch, Highland herbs, and heather honey. It is about 80 proof.

Escorial
A green herb-flavored liqueur from Germany.

Frangelico
This amber-colored Italian herb liqueur is made from hazelnuts, herbs, and berries.

Galliano
Galliano is one of the most famous Italian liqueurs. More than 70 different herbs and plant extracts lend the golden-yellow liqueur its unique flavor. Its alcohol content is 35 percent by volume, or 70 proof. Galliano is also available as a colorless, orange-flavored liqueur, and as a brownish, almond-flavored variety.

Goldwasser
This clear, colorless liqueur, spiced with caraway and aniseed, is produced according to a 400-year-old recipe, originally in Poland, but now in Germany. What is special about it are the pieces of genuine 22-carat gold leaf which float, glittering, in the liquid, and which are supposed to bring luck. (The gold leaf is safe to consume.) The alcohol content is 76 proof.

Grand Marnier
Caribbean bitter oranges flavor this French orange liqueur. There is a clear Grand Marnier and a red variety (Grand Marnier Cordon Rouge), and both are about 80 proof. Grand Marnier is either served neat at room temperature in a brandy snifter or chilled over ice in a rocks glass. It is also ideally suited for mixing.

Irish Mist
This whiskey liqueur, produced from Irish whiskey, herbs, and Irish heather, is 70 proof.

Jägermeister
A popular German herbal liqueur. If you can not find this, Fernet-Branca is a slightly more bitter-tasting alternative.

Kontiki
An alcoholic-tropical drink which combines gin with lemons and grapefruit.

Ingredients

Lemon liqueur
This fruit-flavored liqueur is produced from ripe lemons. To be labeled "triple" or "triple sec," the liqueur must be at least 70 proof; ordinary lemon liqueur is 60 proof.

Maraschino
This clear cherry liqueur, which is 60 to 70 proof, tastes slightly of bitter almonds, although it is made with sour almonds. Italians enjoy drinking it "on the rocks" after meals as a digestive.

Parfait Amour
A sweet, mauve-colored fruit liqueur produced from violets and exotic ingredients, with a hint of citrus flavor.

Passion-fruit liqueur
Jambosala is the best-known brand of this tropical-fruit drink, which is at least 25 percent alcohol by volume, or 50 proof.

Peach brandy
Clear and almost colorless, this is classified as a liqueur rather than a brandy.

Peppermint liqueur
Consists of natural peppermint extracts, alcohol, and sugar.

Pisang Ambon
This Dutch liqueur is produced from bananas that grow on the tiny Indonesian island of Ambon. Bright green, it is flavored with herbs, and is 44 proof.

Sambuca
In Italy, you will see Italians drinking this licorice-flavored liqueur "on the rocks" with water. Sambuca is one of numerous aniseed-flavored drinks but, in this case, elderberries contribute a unique taste.

Southern Comfort
This classic whiskey liqueur, invented more than 130 years ago in New Orleans, has a distinctive orange-peach flavor. It is 80 proof.

Strega
This is often called "la strega" (the witch) and is one of Italy's best-known herbal liqueurs. Its bittersweet taste comes from herbs, roots, and the rinds of plants from the valleys of the Apennine Mountains.

Swedish Punsch
Blended from arrak, wine, and neutral alcohol, this strong liqueur is available up to 100 proof.

There is a huge number of soft spirits and exotic mixtures that do not exactly belong to the liqueur family, but which can not be overlooked. For example, Pimm's No. 1, the English specialty based on gin, is already mixed when you buy it. Often rumored to be the favorite drink of Queen Elizabeth II, this drink just needs to be topped up with sparkling mineral water, ginger ale, or lemonade. Pimm's No. 2 is based on whiskey; No. 3 brandy; No. 4 light rum; and No. 5 on vodka.

SPARKLING WINES

"Sparkling wine" is the decidedly bare generic term for an extremely bubbly pleasure, as French champagne and crémant, Italian spumante, German sekt, and Spanish cava bubble under this name. They are all sparkling wines that are produced from wine through fermentation (either in the bottle or in tanks) or by the addition of carbonic acid, and exhibit a pressure of at least three bar when stored in closed containers at 68°F.

Champagne
The king of sparkling wines, champagne takes its name from the region in northern France where it is produced. Only the sparkling wines from a specific growing area around Rheims and Epernay can be labeled as "champagne." The production process is very laborious because champagne has to ferment in the bottle in which it is sold (*méthode champenoise*).
Extra brut is a very dry champagne, brut is very dry to dry, extra dry is a dry to off-dry, sec is medium dry to sweet, demi-sec is sweet, and doux very sweet.

Ingredients

Cava
This is the name for sparkling Spanish wine produced according to the *méthode champenoise*.

Crémant
This sparkling wine, which is also called vin mousseux, does not come from the Champagne region, but it is also produced according to the *méthode champenoise*.

Crimean sparkling wine
This white or red sparkling wine is produced from muscatel grapes, which only grow on the Crimean peninsula in the Ukraine. True Crimean sparkling wine ferments in the bottle.

Sekt
Germany produces this version of sparkling wine, and the minimum maturation period is nine months. After official testing, it is granted an official test number which has to appear on the label. Prädikatssekt is a quality sparkling wine produced from at least 60 percent German wine. Winzersekt is a sekt produced exclusively by the wine grower, or by a producer's cooperative using the same procedures as the French *méthode champenoise*.

Spumante
This is a sweet Italian sparkling wine. The best-known, oldest representative is Asti Spumante.

FORTIFIED WINES

Fortified wines are given better keeping properties than ordinary wines by the addition of herbs, sugar, and other preservatives. They are ideal to drink as aperitifs.

Madeira
This golden fortified wine (30 to 40 proof) is only produced on the Portuguese island of Madeira, off the west coast of Africa. There are four different types with varying degrees of sweetness, which are named according to the variety of grape used in their production— bual (boal), a light, not very sweet wine; verdelho, a medium wine which tastes faintly of honey; malvasia (malmsey), the sweetest Madeira; and sercial, the driest Madeira.

Malaga
This Spanish wine was originally only produced in the area around Malaga on the Costa del Sol. Today, however, it is also produced on the eastern coast of Spain. As a young wine it is straw colored, but becomes brownish yellow as it ages. Dulce on the label means that it is very sweet; seco, on the other hand, means dry. It is 34 proof and mostly drunk as a digestive after meals.

Marsala
This wine (at least 24 proof) is only produced in the western Sicilian region of Trapani and in parts of Agrigent and Palermo.

Port
One of the most famous fortified wines in the world, port wine originates in northern Portugal. Red and ruby ports are young blends with a sweet and fruity taste. They are ideal to serve as dessert wines. White port, matured for several years in oak casks before bottling, makes an outstanding aperitif.

Samos
This very sweet dessert wine is named after the Greek island of Samos. Serve it in small dessert-wine glasses, like a liqueur.

Sherry
This is a fortified Mediterranean wine produced in the area around Jerez, whence it gets its name, that is strictly defined by law. The

following types of sherry are distinguished according to taste:

Fino is the driest sherry. It is straw yellow, has a delicate scent of almonds, and is 31 to 34 proof.

Manzanilla is a fino from Sanlúcar de Barrameda. It is light, fresh, tangy, and slightly bitter tasting, and is 32 to 33 proof.

Amontillado, amber-colored, is 36 to 50 proof. It is also available as medium and medium dry.

Oloroso is the name given to dark brown, full-bodied sherry that is up to 48 proof. It tastes slightly of walnuts.

Cream sherry is an oloroso that has been sweetened by the addition of wine made from Pedro Ximinez or muscatel grapes. It is very sweet and dark.

Tokaji or tokay

This Hungarian dessert wine originates from the Tokaj, a wine-growing area about 90 miles north of Budapest.

Vermouth

Produced mostly in France and Italy, vermouth is fortified with herbs, alcohol, sugar, and caramel. *Sweet vermouth* is white (bianco) or red (rosso) and is 31 to 32 proof. *Dry vermouth* (dry, extra dry) is always white and at least 36 proof. *Semisweet vermouth* is available as a rosé. Some of the best-known brands of vermouth are: Carpano Punt e Mes, a bittersweet Italian vermouth that is 40 proof; Cinzano, called rosso antico, sold as bianco, rosso, and dry; and Noilly Prat, the driest of vermouths. Noilly Prat comes from France, as does another brand called Picon. Alcohol-free vermouth is also sold.

In addition to classic vermouth, there is also a wealth of wine-based aperitifs, which for the most part owe their flavor to quinine. The best-known representatives from this group are, among others, **Byrrh** (red) and **Dubonnet** (white and red), which are both French.

SYRUPS AND CORDIALS

These play a major role in mixing drinks, because they add color and the correct level of sweetness, and lend many drinks that "certain something." You should be sparing with syrups, though, because in most instances a few drops are sufficient.

Cream of coconut
This is not a syrup in the normal definition of the word, but all the same it is a frequently used ingredient in many cocktails. It is sold in cans, may be either a thick liquid or firm cream, and is perfect for including in exotic drinks to give them a tropical taste. Because it is so sweet, however, it should be diluted with an equal amount of water.

Grenadine
This blood-red, strong fruit syrup is made from pomegranates. Depending on how much you use, it will color drinks anything from blush pink to deep red. (If you can not find any, raspberry, cranberry, and strawberry liqueurs are also suitable for use in cocktails that are supposed to be colored red, as is cassis, which is made from black currants.) Most grenadine is nonalcoholic, but you must check the label carefully if you want an alcohol-free drink because some brands contain small amounts of alcohol.

Rose's Lime Juice Cordial
This is one popular brand of cordial used by bartenders for sweetening and flavoring drinks, often replacing lemon juice and sugar in many cocktails. Cordials are fruit juices sweetened with syrup, made in a variety of flavors. In the United States, "cordials" is also an old-fashioned word for liqueurs. In this book, however, it means a nonalcoholic mixer.

Sugar syrup
Often also called stock syrup, this is frequently used in cocktails. It can be bought, but it is very easy to make yourself: stir five cups of sugar into one quart of boiling water and bring to a boil without stirring after the sugar dissolves. The longer the sugar solution boils, the thicker the syrup will be. Leave to cool, then bottle and store in a cool, dark place.

There are, in fact, as many as **30 different types of syrup**, flavored with mango, papaya, passion fruit, coconut, and kiwi fruit, as well as banana, maple, orange, peach, mandarin, apricot, peppermint, and aniseed. Almond syrup is a specific example of a flavored syrup used by bartenders. Called orgeat in the United States after its French name, and orzata in Italy, this syrup is milky white and has a very intensive and aromatic flavor.

JUICES

Fruit juices are an absolute must in any well-stocked bar, because they lend drinks desirable colors and particular flavors. The classic fruit juices are, as always, lemon and orange. Both should be freshly squeezed, if possible. High-quality fruit juices are now available commercially, too, but read the labels carefully before you buy, because not everything you pour out of a bottle or carton comes from fruit.

Natural fruit juice must be 100 percent from pressed fruit (fresh or frozen). Fruit juices from concentrates also consist of 100 percent fruit, but the juice is made up from fruit juice concentrate.

Fruit nectar is a mixture of fruit juice and/or fruit essence, water, and sugar. In the case of apples, pears, and citrus fruit, the fruit content must be at least 50 percent; and for tropical fruit, black currants, and sea buckthorn at least 25 percent. In diet fruit-juice nectars or light juices, the fruit juice is diluted with water and the sugar replaced with sugar substitute or sweetener.

Fruit-juice drinks have only a minimal proportion of fruit, but instead contain much ordinary or mineral water and sugar.

In addition to fruit juice, you also need vegetable juice to mix savory drinks. The classic example is tomato juice in a Bloody Mary.

CARBONATED BEVERAGES AND MINERAL WATERS

These are used for topping up and diluting, and they add a fizzy, foaming *je ne sais quoi*.

Bitter lemon is produced with an extract from lemon peels and also contains quinine. **Bitter orange** comes from orange peel and **bitter grapefruit** from grapefruit peel; both drinks are used in cocktails.

Unlike fruit juices, carbonated drinks are not legally required to contain fruit juices, but some are made with the natural products. As a general rule, carbonated drinks are high in sugar. **Ginger ale** is an example of a carbonated drink frequently used by bartenders as a mixer in highballs. As well as adding a light effervescence, it has a perky ginger flavor.

Cola drinks are also part of the carbonated drinks family, and, in addition to sugar, water, and other flavorings, they also contain the stimulant caffeine.

Mineral water is available in a range of styles, such as sparkling or still and slightly bitter or salty, with both high and low mineral contents. It is simply a matter of tasting several brands until you find one that appeals to your taste buds.

Sanbitter is an alcohol-free bitter drink from Italy.

Soda water has a high sodium carbonate content. It contains either natural or "artificially injected" carbonic acid.

Tonic water tastes tangy and fresh, and slightly sweet. It contains a trace of quinine.

EGGS, MILK, AND CREAM

These are needed, for example, for eggnogs and shakes, flips, and creamy cocktails, as well as for topping up and garnishing. It may sound strange, but they are essential ingredients for a bartender.

Cream is a good addition if a drink is meant to be especially creamy, but also if you want to decorate it with a whirl or rosette. Light cream is usually used for mixing, but lightly whipped cream may also be used. Other dairy products, such as **buttermilk** and **plain yogurt**, are also very suitable for mixing. You should use full-fat varieties for the best flavor.

Ingredients

Eggs should always be absolutely fresh, and you should not use any egg with a cracked shell. Note that raw eggs may contain salmonella bacteria, which can cause food poisoning. In extreme cases it can be fatal. Drinks containing raw eggs or raw egg yolks should not be drunk by the elderly or young children, or anyone who is pregnant or ill.

Frothee is a runny, neutral-tasting egg-white concentrate that gives drinks an attractive head of froth. If you can not obtain any, use a mixture of egg white and water (in a ratio of 1:1).

Milk tastes best when fresh. If you use whole milk, your drinks will taste especially creamy.

FRUIT, VEGETABLES, AND FLAVORINGS

Whether as a cheerful decoration or an elegant seasoning, fruit, vegetables, spices, and other flavorings also play an important role in mixing drinks. Many of the items you will find listed here will doubtless already be stocked in your kitchen.

Fruit is usually needed for garnishing. **Vegetables**, such as olives and pearl onions, are also used as garnishes.

You also need the following ingredients: celery salt, cinnamon (ground and sticks), cloves, instant coffee, nutmeg (whole nuts or ground), ground paprika, ground black pepper, salt, and sugar (brown sugar, confectioners' sugar, granulated sugar, and sugar cubes), as well as hot-pepper sauce, tomato catsup, and Worcestershire sauce.

ICE

Most mixed drinks are unthinkable without ice. On the one hand it cools down the drink as much as possible during mixing, without diluting it, and on the other it should keep the drinks cool in the glass for as long as possible.

The general rule for ice cubes is the bigger the better. The ice cubes can be removed quickly from either an ice-cube tray with a lever, or from a plastic bag. If you are fussy about serving clear ice, either boil the water before freezing it or use still mineral water.

Crushed ice is best prepared in an electric blender or food processor, but you can manage without one. To crush ice manually, place a few ice cubes in a clean dishtowel and fold in the sides to make a bundle. Place the bundle of ice on a firm surface and bash it several times with a meat mallet. Now put the crushed ice into a large glass or dish and place it in the freezer until required. Because crushed ice melts faster than cubes, you should always prepare it shortly before you need to use it.

You may also want to use **cobbler ice** (roughly crushed ice) and **shaved ice**. These, however, are usually only needed very rarely.

Although it may sound contradictory, the colder the ice, the less its cooling effect. Drinks with ice-cold cubes have to be shaken for longer than those with "warmer" ice. For this reason, professional bartenders use ice cubes at a temperature of around 32°F. Just remember to take the ice-cube tray out of the freezer a little while before you intend to prepare the drinks.

Ingredients

BASIC STOCK FOR A BAR

To give you a head start in enjoying mixed drinks and cocktails, I have put together a list of the basic stock of liquor and liqueurs which will equip you for making many drinks. You can also start with just two or three of your favorite spirits, though, and then gradually stock your bar.

For beginners:
Apricot brandy
Bourbon
Campari
Cognac or brandy
Cointreau
Curaçao (blue)
Crème de cacao
Crème de cassis
Crème de menthe (green)
Curaçao (blue)
Gin
Rum, light and dark
Scotch
Sherry (fino and oloroso)
Sparkling wine
Tequila (white)
Vermouth (bianco, rosso, dry)
Vodka

For those with experience to build up their stock:
Amaretto
Aniseed-flavored liqueur
Benedictine
Calvados
Cherry brandy
Cynar
Drambuie
Galliano
Grand Marnier
Irish whiskey
Pernod
Port wine
Schnapps (unflavored)
Sherry (amontillado, cream)
Southern Comfort

Flavoring and mixing agents such as Angostura and orange bitters, bitter lemon, ginger ale, grenadine, soda or sparkling mineral water, sugar syrup, and tonic water, as well as cream, eggs, fresh mint, and a selection of fresh fruit.

HOW TO MIX COCKTAILS

Preparing drinks in a shaker

This is how cocktails containing ingredients that are difficult to combine—such as eggs, milk, liqueurs, and syrups—are prepared. Fill the cocktail shaker up to two-thirds full with ice cubes and swirl them round briefly. Put the shaker or glass liner in the refrigerator to chill.

Strain any water from the melting ice cubes out of the shaker. Measure out the ingredients according to the recipe, add them to the shaker, and close it tightly. Shake the shaker firmly for a few seconds, moving it in and out from the body. Drinks that are easy to mix should be shaken for about 10 seconds, while drinks using egg yolk need about 20 seconds.

Open the shaker and strain the drink through the bar sieve into a chilled glass. Garnish the drink, if desired. A perfectly shaken cocktail looks cloudy at first, then slowly clears from bottom to top. Ingredients for no more than two cocktails should be shaken together in a Boston shaker (if extra cocktails are required, use more ice).

Mixing

Preparing drinks in a blender
You usually use a blender for mixing drinks that contain cream, eggs, fruit, and ice, as well as for those that are frozen. First chill a suitable glass in the refrigerator. If the drink has an elaborate garnish, assemble it now so the drink can be served as soon as it is blended. Put 1 scoop of crushed ice or 2 or 3 ice cubes into the blender jug.

Measure out the ingredients according to the recipe and put them into the blender jug. Make sure the lid is properly closed. Now run the blender for about 10 seconds on the first setting, then switch to the second setting and blend for 10 seconds longer. If the drink is too thick, add some more crushed ice or ice cubes to the blender jug before switching the blender to setting 2.

Pour the drink into the prepared glass, garnish, and serve immediately.

Preparation in a mixing glass

All drinks which are stirred together with ice cubes, but which are served without ice, are prepared in a mixing glass. First chill a suitable glass. If the drink has an elaborate garnish, assemble it now so the drink can be served as soon as it is mixed.

Put 2 or 3 ice cubes in the mixing glass and swirl them around a few times.

Strain the melted ice water out of the mixing glass. Measure out the ingredients according to the recipe and put them in the mixing glass. Now mix everything together, working from bottom to top, with a long-handled bar spoon.

Strain the drink immediately through the bar sieve into the chilled glass and garnish if desired. If cocktails for several people are being mixed (remember to add more ice), it is better to pour less into the glasses initially, and then share out the rest equally.

Mixing

Preparation in the glass
Generally, drinks whose ingredients combine easily are stirred in the glass in which they will be served. First chill a suitable glass. If the drink has an elaborate garnish, assemble it now so the drink can be served as soon as it is blended. Put 2 or 3 ice cubes into the chilled glass.

Measure out the ingredients according to the recipe and add them to the glass.

Carefully stir the drink with a bar spoon, garnish if desired, and serve immediately.

Flavoring with lemon or orange peel

Many cocktails are flavored in the glass with the zest from a piece of lemon or orange peel. To do this, pare a small, round piece of peel (without any bitter white pith) from an unwaxed, organic citrus fruit. With the peel facing downward, take the piece of peel between your fingers and squeeze. The essential oils from the peel will squirt into the drink, adding a "special" flavor.

Professional tips and hints

- As a novice drinks mixer you should follow the quantities specified in the recipes exactly.

  Frequently used quantities in the recipes are:

  1 dash = the amount which flows out of the dash bottle through the pourer when it is inverted once

  1 shot = 2 teaspoons

  1 tsp. or 1 bar spoon = 1/6 ounce

  1 tbsp. = 1/2 ounce

  For recipes which are prepared for several people (such as bowls and punches), quantities are also given in cups and quarts. When a bottle of wine or liquor is specified, it is a standard 750-ml bottle.

- Unless otherwise specified, the recipes are intended for 1 glass (1 person).

- When mixing drinks, cleanliness is paramount. Wash all equipment, such as the shaker, mixing glass, bar strainer, and bar spoon, thoroughly and immediately after use. Also, use ice tongs, a fork or spoon to put ice cubes or pieces of fruit into glasses, not your fingers.

- If you want to serve drinks in chilled glasses, you have two options. Either put the glasses in the freezer until they are frosted with a film of ice, or chill them with ice cubes. If you are going to use the freezer, however, only use a freezerproof glass.

Mixing

- Cocktails which are served with complicated garnishes, such as fruit kabobs or citrus fruit peel, are best served on a small plate or cocktail napkin. This gives the drinker somewhere to put the garnish when it is removed from the glass.
- According to international conventions, a drink should not contain more than 2 ounces alcohol and no more than five ingredients. The total volume of a long drink should not exceed 9 ounces.
- Champagne and sparkling wines, juices, carbonated beverages, and mineral water should always be kept in the refrigerator.
- Carbonated ingredients, such as soft drinks, soda water, and sparkling wine, should never be shaken in the cocktail shaker, because otherwise they will fizz up and spill over the top.
- Only use unwaxed, organic citrus fruits for garnishes, squeezing, and adding to drinks (even in bowls and punches). These should be washed thoroughly before use, as should all other varieties of fruit.
- When serving long drinks, serve them with a straw and stirrer in the glass.
- Drinks that should be shaken can also be prepared using an electric blender.
- For the sake of simplicity, a cocktail glass is always suggested in the recipes. It is, however, up to you whether you use a cocktail glass or a wide-mouth champagne glass.
- The recipes for bowls, punches, and mulled wines include ingredients that are given in bottles. These are standard 750-ml bottles.
- Some drinks are first prepared with ice cubes and then strained (without ice cubes) into a glass that contains fresh ice cubes. In this way, the drink is not diluted so quickly and remains well chilled. In the recipes, the rule is always to strain the drink into a glass with ice cubes.

GARNISHING

Cocktails should not only taste good, they should also do something for the eye, because it is a well-known fact that the eye drinks with you. Give your imagination and creativity free rein when you get to the final step of cocktail making—garnishing.

There are very few drinks for which a garnish is superfluous or even frowned upon. There are the classics whose garnishes have been predetermined by generations of bartenders, such as the olive in a Dry Martini, the cherry in a Manhattan, the pearl onions in a Gibson, the mint for juleps, and cucumber peel for Pimm's.

For all exotic and tropical drinks, and especially for fancy drinks, you can do whatever your heart desires as far as garnishing is concerned, but you should bear a few rules in mind.

- Only use ingredients for the garnish that are suitable for the drink in terms of both taste and color.
- The garnish is supposed to decorate the drink, not adulterate it, overload it, or even push it into the background. Less is often more. Generally, just a slice of orange perched on the rim of the glass, a wedge of lime, a spiral of lemon peel, a maraschino cherry, or a sprig of mint is enough.
- If you use fresh fruit, make sure that it is ripe and blemish free and that you slice it carefully. Twists of citrus-fruit peel are best cut with a potato peeler or with a citrus zester, which is what professionals use.

When choosing fruit, there is no limit to what you can use, provided it is edible. Small fruit is very suitable, as well as pieces of fruit, such as baby apples or pears (canned), banana slices, black currants, Cape gooseberries, grapes, kumquats, lychees, maraschino cherries, melon balls, and raspberries.

Cherries give you great scope because you can choose between red or green maraschino cherries, which are both readily available from supermarkets. In specialist stores, you might even find golden, orange, and black cherries, as well as sour-tasting Amarena cherries which are preserved in a rum syrup. If you want to use fresh cherries, choose pairs of cherries on the stem, if possible.

Pieces or slices of apricots, citrus fruits, figs, kiwi fruit, peaches, pineapple, and star fruit, as well as wedges of mandarin and lime, are also very attractive. Black and green grapes are extremely decorative.

Garnishing

Strawberries and raspberries look great, too, if they are drizzled with lemon juice and then dipped in sugar; they look as though they are frosted. Fruit can also be dusted with confectioners' sugar for an attractive finish. Slices of apple and pear, on the other hand, are not very suitable for garnishing because they turn brown quickly. If you do want to use them, however, drizzle them with lemon juice to delay the discoloration.

Vegetable garnishes are suitable for savory mixed drinks and include celery sticks, cucumber peel or slices, green olives, pearl onions, and cherry tomatoes. Thin slices of pepperoni also make an interesting garnish for robustly flavored, spicy drinks.

Fresh herbs also provide variety in or on the glass. For example, fresh basil goes very well with mixed drinks including tomato or vegetable juice; lemon balm goes well whenever lemon juice is used; and mint leaves are "the icing on the cake" for drinks based on peppermint liqueur or syrup. A touch of green can be added with pineapple leaves, which are speared on toothpicks or kabob sticks and fanned out, but, of course, you can not eat them.

There are various ways to practice the art of garnishing. Make a single incision in whole fruit or pieces of fruit from the middle to the edge and perch them on the rim of the glass. Other pieces of fruit can then be secured to this with a toothpick. You can put fruit kabobs in the glass or rest them across the rim of the glass. The following are a few suggestions for attractive fruit kabobs.

Pineapple kabob

Cut a slice of pineapple into 8 pieces and cut out the heart. Spear a few pineapple leaves on a large skewer. Alternately skewer pineapple pieces, black grapes, and red maraschino cherries onto the skewer.

Star fruit-kiwi fruit kabob

Spear 1 strawberry with a stem, 1 slice of peeled kiwi fruit, a slice of star fruit, and a sprig of lemon balm leaf on a large toothpick or kabob skewer.

Citrus kabob

Make a single incision from the edge of a slice of lime into the middle, twist the ends in opposite directions, and skewer on a toothpick. Spear 1 red maraschino cherry on each end.

Sugared rim

An absolute necessity for all crustas, but also originally for many other mixed drinks, especially the more exotic ones. Make a 1/2-inch-deep cut in a wedge of lemon. Hold the glass upside down and run the rim of the glass through the cut in the wedge of lemon.

Put some sugar (light brown, granulated, superfine, or multicolored) in a shallow dish and gently roll the still-damp rim of the glass in the sugar. Hold the glass upside down and tap it gently so any loose sugar falls away.

Garnishing

Rims of glasses coated in white shredded coconut, finely grated chocolate, or brown instant coffee also make interesting finishing touches. Savory drinks can be garnished with rims coated in coarse salt, caraway seeds, snipped chives, or paprika. In addition to lemon juice, orange and grapefruit juices, liqueurs, syrup, and honey are all suitable "adhesives" for sugared rims on sweet drinks. For savory drinks, however, it is best to stick with lemon juice. Glasses with sugared rims can be prepared in advance, though only for a short time.

In addition to the garnishes already described, there is a wealth of others you can use, including chopped pistachio nuts, slivered almonds, cocoa powder, and ground cinnamon and grated nutmeg which, for example, can be sprinkled on piped cream toppings for flips and eggnogs. Attractive, colorful straws and pretty stirrers can also make every drink a feast for the eyes.

CLASSIC COCKTAILS

ALEXANDER

SIDE CAR

COGNAC COLLINS

HONEYMOON

Brandy-based drinks

ZOOM

STINGER

BREAKFAST EGG-NOG

BRANDY FLIP

BERMUDA HIGHBALL

COGNAC CASSIS

ALEXANDER

Creamy drink for the evening
• Cocktail glass
• Shaker

¾ ounce brandy or cognac
¾ ounce brown crème de cacao
¾ ounce light cream
• Extra:
Grated nutmeg

Shake all the ingredients together firmly, with ice, in the shaker and strain into the glass. Sprinkle with a little nutmeg.

SIDECAR

Sharp-tasting aperitif
• Cocktail glass
• Shaker

¾ ounce brandy or cognac
¾ ounce Cointreau or other orange-flavored liqueur
¾ ounce lemon juice

Shake the ingredients together, with ice, in the shaker and strain into the cocktail glass.

STINGER

Spicy, fresh after-dinner drink
• Cocktail glass
• Mixing glass

1½ ounces brandy or cognac
¾ ounce white crème de menthe

Mix the ingredients together in the mixing glass, with ice, and strain into the cocktail glass.

ZOOM

Sweet after-dinner drink
• Cocktail glass
• Shaker

1½ ounces brandy
¾ ounce light cream
2 tsp. honey

Shake the ingredients together firmly, with ice, in the shaker and strain into the cocktail glass.

B AND B

Strong, short after-dinner drink or to accompany coffee
• Cocktail glass

1 ounce brandy
1 ounce Benedictine

Mix the ingredients together in the cocktail glass. Add ice to taste.

ECSTASY

Aromatic, short aperitif
• Cocktail glass
• Mixing glass

¾ ounce brandy
¾ ounce Drambuie
¾ ounce dry vermouth

Mix the ingredients together, with plenty of ice, in the mixing glass and strain into the cocktail glass.

Brandy

Alexander (back), Sidecar (middle), Ecstasy (front)

PANAMAC

Creamy drink for the evening
- Cocktail glass
- Shaker

¾ *ounce cognac or brandy*
¾ *ounce brown crème de cacao*
¾ *ounce light cream*
- *Extra:*
Grated nutmeg

Shake all the ingredients together firmly, with ice, in the shaker and strain into the cocktail glass. Sprinkle with a little nutmeg.

IBU COCKTAIL

Refreshing champagne cocktail for the evening
- Champagne flute or glass
- Shaker

¾ *ounce brandy*
¾ *ounce apricot brandy*
¾ *ounce orange juice*
Champagne or dry sparkling wine for topping up
- *Garnish:*
½ *slice of orange*

Shake all the ingredients, except the champagne or sparkling wine, together in the shaker, with ice, and strain into the glass. Top up with sparkling wine or champagne. Perch the slice of orange on the rim.

PRINCE OF WALES

Aromatic champagne cocktail for the evening
- Silver goblet or highball/Collins glass

¾ *ounce brandy or cognac*
2 tsp. orange curaçao
1 dash Angostura bitters
Champagne or sparkling wine for topping up
- *Extra:*
½ *slice of orange*
½ *slice of lemon*
2 maraschino cherries

Mix all the ingredients together in the goblet or glass, with ice. Put the fruit in the glass. Serve the drink with a stirrer.

HAUTE COUTURE

Strong, short after-dinner drink
- Cocktail glass
- Mixing glass

¾ *ounce brandy*
¾ *ounce Benedictine*
¾ *ounce brown crème de cacao*

Stir all the ingredients together in the mixing glass, with ice, and strain into the cocktail glass.

Brandy

BRANDY FLIP

Creamy flip for the afternoon
• Champagne flute
• Shaker

1½ ounces brandy
1 tsp. sugar syrup
1 egg yolk
• *Extra:*
Grated nutmeg

Shake all the ingredients together firmly, with ice, in the shaker and strain into the glass. Sprinkle with a little nutmeg.

RITZ COCKTAIL

Aromatic champagne cocktail to serve as an aperitif or after-dinner drink
• Champagne glass or flute
• Shaker

¾ ounce brandy or cognac
¾ ounce Cointreau or other orange-flavored liqueur
¾ ounce orange juice
Champagne or sparking wine for topping up
• *Garnish:*
½ slice of orange

Shake all the ingredients, except the champagne, together, with ice, in the shaker and strain into the glass. Top up with champagne or sparkling wine. Perch the slice of orange on the rim of the glass.

RED MOON

Sweetish, fruity champagne cocktail for a reception
• Champagne glass or flute
• Shaker

¾ ounce brandy or cognac
¾ ounce passion-fruit juice
2 tsp. strawberry syrup
Champagne or sparkling wine for topping up
• *Garnish:*
1 maraschino cherry

Shake all the ingredients, except the champagne or sparkling wine, together, with ice, in the shaker. Strain into the champagne glass and top up with champagne or sparkling wine. Spear the cherry on a toothpick and add it to the glass.

FRENCH CONNECTION I

Bittersweet after-dinner drink
• Rocks glass

1 ounce cognac
¾ ounce amaretto

Stir the cognac and amaretto together in the glass with ice cubes.

BETWEEN THE SHEETS

Tangy, fruity short drink for the evening
- Cocktail glass
- Shaker

¾ ounce cognac
¾ ounce light rum
¾ ounce Cointreau or other orange-flavored liqueur
1 dash lemon juice

Shake all the ingredients together, with ice, in the shaker and strain into the cocktail glass.

NIKOLASCHKA

Spicy drink for the afternoon
- Pousse-café glass

¾ ounce brandy or cognac
1 slice of lemon, peeled
1 tsp. sugar
1 tsp. ground coffee

Put the brandy in the glass, place the slice of lemon on the rim of the glass, and sprinkle one half with sugar and the other with ground coffee.

MOONLIGHT

Creamy, sweet after-dinner drink
- Cocktail glass
- Mixing glass

½ ounce light cream
2 tsp. cognac
2 tsp. mandarin-flavored liqueur
2 tsp. sugar syrup
5 tsp. cold black coffee
- *Extra:*
1 piece of mandarin peel
1 orange peel spiral

Mix all the ingredients, except the coffee and cream, together, with ice, in the mixing glass and strain into the cocktail glass. Add the coffee, stir, and float the cream on top. Squeeze the mandarin peel into the drink. Hang the spiral of orange peel over the edge of the glass.

OLYMPIC

Medium-dry, fruity aperitif or after-dinner drink
- Cocktail glass
- Shaker

¾ ounce brandy or cognac
¾ ounce triple sec
¾ ounce orange juice

Shake the ingredients together, with ice, in the shaker and strain into the glass.

Brandy

Pisco Sour (left), Queen Mary (right)

PISCO SOUR

Refreshing, sharp short drink for parties
• Rocks glass with sugared rim
• Shaker

1½ ounces pisco
¾ ounce lemon juice
1 tsp. sugar or 1 dash lemon syrup, to
taste
• *Garnish:*
1 slice of lemon
1 maraschino cherry

Shake all the ingredients together, with
ice, in the shaker and strain into the
glass with the sugared rim. Perch the
fruit on the rim of the glass.

QUEEN MARY

Elegant, sweet aperitif or after-dinner
drink
• Cocktail glass
• Shaker

1 ounce cognac
1 ounce Cointreau or other orange-
flavored liqueur
1 dash anisette
1 dash grenadine
• *Garnish:*
1 maraschino cherry

Shake all the ingredients together, with
ice, in the shaker and strain into the
cocktail glass. Perch the cherry on the
rim of the glass.

B AND P

Elegant, tangy drink for the evening
• Rocks glass

¾ ounce brandy
¾ ounce port

Stir the ingredients together in the glass with ice cubes.

SARATOGA

Tangy aperitif
• Cocktail glass
• Mixing glass

1½ ounces brandy
2 dashes Angostura bitters
2 dashes maraschino

Mix the ingredients together, with ice, in the mixing glass and strain into the cocktail glass.

BRANDY ZOOM

Sweet after-dinner drink
• Cocktail glass
• Shaker

1½ ounces brandy
¾ ounce light cream
2 tsp. honey

Shake all the ingredients together, with ice cubes, in the shaker and strain into the cocktail glass.

CORONADO

Creamy, sweet after-dinner drink
• Cocktail glass
• Shaker

¾ ounce light cream
½ ounce crème de banane
½ ounce peach-flavored liqueur
2 tsp. brandy
• Garnish:
1 chocolate cookie
Grated chocolate

Shake the ingredients together firmly, with ice, in the shaker and strain into the cocktail glass. Garnish the drink with the chocolate cookie and a little grated chocolate.

LADY BE GOOD

Medium-dry aperitif
• Cocktail glass
• Shaker

¾ ounce brandy
¾ ounce dry vermouth
¾ ounce orange juice
1 tsp. white crème de menthe
1 tsp. grenadine

Shake the ingredients together, with ice, in the shaker and strain into the glass.

Brandy

ROLLS ROYCE

Fruity aperitif
- Cocktail glass
- Shaker

¾ ounce brandy
¾ ounce Cointreau or other orange-flavored liqueur
¾ ounce orange juice

Shake the ingredients together, with ice, in the shaker and strain into the cocktail glass.

QUEEN ELIZABETH

Medium-dry aperitif
- Cocktail glass
- Mixing glass

¾ ounce brandy
¾ ounce sweet red vermouth
1 tsp. triple sec

Stir the ingredients together, with ice, in the mixing glass and strain into the cocktail glass.

COGNAC FLIP

Delicate, tangy flip for the evening
- Cocktail glass
- Shaker

2 ounces cognac
1 egg yolk
2 tbsp. sugar

Shake all the ingredients together firmly and briefly in the shaker and strain into the cocktail glass.

EAST INDIA

Fruity aperitif
- Cocktail glass
- Shaker

1 ounce brandy
¾ ounce pineapple juice
2 tsp. orange curaçao
1 dash Angostura bitters
- *Garnish:*
1 maraschino cherry

Shake the ingredients together, with plenty of ice, in the shaker and strain into the cocktail glass. Drop the cherry into the glass.

NEW ORLEANS SIDECAR

Elegant, dry drink for parties
- Cocktail glass
- Shaker

¾ ounce brandy
¾ ounce light rum
¾ ounce lemon juice
2 tsp. triple sec
1 dash pastis
1 dash grenadine

Shake all the ingredients together firmly, with ice cubes, in the cocktail shaker and strain into the cocktail glass.

CHÂTEAU SARRE

Aromatic drink for parties
• Cocktail glass
• Shaker

1½ ounces brandy
½ ounce crème de banane
½ ounce maraschino
• Garnish:
1 maraschino cherry

Shake the ingredients together, with ice, in the shaker and strain into the cocktail glass. Put the cherry in the glass.

GLORIA

Dry aperitif
• Cocktail glass
• Mixing glass

½ ounce brandy
½ ounce scotch
½ ounce Campari
2 tsp. vermouth
2 tsp. amaretto
• Garnish:
1 piece of lemon peel
1 green maraschino cherry

Stir the ingredients together in the mixing glass, with ice, and strain into the cocktail glass. Spear the lemon peel and cherry on a toothpick and lay the garnish across the rim of the glass.

Brandy

FAR WEST

Mild, spicy drink for the evening
• Cocktail glass
• Shaker

¾ ounce cognac
¾ ounce advocaat
¾ ounce sweet white vermouth
• *Extra:*
Ground cinnamon

Shake all the ingredients together
firmly, with ice cubes, in the shaker and
strain into the cocktail glass. Sprinkle
with a pinch of cinnamon.

ALBA

Fruity, elegant, tangy drink for the
evening
• Cocktail glass
• Shaker

1½ ounces cognac
¾ ounce orange juice
2 tsp. raspberry cordial
• *Garnish:*
½ slice of orange

Shake all the ingredients together, with
ice cubes, in the shaker and strain into
the chilled cocktail glass. Perch the slice
of orange on the rim of the glass.

WILLEM VON ORANIEN

Slightly bitter aperitif
• Cocktail glass
• Mixing glass

¾ ounce brandy
2 tsp. triple sec
2 tsp. orange bitters
• Extra:
1 piece of orange peel

Mix the ingredients together in the mixing glass, with ice, and strain into the cocktail glass. Squeeze the orange peel over the drink.

CHERRY BLOSSOM I

Refined, dry drink for the evening
• Cocktail glass
• Shaker

¾ ounce cognac
¾ ounce cherry brandy
¾ ounce lemon juice
2 tsp. Cointreau or other orange-flavored liqueur
2 tsp. grenadine

Shake all the ingredients together firmly, with ice cubes, in the shaker and strain into the glass.

COFFEE

Strong after-dinner drink
• Red wine glass
• Shaker

1½ ounces cold, strong black coffee
¾ ounce brandy
¾ ounce triple sec
• Extra:
Possibly a little light cream

Shake the ingredients together firmly, with ice, in the shaker and strain into the red wine glass. Float a little cream on top, if liked.

GREEN LOVE

Fruity, bittersweet drink for the evening
• Cocktail glass
• Shaker

¾ ounce cognac
¾ ounce blue curaçao
¾ ounce mandarin-flavored liqueur
¾ ounce lemon juice
• Garnish:
1 slice of lemon

Shake all the ingredients together firmly, with ice cubes, in the shaker and strain into the cocktail glass. Put the slice of lemon on the rim of the glass.

Brandy

PICASSO

Tangy, fruity drink for the evening
- Cocktail glass
- Shaker

1 ounce cognac

¾ ounce Dubonnet

2 tsp. lemon juice

4 dashes sugar syrup

Shake all the ingredients together firmly, with ice cubes, in the shaker and strain into the cocktail glass.

AMERICAN SEA

Fruity, refined, dry aperitif
- Cocktail glass
- Shaker

1 ounce orange juice

¾ ounce cognac

¾ ounce dry vermouth

2 tsp. white crème de menthe

Shake the ingredients together firmly, with ice cubes, in the shaker and strain into the cocktail glass.

GREEN DRAGON

Fresh, spicy after-dinner drink
- Cocktail glass
- Shaker

1½ ounces cognac

2 tsp. green crème de menthe

Shake the cognac and liqueur together well, with ice cubes, in the shaker and strain into the glass.

DAISY

Fruity, elegant, tangy aperitif
- Cocktail glass
- Mixing glass

1 ounce gin

¾ ounce cognac

2 tsp. apricot brandy

- *Garnish:*

½ slice of lemon

Stir all the ingredients together in the mixing glass, with ice cubes, and strain into the cocktail glass. Perch the slice of lemon on the edge of the glass.

COGNAC CASSIS

Fruity, sweet drink for the evening
- Cocktail glass
- Shaker

1 ounce cognac

1 ounce crème de cassis

Shake the cognac and crème de cassis together, with ice, in the shaker and strain into the cocktail glass.

JAMES

Delicate, dry after-dinner drink
• Cocktail glass
• Mixing glass

¾ ounce cognac
¾ ounce gin
¾ ounce yellow Chartreuse
• *Garnish:*
1 green maraschino cherry

Mix all the ingredients together, with ice cubes, in the mixing glass and strain into the cocktail glass. Perch the cherry on the rim of the glass.

BRANDY COCKTAIL

Delicate, dry cocktail for the evening
• Cocktail glass
• Mixing glass

1½ ounces brandy
1 tsp. sugar syrup
3 dashes Angostura bitters
• *Garnish:*
1 green maraschino cherry

Stir all the ingredients together in the mixing glass, with ice, and strain into the cocktail glass. Perch the cherry on the rim of the glass.

HONEYMOON II

Fruity, delicately dry cocktail for the evening
• Cocktail glass
• Mixing glass

1½ ounces cognac
2 tsp. Cointreau or other orange-flavored liqueur
2 tsp. white wine
• *Garnish:*
1 slice of orange

Stir all the ingredients together in the mixing glass, with ice, and strain into the cocktail glass. Perch the slice of orange on the rim of the glass.

BREAKFAST EGGNOG

Sweet eggnog for any time of year
• Highball/Collins glass
• Shaker

1½ ounces cognac
¾ ounce white curaçao
½ ounce sugar syrup
1 egg
Milk for topping up

Shake all the ingredients, except the milk, together, with ice, in the shaker and strain into the glass. Top up with milk and stir.

Brandy

James (back left), Honeymoon II (back right), Brandy Cocktail (front left), Breakfast Eggnog (front right)

EGG SOUR

Nourishing sour for the evening
• Highball/Collins glass
• Shaker

1 ounce brandy
¾ ounce lemon juice
2 tsp. triple sec
2 tsp. sugar syrup
1 egg
• Garnish:
½ slice of orange
1 maraschino cherry

Shake the ingredients together firmly, with ice, in the shaker and strain into the glass. Spear the slice of orange and the cherry on a toothpick and place across the rim of the glass.

BRANDY EGGNOG

Nourishing eggnog for the afternoon
• Rocks glass
• Shaker

3½ ounces milk
1½ ounces brandy
2 tsp. sugar syrup
1 egg yolk
• Extra:
Grated nutmeg

Shake the ingredients together firmly, with ice, in the shaker and strain into the glass. Sprinkle with nutmeg.

LUMUMBA I

Spicy drink for the summer
• Highball glass

1½ ounces brandy
Cold cocoa for topping up
• Garnish:
½ ounce whipped cream
Cocoa powder

Pour the brandy into the highball glass, top up with cocoa, and stir briefly. Heap whipped cream on top and dust with cocoa powder.

HORSE'S NECK III

Refreshing long drink for any occasion
• Highball/Collins glass

1½ ounces brandy
1 dash Angostura bitters
Ginger ale for topping up
• Garnish:
1 lemon peel spiral

Pour the brandy and Angostura bitters into the highball glass with some ice. Top up with ginger ale and stir. Hang the lemon peel spiral over the edge of the glass and serve the drink with a stirrer.

Brandy

Brandy Eggnog (left), Brandy Cola (right)

BRANDY COLA

Sweet, long drink for the evening
• Highball/Collins glass

1½ ounces brandy
Cola for topping up
• *Garnish:*
½ slice of lemon

Pour the brandy into the highball glass, with ice cubes. Top up with cola and stir briefly. Add the slice of lemon to the glass.

COCO DE MARTINIQUE

Fruity, sweet long drink for the evening
• Highball/Collins glass
• Shaker

2¾ ounces orange juice
1¾ ounces cream of coconut
1 ounce Armagnac
1 ounce Benedictine

Shake all the ingredients together firmly, with ice cubes, in the shaker and strain into the highball glass over crushed ice.

BERMUDA HIGHBALL

Spicy, mild drink for the evening
• Highball/Collins glass
• Mixing glass

1 ounce brandy
¾ ounce gin
1 dash orange bitters
Ginger ale for topping up
• *Extra:*
1 kumquat

Stir together the brandy, gin, and orange bitters in the mixing glass, with ice, and strain into the glass. Top up with ginger ale and add the kumquat to the glass.

PIERRE COLLINS

Refreshing Collins for any time of day
• Collins/highball glass

1½ ounces brandy
¾ ounce lemon juice
2 tsp. sugar syrup
Soda water for topping up
• *Garnish:*
½ slice of lemon
1 maraschino cherry

Stir together the brandy, lemon juice, and sugar syrup in the highball glass with ice. Top up with soda water and stir until the glass condenses. Put the fruit on the rim of the glass.

COGNAC COLLINS

Dry, fruity Collins for the evening
• Collins/highball glass

1½ ounces cognac
¾ ounce lemon juice
2 tsp. sugar
Soda water for topping up
• *Extra:*
1 slice of lemon
½ slice of orange
1 maraschino cherry

Stir the cognac, sugar, and lemon juice together in the highball glass, with ice cubes. Top up with soda water and stir briefly. Add the fruit to the glass.

DRY MANHATTAN

GODFATHER

SWEET MANHATTAN

Whiskey-based Drinks

ROB ROY

RUSTY NAIL

OHIO OLD-FASHIONED

BOURBON HIGHBALL

MINT JULEP

MANHATTAN

Classic aperitif
• Cocktail glass
• Mixing glass

1½ ounces Canadian whisky
¾ ounce sweet red vermouth
1 dash Angostura bitters
• Extra:
1 maraschino cherry
1 piece of lemon peel (optional)

Stir the ingredients together in the mixing glass, with ice, and strain into the cocktail glass. Spear the cherry on a toothpick, put it in the drink, and squeeze the lemon peel over the drink, if liked.

SWEET MANHATTAN

Delicate, dry aperitif
• Cocktail glass
• Mixing glass

1½ ounces Canadian whisky
¾ ounce sweet red vermouth
1 dash orange bitters
2 dashes white curaçao
• Garnish:
1 green maraschino cherry

Stir the ingredients together, with ice, in the mixing glass and strain into the cocktail glass. Perch the cherry on the rim of the glass.

DRY MANHATTAN

Classic aperitif
• Cocktail glass
• Mixing glass

1½ ounces Canadian whisky
¾ ounce dry vermouth
• Extra:
1 green olive
1 piece of lemon peel (optional)

Stir the ingredients together in the mixing glass, with ice, and strain into the cocktail glass. Spear the olive on a toothpick, put it in the drink, and squeeze the lemon peel over the drink, if liked.

PERFECT MANHATTAN

Aromatic drink for the evening
• Cocktail glass
• Mixing glass

1½ ounces bourbon
2 tsp. dry vermouth
2 tsp. sweet red vermouth

Stir the ingredients together in the mixing glass, with ice, and strain into the cocktail glass.

Whiskey

Sweet Manhattan (top), Dry Manhattan (front left), Esquire Manhattan (front right)

JIMMY LOPEZ MANHATTAN

Delicate, dry aperitif
- Cocktail glass
- Mixing glass

1 ounce bourbon

¾ ounce dry vermouth

1 tsp. apricot brandy

• Garnish:

1 maraschino cherry

Stir the ingredients together in the mixing glass, with ice, and strain into the cocktail glass. Add the cherry to the glass.

ESQUIRE MANHATTAN

Delicate, dry aperitif
- Cocktail glass
- Mixing glass

¾ ounce bourbon

¾ ounce sweet red vermouth

1 dash orange bitters

• Garnish:

1 green maraschino cherry

Stir the ingredients together in the mixing glass, with ice, and strain into the cocktail glass. Perch the cherry on the rim of the glass.

GODFATHER

Sweet short drink for all occasions
• Rocks glass

1¾ ounces bourbon
¾ ounce amaretto

Mix all the ingredients together in the glass, with ice, and serve the drink with a stirrer.

SCOTCH ON THE ROCKS

Aromatic drink
• Rocks glass

1½ ounces scotch

Pour the scotch into the glass over ice cubes and serve the drink with a stirrer.

RUSTY NAIL

Sweet after-dinner drink
• Rocks glass

1 ounce scotch
1 ounce Drambuie

Mix all the ingredients together in the glass, with ice cubes, and serve with a stirrer.

JOKER

Aromatic aperitif
• Cocktail glass
• Mixing glass

1 ounce scotch
½ ounce Grand Marnier
½ ounce Dubonnet

Stir the ingredients together, with ice, in the mixing glass and strain into the cocktail glass.

OHIO OLD-FASHIONED

Slightly bitter after-dinner drink
• Old-fashioned glass

1¾ ounces bourbon
1 dash Angostura bitters

Mix together the bourbon and Angostura bitters in the glass, with 2 ice cubes.

ROB ROY

Aromatic drink
• Cocktail glass
• Mixing glass

1½ ounces scotch
¾ ounce sweet red vermouth
1 dash Angostura bitters
• Garnish:
1 maraschino cherry

Mix the ingredients together, with ice, in the mixing glass and strain into the cocktail glass. Spear the cherry on a toothpick and add it to the glass.

Godfather (left), Ohio Old-Fashioned (middle), Rob Roy (right)

OLD-FASHIONED BOURBON COCKTAIL

Strong aperitif
• Old-fashioned glass

1 sugar lump
3 dashes Angostura bitters
1½ ounces bourbon
Water or still mineral water
• Garnish:
½ slice of lemon
½ slice of orange
2 maraschino cherries

Put the sugar lump in the glass, drizzle the Angostura bitters over it, and crush it. Add a few ice cubes to the glass and pour the bourbon over them. Add a little water and stir. Add the fruit to the glass. Serve with a stirrer.

MINT JULEP

Refreshing julep for a party
• Rocks glass

A few mint leaves
2 tsp. water or still mineral water
2 tsp. sugar syrup
1½ ounces bourbon
• Garnish:
1 maraschino cherry

Crush the mint leaves in the glass, add the water and sugar syrup, and stir well. Add plenty of crushed ice and top up with the bourbon. Spear the cherry on a toothpick and balance it on the rim of the glass.

SWEET LADY

A fruity, mild drink for any time of year
• Cocktail glass
• Shaker

1½ ounces scotch
2 tsp. white crème de cacao
2 tsp. peach brandy

Shake all the ingredients together, with ice, in the shaker and strain into the cocktail glass.

CONTINENTAL SOUR

Fruity, mild, dry sour for the evening
• Rocks glass
• Shaker

1¾ ounces bourbon
1 ounce grenadine
¾ ounce lemon juice
1 egg white
1 dash red wine
• Garnish:
1 slice of orange

Shake all the ingredients, except the red wine, together well, with ice, in the shaker and strain into the glass. Add the red wine and stir. Perch the slice of orange on the rim of the glass.

Whiskey

IRISH ROSE

Strong aperitif
- Cocktail glass
- Shaker

1½ ounces Irish whiskey
¾ ounce lemon juice
2 tsp. grenadine

Shake the ingredients together, with ice, in the shaker and strain into the cocktail glass.

DANDY

Aromatic aperitif
- Cocktail glass
- Mixing glass

1 ounce rye
1 ounce Dubonnet
3 dashes Angostura bitters
1 dash lemon juice
- *Extra:*
1 piece each of lemon and orange peel

Mix the ingredients together, with ice, in the mixing glass and strain into the cocktail glass. Squeeze the lemon and orange peels over the drink and add the peels to the glass.

QUATTRO

Aromatic aperitif or after-dinner drink
- Cocktail glass
- Mixing glass

½ ounce Canadian whisky
½ ounce amaretto
½ ounce crème de cassis
½ ounce dry vermouth
- *Garnish:*
1 maraschino cherry
1 piece of orange peel

Mix the ingredients together, with ice, in the mixing glass and strain into the cocktail glass. Add the cherry and the piece of orange peel to the glass.

KING'S CROSS

Medium-dry aperitif
- Cocktail glass
- Mixing glass

1 ounce bourbon
1 ounce sweet red vermouth
1 dash Benedictine
- *Extra:*
1 piece of lemon peel

Shake the ingredients together, with ice, in the shaker and strain into the cocktail glass. Squeeze the lemon peel over the drink and add the peel to the glass.

UP TO DATE

Medium-dry aperitif
- Cocktail glass
- Mixing glass

1 ounce Canadian whisky
¾ ounce dry vermouth
2 tsp. Grand Marnier
1 dash Angostura bitters
• Extra:
1 piece of lemon peel, if liked

Stir the ingredients together, with ice, in the mixing glass and strain into the glass. Squeeze the lemon peel over the cocktail, if liked.

OLYMPIA

Sweet aperitif or after-dinner drink
- Cocktail glass
- Shaker

½ ounce Canadian whisky
½ ounce dry vermouth
2 tsp. green Chartreuse
2 tsp. Escorial or other herb-flavored liqueur
2 tsp. greengage cordial
• Garnish:
1 black grape

Shake the ingredients together, with ice, in the shaker and strain into the cocktail glass. Put the grape in the glass.

NEW YORKER

Fruity aperitif
- Cocktail glass
- Shaker

1½ ounces bourbon
¾ ounce lemon juice
2 tsp. grenadine

Shake the ingredients together, with ice, in the shaker and strain into the cocktail glass.

ZAZARAC I

Strong, aniseed-flavored aperitif
- Cocktail glass
- Mixing glass

¾ ounce scotch
¾ ounce anisette
¾ ounce light rum
1 dash Angostura bitters
1 dash grenadine

Mix the ingredients together, with ice, in the mixing glass and strain into the cocktail glass.

BLINKER

Fruity aperitif
- Cocktail glass
- Shaker

1 ounce Canadian whisky
1 ounce grapefruit juice
¾ ounce grenadine

Shake the ingredients together, with ice, in the shaker and strain into the glass.

Whiskey

HANDLEBAR

Dry drink for the evening
• Cocktail glass
• Shaker

1 ounce scotch
2 tsp. Drambuie
2 tsp. lime juice

Shake all the ingredients together, with ice, in the shaker and strain into the glass.

HURRICANE I

Delicate, dry drink for the evening
• Cocktail glass
• Mixing glass

¾ ounce bourbon
¾ ounce gin
¾ ounce peppermint-flavored liqueur

Stir all the ingredients together, with ice, in the mixing glass and strain into the glass.

TORONTO

Delicate, dry after-dinner drink
• Cocktail glass
• Shaker

2 ounces Canadian whisky
¾ ounce Fernet Branca or other herbal bitters
1 tsp. sugar syrup
1 dash Angostura bitters

Shake all the ingredients together, with ice, in the shaker and strain into the glass.

CHURCHILL

Delicate, dry drink for the evening
• Cocktail glass
• Shaker

2 ounces scotch
¾ ounce sweet red vermouth
1 dash triple sec
1 dash lemon juice
• Garnish:
1 slice of lemon

Shake all the ingredients together, with ice, in the shaker and strain into the cocktail glass. Perch the slice of lemon on the rim of the glass.

CHAMPION

Medium-dry drink for parties
• Cocktail glass
• Mixing glass

¾ ounce scotch
¾ ounce dry vermouth
2 tsp. Benedictine
2 tsp. triple sec

Stir the ingredients together, with ice, in the mixing glass and strain into the cocktail glass.

LORD BYRON

Spicy, fruity drink for the evening
• Rocks glass
• Mixing glass

1 ounce scotch

2 tsp. orange-flavored liqueur

2 tsp. sweet red vermouth

1 dash Angostura bitters

• Garnish:

1 slice of orange

Stir all the ingredients together, with ice, in the mixing glass and strain into the glass. Add the slice of orange to the glass. Serve immediately.

NEW YORK FLIP

Sweet after-dinner drink
• Cocktail glass
• Shaker

1 ounce bourbon

¾ ounce port

¾ ounce light cream

2 tsp. sugar syrup

1 egg yolk

• Extra:

Grated nutmeg

Shake the ingredients together very firmly, with ice, in the shaker and strain into the cocktail glass. Sprinkle a little grated nutmeg over the drink and serve immediately.

Whiskey

LENA

Medium-dry aperitif
- Cocktail glass
- Mixing glass

1 ounce bourbon

½ ounce sweet red vermouth

2 tsp. Galliano

2 tsp. Campari

2 tsp. dry vermouth

• Garnish:

1 maraschino cherry

Stir all the ingredients together, with ice, in the mixing glass and strain into the chilled cocktail glass. Add the maraschino cherry to the glass.

TUTIOSI

Sweet after-dinner drink
- Cocktail glass
- Mixing glass

¾ ounce Canadian whisky

½ ounce brandy

½ ounce sweet red vermouth

2 tsp. Galliano

2 tsp. mandarin-flavored liqueur

• Extra:

1 piece of orange peel

Stir the ingredients together, with ice, in the mixing glass and strain into the cocktail glass. Squeeze the orange peel over the drink and add the peel to it.

YANKEE DUTCH

Strong drink for parties
• Cocktail glass
• Mixing glass

½ ounce bourbon
½ ounce cherry brandy
½ ounce triple sec
½ ounce vodka
• *Extra:*
1 piece of orange peel

Stir all the ingredients together, with ice, in the mixing glass and strain into the cocktail glass. Squeeze the orange peel over the drink and add it to the glass.

MR. BEAR

Sweet, short drink for parties
• Cocktail glass
• Shaker

1½ ounces Canadian whisky
2 tsp. honey
• *Extra:*
1 piece of lemon peel

Shake all the ingredients together, with ice, in the shaker and strain into the cocktail glass. Squeeze the lemon peel over the drink and add it to the glass.

A. M. B. A.

Very strong after-dinner drink
• Cocktail glass
• Mixing glass

¾ ounce scotch
¾ ounce dark rum
2 tsp. sweet red vermouth
1 tsp. Cointreau or other orange-flavored liqueur
• *Extra:*
1 piece of lemon peel
1 maraschino cherry

Stir all the ingredients together, with ice, in the mixing glass and strain into the cocktail glass. Squeeze the lemon peel over the drink and put the cherry into the glass.

IZCARAGUA

Medium-dry after-dinner drink
• Cocktail glass
• Mixing glass

½ ounce scotch
½ ounce dry vermouth
½ ounce amaretto
½ ounce crème de banane
• *Extra:*
1 piece of lemon peel

Stir all the ingredients together, with ice, in the mixing glass and strain into the cocktail glass. Add the lemon peel to the glass.

Whiskey

TENNESSEE

Fruity, delicately dry drink for the evening
• Cocktail glass
• Shaker

1½ ounces bourbon
2 tsp. maraschino
1 dash lemon juice
• Garnish:
1 maraschino cherry

Shake all the ingredients together, with ice, in the shaker and strain into the cocktail glass. Perch the cherry on the rim of the glass.

EXPLORATION

Fruity, delicately dry drink for the evening
• Rocks glass
• Shaker

1 ounce scotch
¾ ounce dry sherry
2 tsp. amaretto
2 tsp. lemon juice
• Extra:
1 piece of lemon peel

Shake all the ingredients together, with ice, in the shaker and strain into the glass. Squeeze the lemon peel over the drink and add it to the glass.

LAFAYETTE

Delicate, dry aperitif
• Cocktail glass
• Mixing glass

1 ounce bourbon
2 tsp. dry vermouth
2 tsp. Dubonnet
2 dashes Angostura bitters

Stir all the ingredients together, with ice, in the mixing glass and strain into the cocktail glass.

GOLDEN NAIL

Fruity, spicy after-dinner drink
• Rocks glass

1 ounce bourbon
¾ ounce Southern Comfort

Mix all the ingredients together in the glass with ice cubes.

MISSOURI MULE

Fruity, delicately dry drink for the evening
• Cocktail glass
• Shaker

1½ ounces bourbon
2 tsp. crème de cassis
2 tsp. lemon juice
• Garnish:
1 slice of lemon

Shake all the ingredients together firmly, with ice, in the shaker and strain into the cocktail glass. Perch the lemon on the rim of the glass.

KENTUCKY BOURBON

Delicate, dry after-dinner drink
• Cocktail glass
• Mixing glass

1½ ounces bourbon
¾ ounce Benedictine
• Garnish:
1 maraschino cherry

Stir all the ingredients together, with ice, in the mixing glass and strain into the cocktail glass. Perch the cherry on the rim of the glass.

UNION CLUB

Fruity, dry drink for the evening
• Cocktail glass
• Shaker

1½ ounces bourbon
¾ ounce triple sec
¾ ounce lemon juice
1 tsp. egg white
2 dashes grenadine

Shake all the ingredients together, with ice, in the shaker and strain into the cocktail glass.

MONTE CARLO

Delicate, dry after-dinner drink
• Cocktail glass
• Mixing glass

1½ ounces bourbon
¾ ounce Benedictine
1 dash Angostura bitters

Stir all the ingredients together, with ice, in the mixing glass and strain into the cocktail glass.

Whiskey

Missouri Mule (left), Union Club (right)

BELLRIVE JUBILEE COCKTAIL

Delicate, dry aperitif
- Cocktail glass
- Mixing glass

1½ ounces bourbon
¾ ounce sweet red vermouth
1 dash triple sec
• Garnish:
½ slice of orange

Stir all the ingredients together, with ice, in the mixing glass and strain into the cocktail glass. Perch the slice of orange on the rim of the glass.

OLD PALE

Spicy, dry drink for the evening or as an aperitif
- Cocktail glass with sugared rim
- Mixing glass

1 ounce bourbon
¾ ounce Campari
1 tsp. lime syrup
• Extra:
1 piece of lemon peel

Stir all the ingredients together, with ice, in the mixing glass and strain into the cocktail glass. Add the piece of lemon peel to the glass.

BARETT

Spicy, sweet drink for the evening
- Rocks glass

1½ ounces bourbon
2 tsp. Galliano
2 tsp. amaretto

Stir all the ingredients together, with ice cubes, in the glass.

DANNY'S SPECIAL COCKTAIL

Fruity, delicate, dry after-dinner drink
- Cocktail glass
- Shaker

¾ ounce bourbon
¾ ounce Grand Marnier
2 tsp. lemon juice

Shake all the ingredients together, with ice, in the shaker and strain into the cocktail glass.

ERANS

Fruity, sweet drink for the evening
- Cocktail glass
- Mixing glass

1½ ounces bourbon
2 tsp. apricot brandy
2 tsp. Cointreau or other orange-flavored liqueur

Stir all the ingredients together, with ice, in the mixing glass and strain into the cocktail glass.

Whiskey

BRAINSTORMING

Delicate, dry drink for the evening
• Cocktail glass
• Mixing glass

1¾ ounces Irish whiskey

2 dashes Benedictine

2 dashes dry vermouth

• Extra:

1 piece of orange peel

Stir all the ingredients together, with ice, in the mixing glass and strain into the cocktail glass. Squeeze the orange peel over the drink and add it to the glass.

CREOLE

Mild, spicy drink for the evening
• Cocktail glass
• Mixing glass

¾ ounce bourbon

¾ ounce sweet red vermouth

2 tsp. Benedictine

• Garnish:

1 slice of lemon

Stir all the ingredients together, with ice, in the mixing glass and strain into the cocktail glass. Perch the slice of lemon on the rim of the glass.

OPENING I

Sweet, short drink for the evening
• Cocktail glass
• Shaker

1½ ounces bourbon

¾ ounce sweet red vermouth

2 tsp. grenadine

Shake all the ingredients together, with ice, in the shaker and strain into the cocktail glass.

DON JOSÉ

Spicy, short drink for the evening
• Cocktail glass
• Shaker

¾ ounce bourbon

¾ ounce sweet red vermouth

2 tsp. banana-flavored liqueur

Shake all the ingredients together, with crushed ice, in the shaker and pour into the cocktail glass.

OLD PAL

Spicy, bitter aperitif
• Cocktail glass
• Mixing glass

¾ ounce bourbon

¾ ounce Campari

¾ ounce dry vermouth

Stir all the ingredients together, with ice, in the mixing glass and strain into the glass.

DELTA

Fruity, sweet drink for the evening
• Rocks glass
• Shaker

1 ounce bourbon
2 tsp. Southern Comfort
2 tsp. lime syrup
• Garnish:
½ slice of orange
1 maraschino cherry

Shake all the ingredients together well, with ice, in the shaker and strain into the glass half filled with crushed ice. Perch the fruit on the rim of the glass.

COAXER

Fruity, dry drink for any time of year
• Rocks glass
• Shaker

1¾ ounces bourbon
2 tsp. sugar syrup
¾ ounce lemon juice
1 egg white

Shake all the ingredients together firmly, with crushed ice, in the shaker and pour into the glass.

BROOKLYN

Dry, spicy aperitif
• Cocktail glass
• Mixing glass

1½ ounces Canadian whisky
¾ ounce dry vermouth
2 dashes maraschino

Stir all the ingredients together, with ice, in the mixing glass and strain into the glass.

DREAM OF NAPLES

Dry, spicy drink for the evening
• Cocktail glass
• Mixing glass

1 ounce bourbon
2 tsp. Campari
2 tsp. triple sec
1 dash Angostura bitters
• Garnish:
1 maraschino cherry

Stir all the ingredients together, with ice, in the mixing glass and strain into the cocktail glass. Perch the cherry on the rim of the glass.

Whiskey

Gloom Lifter (left), Bourbon Flip (right)

GLOOM LIFTER

Sharp, fruity drink for the evening
• Cocktail glass
• Shaker

1 ounce Irish whiskey
2 tsp. lemon juice
2 tsp. sugar syrup
1 dash of egg white
• Garnish:
1 slice of lemon

Shake all the ingredients together firmly, with ice, in the shaker and strain into the cocktail glass. Perch the slice of lemon on the rim of the glass.

BOURBON FLIP

Creamy, sweet after-dinner drink
• Cocktail glass
• Shaker

1 ounce bourbon
1 ounce light cream
2 tsp. dark rum
2 tsp. sugar syrup
1 egg yolk
• Extra:
Grated nutmeg

Shake all the ingredients together firmly, with ice, in the shaker and strain into the cocktail glass. Sprinkle a little grated nutmeg on top.

RITZ OLD-FASHIONED

Fruity, mild drink for the evening
• Old-fashioned glass with sugared rim
• Shaker

1½ ounces bourbon
¾ ounce Grand Marnier
1 dash lemon juice
1 dash maraschino

Shake all the ingredients together, with ice, in the shaker and strain into the glass.

HAWK

Fruity, dry drink for the evening
• Cocktail glass
• Shaker

¾ ounce bourbon
¾ ounce gin
2 tsp. lemon juice
• Garnish:
1 maraschino cherry

Shake all the ingredients together, with ice, in the shaker and strain into the glass. Perch the cherry on the rim of the glass.

CAMERON'S KICK

Nutty, delicately dry drink for the evening
• Cocktail glass
• Shaker

¾ ounce Irish whiskey
¾ ounce scotch
2 tsp. almond syrup
2 tsp. lemon juice

Shake all the ingredients together firmly, with ice, in the shaker and strain into the glass.

NIGHT SHADOWS

Fruity, delicately dry drink for the evening
• Rocks glass
• Shaker

1 ounce bourbon
2 tsp. sweet red vermouth
2 tsp. orange juice
1 tsp. yellow Chartreuse
• Garnish:
½ slice of orange
1 lemon wedge

Shake all the ingredients together, with ice, in the shaker and strain into the glass filled one-third full with crushed ice. Add the fruit to the glass.

Whiskey

DE RIGUEUR

Fruity, dry drink for the evening
- Cocktail glass
- Shaker

1½ ounces bourbon

1½ ounces grapefruit juice

2 tsp. honey

Shake all the ingredients together firmly, with ice, in the shaker and strain into the cocktail glass.

AMERICA

Delicate, dry drink for the evening
- Cocktail glass
- Shaker

1¾ ounces bourbon

½ ounce lime juice

2 tsp. grenadine

• Extra:

1 piece of lime peel

Shake all the ingredients together, with ice, in the shaker and strain into the glass. Squeeze the lime peel over the drink and add it to the glass.

HIGHLAND MOON

Spicy, mild drink for the evening
- Rocks glass
- Mixing glass

1 ounce scotch

1 ounce Drambuie

• Garnish:

1 slice of lemon

1 maraschino cherry

Stir all the ingredients together, with ice, in the mixing glass and strain into the glass. Spear the fruit on a toothpick and balance across the rim of the glass.

ROBBY

Delicate, dry aperitif
- Rocks glass
- Mixing glass

¾ ounce Canadian whisky

½ ounce dry vermouth

½ ounce sweet white vermouth

• Garnish:

1 maraschino cherry

Stir all the ingredients together, with ice, in the mixing glass and strain into the glass. Spear the cherry on a toothpick and add it to the glass.

BISHOP

Fruity, delicate, tangy drink for the evening
• Cocktail glass
• Shaker

1 ounce Canadian whisky
2 tsp. sweet red vermouth
2 tsp. orange juice
1 tsp. green Chartreuse

Shake all the ingredients together, with ice, in the shaker and strain into the glass.

CANADA

Fruity, mild drink for the evening
• Cocktail glass
• Shaker

1 ounce Canadian whisky
2 tsp. triple sec
2 tsp. maple syrup
2 dashes Angostura bitters

Shake all the ingredients together, with ice, in the shaker and strain into the cocktail glass.

BOURBON CAR

Fruity, sourish drink for the evening
• Cocktail glass
• Shaker

1½ ounces bourbon
¾ ounce Cointreau or other orange-flavored liqueur
¾ ounce lemon juice
• Garnish:
1 maraschino cherry

Shake all the ingredients together firmly, with ice, in the shaker and strain into the cocktail glass. Perch the cherry on the rim of the glass.

BOURBON SKIN

Fruity, dry drink for the evening
• Cocktail glass
• Shaker

1¾ ounces bourbon
¾ ounce lemon juice
1 tsp. grenadine
• Garnish:
1 maraschino cherry

Shake all the ingredients together, with crushed ice, in the shaker and pour into the cocktail glass. Perch the cherry on the rim of the glass.

Whiskey

Barbicane (left), Whiskey Twist (right)

BARBICANE

Fruity, mild drink for a party
• Cocktail glass
• Shaker

1 ounce scotch
1 ounce passion-fruit nectar
2 tsp. Drambuie
1 dash lemon juice
• Garnish:
1 maraschino cherry

Shake all the ingredients together, with ice cubes, in the shaker and strain into the cocktail glass. Perch the cherry on the rim of the glass.

WHISKEY TWIST

Fruity, slightly sour drink for the evening
• Cocktail glass
• Mixing glass

1½ ounces Irish whiskey
2 tsp. lemon juice
1 tsp. cherry brandy
1 tsp. raspberry syrup
• Garnish:
1 maraschino cherry

Stir all the ingredients together, with ice cubes, in the mixing glass and strain into the cocktail glass. Perch the cherry on the rim of the glass.

COWBOY COCKTAIL

Creamy after-dinner drink
• Cocktail glass
• Shaker

1½ ounces bourbon
¾ ounce light cream

Shake all the ingredients together, with ice, in the shaker and strain into the glass.

ADELLE SPECIAL

Fruity drink for the evening
• Cocktail glass
• Shaker

1¾ ounces scotch
2 tsp. orange-flavored liqueur

Shake all the ingredients together, with ice, in the shaker and strain into the glass.

FRISCO SOUR

Spicy, sour after-dinner drink
• Sour glass
• Shaker

1½ ounces bourbon
¾ ounce Benedictine
1 ounce lemon juice

Shake all the ingredients together, with ice cubes, in the shaker and strain into the glass.

McKINLEY'S DELIGHT

Fruity, dry drink for the evening
• Cocktail glass
• Mixing glass

1 ounce bourbon
1 ounce dry vermouth
2 tsp. cherry-flavored liqueur
1 tsp. Pernod
• Garnish:
1 maraschino cherry

Stir all the ingredients together, with ice, in the mixing glass and strain into the cocktail glass. Perch the cherry on the rim of the glass.

4TH OF JULY

Fruity, slightly dry drink for the evening
• Rocks glass
• Shaker

1¾ ounces orange juice
1 ounce bourbon
2 tsp. apricot brandy
2 tsp. lemon juice
• Garnish:
1 slice of orange
1 slice of lemon

Shake all the ingredients together well, with ice cubes, in the shaker and strain into the glass. Perch the fruit on the rim of the glass.

Cowboy Cocktail (back left), Adelle Special (back right), 4th of July (front)

PRINCE CHARLIE

Fruity, dry drink for the evening
• Cocktail glass
• Shaker

1 ounce scotch
¾ ounce Drambuie
2 tsp. lemon juice
• Garnish:
1 maraschino cherry

Shake all the ingredients together firmly, with ice cubes, in the shaker and strain into the cocktail glass. Spear the maraschino cherry with a toothpick and add it to the glass.

WHISKEY SANGAREE

Fruity, sweet drink for the evening
• Cocktail glass
• Shaker

1½ ounces bourbon
2 tsp. cherry brandy
1 tsp. honey
• Extra:
Grated nutmeg

Shake all the ingredients together firmly, with ice, in the shaker and strain into the cocktail glass. Sprinkle with grated nutmeg.

BOURBONNAISE

Fruity, spicy drink for the evening or as an aperitif
• Rocks glass
• Shaker

1½ ounces bourbon
2 tsp. dry vermouth
2 tsp. crème de cassis
2 tsp. lemon juice

Shake all the ingredients together, with ice cubes, in the shaker and strain into the glass, which should be half filled with ice cubes.

WEMBLEY

Fruity, spicy drink for the evening
• Cocktail glass
• Shaker

¾ ounce scotch
¾ ounce dry vermouth
¾ ounce pineapple juice
• Garnish:
1 pineapple piece

Shake all the ingredients together, with ice, in the shaker and strain into the cocktail glass. Perch the pineapple segment on the rim of the glass.

Whiskey

MODERN GIRL

Spicy, dry drink for the evening
• Rocks glass
• Shaker

¾ ounce bourbon
2 tsp. lemon juice
1 tsp. light rum
1 tsp. Pernod
1 tsp. orange bitters
• Extra:
1 piece of lemon peel

Shake all the ingredients together, with ice, in the shaker and strain into the glass over ice cubes. Squeeze the lemon peel over the drink and add it to the glass.

PIERRE

Delicate, dry drink for the evening
• Cocktail glass
• Mixing glass

1 ounce bourbon
¾ ounce apricot brandy
2 tsp. lemon juice
• Extra:
1 piece of lemon peel

Mix all the ingredients together, with ice, in the mixing glass and strain into the cocktail glass. Add the lemon peel to the glass.

YORK

Delicate, dry drink for the evening
• Cocktail glass
• Mixing glass

2 ounces bourbon
¾ ounce sweet red vermouth
3 dashes Angostura bitters
• Garnish:
1 maraschino cherry

Mix all the ingredients together, with ice, in the mixing glass and strain into the cocktail glass. Perch the cherry on the rim of the glass.

WHISKY CRUSTA

Fruity, sweet-and-sour drink for the evening
• Cocktail glass with sugared rim
• Shaker

1 ounce scotch
½ ounce maraschino
4 tsp. lemon juice
1 tsp. sugar
1 dash Angostura bitters

Shake all the ingredients together, with ice, in the shaker and strain into the glass.

COCKTAIL NO. 13

Fruity, mild drink for the evening
• Cocktail glass
• Shaker

¾ ounce scotch
¾ ounce apricot-flavored liqueur
¾ ounce orange juice
• Garnish:
1 maraschino cherry

Shake all the ingredients together, with ice cubes, in the shaker and strain into the glass. Perch the cherry on the rim of the glass.

EVERYTHING BUT

Fruity, slightly dry flip for the evening
• Balloon or wine glass
• Shaker

1 ounce bourbon
1 ounce gin
¾ ounce lemon juice
¾ ounce orange juice
½ ounce apricot brandy
½ ounce sugar syrup
1 egg yolk

Shake all the ingredients together firmly, with ice, in the shaker and strain into the glass.

FOOTBALL PLAYER

Fruity, slightly dry drink for the evening
• Cocktail glass
• Shaker

1 ounce scotch
2 tsp. Cointreau or other orange-flavored liqueur
2 tsp. grapefruit juice

Shake all the ingredients together firmly, with ice cubes, in the shaker and strain into the cocktail glass.

WHISKEY SOUR

Refreshing sour for the evening
• Medium sour glass
• Mixing glass

1½ ounces bourbon
¾ ounce lemon juice
2 tsp. sugar syrup
1 dash Angostura bitters
• Garnish:
½ slice of orange
1 maraschino cherry

Shake all the ingredients together, with ice, in the shaker and strain into the glass. Perch the fruit on the rim of the glass.

Whiskey

MINT COOLER

Refreshing cooler for hot days
• Highball/Collins glass

1½ ounces scotch
1 tsp. white or green crème de menthe
Sparkling mineral water for topping up

Put the whiskey and crème de menthe in the glass with ice cubes and top up with mineral water. Serve with a stirrer.

MORNING GLORY FIZZ

Refreshing fizz for all occasions
• Rocks glass
• Shaker

1½ ounces scotch
¾ ounce lemon juice
2 tsp. Pernod
2 tsp. sugar syrup
1 egg white
Soda water for topping up

Except for the soda water, shake all the ingredients together firmly, with ice, in the shaker and strain into the glass. Top up with soda water.

LONDON SOUR

Fruity drink for any occasion
• Highball/Collins glass
• Shaker

1 ounce scotch
¾ ounce lemon juice
¾ ounce orange juice
2 tsp. almond syrup
2 tsp. sugar syrup
• Garnish:
½ slice of orange
1 maraschino cherry

Shake all the ingredients together, with ice, in the shaker and strain into the glass. Spear the slice of orange and cherry on a toothpick and lay the garnish across the rim of the glass.

BOURBON HIGHBALL

Sweet, spicy drink for any time of year
• Highball/Collins glass

1½ ounces bourbon
1 piece of lemon peel
Ginger ale for topping up
• Garnish:
1 lemon peel spiral

Put the whiskey in the glass with ice cubes. Squeeze the lemon peel over the whiskey and add it to the glass. Top up with ginger ale. Hang the lemon peel spiral over the rim of the glass.

WHISKY & SODA

Refreshing drink for any day
• Rocks glass

1½ ounces scotch
Soda water for topping up

Pour the whisky into a glass with ice cubes and top up with soda water to taste.

CANADIAN SUMMER

Fresh, spicy long drink for any time of year
• Large rocks glass

1 ounce Canadian whisky
¾ ounce white crème de cacao
2 tsp. green crème de menthe
Soda water for topping up

Stir the whisky and liqueurs together in the glass. Add a few ice cubes and top up with soda water.

CANADIAN GINGER

Refreshing drink for a summer party
• Highball/Collins glass

1½ ounces Canadian whisky
Ginger ale for topping up

Pour the whisky into the glass, with ice cubes, and top up with ginger ale.

WHISKY FIZZ

Refreshing fizz for a party
• Rocks glass
• Shaker

1½ ounces scotch
¾ ounce lemon juice
2 tsp. sugar syrup
Sparkling mineral water for topping up

Shake all the ingredients, except the mineral water, together, with ice, in the shaker and strain into the glass. Top up with mineral water.

BOURBON SILVER FIZZ

Fruity, delicate, dry drink for the afternoon and evening
• Large rocks glass
• Shaker

1 ounce bourbon
1 tsp. lemon juice
1 tsp. lime juice
1 tsp. sugar syrup
1 egg white
Soda water for topping up
• Garnish:
1 slice of lemon

Shake all the ingredients together, with ice, in the shaker and strain into the glass. Top up with soda water and stir. Perch the slice of lemon on the rim of the glass.

Whiskey

Canadian Summer (back), Whisky Soda (front left), Bourbon Silver Fizz (front right)

FREEFALL

Fruity drink for a summer party
• Highball/Collins glass
• Shaker

2 ounces pineapple juice
1 ounce scotch
*¾ ounce Malibu or other coconut-
flavored liqueur*
2 tsp. passion-fruit syrup
2 tsp. lemon juice
• *Garnish:*
1 piece of pineapple
1 maraschino cherry

Shake all the ingredients together, with
ice, in the shaker and strain into the
highball/Collins glass with ice cubes.
Spear the fruit on a toothpick and lay
across the rim of the glass.

CANADIAN SOUR

Refreshing drink for a party
• Rocks glass
• Shaker

1½ ounces Canadian whisky
¾ ounce lemon juice
2 tsp. sugar syrup
Sparkling mineral water (optional)
• *Garnish:*
½ slice of orange
1 orange peel spiral
1 maraschino cherry

Shake all the ingredients together, with
ice, in the shaker and strain into the
glass. Add a little mineral water. Perch
the slice of orange on the rim of the
glass; spear the cherry and orange peel
spiral on a toothpick and insert it into
the slice of orange. Add to the drink.

Whiskey

SANDY COLLINS

Refreshing Collins for any time of day
• Highball/Collins glass

1½ ounces scotch

¾ ounce lemon juice

2 tsp. sugar syrup

Soda water for topping up

• Garnish:

½ slice of lemon

1 maraschino cherry

Mix all the ingredients, except the soda water, together, with ice, in the high-ball/Collins glass. Top up with soda water and stir until the glass condenses. Spear the fruit on a toothpick and lay the garnish across the rim of the glass.

HIGHLAND COOLER

Light cooler for a summer party
• Highball/Collins glass
• Shaker

1½ ounces scotch

¾ ounce lemon juice

2 dashes Angostura bitters

2 tsp. sugar syrup

Ginger ale for topping up

• Garnish:

½ slice of lemon

Shake all the ingredients, except the ginger ale, together, with ice, in the shaker and strain into the highball/Collins glass over ice cubes. Top up with ginger ale. Add the slice of lemon to the glass.

OPENING II

Sweet drink for a party
• Cocktail glass
• Mixing glass

1 ounce Canadian whisky
½ ounce sweet red vermouth
2 tsp. grenadine

Stir the ingredients together in the mixing glass, with ice, and strain into the cocktail glass.

HANSEATIC COG

Fruity drink for a party
• Highball/Collins glass
• Shaker

1 ounce scotch
1½ ounces orange juice
1½ ounces passion-fruit juice
2 tsp. mandarin syrup
2 tsp. lemon juice
• Garnish:
½ slice of orange
2 maraschino cherries
1 mint leaf

Shake the ingredients together, with ice, in the shaker and strain into the highball/Collins glass, with ice. Spear the fruit and mint leaf on a toothpick and put it in the glass with a long stirrer.

ROYAL TURKEY

Fruity drink for a summer party
• Highball/Collins glass
• Shaker

1½ ounces pineapple juice
¾ ounce bourbon
¾ ounce apricot brandy
¾ ounce gin
Lemonade for topping up
• Garnish:
1 maraschino cherry

Shake all the ingredients, except the lemonade, with ice, in the shaker and strain into the highball/Collins glass over ice cubes. Top up with lemonade and stir. Add the maraschino cherry to the glass and serve the drink with a stirrer.

19TH HOLE

Refreshing, fruity drink for a summer party
• Highball/Collins glass
• Shaker

2¾ ounces passion-fruit juice
1 ounce scotch
¾ ounce Southern Comfort
2 tsp. mandarin syrup
2 tsp. lemon juice
• Garnish:
1 Cape gooseberry

Shake the ingredients together, with ice, in the shaker and strain into the highball/Collins glass over crushed ice. Perch the Cape gooseberry on the rim of the glass.

Whiskey

LOS ANGELES (L. A.)

Fruity drink for a party
- Highball/Collins glass
- Shaker

1 ounce scotch
¾ ounce lemon juice
2 tsp. sugar syrup
1 dash sweet white vermouth
1 egg

Shake the ingredients together firmly, with ice, in the shaker and strain into the highball/Collins glass.

NEW ORLEANS SAZERAC

Refreshing drink for any time of day
- Rocks glass

1 sugar cube
1 dash Angostura bitters
1½ ounces bourbon
2 tsp. Pernod
Water or still mineral water for topping up
- *Extra:*
1 piece of lemon peel

Put the sugar cube into the glass with ice cubes and saturate with the Angostura bitters. Add the spirits, top up with water, and stir well. Squeeze the lemon peel over the drink, and stir with a stirrer.

BIG JOHN

Fruity drink for a party
- Highball/Collins glass
- Shaker

1½ ounces orange juice
1 ounce scotch
¾ ounce passion-fruit syrup
¾ ounce lemon juice
¾ ounce pineapple juice
- *Garnish:*
½ slice of orange
½ slice of lemon
¼ slice of pineapple
1 maraschino cherry
3 dashes amaretto

Shake the ingredients together, with ice, in the shaker and strain into the highball/Collins glass. Spear the fruit on a toothpick and lay across the rim of the glass. Drizzle the amaretto over the cherry.

HORSE'S NECK II

Mild drink for the evening
- Large rocks glass

1½ ounces bourbon
2 dashes Angostura bitters
Ginger ale for topping up
- *Garnish:*
1 lemon peel spiral

Stir the bourbon and Angostura bitters in the glass, with ice. Top up with ginger ale and stir briefly. Add the lemon peel spiral to the glass.

WALDORF ASTORIA

Strong, sweet eggnog for every day
• Rocks glass
• Shaker

3½ ounces milk
1½ ounces bourbon
¾ ounce port
2 tsp. sugar syrup
2 tsp. light cream
2 egg yolks
• Extra:
Grated nutmeg

Shake the ingredients together very firmly, with ice, in the shaker and pour into the glass. Sprinkle a little grated nutmeg on top.

SCOTTIE

Fruity drink for a summer party
• Highball/Collins glass
• Shaker

2 ounces pineapple juice
1½ ounces passion-fruit juice
1 ounce scotch
¾ ounce peach-flavored liqueur
2 tsp. grenadine
• Garnish:
1 slice of pineapple
1 maraschino cherry

Shake the ingredients together, with ice, in the shaker and pour into the highball/Collins glass. Perch the piece of pineapple on the rim of the glass and fasten the maraschino cherry to it with a toothpick.

PICNIC

Fruity drink for a summer party
• Highball/Collins glass
• Shaker

1½ ounces pineapple juice
2 tsp. Canadian whisky
2 tsp. mandarin-flavored liqueur
Ginger ale for topping up
• Garnish:
Selection of pieces of fresh fruit

Shake all the ingredients, except the ginger ale, together, with ice, in the shaker and strain into the highball/Collins glass over ice cubes. Top up with ginger ale and stir. Spear the pieces of fruit on a toothpick and lay the garnish across the rim of the glass. Serve with a stirrer.

BOURBON-COLA HIGHBALL

Sweet drink for any time of year
• Highball/Collins glass

1½ ounces bourbon
Cola for topping up
• Garnish:
1 lemon peel spiral

Pour the bourbon into the glass over ice cubes. Top up with cola and stir briefly. Add the lemon peel spiral to the glass.

Whiskey

DEEP DREAM

Fruity, delicate, dry drink for the
evening
• Highball/Collins glass
• Shaker

1 ounce bourbon
¾ ounce apricot brandy
2 tsp. dry vermouth
Orange juice for topping up
• Garnish:
1 slice of orange

Shake all the ingredients, except the
orange juice, with ice, in the shaker
and strain into the glass. Top up with
orange juice. Perch the slice of orange
on the rim of the glass. Serve with a
stirrer.

WARD EIGHT

Refreshing, fruity drink for a party
• Small wine glass
• Shaker

1½ ounces bourbon
¾ ounce lemon juice
¾ ounce orange juice
2 tsp. grenadine
1 tsp. sugar syrup
• Garnish:
1 slice of lemon
1 maraschino cherry

Shake the ingredients together, with
crushed ice, in the shaker and pour
into the glass. Float the slice of lemon
and maraschino cherry in the glass.

SWEET SCOTCH

Mild drink for the evening
• Large rocks glass

1 ounce scotch
¾ ounce white crème de cacao
Soda water for topping up
• Garnish:
1 kumquat

Mix together the whisky and crème de
cacao, with ice cubes, in the glass. Top
up with soda water and stir. Perch the
kumquat on the rim of the glass.

ICE RICKEY

Fruity, delicate, dry drink for hot days
• Highball/Collins glass
• Shaker

1 scoop lemon sorbet
1½ ounces scotch
1 ounce lime cordial
¾ ounce lemon juice
1 dash grenadine
Soda water for topping up
• Garnish:
1 slice of lime

Put the scoop of sorbet into the highball glass. Shake all the ingredients, except the soda water, together, with ice, in the shaker and strain into the glass. Top up with soda water and stir briefly. Perch the slice of lime on the rim of the glass. Serve with a spoon.

BLUEGRASS

Aromatic drink for a party
• Highball/Collins glass
• Shaker

1 ounce bourbon
1 ounce lemon juice
¾ ounce lime juice
½ ounce blue curaçao
½ ounce Southern Comfort
• Garnish:
1 piece of lemon peel
1 maraschino cherry

Shake the ingredients together, with ice, in the shaker and strain into the highball/Collins glass with ice. Add the lemon peel and maraschino cherry to the glass.

FLOATER

Refreshing drink for the afternoon and evening
• Highball/Collins glass

Soda water
1 ounce scotch

Pour a little soda water into the glass, then slowly pour the scotch over the back of a spoon on top of the soda water. The two liquids should not mix.

HILL STREET

Fruity, mild drink for any time of year
• Rocks glass
• Shaker

1¾ ounces passion-fruit juice
1½ ounces bourbon
¾ ounce pineapple juice
2 tsp. dark rum
• Garnish:
1 maraschino cherry

Shake all the ingredients together, with ice cubes, in the shaker and strain into the glass over ice cubes. Perch the cherry on the rim of the glass.

Whiskey

Ice Rickey (left), Bluegrass (middle), Hill Street (right)

RICKEY

Fruity, slightly sour drink for the evening
- Highball/Collins glass
- Shaker

1½ ounces scotch
2 tsp. lemon juice
2 tsp. lime cordial
Soda water for topping up
- *Garnish:*
1 slice of lime
1 slice of lemon

Shake all the ingredients, except the soda water, with ice, in the shaker and strain into the glass. Top up with soda water and stir briefly. Perch the slices of fruit on the rim of the glass.

CANADIAN SQUASH

Fruity, delicate, dry drink for a party
- Highball/Collins glass

2 ounces orange juice
1½ ounces Canadian whisky
¾ ounce grapefruit juice
2 tsp. Drambuie
1 tsp. lemon juice
- *Garnish:*
½ slice of orange

Stir all the ingredients together, with ice cubes, in the highball/Collins glass. Perch the slice of orange on the rim of the glass.

ONE IRELAND

Delicate, dry drink for the evening
- Highball/Collins glass
- Shaker

2 scoops vanilla ice cream
1½ ounces Irish whiskey
2 tsp. white crème de menthe
Milk for topping up

Put the vanilla ice cream in the highball glass. Shake the whiskey and crème de menthe together well in the shaker, pour over the vanilla ice cream, top up with milk, and stir.

COLONEL COLLINS

Fruity, sweet-and-sour Collins for the summer
- Collins/highball glass

2 ounces bourbon
1 ounce lemon juice
¾ ounce sugar syrup
Soda water for topping up
- *Garnish:*
1 slice of lemon
1 maraschino cherry

Mix together the bourbon, lemon juice, and sugar syrup, with ice cubes, in the Collins glass. Top up with soda water and stir briefly. Perch the slice of lemon on the rim of the glass and fasten the cherry to it with a toothpick.

Whiskey

SOFTY

Fruity long drink for a party
- Rocks glass
- Shaker

| 2 ounces orange juice |
| 1½ ounces scotch |
| 2 tsp. Drambuie |
| • Garnish: |
| 1 slice of orange |
| 1 maraschino cherry |

Shake all the ingredients together well,
with ice cubes, in the shaker and strain
into the glass with ice cubes. Perch the
fruit on the rim of the glass.

WILD IRISH ROSE

Fruity drink for the summer
- Large rocks glass
- Shaker

| 1½ ounces Irish whiskey |
| 2 tsp. lemon juice |
| 2 tsp. grenadine |
| Soda water for topping up |
| • Garnish: |
| 1 slice of orange |

Shake all the ingredients, except the
soda water, with ice, in the shaker. Half
fill the glass with ice cubes and strain
the cocktail into the glass. Top up with
soda water and stir briefly. Add the slice
of orange to the glass.

KENTUCKY LEMON

Dry, fruity drink for the evening
- Highball/Collins glass

| 1½ ounces bourbon |
| ¾ ounce lemon juice |
| Bitter lemon for topping up |
| • Garnish: |
| ½ slice of orange |

Mix together the bourbon and lemon
juice, with ice cubes, in the highball
glass. Top up with bitter lemon and stir.
Perch the slice of orange on the rim of
the glass.

WHISKEY SLING

Fruity, mild drink for a summer's
evening.
- Large rocks glass

| 1½ ounces bourbon |
| 1½ ounces sugar syrup |
| ¾ ounce lemon juice |
| Soda water for topping up |

Mix together the bourbon, sugar syrup,
and lemon juice, with ice cubes, in the
glass. Top up with soda water and stir
briefly.

CHERRY BLOSSOM II

Fruity, delicate, dry drink for the evening
- Rocks glass
- Shaker

1½ ounces Irish whiskey
2 tsp. lemon juice
2 tsp. grenadine
1 tsp. egg white
Soda water for topping up

Shake all the ingredients, except the soda water, with ice, in the shaker and strain into the glass. Top up with soda water and stir briefly.

IRISH ORANGE

Fruity, dry drink for the evening
- Large rocks glass
- Shaker

1½ ounces Irish whiskey
2 tsp. lemon juice
2 tsp. grenadine
Bitter orange for topping up
- *Garnish:*
1 orange peel spiral

Shake all the ingredients, except the bitter orange, together, with ice, in the shaker and strain into the glass over ice cubes. Top up with bitter orange and stir. Hang the orange peel spiral over the rim of the glass.

BOURBON DREAM

Fruity, mild drink for the evening
- Highball/Collins glass
- Shaker

1 ounce bourbon
1 ounce apricot brandy
Orange juice for topping up
- *Garnish:*
1 slice of orange
1 maraschino cherry

Shake the bourbon and apricot brandy together, with ice cubes, in the shaker and strain into the highball glass. Top up with orange juice and stir briefly. Perch the slice of orange on the rim of the glass and fasten the maraschino cherry to it with a toothpick.

HOLIDAY EGGNOG

Sweet eggnog also enjoyable throughout the year
- Highball/Collins glass
- Shaker

1½ ounces bourbon
1½ ounces milk
¾ ounce dark rum
2 tsp. sugar syrup
1 egg
- *Extra:*
Grated nutmeg

Shake all the ingredients together, with ice, in the shaker and strain into the glass. Sprinkle with a little grated nutmeg.

GODMOTHER

VODKATINI

Vodka-based drinks

BLACK RUSSIAN

VODKA GIBSON

FLYING GRASSHOPPER

HAIR RAISER

BARBARA

Sweet, creamy drink
- Cocktail glass
- Shaker

¾ ounce vodka
¾ ounce white crème de cacao
¾ ounce light cream
- *Extra:*
Grated nutmeg

Shake the ingredients together firmly, with ice, in the shaker and strain into the glass. Sprinkle a little grated nutmeg on top.

GREEN SEA

Medium-dry aperitif
- Cocktail glass
- Mixing glass

½ ounce vodka
½ ounce green crème de menthe
½ ounce dry vermouth

Mix the ingredients together, with ice, in the mixing glass and strain into the cocktail glass.

GOSPODIN

Aromatic drink for the afternoon
- Rocks glass

1 ounce vodka
¾ ounce apricot brandy

Mix the ingredients together, with ice, in the glass. Serve with a stirrer.

VODKATINI

Dry drink for a party
- Cocktail glass
- Mixing glass

1½ ounces vodka
¾ ounce dry vermouth
- *Extra:*
1 olive

Mix the ingredients together, with ice, in the mixing glass and strain into the cocktail glass. Spear the olive on a toothpick and add it to the glass.

BLACK RUSSIAN

Sweet, short drink for the evening
- Cocktail glass
- Mixing glass

1½ ounces vodka
¾ ounce coffee-flavored liqueur

Mix the ingredients together, with ice, in the mixing glass and strain into the cocktail glass.

GODMOTHER

Aromatic drink for any time of day
- Rocks glass

1½ ounces vodka
¾ ounce amaretto

Mix the ingredients together, with ice, in the glass. Serve with a stirrer.

Vodka

Barbara (left), Green Sea (middle), Vodkatini (right)

FINLADY

Fruity, delicate, dry drink for the
evening
• Cocktail glass
• Shaker

1½ ounces vodka
¾ ounce apricot brandy
2 tsp. lemon juice

Shake all the ingredients, with ice, in
the shaker and strain into the glass.

VODKA GIBSON

Dry, short aperitif
• Cocktail glass
• Mixing glass

1½ ounces vodka
2 tsp. dry vermouth
• Extra:
1 pearl onion

Stir the ingredients together, with ice, in
the mixing glass and strain into the
cocktail glass. Add the onion to the glass.

SMIRNOFF COCKTAIL

Creamy drink for a party
• Cocktail glass
• Shaker

1¾ ounces Smirnoff vodka or other
unflavored vodka
½ ounce white crème de cacao
½ ounce green crème de menthe
½ ounce light cream

Shake the ingredients together, with ice,
in the shaker and strain into the glass.

BERENTZ PARADISE COCKTAIL

Medium-dry aperitif
• Cocktail glass
• Shaker

¾ ounce vodka
¾ ounce apple-flavored liqueur
½ ounce orange juice
1 dash Campari
• Garnish:
1 slice of apple
1 maraschino cherry
Sprig of mint

Shake the ingredients together, with ice,
in the shaker and strain into the glass.
Spear the slice of apple, the cherry, and
the sprig of mint on a toothpick and lay
the garnish across the rim of the glass.

TARANTELLA

Bitter champagne cocktail for a
reception
• Champagne glass or flute
• Mixing glass

½ ounce vodka
½ ounce triple sec
½ ounce Campari
Dry champagne or sparkling wine for
topping up
• Garnish:
1 piece of pineapple
1 maraschino cherry

Mix all the ingredients, except the
champagne, together, with ice, in the
mixing glass. Strain into the champagne
glass and top up with champagne. Perch
the piece of pineapple on the rim of the
glass and fasten the maraschino cherry
to it with a toothpick.

Vodka

OVIDIO

Refreshing, dry champagne cocktail for a party
• Champagne glass
• Shaker

1 ounce vodka
¾ ounce blue curaçao
¾ ounce grapefruit juice
Dry champagne or sparkling wine for topping up
• *Garnish:*
½ slice of lemon
1 mint leaf

Shake all the ingredients, except the champagne, together, with ice, in the shaker. Strain into the cocktail glass and top up with champagne. Perch the slice of lemon on the rim of the glass and place the mint leaf on top of the drink.

SNAP

Medium-dry aperitif
• Cocktail glass
• Mixing glass

¾ ounce vodka
¾ ounce dry vermouth
¾ ounce lime juice
• *Extra:*
1 piece of lime peel

Mix the ingredients together, with ice, in the mixing glass and strain into the cocktail glass. Squeeze the lime peel over the drink and add the peel to the glass.

HAIR RAISER

Delicate, dry drink for the evening
• Rocks glass

¾ ounce vodka
¾ ounce Dubonnet
¾ ounce tonic water

Mix all the ingredients together slowly, with ice cubes, in the glass.

RUSSIAN CAR

Creamy, sweet after-dinner drink
• Large cocktail glass
• Shaker

1½ ounces vodka
1½ ounces light cream
2 tsp. Galliano
2 tsp. white crème de cacao

Shake all the ingredients together, with ice, in the shaker and strain into the glass.

NORTH POLE

Tangy, spicy drink for the evening
• Cocktail glass
• Shaker

1 ounce vodka
2 tsp. Drambuie
2 tsp. Campari

Shake all the ingredients together, with ice, in the mixing glass and strain into the cocktail glass.

WHITE RUSSIAN

Creamy drink for any time of day
• Cocktail glass
• Mixing glass

1 ounce vodka
¾ ounce coffee-flavored liqueur
2 tsp. light cream

Mix the vodka and liqueur together,
with ice, in the mixing glass and strain
into the cocktail glass. Lightly whip the
cream and put it on top of the drink.
This cocktail can also be drunk with
ice cubes; if you do, serve it in a
rocks glass.

MONTE ROSA

Light, short aperitif
• Cocktail glass
• Shaker

¾ ounce vodka
2 tsp. triple sec
2 tsp. Campari
2 tsp. orange juice

Shake the ingredients together, with
ice, in the shaker and strain into the
cocktail glass.

Vodka

FLYING GRASSHOPPER

Spicy, sweet drink for the evening
- Cocktail glass
- Mixing glass

¾ ounce vodka

2 tsp. white crème de cacao

2 tsp. green crème de menthe

• Garnish:

1 green maraschino cherry

Mix all the ingredients together, with ice, in the mixing glass and strain into the glass. Perch the cherry on the rim of the glass.

BALANCE

Fruity, delicate, dry crusta for the evening
- Cocktail glass with a sugared rim
- Shaker

¾ ounce vodka

2 tsp. light rum

2 tsp. triple sec

1 tsp. grenadine

• Garnish:

1 maraschino cherry

Shake all the ingredients together, with ice, in the shaker and strain into the glass with the sugared rim. Spear the cherry with a toothpick and add it to the glass.

VODKA NIKOLASCHKA

Mild, fruity drink for a party
• Shot glass

¾ ounce vodka

1 slice of orange, peeled

1 tsp. confectioners' sugar

Dash Grand Marnier

Pour the vodka into the glass. Place the slice of orange on top of the glass, sprinkle confectioners' sugar on top and drizzle Grand Marnier over. You are supposed to eat the orange and drink the vodka at the same time.

EAST WIND

Spicy, delicate, dry aperitif
• Cocktail glass
• Mixing glass

¾ ounce vodka

¾ ounce dry vermouth

¾ ounce sweet red vermouth

• Garnish:

½ slice of orange

½ slice of lemon

Stir all the ingredients together, with ice cubes, in the cocktail glass. Perch the slices of fruit on the rim of the glass.

YELLOW SEA

Spicy short drink for a party
• Cocktail glass
• Shaker

1¾ ounces vodka

½ ounce light rum

½ ounce Galliano

2 tsp. lime juice

1 tsp. maraschino

1 tsp. sugar syrup

Shake the ingredients together, with ice, in the shaker and strain into the glass.

RED RUSSIAN

Fruity, sweet after-dinner drink
• Rocks glass

1 ounce vodka

¾ ounce cherry-flavored liqueur

Mix the ingredients together, with ice, in the glass.

VODKA SPECIAL

Medium-dry aperitif for the evening
• Cocktail glass
• Shaker

1 ounce vodka

2 tsp. white crème de cacao

2 tsp. lemon juice

Shake all the ingredients together, with ice, in the shaker and strain into the glass.

Vodka

RUSSIAN COCKTAIL

Spicy, sweet drink for the evening
• Cocktail glass
• Shaker

1½ ounces vodka
¾ ounce brown crème de cacao

Shake all the ingredients together, with ice, in the shaker and strain into the glass.

VODKA STINGER

Spicy, fresh drink for the evening
• Rocks glass

1 ounce vodka
¾ ounce green crème de menthe

Stir the ingredients together, with ice cubes, in the glass.

VODKA SIDECAR

Bittersweet drink for the evening
• Cocktail glass
• Shaker

¾ ounce vodka
¾ ounce triple sec
1 tsp. lemon juice

Shake all the ingredients together, with ice, in the shaker and strain into the cocktail glass.

MARAWOD

Fruity, delicate, sweet drink for the evening
• Cocktail glass
• Mixing glass

1 ounce vodka
2 tsp. cherry eau-de-vie
2 tsp. maraschino
• Garnish:
1 maraschino cherry

Mix all the ingredients together, with ice, in the mixing glass and strain into the glass. Spear the cherry on a toothpick and add it to the glass.

FINLANDIA BITE

Piquant, sweet after-dinner drink
• Cocktail glass
• Shaker

1 ounce vodka
1 ounce Southern Comfort
¾ ounce light cream
1 dash lemon juice
• Extra:
Grated nutmeg

Shake all the ingredients together, with ice, in the shaker and strain into the cocktail glass. Sprinkle with grated nutmeg.

RUSSIAN FRUIT

Fruity, sweet after-dinner drink
• Rocks glass

1½ ounces vodka
¾ ounce raspberry cordial

Mix the ingredients together, with ice cubes, in the glass.

HEAVEN SO SWEET

Mild, spicy after-dinner drink
• Cocktail glass
• Shaker

1½ ounces vodka
2 tsp. amaretto
2 tsp. Galliano

Shake the ingredients together firmly, with ice, in the shaker and strain into the champagne glass.

MORTON'S SPECIAL

Fruity drink for the evening
• Cocktail glass
• Shaker

1½ ounces vodka
1½ ounces orange juice
¾ ounce tequila
1 dash grenadine

Shake all the ingredients together, with ice cubes, in the shaker and strain into the cocktail glass.

FREEDOM

Fruity, elegant, dry drink for any time of year
• Cocktail glass
• Shaker

¾ ounce vodka
2 tsp. triple sec
2 tsp. crème de cassis
2 tsp. lemon juice
• Extra:
1 piece of lemon peel

Shake the ingredients together well, with ice, in the shaker and strain into the glass. Squeeze the lemon peel over the drink and add the peel to the glass.

FINNISH VIRGIN

Fruity, bittersweet drink for the evening
• Cocktail glass
• Shaker

1¾ ounces vodka
1 tsp. orange juice
1 tsp. almond syrup
1 tsp. lime juice
• Garnish:
1 maraschino cherry

Shake all the ingredients together, with ice, in the shaker and strain into the glass. Perch the cherry on the rim of the glass.

Vodka

Heaven So Sweet (back left), **Finnish Virgin** (back right), **Russian Fruit** (front)

CRISTA SOLAR

Piquant drink for a party
• Cocktail glass
• Mixing glass

1 ounce vodka
2 tsp. triple sec
2 tsp. port
2 tsp. dry vermouth
2 dashes Angostura bitters
• *Extra:*
1 pearl onion
1 piece of orange peel

Mix the ingredients together, with ice, in the mixing glass and strain into the cocktail glass. Squeeze the orange peel over the drink; spear the onion on a toothpick and add it to the glass.

KANGAROO

Medium-dry aperitif
• Cocktail glass
• Mixing glass

1½ ounces vodka
¾ ounce dry vermouth
• *Extra:*
1 piece of lemon peel

Mix the ingredients together, with ice, in the mixing glass and strain into the cocktail glass. Squeeze the lemon peel over the drink and add the peel to the glass.

GREEN HOPE

Medium-dry aperitif
• Cocktail glass
• Shaker

1 ounce vodka
½ ounce green curaçao
2 tsp. crème de banane
2 tsp. grape juice
2 tsp. lemon juice
• *Garnish:*
1 red maraschino cherry
1 green maraschino cherry

Shake the ingredients together, with ice, in the shaker and strain into the glass. Spear the cherries on a toothpick and lay the garnish across the rim of the glass.

VODKA ALEXANDER

Piquant, sweet after-dinner drink
• Cocktail glass
• Shaker

1 ounce vodka
½ ounce white crème de cacao
½ ounce light cream
• *Garnish:*
Unsweetened cocoa powder

Shake all the ingredients together, with ice, in the shaker and strain into the glass. Dust the drink with cocoa powder.

Vodka

PEDI COCKTAIL

Piquant aperitif
• Cocktail glass
• Mixing glass

1 ounce vodka
¾ ounce Campari
2 tsp. triple sec
• *Garnish:*
1 maraschino cherry
½ slice of lemon

Mix the ingredients together, with ice, in the mixing glass and strain into the cocktail glass. Spear the slice of lemon and maraschino cherry on a toothpick and lay the garnish across the rim of the glass.

RUSSIAN NIGHT

Delicately piquant, mild drink for the evening
• Cocktail glass
• Shaker

1½ ounces vodka
2 tsp. blue curaçao
1 dash Pernod
• *Garnish:*
1 maraschino cherry

Shake all the ingredients together, with ice, in the shaker and strain into the glass. Spear the maraschino cherry on a toothpick and add it to the glass.

GALWAY SUNRISE

Fruity drink for a party
• Cocktail glass
• Shaker

1 ounce Drambuie
¾ ounce orange juice
½ ounce vodka
2 tsp. triple sec
1 dash of Frothee

Shake the ingredients together, with ice, in the shaker and strain into the cocktail glass.

DAY DREAMER

Piquant, dry aperitif
• Cocktail glass
• Mixing glass

1 ounce vodka
2 tsp. dry vermouth
2 tsp. dry sherry
• *Extra:*
1 piece of lemon peel

Mix the ingredients together well, with ice, in the mixing glass and strain into the glass. Squeeze the lemon peel over the drink and add the peel to the glass.

TRIP

Dry aperitif
• Cocktail glass
• Mixing glass

¾ ounce vodka
¾ ounce lime cordial
¾ ounce Noilly Prat or other dry vermouth
• Extra:
1 piece of lime peel

Mix the ingredients together, with ice, in the mixing glass and strain into the cocktail glass. Squeeze the lime peel over the drink and add the peel to the glass.

AMATO

Fruity, delicate, dry drink for the evening
• Large cocktail glass
• Mixing glass

¾ ounce vodka
¾ ounce dry vermouth
¾ ounce mandarin-flavored liqueur
• Extra:
1 piece of orange peel

Mix all the ingredients together, with ice, in the mixing glass and strain into the glass over ice cubes. Squeeze the orange peel over the drink and add the peel to the glass.

SIMINEN RAKKAUS

Fruity drink for a party
• Cocktail glass
• Shaker

¾ ounce vodka
¾ ounce crème de banane
2 tsp. Parfait Amour
2 tsp. lemon juice
• Garnish:
1 maraschino cherry

Shake the ingredients together, with ice, in the shaker and strain into the glass. Spear the cherry on a toothpick and add it to the glass.

VODKA GIMLET

Medium-dry aperitif
• Cocktail glass
• Mixing glass

1½ ounces vodka
¾ ounce lime juice
• Extra:
½ slice of lime

Mix the ingredients together, with ice, in the mixing glass and strain into the cocktail glass. Add the slice of lime to the glass.

Vodka

Vodka Orange (left), Pacific Blue (right)

VODKA ORANGE

Fruity, delicately dry drink for any time of year
• Cocktail glass
• Mixing glass

1 ounce vodka
2 tsp. orange-flavored liqueur
2 tsp. lime juice
• Garnish:
½ slice of orange

Mix all the ingredients together, with ice, in the mixing glass and strain into the glass. Perch the slice of orange on the rim of the glass.

PACIFIC BLUE

Sweet drink for a party
• Cocktail glass with sugared rim
• Mixing glass

¾ ounce crème de banane
¾ ounce blue curaçao
2 tsp. vodka
2 tsp. coconut-flavored liqueur
• Garnish:
1 maraschino cherry

Mix the ingredients together, with ice, in the mixing glass and strain into the glass with the sugared rim. Perch the cherry on the rim of the glass.

AVIATION

Medium-dry aperitif
• Cocktail glass
• Shaker

1 ounce vodka
½ ounce lemon juice
1 tsp. apricot brandy
2 dashes maraschino

Shake the ingredients together, with ice, in the shaker and strain into the cocktail glass.

GOLDFINGER

Fruity, delicately piquant drink for the evening
• Cocktail glass
• Shaker

1½ ounces Cinzano (rosso antico)
¾ ounce vodka
2 tsp. orange juice
1 dash orange bitters

Shake all the ingredients together, with ice, in the shaker and strain into the glass.

ROBERTA

Medium-dry aperitif
• Cocktail glass
• Mixing glass

¾ ounce vodka
¾ ounce dry vermouth
¾ ounce cherry-flavored liqueur
2 dashes Campari
2 dashes crème de banane
• Extra:
1 piece of orange peel

Mix the ingredients together, with ice, in the mixing glass and strain into the cocktail glass. Squeeze the orange peel over the drink.

FESTRUS

Medium-dry aperitif
• Cocktail glass
• Mixing glass

¾ ounce vodka
¾ ounce Grand Marnier
¾ ounce Cinzano
• Extra:
1 piece of orange peel

Mix the ingredients together, with ice, in the mixing glass and strain into the cocktail glass. Squeeze the orange peel over the drink and add it to the glass.

Vodka

VOLGA CLIPPER

Fruity, sweet drink for the evening
• Cocktail glass
• Shaker

1 ounce vodka

1 ounce orange juice

¾ ounce apricot brandy

Shake the ingredients together, with ice, in the shaker and strain into the cocktail glass.

TRIPLE SUN

Aromatic drink for a party
• Cocktail glass
• Mixing glass

½ ounce vodka

½ ounce banana-flavored liqueur

½ ounce sweet white vermouth

½ ounce dry vermouth

2 dashes grenadine

• Garnish:

1 maraschino cherry

Mix the ingredients together, with ice, in the mixing glass and strain into the cocktail glass. Add the cherry to the glass.

E. P. U.

Spicy, piquant pick-me-up
• Sherry glass

1 egg yolk

Freshly ground black pepper

Salt

Hot-pepper sauce

¾ ounce vodka

¾ ounce Sangrita

Put the egg yolk into the sherry glass. Add the seasonings, vodka, and Sangrita. The drink should be tossed back and consumed in one swallow.

COLONEL KREMLIN

Fruity, delicate, dry drink for the evening
• Cocktail glass
• Shaker

1½ ounces vodka

2 tsp. lime juice

2 tsp. sugar syrup

• Extra:

3 mint leaves

Shake the ingredients together firmly, with ice, in the shaker and strain into the glass. Finely chop the mint and add it to the glass.

BLUE DAY

Mild, fruity drink for the evening
• Champagne or cocktail glass
• Shaker

1½ ounces vodka
¾ ounce blue curaçao
1 dash orange bitters
• Garnish:
½ slice of orange

Shake all the ingredients together, with ice, in the shaker and strain into the glass. Perch the slice of orange on the rim of the glass.

BABYFACE

Fruity, sweet after-dinner drink
• Champagne or cocktail glass
• Shaker

¾ ounce vodka
¾ ounce light cream
¾ ounce crème de cassis

Shake all the ingredients together firmly, with ice, in the shaker and strain into the glass.

Vodka

GRAND DUCHESSE

Bittersweet drink for the evening
- Champagne or cocktail glass
- Shaker

1 ounce vodka
2 tsp. light rum
2 tsp. lemon juice
1 tsp. grenadine

Shake all the ingredients together, with ice, in the shaker and strain into the glass.

SONIA COCKTAIL

Spicy after-dinner drink
- Champagne or cocktail glass
- Shaker

1 ounce vodka
1 ounce green peppermint-flavored liqueur
• Garnish:
1 sprig of mint

Shake all the ingredients together, with ice, in the shaker and strain into the glass. Perch the sprig of mint on the rim of the glass.

WHITE CAP

Creamy drink for the afternoon
• Cocktail glass
• Shaker

1 ounce vodka
2 tsp. mocha-flavored liqueur
2 tsp. port
2 tsp. lightly whipped cream

Shake all the ingredients, except the cream, together, with ice, in the shaker and strain into the cocktail glass. Top the drink with the cream.

CAIPIROSKA

Dry drink for the evening
• Rocks glass

1 lime
1 tsp. brown sugar
1¾ ounces vodka

Cut the lime into quarters, put them into the glass and crush with a mortar or the end of a bar spoon. Add the sugar, top up with crushed ice, add the vodka, and stir thoroughly.

INDIANAPOLIS

Creamy drink for the evening
• Cocktail glass
• Shaker

¾ ounce vodka
¾ ounce blue curaçao
¾ ounce light cream

Shake the ingredients together firmly, with ice, in the shaker and strain into the cocktail glass.

RED DREAMS I

Fruity, delicate, dry drink for the evening
• Cocktail glass
• Shaker

1 ounce vodka
2 tsp. cherry-flavored liqueur
2 tsp. lime juice
• Garnish:
1 maraschino cherry

Shake the ingredients together, with ice, in the shaker and strain into the glass. Perch the cherry on the rim of the glass.

Vodka

FINNISH COCKBULL

Spicy, sweet drink for the evening
• Cocktail glass
• Mixing glass

1 ounce vodka
¾ ounce amaretto
2 tsp. coffee-flavored liqueur
• Garnish:
¼ slice of pineapple

Mix all the ingredients together, with ice, in the mixing glass and strain into the cocktail glass. Perch the slice of pineapple on the rim of the glass.

RED SQUARE

Piquant, delicate, dry drink for any time of year
• Cocktail glass
• Shaker

¾ ounce vodka
¾ ounce white crème de cacao
2 tsp. lemon juice
1½ tsp. grenadine
• Garnish:
1 maraschino cherry

Shake all the ingredients together firmly, with ice, in the shaker and strain into the glass. Perch the cherry on the rim of the glass.

LOVER'S NOCTURNE

Delicate, dry after-dinner drink
• Cocktail glass
• Mixing glass

1½ ounces vodka
2 tsp. Drambuie
1 dash Angostura bitters

Mix all the ingredients together, with ice, in the mixing glass and strain into the cocktail glass.

PLAZA

Refreshing drink for the summer
• Highball/Collins glass

1½ ounces vodka
¾ ounce passion-fruit-flavored
liqueur
¾ ounce cream of coconut
Soda water for topping up
• *Garnish:*
1 slice of orange
1 maraschino cherry

Carefully mix the ingredients together,
with ice cubes, in the highball glass.
Perch the slice of orange on the rim of
the glass and fasten the cherry to it with
a toothpick. Put a stirrer in the glass and
serve the drink immediately.

FOLK BOAT COCKTAIL

Fruity drink for the summer
• Highball/Collins glass
• Shaker

2 ounces pineapple juice
1½ ounces vodka
¾ ounce blue curaçao
2 tsp. passion-fruit syrup
1 dash lime juice
• *Garnish:*
½ slice of orange
1 green maraschino cherry

Shake the ingredients together, with
ice, in the shaker and strain into the
highball glass. Perch the slice of orange
and the cherry on the rim of the glass.

Vodka

IVAN COLLINS

Refreshing drink for any time of day
• Collins/highball glass

1½ ounces vodka
¾ ounce lemon juice
2 tsp. sugar syrup
Soda water for topping up
• Garnish:
½ slice of lemon
1 green maraschino cherry

Put all the ingredients, except the soda water, in the Collins glass with ice cubes, top up with soda water, and stir well. Perch the slice of lemon on the rim of the glass and add the cherry to the glass. Serve with a long stirrer.

ROULETTE

Fruity, bitter after-dinner drink
• Highball/Collins glass

1 ounce vodka
1 ounce Campari
1 ounce orange juice
2 tsp. grenadine
• Extra:
½ slice of orange

Mix the ingredients together, with ice, in the highball glass. Add the slice of orange to the glass. Serve with a stirrer.

SERRERA

Refreshing drink for the summer
• Highball/Collins glass
• Shaker

1 ounce vodka
¾ ounce blue curaçao
2 tsp. lemon juice
Soda water for topping up
• Garnish:
¼ slice of pineapple
1 piece of orange peel
1 maraschino cherry

Shake all the ingredients, except the soda water, together, with ice, in the shaker. Strain into the highball glass over ice cubes, and top up with soda water. Spear the slice of pineapple, orange peel, and cherry on a toothpick and perch the garnish on the rim of the glass. Serve with a stirrer.

HAPPY FIN

Fruity, refreshing drink for the summer
• Highball/Collins glass

1½ ounces vodka
¾ ounce peach-flavored liqueur
Orange juice for topping up
• Garnish:
½ slice of orange
1 maraschino cherry

Mix the ingredients together, with ice cubes, in the highball glass. Spear the slice of orange and maraschino cherry on a toothpick and perch the garnish on the rim of the glass.

MOSCOW MULE

Mild, piquant drink for the evening
• Highball/Collins glass

2 ounces vodka
1 dash lemon juice
Ginger ale for topping up
• Extra:
1 piece of lemon peel

Mix the ingredients together, with ice cubes, in the highball glass. Add the lemon peel to the glass. Serve with a stirrer.

BALTIC

Fruity drink for the summer
• Highball/Collins glass

1 ounce plus 1 tsp. vodka
1 tsp. blue curaçao
½ ounce passion-fruit juice
1 tsp. lemon juice
Orange juice for topping up
• Garnish:
½ slice of orange
1 maraschino cherry

Stir the ingredients together, with ice cubes, in the highball glass. Spear the slice of orange and cherry on a toothpick, and perch the garnish on the rim of the glass.

Vodka

BLUE AEGEAN

Fruity drink for the summer
• Highball/Collins glass

¾ ounce vodka
¾ ounce blue curaçao
¾ ounce Grand Marnier
Mixture of pineapple and lemon
juices (1:1) for topping up
• Garnish:
½ slice of pineapple
1 maraschino cherry
Sprig of mint

Mix the spirits together thoroughly, with ice cubes, in the highball glass and top up with the mixture of pineapple and lemon juices. Spear the slice of pineapple, maraschino cherry, and sprig of mint on a toothpick and perch the garnish on the rim of the glass.

SCREWDRIVER

Fruity aperitif or after-dinner drink
• Rocks glass

1½ ounces vodka
Orange juice for topping up
• Garnish:
½ slice of orange

Pour the vodka into the glass, with ice cubes, and top up with orange juice. Perch the slice of orange on the rim of the glass.

SALTY DOG

Fruity aperitif or after-dinner drink
• Rocks glass with a salt-coated rim

1½ ounces vodka
Grapefruit juice for topping up

Pour the vodka into the glass with the salted rim and top up with grapefruit juice.

MANBOLS

Fruity drink for hot days
• Highball/Collins glass

1½ ounces mandarin-flavored liqueur
¾ ounce vodka
¾ ounce lemon juice
2 tsp. grenadine
Tonic water for topping up
• Garnish:
1 slice of mandarin orange
1 slice of lemon
1 maraschino cherry

Stir the ingredients together, with ice cubes, in the highball glass. Spear the slices of mandarin orange, lemon, and the cherry on a toothpick and lay the garnish across the rim of the glass. Serve with a stirrer.

GREEN PEACE I

Sweet drink for the summer
• Highball/Collins glass

½ ounce vodka
½ ounce dry vermouth
½ ounce Pisang Ambon
2 tsp. apricot brandy
Pineapple juice for topping up
• Garnish:
1 maraschino cherry

Stir the ingredients together, with crushed ice or ice cubes, in the highball glass. Perch the cherry on the rim of the glass. Serve with a stirrer.

BITTERSWEET I

Fruity, delicate, dry drink for the summer
• Highball/Collins glass

1 large scoop lemon sorbet
¾ ounce vodka
¾ ounce grapefruit juice
¾ ounce lemon cordial
Soda water for topping up

Mix together the scoop of sorbet, vodka, grapefruit juice, and lemon cordial in the highball glass. Top up with soda water and stir briefly. Serve with a spoon.

LONG VOLGA CLIPPER

Fruity, delicate, dry drink for a party
• Highball/Collins glass
• Shaker

1 ounce vodka
1 ounce orange juice
¾ ounce apricot brandy
Bitter orange for topping up
• Garnish:
1 kumquat

Shake the vodka, orange juice, and apricot brandy together well, with ice cubes, in the shaker and strain into the highball glass. Top up with bitter orange and stir briefly. Perch the kumquat on the rim of the glass.

NORDIC SUMMER

Fruity, delicate, dry drink for a party
• Highball/Collins glass

2¾ ounces orange juice
1½ ounces vodka
¾ ounce passion-fruit syrup
¾ ounce lime juice
1 dash grenadine (optional)
• Garnish:
1 slice of lime
1 maraschino cherry

Carefully stir all the ingredients together, with ice, in the highball glass. Perch the fruit on the rim of the glass.

Vodka

Nordic Summer (back), **Green Peace I** (middle left), **Bittersweet** (middle right), **Long Volga Clipper** (front)

NIKKO

Fruity drink for the summer
• Highball/Collins glass
• Shaker

1 ounce plus 1 tsp. vodka
½ ounce blue curaçao
1 tsp. lemon juice
1 tsp. pineapple juice
Orange juice for topping up
• Garnish:
Sprig of mint

Shake all the ingredients, except the orange juice, together, with ice, in the shaker. Strain into the highball glass over ice cubes, top up with orange juice, and stir. Add the sprig of mint and a stirrer to the glass.

GREYHOUND

Dry, fruity aperitif
• Highball/Collins glass

2 ounces vodka
2 ounces grapefruit juice

Pour the ingredients into the highball glass over ice cubes. Serve the drink with a stirrer.

VODKA SILVER FIZZ

Fruity, slightly bitter fizz for the summer
• Highball/Collins glass
• Shaker

2 ounces vodka
1 ounce lemon juice
¾ ounce sugar syrup
1 egg white
Soda water for topping up

Shake all the ingredients, except the soda water, together, with ice, in the shaker and strain into the glass. Top up with soda water.

BLUE LAGOON

Fruity, sweet drink for the summer
• Highball/Collins glass

1½ ounces vodka
¾ ounce blue curaçao
1 tsp. lemon juice
Lemonade for topping up
• Garnish:
1 slice of lemon

Mix all the ingredients, except the lemonade, together, with ice cubes, in the highball glass. Top up with lemonade and stir briefly. Perch the slice of lemon on the rim of the glass.

Vodka

VODKA AND PEPPERMINT

Dry, spicy drink for a party
• Highball/Collins glass
• Shaker

¾ ounce vodka
¾ ounce peppermint cordial
Tonic water for topping up
• Garnish:
1 lemon peel spiral

Shake the vodka and cordial together, with ice, in the shaker and strain into the glass. Top up with tonic and stir briefly. Hang the lemon peel spiral over the rim of the glass.

SWINGER

Bittersweet drink for a party
• Highball/Collins glass
• Shaker

2¾ ounces orange juice
1½ ounces vodka
¾ ounce amaretto
2 tsp. lime juice
• Garnish:
1 slice of orange

Shake all the ingredients together firmly, with ice cubes, in the shaker and strain into the highball glass. Perch the slice of orange on the rim of the glass.

CONSUL

Dry, fruity drink for a party
• Highball/Collins glass
• Shaker

1½ ounces grapefruit juice
1 ounce vodka
¾ ounce raspberry-flavored liqueur
2 tsp. lemon juice

Shake the ingredients together, with ice, in the shaker and strain into the highball glass over ice cubes.

VODKA SOUR

Refreshing drink for a party
• Rocks glass
• Shaker

1½ ounces vodka
¾ ounce lemon juice
2 tsp. sugar syrup
• Extra:
½ slice of lemon
1 maraschino cherry

Shake the ingredients together, with ice, in the shaker and strain into the glass. Add the fruit to the glass. Add a little mineral water, too, if liked.

CASABLANCA

Fruity, creamy drink for the evening
• Highball/Collins glass
• Shaker

1½ ounces orange juice

1 ounce vodka

¾ ounce advocaat

¾ ounce lemon juice

Shake all the ingredients together well, with ice cubes, in the shaker. Half fill the highball glass with crushed ice and strain the cocktail into it.

CAMURAI

Creamy drink for the summer
• Highball/Collins glass

1 ounce vodka

½ ounce blue curaçao

½ ounce cream of coconut

Soda water for topping up

• Garnish:

1 maraschino cherry

1 piece of orange peel

1 piece of lemon peel

Carefully mix the ingredients together in the highball glass. Spear the cherry and slices of citrus fruit on a toothpick and lay the garnish across the rim of the glass. Serve with a stirrer.

Vodka

HARVEY WALLBANGER

Fruity aperitif or after-dinner drink
• Highball/Collins glass

1 ounce vodka
Orange juice for topping up
2 tsp. Galliano
• Garnish:
½ slice of orange

Pour the vodka into the glass over ice cubes. Top up with orange juice, stir the drink, and pour the Galliano on top. Perch the slice of orange on the rim of the glass. Serve with a stirrer.

GREEN SPIDER

Spicy, fresh drink for the summer
• Highball/Collins glass

1½ ounces vodka
¾ ounce peppermint cordial
Soda water for topping up
• Garnish:
Sprig of mint

Mix the vodka and cordial together, with ice, in the highball glass. Top up with soda water and stir briefly. Perch the sprig of mint on the rim of the glass.

BULL SHOT

Spicy, piquant pick-me-up
• Highball/Collins glass

3½ ounces beef consommé
1½ ounces vodka

Mix the ingredients together
thoroughly, with ice cubes, in the
highball glass.

LE MANS

Delicate, dry drink for a party
• Large rocks glass

1 ounce vodka
*1 ounce Cointreau or other orange-
flavored liqueur*
Soda water for topping up
• Garnish
1 slice of lemon

Mix the vodka and Cointreau together,
with ice cubes, in the glass. Top up with
soda water and stir briefly. Perch the
slice of lemon on the rim of the glass.

BLOODY MARY

Spicy, piquant pick-me-up
• Highball/Collins glass

1¾ ounces tomato juice
1½ ounces vodka
2 tsp. lemon juice
Worcestershire sauce
Salt
Freshly ground black pepper
Hot-pepper sauce
Celery salt
• Garnish:
1 small celery stalk (optional)

Mix the ingredients together, with ice
cubes, in the highball glass. Add a small
celery stalk to the glass, if liked.

APRICOT DAILY

Dry, fruity drink for the evening
• Highball/Collins glass
• Shaker

1½ ounces vodka
¾ ounce apricot brandy
2 tsp. lemon juice
Bitter lemon for topping up

Shake all the ingredients, except the
bitter lemon, together, with ice, in the
shaker and strain into the glass. Top up
with bitter lemon and stir briefly.

GIN STINGER

GIMLET

Gin-based drinks

MARTINI EXTRA DRY

SWEET MARTINI

FLYING

ANGEL'S FACE

ORIGINAL SINGAPORE SLING

DRY MARTINI

Dry aperitif
• Cocktail glass
• Mixing glass

1½ ounces gin
¾ ounce dry vermouth
• Garnish:
1 olive

Mix the ingredients together, with ice, in the mixing glass and strain into the cocktail glass. Spear the olive on a toothpick and add it to the glass.

EXTRA-DRY MARTINI

Very strong aperitif
• Cocktail glass
• Mixing glass

1¾ ounces gin
2 tsp. dry vermouth
• Garnish:
1 olive
1 piece of lemon peel (optional)

Mix the ingredients together, with ice, in the mixing glass and strain into the cocktail glass. Spear the olive on a toothpick, add it to the glass and, if liked, squeeze the lemon peel over the drink.

MEDIUM-DRY MARTINI

Medium-dry drink
• Cocktail glass
• Mixing glass

1½ ounces gin
2 tsp. dry vermouth
2 tsp. sweet red vermouth
• Garnish:
1 olive
1 piece of lemon peel (optional)

Mix the ingredients together, with ice, in the mixing glass and strain into the cocktail glass. Spear the olive on a toothpick, add it to the glass, and, if liked, squeeze the lemon peel over the drink.

SWEET MARTINI

Sweet aperitif
• Cocktail glass
• Mixing glass

1½ ounces gin
¾ ounce sweet red vermouth
• Garnish:
1 maraschino cherry
1 piece of lemon peel (optional)

Mix the ingredients together, with ice, in the mixing glass and strain into the cocktail glass. Spear the cherry on a toothpick and add it to the glass, and, if liked, squeeze the lemon peel over the drink.

Gin

Dry Martini (above), Sweet Martini (below)

BRONX

Dry, short aperitif
• Cocktail glass
• Shaker

¾ ounce gin
2 tsp. sweet red vermouth
2 tsp. dry vermouth
¾ ounce orange juice

Shake all the ingredients together
firmly, with ice cubes, in the shaker and
strain into the cocktail glass.

WHITE WINGS

Tangy, dry aperitif
• Cocktail glass
• Mixing glass

1 ounce gin
½ ounce white crème de menthe

Mix the ingredients together, with ice,
in the mixing glass and strain into the
cocktail glass.

GIN STINGER

Aromatic aperitif or after-dinner drink
• Cocktail glass
• Mixing glass

1 ounce gin
1 ounce green crème de menthe

Mix the ingredients together, with ice,
in the mixing glass and strain into the
cocktail glass.

FRENCH 75

Aromatic champagne cocktail for
aperitif or after-dinner drink
• Champagne glass or flute
• Shaker

¾ ounce gin
¾ ounce Cointreau or other orange-
flavored liqueur
¾ ounce lemon juice
1 dash Pernod
Champagne or sparkling wine for
topping up
• Garnish:
½ slice of orange
1 maraschino cherry

Shake all the ingredients, except the
champagne, together, with ice, in the
shaker and strain into the champagne
glass. Top up with champagne. Spear
the slice of orange and cherry on a
toothpick, and perch the garnish on the
rim of the glass.

NEGRONI

Slightly sweet drink for the evening
• Rocks glass

¾ ounce gin
¾ ounce Campari
¾ ounce sweet red vermouth
• Garnish:
1 slice of orange

Mix all the ingredients together, with
ice, in the glass. Perch the slice of
orange on the rim of the glass.

Gin

RESOLUTE

Medium-dry drink
• Cocktail glass
• Shaker

¾ ounce gin
2 tsp. apricot brandy
2 tsp. lemon juice

Shake the ingredients together, with ice, in the shaker and strain into the cocktail glass.

ANGEL'S FACE

Sweet aperitif
• Cocktail glass
• Mixing glass

¾ ounce gin
¾ ounce Calvados
¾ ounce apricot brandy

Mix all the ingredients together, with ice, in the mixing glass and strain into the cocktail glass.

ATTA BOY

Dry aperitif
• Cocktail glass
• Mixing glass

1 ounce gin
½ ounce dry vermouth
1 tsp. grenadine

Mix the ingredients together, with ice, in the mixing glass and strain into the cocktail glass.

BALLA BALLA

Dry, bitter champagne cocktail for a reception
• Champagne glass or flute
• Mixing glass

½ ounce gin
½ ounce triple sec
½ ounce Campari
Dry champagne or sparkling wine for topping up
• *Garnish:*
½ slice of orange
1 maraschino cherry

Mix all the ingredients, except the champagne, together, with ice, in the mixing glass. Strain into the champagne glass and top up with champagne. Add the fruit to the glass.

MANDY

Medium-dry aperitif
• Cocktail glass
• Shaker

1 ounce plus 1 tsp. orange juice
¾ ounce gin
1 tsp. peach-flavored liqueur
1 tsp. orange curaçao
1 tsp. lemon juice
• *Garnish:*
1 maraschino cherry
1 small sprig of mint

Shake the ingredients together, with ice, in the shaker and strain into the cocktail glass. Perch the cherry and sprig of mint on the rim of the glass.

HONEYMOON I

Dry aperitif
- Cocktail glass
- Shaker

1½ ounces gin
¾ ounce apricot brandy
1 tsp. lemon juice
1 tsp. grenadine
- Garnish:
1 maraschino cherry

Shake the ingredients together, with plenty of ice, in the shaker and strain into the cocktail glass. Add the cherry to the glass.

HAWAIIAN COCKTAIL

Fruity aperitif
- Cocktail glass
- Shaker

1 ounce gin
¾ ounce orange juice
2 tsp. triple sec

Shake the ingredients together, with plenty of ice, in the shaker and strain into the cocktail glass.

ISLE OF SKYE

Sweet aperitif
- Cocktail glass
- Shaker

¾ ounce gin
¾ ounce Drambuie
¾ ounce lemon juice

Shake the ingredients together, with ice, in the shaker and strain into the cocktail glass.

ORANGE BLOSSOM

Fruity aperitif
- Cocktail glass
- Shaker

1 ounce gin
1 ounce orange juice

Shake the ingredients together, with ice, in the shaker and strain into the cocktail glass.

BLUE LADY

Fruity, sweet drink for the evening
- Cocktail glass with sugared rim
- Shaker

¾ ounce gin
¾ ounce blue curaçao
¾ ounce lemon juice

Shake the ingredients together, with ice, in the shaker and strain into the cocktail glass with the sugared rim. Serve immediately.

MAY FAIR

Fruity aperitif or after-dinner drink
- Cocktail glass
- Shaker

1 ounce gin
1 ounce orange juice
3 dashes apricot brandy

Shake the ingredients together, with ice, in the shaker and strain into the cocktail glass.

Gin

Blue Lady (left), Gimlet (right)

FLYING I

Refreshing champagne cocktail for an aperitif or after-dinner drink
• Champagne flute
• Shaker

¾ ounce gin
¾ ounce Cointreau or other orange-flavored liqueur
¾ ounce lemon juice
Champagne or dry sparkling wine for topping up
• Garnish:
1 maraschino cherry

Shake all the ingredients, except the champagne, together, with plenty of ice, in the shaker and strain into the champagne flute. Top up, then add the cherry to the glass.

GIMLET

Slightly dry aperitif
• Cocktail glass
• Mixing glass

1½ ounces gin
¾ ounce Rose's lime juice cordial
• Extra:
1 maraschino cherry
1 piece of lime peel
1 piece of lemon peel

Mix the ingredients, with plenty of ice, in the mixing glass and strain into the cocktail glass. Add the cherry to the glass. Squeeze the lime and lemon peels over the drink and add the peel to the glass.

153

QUEBEC

Aromatic drink
• Cocktail glass
• Shaker

¾ ounce gin
¾ ounce Canadian whisky
¾ ounce lemon juice
1 dash Angostura bitters

Shake the ingredients together, with ice, in the shaker and strain into the glass.

QUEEN'S COCKTAIL

Fruity aperitif
• Cocktail glass
• Shaker

¾ ounce gin
¾ ounce pineapple juice
2 tsp. sweet red vermouth
2 tsp. dry vermouth

Shake the ingredients together, with ice, in the shaker and strain into the cocktail glass.

XANTHIA

Sweet aperitif
• Cocktail glass
• Mixing glass

¾ ounce gin
¾ ounce green Chartreuse
¾ ounce cherry brandy

Mix the ingredients together, with ice, in the mixing glass and strain into the cocktail glass.

THEATER

Medium-dry, refreshing champagne cocktail for a reception
• Champagne glass or flute
• Shaker

¾ ounce gin
¾ ounce peach brandy
2 tsp. banana-flavored liqueur
2 tsp. pineapple juice
1 dash lemon juice
Dry champagne or sparkling wine for topping up
• Garnish:
1 strawberry
Sprig of mint

Shake all the ingredients together, with ice, in the shaker, and strain into the champagne glass. Top up with champagne or sparkling wine. Spear the strawberry and the sprig of mint on a toothpick and lay the garnish across the rim of the glass.

INSPIRATION

Dry aperitif
• Cocktail glass
• Mixing glass

½ ounce gin
½ ounce dry vermouth
½ ounce Calvados
½ ounce Grand Marnier
• Garnish:
1 maraschino cherry

Mix the ingredients together, with ice, in the mixing glass and strain into the cocktail glass. Spear the cherry on a toothpick and add it to the glass.

Gin

NET ROLLER

Refreshing, fruity champagne cocktail
for a reception
• Champagne glass or flute
• Shaker

¾ ounce gin
¾ ounce passion-fruit-flavored
liqueur
¾ ounce orange juice
Dry sparkling wine for topping up
• *Garnish:*
½ slice of orange
1 maraschino cherry

Shake all the ingredients, except the
sparkling wine, together, with ice, in
the shaker. Strain into the champagne
glass and top up with sparkling wine.
Perch the slice of orange on the rim of
the glass. Fasten the cherry to the slice
of orange with a toothpick.

EXTERMINATOR

Dry champagne cocktail for a
reception
• Large champagne glass or flute
• Shaker

1½ ounces grapefruit juice
1 ounce gin
¾ ounce Cointreau or other orange-
flavored liqueur
Dry champagne or sparkling wine for
topping up
• *Garnish:*
1 maraschino cherry

Shake all the ingredients, except the
champagne, together, with ice, in the
shaker. Strain into the champagne glass
and top up with sparkling wine. Add
the cherry to the glass.

PARADISE

Medium-dry, fruity after-dinner drink
• Cocktail glass
• Shaker

¾ ounce gin
¾ ounce apricot brandy
¾ ounce orange juice

Shake the ingredients together, with
ice, in the shaker and strain into the
cocktail glass.

ZAZA

Dry aperitif
• Cocktail glass
• Mixing glass

1 ounce gin
1 ounce Dubonnet
1 dash Angostura bitters

Shake the ingredients together, with
ice, in the shaker and strain into the
cocktail glass.

TRINITY

Tangy aperitif
• Cocktail glass
• Mixing glass

¾ ounce gin
¾ ounce sweet red vermouth
¾ ounce dry vermouth

Mix the ingredients together, with ice,
in the mixing glass and strain into the
cocktail glass.

LADY DI

Fruity, sparkling champagne cocktail for a reception
• Champagne glass with sugared rim
• Shaker

¾ ounce gin
2 tsp. Benedictine
2 tsp. orange juice
1 tsp. grenadine
2 dashes orange bitters
Champagne or dry sparkling wine for topping up
• *Garnish:*
½ slice of orange
1 maraschino cherry

Shake all the ingredients, except the champagne, together, with ice, in the shaker. Strain into the champagne glass with the sugared rim and top up with champagne. Spear the fruit on a toothpick and lay the garnish across the rim of the glass.

BLUE DIAMOND

Fruity champagne cocktail for a reception
• Champagne glass or flute
• Shaker

¾ ounce gin
¾ ounce blue curaçao
¾ ounce lemon juice
Champagne or sparkling wine for topping up
• *Garnish:*
1 maraschino cherry

Shake the ingredients, except the champagne, together, with ice, in the shaker and strain into the champagne glass. Spear the cherry on a toothpick and add it to the glass.

Gin

SUZY WONG

Refreshing, fruity, medium-dry
champagne cocktail for a reception
• Champagne glass with sugared rim
• Shaker

¾ ounce gin
¾ ounce mandarin-flavored liqueur
¾ ounce lemon juice
Champagne or dry sparkling wine for
topping up
• Garnish:
½ slice of orange

Shake all the ingredients, except the
champagne, together, with ice, in the
shaker. Strain into the champagne glass
and top up with champagne. Perch the
slice of orange on the rim of the glass.

IMPERIAL

Very dry aperitif
• Cocktail glass
• Mixing glass

1 ounce gin
1 ounce dry vermouth
1 dash Angostura bitters
1 dash maraschino
• Garnish:
1 olive

Mix the ingredients together, with ice,
in the mixing glass and strain into the
cocktail glass. Spear the olive on a
toothpick and add it to the glass.

FLAMINGO

Spicy, fruity aperitif
• Cocktail glass
• Shaker

1½ ounces gin
¾ ounce apricot brandy
¾ ounce lemon juice
2 dashes grenadine

Shake all the ingredients together, with ice, in the shaker and strain into the cocktail glass.

EMERALD

Spicy aperitif
• Cocktail glass
• Mixing glass

1 ounce gin
2 tsp. green Chartreuse
2 tsp. yellow Chartreuse
• Garnish:
1 green olive, stuffed with pimiento

Mix the ingredients together well, with ice, in the mixing glass and strain into the cocktail glass. Add the olive to the glass.

GIN COCKTAIL

Spicy aperitif
• Cocktail glass
• Mixing glass

1¾ ounces gin
3 dashes orange bitters

Mix the ingredients together, with ice, in the mixing glass and strain into the cocktail glass.

RED LION COCKTAIL

Fruity, dry drink for the evening
• Cocktail glass with sugared rim
• Shaker

¾ ounce gin
¾ ounce Grand Marnier
2 tsp. orange juice
2 tsp. lemon juice

Shake the ingredients together, with ice, in the shaker and strain into the cocktail glass.

HOARFROST I

Alcoholic after-dinner drink
• Cocktail glass with sugared rim
• Shaker

2 tsp. gin
2 tsp. white curaçao
2 tsp. light rum
2 tsp. grenadine
2 tsp. lemon juice

Shake the ingredients together, with ice, in the shaker and strain into the cocktail glass with the sugared rim.

Gin

ST. VINCENT

Spicy, sweet after-dinner drink
• Cocktail glass
• Shaker

¾ ounce gin
¾ ounce light cream
¾ ounce Galliano
3 dashes grenadine

Shake all the ingredients together well, with ice, in the mixing glass and strain into the glass.

GAME

Fruity, mild drink for the evening
• Rocks glass

1 ounce gin
2 tsp. apricot brandy
2 tsp. amaretto

Mix all the ingredients together, with ice cubes, in the glass.

HONOLULU

Mild, fruity drink for the evening
• Cocktail glass
• Shaker

¾ ounce gin
2 tsp. Benedictine
2 tsp. maraschino

Shake all the ingredients together, with ice, in the shaker and strain into the glass.

HOLLAND HOUSE

Medium-dry aperitif
• Cocktail glass
• Shaker

1 ounce gin
½ ounce dry vermouth
2 tsp. lemon juice
4 dashes maraschino
• Garnish:
1 small piece of pineapple

Shake the ingredients together, with ice, in the shaker and strain into the glass. Add the piece of pineapple to the glass.

ORANGE FLIP

Creamy drink for the afternoon
• Goblet or flip glass
• Shaker

1½ ounces orange juice
¾ ounce gin
¾ ounce triple sec
2 tsp. light cream
1 egg yolk
• Extra:
Grated nutmeg

Shake the ingredients together firmly, with ice, in the shaker and strain into the goblet or flip glass. Sprinkle grated nutmeg on top.

CLOVER CLUB

Fruity aperitif
- Cocktail glass
- Shaker

1 ounce gin
¾ ounce lemon juice
2 tsp. grenadine
1 tsp. egg white

Shake all the ingredients together firmly, with ice, in the shaker and strain into the cocktail glass.

CASINO

Dry aperitif
- Cocktail glass
- Mixing glass

1½ ounces gin
2 tsp. maraschino
2 tsp. lemon juice
1 dash orange bitters
• Garnish:
1 maraschino cherry

Shake the ingredients together, with plenty of ice, in the shaker and strain into the cocktail glass. Add the cherry to the glass.

OPERA

Slightly dry aperitif
- Cocktail glass
- Mixing glass

1½ ounces gin
2 tsp. Dubonnet
2 tsp. maraschino
• Extra:
1 piece of orange peel

Mix the ingredients together, with ice, in the mixing glass and strain into the cocktail glass. Squeeze the orange peel over the drink and add the peel to the glass.

EMPIRE

Very alcoholic after-dinner drink
- Cocktail glass
- Mixing glass

1 ounce gin
½ ounce Calvados
½ ounce apricot brandy
• Garnish:
1 maraschino cherry

Mix the ingredients together, with plenty of ice, in the mixing glass and strain into the cocktail glass. Spear the cherry on a toothpick and add it to the glass.

Gin

Casino (back), Clover Club (middle), Opera (front)

FALLEN ANGEL

Very fruity, dry aperitif
• Cocktail glass
• Shaker

1½ ounces gin
¾ ounce lemon juice
2 dashes green crème de menthe
1 dash Angostura bitters

Shake all the ingredients together, with plenty of ice, in the shaker and strain into the glass.

ALCUDIA

Fruity drink for the summer
• Cocktail glass
• Shaker

¾ ounce gin
½ ounce banana-flavored liqueur
½ ounce Galliano
½ ounce grapefruit juice
• Garnish:
¼ slice of orange
1 maraschino cherry

Shake the ingredients together, with ice, in the shaker and strain into the cocktail glass. Perch the slice of orange on the rim of the glass and fasten the cherry to it with a toothpick.

MILLION DOLLAR

Sweet aperitif
• Cocktail glass
• Shaker

1 ounce gin
1 ounce sweet red vermouth
1 tsp. grenadine
1 tsp. pineapple juice
1 tsp. egg white

Shake the ingredients together firmly, with ice, in the shaker and strain into the glass.

GIN AND FRENCH

Very dry aperitif
• Cocktail glass
• Mixing glass

1½ ounces gin
¾ ounce dry French vermouth
• Extra:
1 piece of lemon peel

Mix the ingredients together, with ice, in the mixing glass and strain into the cocktail glass. Squeeze the lemon peel over the drink and add the peel to the glass.

Gin

CLARIDGE

Medium-dry drink for any occasion
- Cocktail glass
- Mixing glass

½ ounce gin
½ ounce dry vermouth
2 tsp. apricot brandy
2 tsp. triple sec
- Garnish:
1 maraschino cherry

Mix the ingredients together, with ice, in the mixing glass and strain into the glass. Add the cherry to the glass.

WHITE LADY

Aromatic aperitif
- Cocktail glass
- Shaker

¾ ounce gin
¾ ounce Cointreau or other orange-flavored liqueur
¾ ounce lemon juice
- Garnish:
1 maraschino cherry

Shake the ingredients together, with ice, in the shaker and strain into the cocktail glass. Add the cherry to the glass.

RHINE GOLD

Dry, slightly bitter aperitif
- Cocktail glass
- Mixing glass

¾ ounce gin
½ ounce Cointreau or other orange-flavored liqueur
2 tsp. dry vermouth
2 tsp. Campari
- Garnish:
1 piece of orange peel

Mix the ingredients together, with ice, in the mixing glass and strain into the cocktail glass. Squeeze the orange peel over the drink.

HAPPY BIRTHDAY

Fruity, champagne cocktail for a reception
- Champagne flute
- Shaker

1½ ounces gin or genever
½ ounce orange curaçao
½ ounce light rum
½ ounce peach-flavored liqueur
½ ounce pineapple juice
Champagne or sparkling wine for topping up
- Garnish:
½ slice of lemon
1 maraschino cherry

Shake all the ingredients, except the champagne, together, with ice, in the shaker and strain into the champagne flute. Top up with champagne. Perch the slice of lemon on the rim of the glass and fasten the cherry to it with a toothpick.

PINK GIN

Strong drink for the evening
• Rocks glass

1 dash Angostura bitters
1½ ounces gin
Iced water (optional)

Rinse the glass out with the Angostura bitters and then pour the gin into the glass. Add 2 ice cubes to the glass. Add iced water to the drink, if desired.

YELLOW DAISY

Medium-dry aperitif
• Cocktail glass
• Mixing glass

1 ounce gin
¾ ounce dry vermouth
2 tsp. Grand Marnier

Mix the ingredients together, with ice, in the mixing glass and strain into the cocktail glass.

MAXIM COCKTAIL

Spicy, mild after-dinner drink
• Cocktail glass
• Mixing glass

1 ounce gin
¾ ounce sweet red vermouth
2 tsp. white crème de cacao

Mix the ingredients together, with ice, in the mixing glass and strain into the glass.

CONCA D'ORO

Sweet after-dinner drink
• Cocktail glass
• Mixing glass

1½ ounces gin
2 tsp. cherry brandy
2 tsp. maraschino
2 tsp. white curaçao
• Extra:
1 piece of orange peel

Mix the ingredients together, with ice, in the mixing glass and strain into the cocktail glass. Squeeze the orange peel over the drink and add the peel to the glass.

INES

Medium-dry aperitif
• Cocktail glass
• Mixing glass

¾ ounce gin
¾ ounce dry vermouth
¾ ounce sweet red vermouth
2 tsp. amaretto
• Garnish:
1 green olive, stuffed with pimiento

Mix the ingredients together, with ice, in the mixing glass and strain into the cocktail glass. Add the olive to the glass.

Gin

AMOUR MARIE

Fruity drink for the summer
• Cocktail glass
• Mixing glass

1 ounce gin
½ ounce Parfait Amour
½ ounce dry vermouth
• *Garnish:*
1 maraschino cherry

Mix the ingredients together, with ice, in the mixing glass and strain into the cocktail glass. Add the cherry to the glass.

ALASKA

Aromatic aperitif
• Cocktail glass
• Mixing glass

1½ ounces gin
¾ ounce yellow Chartreuse
• *Extra:*
1 piece of lemon peel

Mix the ingredients together, with ice, in the mixing glass, strain into the cocktail glass and squeeze the lemon peel over the drink.

BANANZAS

Sweet drink for a party
• Cocktail glass
• Shaker

¾ ounce gin
½ ounce crème de banane
½ ounce Drambuie
½ ounce grapefruit juice
• *Garnish:*
1 maraschino cherry

Shake the ingredients together, with ice, in the shaker and strain into the cocktail glass. Add the cherry to the glass.

PINK LADY

Fruity aperitif or after-dinner drink
• Cocktail glass
• Shaker

1½ ounces gin
¾ ounce lemon juice
2 tsp. grenadine
½ egg white

Shake the ingredients together firmly, with ice, in the shaker and strain into the glass.

TANGO

Medium-dry aperitif
- Champagne or cocktail glass
- Shaker

1 ounce gin
½ ounce sweet red vermouth
½ ounce dry vermouth
2 tsp. orange juice
2 dashes orange curaçao
• Extra:
1 piece of orange peel

Shake the ingredients together, with ice, in the shaker and strain into the glass. Add the piece of orange peel to the glass.

ADAM & EVE

Fruity, spicy drink for the evening
- Champagne or cocktail glass
- Shaker

¾ ounce gin
¾ ounce Drambuie
¾ ounce Angostura bitters
2 tsp. lemon juice
1 dash grenadine
• Garnish:
1 slice of lemon
1 maraschino cherry

Shake all the ingredients together, with ice cubes, in the shaker and strain into the glass. Spear the fruit on a toothpick and lay the garnish across the rim of the glass.

Gin

ADMIRAL COCKTAIL

Fruity, spicy drink for any time of year
• Champagne or cocktail glass
• Shaker

1½ ounces gin
¾ ounce cherry-flavored liqueur
¾ ounce lemon juice
• Garnish:
1 maraschino cherry

Shake all the ingredients together, with ice cubes, in the shaker and strain into the glass. Perch the cherry on the rim of the glass.

LEMON FLIP

Refreshing after-dinner drink
• Champagne flute
• Shaker

1½ ounces lemon juice
1 ounce gin
¾ ounce triple sec
1 egg yolk
• Garnish:
½ slice of lemon

Shake the ingredients together firmly, with ice, in the shaker and strain into the champagne flute. Perch the slice of lemon on the edge of the glass.

MAR DEL PLATA

Medium-dry aperitif
• Cocktail glass
• Mixing glass

1 ounce gin
¾ ounce dry vermouth
2 tsp. Benedictine
• Extra:
1 piece of lemon peel

Mix the ingredients together, with ice, in the mixing glass and strain into the cocktail glass. Squeeze the lemon peel over the drink.

GIN AND IT

Medium-dry aperitif
• Cocktail glass
• Mixing glass

1 ounce gin
1 ounce sweet red vermouth
• Garnish:
1 maraschino cherry

Mix the ingredients together, with plenty of ice, in the mixing glass and strain into the cocktail glass. Spear the cherry on a toothpick and add it to the glass.

PINK ROSE COCKTAIL

Fruity drink for any time of year
• Cocktail glass
• Shaker

1½ ounces gin
1 tsp. grenadine
1 tsp. lemon juice
1 tsp. light cream
1 egg white

Shake all the ingredients together, with ice, in the shaker and strain into the cocktail glass.

SILVER JUBILEE

Spicy, sweet after-dinner drink
• Cocktail glass
• Shaker

1½ ounces gin
1½ ounces light cream
¾ ounce banana-flavored liqueur
• Garnish:
1 slice of banana

Shake all the ingredients together well, with ice, in the shaker and strain into the cocktail glass. Spear the slice of banana on a toothpick and add it to the glass.

Gin

BLUE DEVIL

Fruity, mild drink for a party
- Cocktail glass
- Shaker

1½ ounces gin
¾ ounce blue curaçao
¾ ounce lemon juice
2 tsp. sugar syrup
- Garnish:
1 maraschino cherry

Shake all the ingredients together, with ice cubes, in the shaker and strain into the cocktail glass. Perch the cherry on the rim of the glass.

BANJINO COCKTAIL

Fruity, spicy drink for a party
- Cocktail glass
- Shaker

1 ounce gin
1 ounce orange juice
1 dash banana-flavored liqueur
- Garnish:
1 slice of orange

Shake all the ingredients together, with ice, in the shaker and strain into the glass. Perch the slice of orange on the rim of the glass.

GIN AND SIN

Fruity, spicy drink for any time of year
- Rocks glass
- Shaker

1½ ounces gin
¾ ounce orange juice
¾ ounce lemon juice
2 tsp. grenadine
- Garnish:
½ slice of orange

Shake all the ingredients together firmly, with ice, in the shaker and strain into the glass. Perch the slice of orange on the rim of the glass.

BARFLY'S DREAM

Mild, spicy drink for the evening
- Cocktail glass
- Shaker

¾ ounce gin
¾ ounce dark rum
¾ ounce pineapple juice

Shake all the ingredients together, with ice, in the shaker and strain into the glass.

ALEXANDRA COCKTAIL

Sweet drink for the afternoon
• Champagne or cocktail glass
• Shaker

¾ ounce gin
¾ ounce white or brown crème de cacao
¾ ounce light cream

Shake all the ingredients together, with ice, in the shaker and strain into the glass.

MY FAIR LADY

Dry, spicy drink for the evening
• Cocktail glass
• Shaker

1 ounce gin
2 tsp. orange juice
2 tsp. lemon juice
1 tsp. egg white
1 dash grenadine
• Garnish:
½ slice of orange

Shake all the ingredients together, with ice, in the shaker and strain into the cocktail glass. Perch the slice of orange on the rim of the glass.

RED GIN

Medium-dry aperitif or after-dinner drink
• Cocktail glass
• Shaker

1½ ounces gin
2 tsp. cherry brandy
• Garnish:
1 slice of orange

Shake the ingredients together well, with ice cubes, in the shaker and strain into the cocktail glass. Perch the slice of orange on the rim of the glass.

PALL MALL COCKTAIL

Spicy aperitif
• Cocktail glass
• Mixing glass

1½ ounces gin
2 tsp. sweet red vermouth
2 tsp. dry vermouth
• Garnish:
1 maraschino cherry

Mix the ingredients together, with ice, in the mixing glass and strain into the cocktail glass. Add the cherry to the glass.

Gin

Alexandra Cocktail (left), Lady Brown (middle), Royal Cocktail (right)

LADY BROWN

Fruity, dry drink for any time of year
- Champagne or cocktail glass
- Shaker

1 ounce gin

½ ounce Grand Marnier

½ ounce lemon juice

• Garnish:

½ slice of orange

Shake all the ingredients together, with ice cubes, in the shaker and strain into the cocktail glass. Add the slice of orange to the glass.

ROYAL COCKTAIL

Fruity, spicy aperitif and after-dinner drink
- Cocktail glass
- Shaker

¾ ounce gin

¾ ounce dry vermouth

¾ ounce cherry brandy

1 dash maraschino

• Garnish:

1 green maraschino cherry

Shake all the ingredients together, with ice, in the shaker and strain into the cocktail glass. Perch the cherry on the rim of the glass.

MOULIN ROUGE

Fruity, delicate, dry drink for any time of year
- Cocktail glass
- Shaker

¾ *ounce gin*
¾ *ounce apricot brandy*
¾ *ounce lemon juice*
1 tsp. grenadine
- ***Garnish:***
1 maraschino cherry

Shake all the ingredients together, with ice, in the shaker and strain into the cocktail glass. Add the cherry to the glass.

DRY GIBSON

Dry aperitif
- Cocktail glass
- Mixing glass

1½ ounces gin
¾ *ounce dry vermouth*
- ***Garnish:***
2 pearl onions

Mix the ingredients together, with plenty of ice, in the mixing glass and strain into the cocktail glass. Spear the onions on a toothpick and add it to the glass.

AFTER THE STORM

Mild, spicy after-dinner drink
- Cocktail glass
- Shaker

¾ *ounce gin*
¾ *ounce light cream*
2 tsp. scotch
2 tsp. white crème de cacao
- ***Garnish:***
1 maraschino cherry

Shake all the ingredients together firmly, with ice, in the shaker and strain into the glass. Perch the cherry on the rim of the glass.

ASTORIA COCKTAIL

Dry, spicy aperitif
- Cocktail glass
- Mixing glass

1½ ounces gin
¾ *ounce dry vermouth*
2 dashes orange bitters
- ***Garnish:***
1 green olive

Mix all the ingredients together, with ice, in the mixing glass and strain into the glass. Add the olive to the glass.

Gin

MISSISSIPPI I

Mild, fruity drink for the evening
• Cocktail glass
• Shaker

1 ounce gin
1 ounce crème de cassis
4 dashes orange juice

Shake all the ingredients together, with ice, in the shaker and strain into the cocktail glass.

EMPIRE STATE

Spicy, delicate, dry drink for the evening
• Cocktail glass
• Mixing glass

1½ ounces gin
¾ ounce cognac
¾ ounce apricot brandy
1 dash orange bitters
• Garnish:
1 maraschino cherry

Mix all the ingredients together, with ice, in the mixing glass and strain into the cocktail glass. Perch the cherry on the rim of the glass.

BERMUDA

Delicately spicy drink for any time of year
• Cocktail glass
• Shaker

2 ounces gin
¾ ounce peach brandy
1 tsp. blue curaçao
1 tsp. orange juice
• Garnish:
½ slice of orange

Shake all the ingredients together, with ice, in the shaker and strain into the cocktail glass. Perch the slice of orange on the rim of the glass.

PICCADILLY

Spicy, delicate dry drink for the evening or as an aperitif
• Cocktail glass
• Mixing glass

1½ ounces gin
¾ ounce dry vermouth
1 dash grenadine
1 dash Pernod

Mix the ingredients together, with ice, in the mixing glass and strain into the cocktail glass.

TAKE FIVE

Fruity, delicate dry drink for a party
- Champagne glass or flute
- Shaker

1 ounce gin
1 ounce lemon juice
¾ ounce sugar syrup
2 tsp. orange juice
2 tsp. grenadine
• Garnish:
1 slice of lime

Shake all the ingredients together, with ice, in the shaker and strain into the champagne glass. Perch the slice of lime on the rim of the glass.

ENGLISH ROSE

Medium-dry aperitif
- Cocktail glass
- Shaker

¾ ounce gin
2 tsp. apricot brandy
2 tsp. dry vermouth
1 tsp. grenadine
3 dashes lemon juice

Shake the ingredients together, with ice, in the shaker and strain into the cocktail glass.

HABERFIELD

Spicy, dry aperitif
- Cocktail glass
- Shaker

1½ ounces gin
2 tsp. dry vermouth
2 tsp. lemon juice

Shake all the ingredients together firmly, with ice cubes, in the shaker and strain into the cocktail glass.

VIRGIN COCKTAIL

Sweet after-dinner drink
- Cocktail glass
- Mixing glass

¾ ounce gin
¾ ounce white crème de menthe
¾ ounce triple sec

Mix the ingredients together, with ice, in the mixing glass and strain into the cocktail glass.

BERMUDA ROSE

Dry aperitif
- Cocktail glass
- Shaker

1½ ounces gin
2 tsp. lemon juice
1 tsp. apricot brandy
2 dashes grenadine

Shake the ingredients together, with ice, in the shaker and strain into the cocktail glass.

Take Five (back left), Bermuda Rose (back right), Haberfield (front)

CONCORDE

Fruity, delicate dry drink for any time of year
• Cocktail glass
• Shaker

1 ounce gin
2 tsp. apricot brandy
2 tsp. Campari
2 tsp. grenadine
• Garnish:
1 maraschino cherry

Shake all the ingredients together, with ice cubes, in the shaker and strain into the cocktail glass. Perch the cherry on the rim of the glass.

BUTTERFLY

Aromatic drink for the evening
• Rocks glass
• Shaker

¾ ounce gin
¾ ounce pineapple juice
2 tsp. vodka
2 tsp. crème de banane
1 dash of Frothee
• Garnish:
1 strawberry

Shake the ingredients together, with ice, in the shaker and strain into the glass, with ice cubes. Finally, perch the strawberry on the rim of the glass.

BLUE VELVET

Dry drink for the evening
• Cocktail glass
• Mixing glass

¾ ounce gin
¾ ounce blue curaçao
½ ounce dry vermouth
• Garnish:
1 slice of star fruit

Mix the ingredients together, with ice, in the mixing glass and strain into the cocktail glass. Finally, perch the slice of star fruit on the rim of the glass.

GREEN PEACE II

Dry, spicy drink for any time of year
• Large cocktail glass
• Shaker

1 ounce gin
½ ounce lemon juice
2 tsp. green crème de menthe
2 tsp. sugar
1 egg white

Shake all the ingredients together, with ice, in the shaker and strain into the glass.

Gin

WEDDING BELLS

Drink for any time of day
• Cocktail glass
• Shaker

¾ ounce gin

¼ ounce Dubonnet

¼ ounce orange juice

2 tsp. brandy

Shake the ingredients together, with ice, in the shaker and strain into the glass.

CARIN

Sweet after-dinner drink
• Cocktail glass
• Mixing glass

1 ounce gin

½ ounce Dubonnet

½ ounce mandarin-flavored liqueur

• Extra:

1 piece of lemon peel

Mix the ingredients together, with ice, in the mixing glass and strain into the cocktail glass. Squeeze the piece of lemon peel over the drink and add the peel to the glass.

MONTE CARLO IMPERIAL

Refreshing champagne cocktail for a reception
• Champagne flute
• Shaker

¾ ounce gin

2 tsp. white crème de menthe

Champagne or sparkling wine for topping up

Shake the ingredients, except the champagne, together, with ice, in the shaker and strain into the champagne flute. Top up with champagne.

NORTHERN LIGHT 02

Slightly sweet drink for all occasions
• Cocktail glass
• Shaker

1 ounce gin

2 tsp. cassis

2 tsp. triple sec

2 tsp. lemon juice

1 dash Frothee

• Garnish:

1 maraschino cherry

Shake the ingredients together, with ice, in the shaker and strain into the cocktail glass. Add the cherry to the glass.

WESTERN ROSE

Tangy, dry drink for the evening
- Cocktail glass
- Shaker

¾ ounce gin
2 tsp. apricot brandy
2 tsp. dry vermouth
3 dashes lemon juice

Shake the ingredients together, with ice, in the shaker and strain into the cocktail glass.

YELLOW FINGER

Fruity, mild drink for any time of year
- Cocktail glass
- Shaker

¾ ounce gin
¾ ounce blackberry brandy
2 tsp. banana-flavored liqueur
1 dash light cream

Shake all the ingredients together firmly, with ice, in the shaker and strain into the cocktail glass.

BIJOU

Spicy after-dinner drink
- Cocktail glass
- Mixing glass

1 ounce gin
¾ ounce dry vermouth
2 tsp. green Chartreuse

Mix all the ingredients together, with ice cubes, in the mixing glass and strain into the cocktail glass.

BARNUM

Medium-dry aperitif
- Cocktail glass
- Shaker

1 ounce gin
¾ ounce apricot brandy
3 dashes lemon juice
2 dashes Angostura bitters

Shake the ingredients together, with ice, in the shaker and strain into the cocktail glass.

Gin

ALEXANDER'S SISTER

Creamy, sweet drink for the afternoon
• Cocktail glass
• Shaker

¾ *ounce gin*
¾ *ounce green crème de menthe*
¾ *ounce light cream*

Shake the ingredients together firmly, with ice, in the shaker and strain into the glass.

EXOTIC

Sweet drink for the evening
• Rocks glass

1 *ounce gin*
½ *ounce brown crème de cacao*
½ *ounce crème de banane*

Mix the ingredients together, with ice cubes, in the glass and serve the drink with a stirrer.

DERBY

Aperitif
• Cocktail glass
• Mixing glass

2 *ounces gin*
2 *dashes peach bitters*
• *Garnish:*
A few mint leaves

Mix all the ingredients together, with ice cubes, in the mixing glass and strain into the cocktail glass. Add the mint leaves to the glass.

GOLDEN DAWN

Fruity drink for any time of year
• Cocktail glass
• Shaker

1 *ounce gin*
¾ *ounce orange juice*
2 *tsp. lemon juice*
1 *tsp. apricot brandy*
3 *dashes grenadine*

Shake all the ingredients together, with ice cubes, in the shaker and strain into the cocktail glass.

PERFECT GIN COCKTAIL

Medium-dry drink for the evening
• Cocktail glass
• Mixing glass

1½ ounces gin
2 tsp. dry vermouth
2 tsp. sweet red vermouth

Mix the ingredients together, with ice cubes, in the mixing glass and strain into the cocktail glass.

HABITANT

Spicy, sweet short drink for any time of year
• Cocktail glass
• Mixing glass

¾ ounce gin
¾ ounce sweet red vermouth
¾ ounce maple syrup
2 dashes Angostura bitters

Mix all the ingredients together firmly, with ice, in the mixing glass and strain into the cocktail glass.

SPENCER

Medium-dry aperitif
• Cocktail glass
• Shaker

¾ ounce gin
¾ ounce apricot brandy
1 tsp. orange juice
1 dash Angostura bitters

Shake the ingredients together, with ice, in the shaker and strain into the cocktail glass.

JOURNALIST

Medium-dry drink for all occasions
• Cocktail glass
• Shaker

1 ounce gin
2 tsp. dry vermouth
2 tsp. sweet red vermouth
1 tsp. triple sec
1 tsp. lemon juice
1 dash Angostura bitters

Shake the ingredients together, with ice, in the shaker and strain into the glass.

Gin

Lady Chatterley (left), Gin Crusta (right)

LADY CHATTERLEY

Medium-dry aperitif
• Champagne glass
• Shaker

1 ounce gin

2 tsp. triple sec

2 tsp. dry vermouth

2 tsp. orange juice

Shake the ingredients together, with
ice, in the shaker and strain into the
glass.

GIN CRUSTA

Spicy, fruity drink for any time of year
• Paris goblet with sugared rim
• Mixing glass

1½ ounces gin

2 tsp. cherry-flavored liqueur

2 dashes Angostura bitters

Mix all the ingredients together, with
ice cubes, in the mixing glass and strain
into the glass with the sugared rim.

JOHN COLLINS

Refreshing drink for hot days
• Collins/highball glass

1½ ounces gin
¾ ounce lemon juice
2 tsp. sugar syrup
Soda water for topping up
• Garnish:
½ slice of lemon
1 maraschino cherry

Mix all the ingredients, except the soda water, together, with ice cubes, in the Collins glass and top up with soda water. Perch the slice of lemon on the rim of the glass and add the cherry to the glass. Serve with a stirrer.

GOLDEN FIZZ

Refreshing fizz for the summer
• Highball/Collins glass
• Shaker

1½ ounces gin
¾ ounce lemon juice
2 tsp. sugar syrup
1 egg yolk
Soda water for topping up

Shake all the ingredients, except the soda water, together, with plenty of ice, in the shaker and pour into the highball glass. Top up with soda water.

HORSE'S NECK I

Delicate, dry drink for any time of year
• Large rocks glass

1½ ounces gin
2 tsp. grenadine
Ginger ale for topping up
• Garnish:
1 lemon peel spiral

Mix the gin and grenadine together, with ice cubes, in the glass. Top up with ginger ale and stir briefly. Hang the lemon peel spiral over the rim of the glass.

TOM COLLINS

Fruity, tangy drink for hot days
• Collins/highball glass

1½ ounces gin
¾ ounce lemon juice
2 tsp. sugar syrup
Soda water for topping up
• Garnish:
½ slice of lemon
1 maraschino cherry

Mix all the ingredients, except the soda water, together, with ice, in the Collins glass and top up with soda water. Perch the slice of lemon on the rim of the glass, add the cherry to the glass. Serve with a long stirrer.

Gin

ORIGINAL SINGAPORE SLING

Fruity drink for hot days
- Highball/Collins glass
- Shaker

1 ounce gin
2 tsp. cherry heering
1 dash Benedictine
1 dash Cointreau or other orange-flavored liqueur
1 dash Angostura bitters
Lime juice and pineapple juice for topping up
- *Garnish:*
1 piece of pineapple
1 maraschino cherry

Shake the ingredients, except the fruit juices, together, with ice, in the shaker and strain into the glass over ice. Top up with lime and pineapple juices. Spear the pineapple and cherry on a toothpick. Lay the garnish across the rim of the glass.

PIMM'S NO. 1

Refreshing drink for a party
- Highball/Collins glass

1½ ounces Pimm's No. 1
Lemonade for topping up
1 piece of cucumber peel
2 maraschino cherries
½ slice of orange
½ slice of lemon

Pour the Pimm's No. 1 into the highball glass over ice cubes and top up with lemonade. Add the cucumber peel and fruit to the glass. Serve with a stirrer.

SINGAPORE GIN SLING

Refreshing drink for hot days
- Highball/Collins glass
- Shaker

1½ ounces gin
¾ ounce Cherry Heering or other cherry-flavored liqueur
¾ ounce lemon juice
Soda water for topping up
- *Garnish:*
½ slice of lemon
1 maraschino cherry

Shake all the ingredients, except the soda water, together, with ice, in the shaker and strain into the highball glass over ice. Top up with soda water. Spear the slice of lemon and the cherry on a toothpick, and lay the garnish across the rim of the glass.

PIMM'S ROYAL

Refreshing drink for the summer
- Highball/Collins glass

1½ ounces Pimm's No. 1
Champagne or sparkling wine for topping up
1 piece of cucumber peel
2 maraschino cherries
½ slice of orange
½ slice of lemon

Pour the Pimm's No. 1 into the highball glass over ice cubes. Top up with champagne or sparkling wine. Add the cucumber peel and fruit to the glass.

NEPTUNE'S FAIR

Fruity, refreshing drink for a party
- Highball/Collins glass
- Shaker

¾ ounce gin
¾ ounce lemon juice
2 tsp. Pisang Ambon
2 tsp. Jambosala or other passion-fruit liqueur
Bitter lemon for topping up
- *Garnish:*
1 slice of lemon
1 green maraschino cherry
1 small sprig of mint

Shake all the ingredients, except the bitter lemon, together, with ice, in the shaker and strain into the highball glass over ice. Top up with bitter lemon. Perch the slice of lemon on the rim of the glass and fasten the cherry to it with a toothpick. Add the sprig of mint to the glass.

GIN AND TONIC

Refreshing drink for any occasion
- Highball/Collins glass

1½ ounces gin
Tonic water for topping up
- *Extra:*
½ slice of lemon

Pour the gin into the highball glass over ice cubes and top up with tonic water. Add the slice of lemon to the glass. Serve with a stirrer.

CHAMPAGNE FIZZ

Sparkling, light fizzy drink for a party
- Champagne flute
- Shaker

1 ounce gin
¾ ounce lemon juice
2 tsp. sugar syrup
2 ounces champagne or sparkling wine
- *Garnish:*
½ slice of lemon

Shake all the ingredients, except the champagne, together, with ice, in the shaker. Strain into the champagne flute and top up with champagne. Perch the slice of lemon on the rim of the glass.

OPTIMIST

Fruity drink for any occasion
- Highball/Collins glass
- Shaker

1 ounce gin
¾ ounce crème de cassis
¾ ounce pineapple juice
Orange juice for topping up
1 dash passion-fruit syrup
- *Garnish:*
½ slice of orange
1 piece of pineapple
1 green maraschino cherry

Shake all the ingredients, except the passion-fruit syrup and orange juice, together, with ice, in the shaker and strain into the highball glass over ice cubes. Top up with orange juice. Float the passion-fruit syrup on top of the drink. Spear the fruit on a toothpick and lay the garnish across the rim of the glass.

Neptune's Fair (back), Gin and Tonic (front left), Champagne Fizz (middle front),
Optimist (front right)

GIN FIZZ

Refreshing, fruity fizz for any occasion
• Rocks glass
• Shaker

1½ ounces gin
¾ ounce lemon juice
2 tsp. sugar syrup
Soda water for topping up
• Garnish:
½ slice of lemon

Shake all the ingredients, except the soda water, together, with plenty of ice, in the shaker. Pour into the glass and top up with soda water. Perch the slice of lemon on the rim of the glass.

GIN SOUR

Strong, refreshing sour for a party
• Rocks glass
• Shaker

1½ ounces gin
¾ ounce lemon juice
2 tsp. sugar syrup
Soda water for topping up (optional)
• Extra:
½ slice of lemon
1 maraschino cherry

Shake all the ingredients, except the soda water, together, with ice, in the shaker and strain into the glass. Add the slice of lemon and the maraschino cherry to the glass. The drink may be topped up with soda water, if desired.

PIRATE

Fruity, medium-dry drink for any occasion
• Highball/Collins glass
• Shaker

1½ ounces passion-fruit juice
1 ounce Cherry Herring or other cherry-flavored liqueur
¾ ounce gin
2 tsp. lemon juice
Tonic water for topping up
• Garnish:
½ slice of orange
2 maraschino cherries

Shake all the ingredients, except the tonic water, together, with ice, in the shaker and strain into the highball glass over ice cubes. Top up with tonic water. Spear both the slice of orange and the maraschino cherries on a long wooden skewer so it looks like a sail and put it in the glass. Serve with a stirrer.

GIN AND ORANGE

Light drink for a party
• Rocks glass

1½ ounces gin
Orange juice for topping up
• Garnish:
½ slice of orange

Pour the gin into the glass over ice cubes and top up with orange juice. Add the slice of orange to the glass. Serve with a stirrer.

Gin

GOLD DIGGER

Fruity drink for a party
- Highball/Collins glass
- Mixing glass

½ ounce gin
½ ounce kiwi-fruit-flavored liqueur
½ ounce melon-flavored liqueur
½ ounce Aperol
Orange juice for topping up

Mix all the ingredients, except the orange juice, together, with ice, in the mixing glass and pour into the highball glass over ice. Top up with orange juice and stir well. Serve with a stirrer.

TROPICAL SUN I

Light, fruity, refreshing drink for a summer party
- Highball/Collins glass
- Shaker

1½ ounces gin
¾ ounce passion-fruit syrup
2 tsp. lemon juice
Tropical bitters or tropical fruit carbonated drink for topping up
1 dash grenadine
- *Garnish:*
½ slice of orange
1 maraschino cherry

Shake all the ingredients, except the tropical bitters and grenadine, together, with ice, in the shaker and strain into the highball glass over ice cubes. Top up with tropical bitters. Float the grenadine on top of the drink. Spear the slice of orange and the maraschino cherry on a long wooden skewer and add it to the glass.

NICKY

Aromatic drink for a party
- Highball/Collins glass

1 ounce gin
1 ounce apricot brandy
3 dashes lemon juice
1 dash dark rum
Soda water for topping up
- *Garnish:*
1 slice of orange
1 maraschino cherry

Mix all the ingredients, except the soda water, together, with ice cubes, in the highball glass. Top up with soda water. Perch the slice of orange on the rim of the glass and fasten the maraschino cherry to it with a toothpick.

NEW ORLEANS FIZZ

Fruity, refreshing fizz for a summer party
- Highball/Collins glass
- Shaker

1½ ounces gin
¾ ounce lemon juice
2 tsp. sugar syrup
2 tsp. light cream
3 dashes orange bitters
1 egg white
Soda water for topping up

Shake all the ingredients, except the soda water, together firmly, with ice, in the shaker and strain into the highball glass. Top up with soda water.

MINE

Fruity, refreshing aperitif or after-dinner drink
• Highball/Collins glass

1 ounce gin
Orange juice for topping up
½ slice of orange
¾ ounce Campari

Pour the gin into the highball glass over ice and top up with orange juice. Place the slice of orange in the glass and pour the Campari on top of it. Do not stir. Serve with a long stirrer.

SILVER FIZZ

Refreshing, fruity fizz for the summer
• Highball/Collins glass
• Shaker

1½ ounces gin
¾ ounce lemon juice
2 tsp. sugar syrup
1 egg white
Soda water for topping up

Shake all the ingredients, except the soda water, together, with ice, in the shaker and strain into the highball glass. Top up with soda water.

Gin

JOHNNIE RED

Fruity drink for the summer
• Highball/Collins glass

1 ounce gin
½ ounce Parfait Amour
½ ounce crème de banane
1 dash grenadine
Orange juice for topping up
• *Garnish:*
1 orange peel spiral

Mix the ingredients together, with ice cubes, in the highball glass. Hang the orange peel spiral over the rim of the glass and serve the drink with a long stirrer.

SEVEN SEAS

Fruity drink for a summer party
• Highball/Collins glass

1½ ounces Pisang Ambon
¾ ounce gin
1 dash crème de banane
Tonic water for topping up
• *Garnish:*
1 maraschino cherry

Mix the ingredients together, with ice cubes, in the highball glass. Add the cherry to the glass and serve the drink with a stirrer.

ROYAL FIZZ

Refreshing fizz for hot days
• Highball/Collins glass
• Shaker

1½ ounces gin
¾ ounce lemon juice
2 tsp. sugar syrup
1 egg
Soda water for topping up

Shake all the ingredients, except the
soda water, together firmly, with ice, in
the shaker and strain into the highball
glass. Slowly top up with soda water.

STARMANIA

Sweet drink for a party
• Highball/Collins glass
• Shaker

¾ ounce gin
2 tsp. apricot brandy
2 tsp. passion-fruit juice
1 tsp. Campari
1 dash green curaçao
Ginger ale for topping up
• Garnish:
Small pieces of fruit

Shake all the ingredients, except the
ginger ale, together, with ice, in the
shaker and strain into the highball glass
over ice. Top up with ginger ale and stir.
Spear the pieces of fruit on a toothpick
and lay the garnish across the rim of the
glass. Serve with an attractive stirrer.

DASH MADNEY

Refreshing drink for the summer
• Highball/Collins glass
• Mixing glass

1 ounce gin
½ ounce maraschino
½ ounce crème de banane
Bitter lemon for topping up
• Garnish:
1 maraschino cherry

Stir all the ingredients, except the bitter
lemon, together, with ice, in the mixing
glass and strain into the highball glass
over ice cubes. Top up with bitter
lemon and stir well. Perch the cherry
on the rim of the glass and serve the
drink with a stirrer.

BABY DOC

Fruity drink for a summer party
• Highball/Collins glass

¾ ounce gin
¾ ounce kiwi-fruit-flavored liqueur
¾ ounce pineapple juice
1 tsp. peppermint-flavored liqueur
Tonic water for topping up
• Garnish:
1 orange peel spiral

Mix all the ingredients together, with
ice cubes, in the highball glass. Hang
the orange peel spiral over the rim of
the glass.

Gin

SWEET MARY

Refreshing drink for hot days
• Highball/Collins glass

1¾ ounces crème de banane
½ ounce gin
1 dash crème de cassis
Lemonade for topping up
• Garnish:
1 maraschino cherry

Mix all the ingredients, except the lemonade, together, with ice cubes, in the highball glass. Top up with lemonade. Spear the maraschino cherry on a toothpick and lay the garnish across the rim of the glass.

LADY KILLER

Fruity, sweet drink for the summer
• Highball/Collins glass
• Shaker

1 ounce passion-fruit juice
1 ounce pineapple juice
¾ ounce gin
2 tsp. Cointreau or other orange-flavored liqueur
2 tsp. apricot brandy
• Garnish:
1 green plum
1 orange peel spiral
1 sprig of mint

Shake all the ingredients together firmly, with ice, in the shaker and strain into the highball glass over ice cubes. Perch the plum on the rim of the glass. Spear the orange peel spiral on a toothpick and lay the garnish across the rim of the glass. Add the sprig of mint to the glass.

ROSETTE MEROLA

Fruity drink for a party
• Highball/Collins glass

½ ounce gin
½ ounce Gold Digger liqueur
½ ounce kiwi-fruit-flavored liqueur
½ ounce Aperol
Orange juice for topping up
• Garnish:
1 maraschino cherry
1 piece of orange peel

Mix all the ingredients, except the orange juice, together, with ice cubes, in the highball glass. Top up with orange juice. Spear the cherry and the orange peel on a toothpick and lay the garnish across the rim of the glass. Serve the drink with a stirrer.

POGO STICK

Tangy, refreshing drink for the summer
• Highball/Collins glass
• Shaker

2 ounces grapefruit juice
1 ounce gin
¾ ounce Cointreau or other orange-flavored liqueur
2 tsp. lemon juice
• Garnish:
½ grapefruit segment

Shake all the ingredients together, with ice, in the shaker and strain into the highball glass over ice cubes. Perch the grapefruit segment on the rim of the glass.

BLUE MOON I

Fruity, refreshing drink for the summer
- Highball/Collins glass
- Shaker

¾ ounce gin
2 tsp. blue curaçao
2 tsp. Cointreau or other orange-
flavored liqueur
2 tsp. pineapple juice
Lemonade for topping up
• Garnish:
¼ slice of pineapple
1 green maraschino cherry

Shake all the ingredients, except the lemonade, together, with ice, in the shaker and strain into the highball glass over ice cubes. Top up with lemonade and stir. Perch the piece of pineapple and the cherry on the rim of the glass.

APRICOT BLOSSOM

Bitter, refreshing drink for the evening
- Highball/Collins glass
- Shaker

¾ ounce gin
¾ ounce apricot-flavored liqueur
1 tsp. lime juice
2 dashes Angostura bitters
Tonic water for topping up
• Garnish:
1 slice of lime

Shake all the ingredients, except the tonic water, together, with ice, in the shaker and strain into the highball glass over ice cubes. Top up with tonic water and stir. Perch the slice of lime on the rim of the glass. Serve the drink immediately.

Gin

LONG ISLAND ICED TEA

Refreshing drink for a party
• Highball/Collins glass

2 tsp. vodka
2 tsp. gin
2 tsp. light rum
2 tsp. triple sec
2 tsp. white tequila
2 tsp. lemon juice
Cola for topping up
• *Garnish:*
½ slice of lemon
1 sprig of mint

Mix all the ingredients, except the cola, together, with ice, in a highball glass and top up with cola. Perch the slice of lemon and the sprig of mint on the rim of the glass. Serve with a stirrer.

BLUE EYES

Spicy, mild drink for a party
• Highball/Collins glass

1 ounce gin
¾ ounce sweet white vermouth
2 tsp. blue curaçao
Ginger ale for topping up
• *Garnish:*
1 slice of orange
1 maraschino cherry

Mix the gin, vermouth, and curaçao together, with ice cubes, in the highball glass. Top up with ginger ale and stir again. Perch the slice of orange on the rim of the glass and fasten the cherry to the slice of orange with a toothpick.

BULLDOG COOLER

Fruity, mild drink for hot days
• Highball/Collins glass
• Shaker

1 ounce gin
1 ounce orange juice
2 tsp. triple sec
Ginger ale for topping up
• *Garnish:*
1 slice of orange

Shake the gin, orange juice, and Curaçao together, with ice cubes, in the shaker and strain into the highball glass. Top up with ginger ale and stir briefly. Perch the slice of orange on the rim of the glass.

RED SUNSHINE

Fruity, delicate, dry drink for a party
• Highball/Collins glass
• Shaker

1 ounce gin
¾ ounce black-currant-flavored liqueur
¾ ounce lemon juice
Soda water for topping up

Shake the gin, black-currant liqueur, and lemon juice together, with ice, in the shaker and strain into the glass over ice cubes. Top up with soda water and stir briefly.

GIN BUCK

Fruity, spicy drink for any time of year
• Rocks glass

1½ ounces gin
¾ ounce lemon juice
Ginger ale for topping up

Mix the gin and lemon juice together in the glass, top up with ginger ale, and stir briefly.

PARADISO

Fruity, spicy drink for a summer party
• Highball/Collins glass
• Shaker

1 ounce gin
¾ ounce apricot brandy
2 tsp. orange juice
• *Garnish:*
1 slice of orange

Shake all the ingredients together firmly, with ice, in the shaker and strain into the highball glass over ice cubes. Perch the slice of orange on the rim of the glass.

Gin

SOUTH PACIFIC

Fruity, refreshing drink for a summer party
• Highball/Collins glass

¾ ounce gin
2 tsp. blue curaçao
2 tsp. Galliano
Bitter lemon for topping up
• Garnish:
1 maraschino cherry
1 sprig of mint

Mix all the ingredients, except the bitter lemon, together, with ice cubes, in the highball glass. Top up with bitter lemon. Add the cherry and the sprig of mint to the glass and serve the drink with a stirrer.

SEX ROUGE

Aromatic drink for a party
• Highball/Collins glass

1 ounce gin
1 ounce Benedictine
1 dash grenadine
Orange juice and ginger ale for topping up (ratio 1:1)
• Garnish:
1 slice of lime
1 maraschino cherry

Mix all the ingredients, except the orange juice and ginger ale, together, with ice cubes, in the highball glass. Top up with equal quantities of orange juice and ginger ale. Spear the slice of lime and the cherry on a toothpick and lay the garnish across the rim of the glass. Serve with an attractive stirrer.

MINT FIZZ

Spicy, fresh drink for any time of year
• Highball/Collins glass
• Shaker

1¾ ounces gin
1 ounce lemon juice
¾ ounce sugar syrup
2 tsp. green crème de menthe
Soda water for topping up

Shake all the ingredients together, except the soda water, long and firmly, with ice cubes, in the shaker. Strain into the highball glass and add a few ice cubes. Top up with soda water and stir briefly.

AMBER GLOW

Fruity, dry drink for a summer party
• Rocks glass

1 ounce gin
1 ounce light rum
1 ounce lime juice
1 tsp. grenadine
Soda water for topping up

Mix together the gin, rum, lime juice, and grenadine, with ice, in the glass. Top up with soda water and stir briefly.

STROUMF

Full-flavored drink for the evening
• Highball/Collins glass
• Shaker

¾ ounce gin
¾ ounce apricot brandy
2 tsp. amaretto
1 dash lemon juice
Orange juice for topping up

Shake all the ingredients, except the orange juice, together, with ice, in the shaker and strain into the highball glass. Top up with orange juice and stir. Serve with a stirrer.

MESSICANO

Fruity, sweet drink for a summer party
• Highball/Collins glass
• Shaker

¾ ounce gin
¾ ounce Galliano
¾ ounce orange juice
1 tsp. amaretto
• Garnish:
1 slice of orange
1 maraschino cherry
1 sprig of mint

Shake all the ingredients together, with ice, in the shaker and strain into the highball glass over ice cubes. Perch the fruit and the sprig of mint on the rim of the glass.

LONDON FEVER

Mild, fruity drink for a party
• Rocks glass

1 ounce gin
1 ounce lime cordial
¾ ounce light rum
1 tsp. grenadine
Soda water for topping up
• Garnish:
½ slice of pineapple
1 maraschino cherry

Mix all the ingredients, except the soda water, together, with ice, in the glass. Top up with soda water and stir briefly. Perch the fruit on the rim of the glass.

PARK LANE

Fruity, mild drink for a party
• Rocks glass
• Shaker

1½ ounces gin
1½ ounces orange juice
¾ ounce apricot brandy
1 dash grenadine
1 dash lemon juice

Shake all the ingredients together well, with ice cubes, in the shaker and strain into the glass.

PLANTER'S COCKTAIL

PLANTER'S PUNCH

PRESIDENT

Rum-based drinks

CAIPIRISSIMA

ROBSON

UPTON

DAIQUIRI

PLANTER'S COCKTAIL I

Fruity, tangy drink for hot days
• Rocks glass
• Shaker

1¾ ounces dark rum
1 ounce orange juice
¾ ounce lemon juice
• *Garnish:*
½ slice of lemon
½ slice of orange

Shake all the ingredients together firmly, with ice, in the shaker and pour into the glass. Perch the slices of fruit on the rim of the glass.

PLANTER'S COCKTAIL II

Fruity, tangy drink for hot days
• Rocks glass
• Shaker

1½ ounces dark rum
¾ ounce lemon juice
½ tsp. confectioners' sugar
• *Garnish:*
½ slice of lemon
½ slice of lime

Shake all the ingredients together, with ice, in the shaker and strain into the glass. Perch the slices of fruit on the rim of the glass.

DAIQUIRI

Tangy, short aperitif
• Cocktail glass
• Shaker

1 ounce light rum
¾ ounce lime or lemon juice
2 tsp. sugar syrup

Shake all the ingredients together, with ice, in the shaker and strain into the glass.

FROZEN DAIQUIRI

Refreshing, fruity drink for a party
• Cocktail glass
• Shaker

1 ounce light rum
¾ ounce lime or lemon juice
2 tsp. sugar syrup
• *Garnish:*
1 maraschino cherry

Shake all the ingredients together, with crushed ice, in the shaker and pour into the glass. Add the cherry to the glass.

BACARDI COCKTAIL

Tangy aperitif
• Cocktail glass
• Shaker

1 ounce Bacardi or other light rum
¾ ounce lemon juice
2 tsp. grenadine

Shake all the ingredients together, with ice, in the shaker and strain into the glass.

Rum

CHERRY DAIQUIRI

Fruity, mild drink for a party
• Cocktail glass
• Mixing glass

1 ounce light rum
¾ ounce cherry brandy
¾ ounce lime cordial
2 tsp. kirsch
• *Garnish:*
1 maraschino cherry

Mix all the ingredients together, with ice, in the mixing glass and strain into the cocktail glass. Add the cherry to the glass.

RUM ALEXANDER COCKTAIL

Sweet after-dinner drink
• Cocktail glass
• Shaker

¾ ounce dark rum
¾ ounce brown crème de cacao
¾ ounce light cream
• *Extra:*
Grated nutmeg

Shake all the ingredients together, with ice cubes, in the shaker and strain into the cocktail glass. Sprinkle a little nutmeg on top of the drink.

FROZEN STRAWBERRY DAIQUIRI

Fruity, refreshing drink for a party
• Large cocktail glass
• Blender

1¼ ounces light rum
¾ ounce lemon juice
2 tsp. strawberry-flavored liqueur
1 tsp. confectioners' sugar
2 large strawberries

Mix all the ingredients together, with a scoop of crushed ice, in the blender. Strain into the cocktail glass.

CAIPIRISSIMA

Tangy drink for the evening
• Rocks glass

1 lime
1 tsp. brown sugar
1¾ ounces light rum

Cut the lime into quarters, put them in the glass, and crush them with a mortar or the end of a bar spoon. Add the sugar and some crushed ice, and then pour the rum on top. Stir the drink to mix everything together.

ROBSON

Medium-dry aperitif
• Cocktail glass
• Shaker

1 ounce dark or light rum
½ ounce grenadine
½ ounce orange juice
2 tsp. lemon juice

Shake the ingredients together, with ice, in the shaker and strain into the glass.

EL PRESIDENTE

Fruity aperitif
• Cocktail glass
• Shaker

1 ounce dark rum
¾ ounce orange juice
2 tsp. dry vermouth
1 dash grenadine
1 dash orange curaçao

Shake all the ingredients together firmly, with ice, in the shaker and strain into the glass.

RUM GIMLET

Fruity, fresh drink for hot days
• Rocks glass

1½ ounces dark rum
¾ ounce lime cordial
• Extra:
1 lime quarter

Mix the ingredients together, with ice cubes, in the glass. Squeeze the juice from the lime quarter over the drink and add the crushed lime to the glass.

DAVIS

Alcoholic drink for a party
• Cocktail glass
• Shaker

¾ ounce dark rum
¾ ounce dry vermouth
2 tsp. grenadine
2 tsp. lemon juice

Shake all the ingredients together, with ice, in the shaker and strain into the cocktail glass.

Davis (left), Robson (back right), Rum Gimlet (front right)

GOLDEN CLIPPER

Fruity, mild drink for a party
• Cocktail glass
• Shaker

1½ ounces light rum
¾ ounce peach brandy
¾ ounce orange juice
• Garnish:
¼ slice of orange

Shake all the ingredients together, with ice cubes, in the shaker and strain into the cocktail glass. Finally perch the slice of orange on the rim of the glass.

CLARENDON COCKTAIL

Fruity, slightly tangy drink for hot days
• Cocktail glass
• Shaker

1½ ounces light rum
¾ ounce grapefruit juice
½ ounce lime cordial
2 tsp. confectioners' sugar
1 tsp. grenadine

Shake all the ingredients together, with ice cubes, in the shaker and strain into the cocktail glass.

HONEYBEE

Sweet drink for any occasion
• Cocktail glass
• Shaker

1 ounce light rum
2 tsp. lemon juice
2 tsp. honey

Shake all the ingredients together firmly, with ice, in the shaker and strain into the cocktail glass.

PRESIDENT

Medium-dry drink for a party
• Cocktail glass
• Shaker

1 ounce light rum
¾ ounce orange juice
1 tsp. grenadine

Shake the ingredients together, with ice, in the shaker and strain into the cocktail glass.

PARISIAN BLONDE

Medium-dry after-dinner drink
• Cocktail glass
• Shaker

¾ ounce dark rum
¾ ounce triple sec
¾ ounce light cream

Shake all the ingredients together, with ice, in the shaker and strain into the glass.

Rum

DUNLOP

Dry aperitif
• Cocktail glass
• Mixing glass

1½ ounces light rum
¾ ounce fino sherry
1 dash Angostura bitters
• Extra:
1 piece of lemon peel

Mix all the ingredients together, with ice, in the mixing glass and strain into the cocktail glass. Squeeze the lemon peel into the drink and add the peel to the glass.

LITTLE PRINCESS

Aperitif
• Cocktail glass
• Mixing glass

¾ ounce light rum
¾ ounce sweet red vermouth
• Garnish:
1 maraschino cherry

Mix all the ingredients together, with ice, in the mixing glass and strain into the cocktail glass. Add the cherry to the glass.

MELISSA

Medium-dry aperitif
• Cocktail glass
• Mixing glass

1 ounce light rum
2 tsp. triple sec
2 tsp. tropical-fruit-flavored liqueur
2 tsp. lime cordial
1 dash grenadine
• Garnish:
½ slice of lime
1 maraschino cherry
1 orange peel spiral

Mix all the ingredients together, with ice, in the mixing glass and strain into the cocktail glass. Spear the fruit on a toothpick and lay the garnish across the rim of the glass.

JAMAICA KISS

Creamy after-dinner drink
• Cocktail glass

¾ ounce dark rum
¾ ounce crème de café
¾ ounce light cream

Pour the rum and crème de café into the cocktail glass. Float the cream on top of the drink.

LITTLE DEVIL

Dry, tangy-fruity aperitif
- Cocktail glass
- Shaker

¾ ounce light rum
¾ ounce gin
2 tsp. Cointreau or other orange-flavored liqueur
2 tsp. lemon juice
• Garnish:
1 maraschino cherry

Shake all the ingredients together, with ice, in the shaker and strain into the glass. Spear the cherry on a toothpick and add it to the glass.

YELLOW BIRD

Sweet aperitif or after-dinner drink
- Cocktail glass
- Shaker

1 ounce light rum
2 tsp. Galliano
2 tsp. Cointreau or other orange-flavored liqueur
2 tsp. lemon juice
• Garnish:
1 maraschino cherry

Shake the ingredients together, with ice, in the shaker and strain into the cocktail glass. Add the cherry to the glass.

UPTON

Fruity aperitif or after-dinner drink
- Cocktail glass
- Shaker

¾ ounce dark rum
¾ ounce pineapple juice
2 tsp. orange juice
2 tsp. lemon juice

Shake all the ingredients together, with ice, in the shaker and strain into the glass.

XYZ

Strong aperitif
- Cocktail glass
- Shaker

1 ounce dark rum
¾ ounce Cointreau or other orange-flavored liqueur
¾ ounce lemon juice

Shake all the ingredients together, with ice, in the shaker and strain into the cocktail glass.

PETITE FLEUR

Fruity aperitif
- Cocktail glass
- Shaker

¾ ounce light rum
¾ ounce Cointreau or other orange-flavored liqueur
¾ ounce grapefruit juice

Shake the ingredients together, with ice, in the shaker and strain into the glass.

Rum

ELISA

Medium-dry after-dinner drink
• Cocktail glass
• Mixing glass

1 ounce dark rum
2 tsp. Amaro Averna bitters
2 tsp. apricot brandy
2 tsp. sweet white vermouth
2 tsp. dry champagne or sparkling wine
• *Garnish:*
1 piece of orange peel
1 maraschino cherry

Mix all the ingredients, except the champagne, together, with ice, in the mixing glass and strain into the glass. Top up with champagne. Spear the orange peel and cherry on a toothpick and lay the garnish across the rim of the glass.

VINTAGE 84

Fruity drink for every day
• Cocktail glass
• Shaker

¾ ounce light rum
½ ounce orange juice
½ ounce pineapple juice
2 tsp. apricot brandy
1 dash grenadine
• *Extra:*
A few small pieces of fruit

Shake the ingredients together, with ice, in the shaker and strain into the cocktail glass. Add the slices of fruit to the glass. Serve with a stirrer.

SWEET MEMORIES

Medium-dry aperitif
• Cocktail glass
• Mixing glass

¾ ounce light rum
¾ ounce orange-flavored liqueur
¾ ounce Noilly Prat or other dry vermouth

Mix the ingredients together, with ice, in the mixing glass and strain into the cocktail glass.

CARDICAS

Medium-dry aperitif
• Cocktail glass
• Mixing glass

1 ounce light rum
½ ounce Cointreau or other orange-flavored liqueur
½ ounce port

Mix the ingredients together, with ice, in the mixing glass and strain into the cocktail glass.

MALLORCA

Medium-dry after-dinner drink
• Cocktail glass
• Mixing glass

1 ounce dark rum
2 tsp. dry vermouth
2 tsp. crème de banane
2 tsp. Drambuie

Mix the ingredients together, with ice, in the mixing glass and strain into the glass.

CALCUTTA FLIP

Creamy, sweet drink for the evening
- Champagne flute or flip glass
- Shaker

1½ ounces dark rum
1½ ounces light cream
¾ ounce sugar syrup
2 tsp. orange-flavored liqueur
1 egg yolk
- *Extra:*
Grated nutmeg

Shake all the ingredients together firmly, with ice, in the shaker and strain into the glass. Sprinkle a little grated nutmeg on top of the drink.

DREAM

Creamy after-dinner drink
- Cocktail glass
- Shaker

¾ ounce light rum
¾ ounce crème de banane
2 tsp. pineapple juice
2 tsp. light cream
1 dash grenadine

Shake the ingredients together firmly, with ice, in the shaker and strain into the cocktail glass.

SHOW

Alcoholic drink for the evening
- Cocktail glass
- Shaker

1 ounce light rum
¾ ounce apricot brandy
1 tsp. green Chartreuse
1 dash grenadine
1 dash lemon juice

Shake the ingredients together, with ice, in the shaker and strain into the cocktail glass.

MARIONETTE

Very strong drink for the evening
- Cocktail glass
- Shaker

¾ ounce light rum
½ ounce apricot brandy
½ ounce dry sherry
½ ounce Cherry Herring or other cherry-flavored liqueur

Shake the ingredients together, with ice, in the shaker and strain into the glass.

RUM STINGER

Spicy drink for the evening
- Cocktail glass
- Mixing glass

1½ ounces dark rum
¾ ounce white crème de menthe

Mix the ingredients together, with ice, in the mixing glass and strain into the glass.

Rum

Dream (back), Show (middle), Marionette (front)

207

RUM KUM

Fruity, mild drink for a party
• Large cocktail glass
• Mixing glass

1½ ounces dark rum
1 ounce lime cordial
¾ ounce orange curaçao
• *Garnish:*
1 kumquat

Mix all the ingredients together in the mixing glass and strain into the cocktail glass. Perch the kumquat on the rim of the glass.

EUPHORIA

Fruity, mild drink for a party
• Cocktail glass
• Shaker

1¾ ounces light rum
¾ ounce grapefruit juice
2 tsp. triple sec
2 tsp. pineapple juice
• *Garnish:*
1 maraschino cherry

Shake all the ingredients together, with ice cubes, in the shaker and strain into the cocktail glass. Perch the cherry on the rim of the glass.

CARIB

Fruity, spicy drink for a party
• Cocktail glass
• Shaker

---

1 ounce dark rum
1 ounce gin
¾ ounce lemon juice
2 tsp. sugar syrup
• *Garnish:*
2 maraschino cherries

Shake all the ingredients together, with ice, in the shaker and strain into the cocktail glass. Spear the cherries on a toothpick and lay across the rim of the glass.

APRICOT LADY

Fruity, delicately tangy drink for a party
• Cocktail glass
• Shaker

---

1 ounce dark rum
¾ ounce apricot brandy
¾ ounce lemon juice
2 tsp. orange curaçao
½ egg white

Shake all the ingredients together, in the shaker, and strain into the glass.

Rum

Euphoria (left), Apricot Lady (right)

ADIOS AMIGOS

Spicy drink for a party
- Cocktail glass
- Shaker

1 ounce light rum
¾ ounce lime juice
2 tsp. dry vermouth
2 tsp. brandy
2 tsp. gin

Shake all the ingredients together, with ice, in the shaker and strain into the glass.

ROBINSON CRUSOE

Fruity, sweet drink for any time of year
- Cocktail glass
- Shaker

1½ ounces light rum
1½ ounces pineapple juice
• Garnish:
¼ baby pineapple

Shake the ingredients together, with ice, in the shaker and strain into the glass. Perch the baby pineapple quarter on the rim of the glass.

BEAU RIVAGE

Fruity, mild short drink for any time of year
• Large cocktail glass
• Shaker

1 ounce orange juice
¾ ounce light rum
¾ ounce gin
2 tsp. dry vermouth
2 tsp. sweet red vermouth
1 dash grenadine

Shake all the ingredients together, with ice cubes, in the shaker and strain into the cocktail glass.

BLUE BOY

Spicy aperitif
• Cocktail glass
• Mixing glass

1 ounce light rum
1 ounce sweet red vermouth
1 dash orange bitters
1 dash Angostura bitters
• Extra:
1 piece of lemon peel

Mix all the ingredients together, with ice, in the mixing glass and strain into the cocktail glass. Squeeze the lemon peel over the drink and add the peel to the glass.

TROPHY

Fruity, bitter drink for the evening
• Cocktail glass
• Shaker

2 ounces dark rum
¾ ounce lime juice
1 tsp. confectioners' sugar
3 dashes Angostura bitters

Shake all the ingredients together in the shaker and strain into the glass.

BEACH

Fruity drink for hot days
• Cocktail glass
• Shaker

1½ ounces light rum
¾ ounce white crème de menthe
2 tsp. lemon juice

Shake all the ingredients together firmly, with ice, in the shaker and strain into the glass.

FOXTROT

Fruity, tangy drink for hot days
• Cocktail glass
• Shaker

1½ ounces light rum
¾ ounce lemon juice
2 tsp. Cointreau or other orange-flavored liqueur

Shake all the ingredients together in the shaker and strain into the glass.

Rum

FLUFFY RUFFLES

Spicy, dry drink for the evening
• Cocktail glass
• Mixing glass

1½ ounces light rum
¾ ounce dry vermouth
• Extra:
1 piece of lemon peel

Mix the ingredients together, with ice cubes, in the mixing glass and strain into the cocktail glass. Squeeze the lemon peel over the drink and add the peel to the glass.

GRADEAL SPECIAL

Medium-dry drink for a party
• Cocktail glass
• Mixing glass

1 ounce light rum
¾ ounce apricot brandy
2 tsp. gin
• Garnish:
¼ apricot

Mix all the ingredients together, with ice, in the mixing glass and strain into the cocktail glass. Spear the apricot quarter on a toothpick and add it to the glass.

HAVANA CLUB

Spicy, mild aperitif
• Cocktail glass
• Mixing glass

1½ ounces light rum
¾ ounce sweet red vermouth
• Extra:
1 piece of lemon peel

Mix all the ingredients together, with ice cubes, in the mixing glass and strain into the glass. Squeeze the lemon peel over the drink.

BATISTA

Aromatic, spicy drink for any time of year
• Cocktail glass
• Mixing glass

1½ ounces dark rum
¾ ounce Grand Marnier
• Extra:
1 piece of orange peel

Mix the ingredients together, with ice cubes, in the mixing glass and strain into the cocktail glass. Squeeze the orange peel over the drink and add the peel to the glass.

HOARFROST II

Spicy, mild crusta for a party
- Cocktail glass with sugared rim
- Shaker

¾ ounce dark rum
¾ ounce gin
2 tsp. lemon juice
2 tsp. triple sec
1 tsp. grenadine

Shake all the ingredients together, with ice cubes, in the shaker and strain into the cocktail glass with the sugared rim.

AMARO

Bittersweet after-dinner drink
- Sherry glass
- Mixing glass

1½ ounces light rum
¾ ounce amaretto
• Garnish:
1 piece of lemon peel
1 tsp. coffee powder

Mix the ingredients together, with ice cubes, in the mixing glass and pour into the sherry glass. Perch the slice of lemon on the rim of the glass and dust with coffee powder.

CHERRY RUM

Fruity, sweet drink for a party
- Large cocktail glass
- Shaker

1 ounce light rum
1 ounce light cream
¾ ounce cherry-flavored liqueur
• Garnish:
2 maraschino cherries

Shake all the ingredients together, with ice, in the shaker and strain into the cocktail glass. Spear the cherries on a toothpick and lay the garnish across the rim of the glass.

WINDJAMMER

Spicy, mild drink for a party
- Cocktail glass with sugared rim
- Mixing glass

1½ ounces light rum
¾ ounce dry vermouth
2 tsp. grenadine
• Garnish:
2 maraschino cherries

Shake the ingredients together, with ice cubes, in the shaker and strain into the cocktail glass with the sugared rim. Add the cherries to the glass. Serve with a toothpick.

Rum

ORACABESSA

Fruity, delicately tangy drink for a party
• Cocktail glass
• Shaker

1½ ounces dark rum
¾ ounce banana-flavored liqueur
1 ounce lemon juice
• Garnish:
3 slices of banana

Shake all the ingredients together, with ice cubes, in the shaker and strain into the cocktail glass. Spear the slices of banana on a toothpick and lay the garnish across the rim of the glass.

SNOW WHITE COCKTAIL

Fruity, tangy drink for a party
• Large cocktail glass
• Shaker

1½ ounces light rum
¾ ounce lemon juice
¾ ounce pineapple juice
1 tsp. sugar syrup
1 egg white

Shake all the ingredients together, with ice, in the shaker and strain into the glass.

RUM FANTASY

Fruity, sweet drink for a party
• Rocks glass

1½ ounces dark rum
¾ ounce lime cordial
2 tsp. peach brandy
• Garnish:
1 slice of lime

Mix all the ingredients together, with ice cubes, in the glass. Add the slice of lime to the glass.

FOUR FLUSH

Mild, spicy drink for any time of year
• Cocktail glass
• Mixing glass

1 ounce light rum
¾ ounce dry vermouth
2 tsp. maraschino
2 dashes grenadine
• Garnish:
1 maraschino cherry

Mix all the ingredients together, with ice cubes, in the mixing glass and strain into the glass. Spear the cherry on a toothpick and add it to the glass.

FIG LEAF

Spicy, tangy drink for the evening
• Champagne or cocktail glass
• Mixing glass

1½ ounces light rum
1 ounce sweet red vermouth
¾ ounce lime juice
• Garnish:
1 maraschino cherry

Mix all the ingredients together, with ice, in the mixing glass and strain into the glass. Spear the cherry on a toothpick and add it to the glass.

BANANA DAIQUIRI COCKTAIL

Fruity drink for a summer party
• Champagne or cocktail glass
• Shaker

1 ounce light or dark rum
1 ounce lemon juice
¾ ounce banana-flavored liqueur
2 tsp. sugar syrup
• Garnish:
1 slice of banana

Shake all the ingredients together, with ice cubes, in the shaker and strain into the glass. Perch the slice of banana on the rim of the glass.

ATLAS

Spicy after-dinner drink
• Champagne or cocktail glass
• Mixing glass

1 ounce dark rum
¾ ounce Cointreau or other orange-
flavored liqueur
2 tsp. Calvados or applejack
1 dash Angostura bitters
• Garnish:
½ slice of orange

Mix all the ingredients together, with ice, in the mixing glass and strain into the glass. Add the slice of orange to the glass.

EL DORADO I

Sweet drink for any time of year
• Champagne or cocktail glass
• Shaker

1½ ounces light rum
¾ ounce advocaat
¾ ounce brown crème de cacao
2 tsp. shredded coconut
• Garnish:
Grated chocolate

Shake all the ingredients together firmly in the shaker and strain into the cocktail glass. Sprinkle grated chocolate on top and serve immediately.

ARAWAK

Spicy, mild drink for a party
• Cocktail glass
• Mixing glass

1 ounce dark rum
1 ounce cream sherry
1 dash Angostura bitters
• Garnish:
1 maraschino cherry

Mix all the ingredients together, with ice, in the mixing glass and strain into the cocktail glass. Spear the cherry on a toothpick and add it to the glass.

COLUMBIA

Fruity, mild drink for hot days
• Cocktail glass
• Shaker

1½ ounces light rum
1 ounce lemon juice
¾ ounce raspberry syrup
• Garnish:
3 raspberries

Shake the ingredients together, with ice, in the shaker and strain into the glass. Add the raspberries and serve with a toothpick.

PIKAKI

Fruity, mild long drink for any time of year
• Rocks glass
• Shaker

1½ ounces dark rum
1 ounce orange juice
¾ ounce lemon juice
2 tsp. grenadine
• Garnish:
¼ baby pineapple

Shake all the ingredients together, with ice, in the shaker and strain into the glass. Add the quarter pineapple to the glass.

PANCHO VILLA

Fruity, sweet drink for a party
• Rocks glass
• Shaker

2 ounces pineapple juice
¾ ounce dark rum
¾ ounce cherry brandy
¾ ounce apricot brandy
• Garnish:
2 maraschino cherries

Shake the ingredients together, with ice, in the shaker and strain into the glass. Spear the cherries on a toothpick and add to the glass.

Rum

Pikaki (left), Pancho Villa (right)

PLANTER'S PUNCH I

Fruity drink for a party
• Large brandy snifter

1¾ ounces dark rum

1½ ounces orange juice

1½ ounces pineapple juice

1 ounce lemon juice

¾ ounce grenadine

2 tsp. sugar syrup

• *Garnish:*

1 maraschino cherry

½ slice of orange

¼ slice of pineapple

½ slice of kiwi fruit

1 thick slice of banana

Sprig of mint

Mix all the ingredients together, with ice cubes, in the brandy snifter. Spear the fruit on a long skewer and add to the glass. Perch the sprig of mint on the rim of the glass. Serve with a straw.

PLANTER'S PUNCH II

Fruity, mild drink for a party
• Highball/Collins glass

1 ounce light rum

¾ ounce dark rum

¾ ounce lemon juice

¾ ounce orange juice

2 tsp. sugar syrup

1 tsp. grenadine

• *Garnish:*

1 slice of orange

1 slice of lemon

1 maraschino cherry

Sprig of mint

Mix all the ingredients together, with ice cubes, in the glass. Spear the slices of fruit, the cherry, and sprig of mint on a long skewer and add to the glass. Serve with a straw.

Rum

PLANTER'S PUNCH III

Fruity, tangy drink for a party
• Highball/Collins glass

2 ounces dark rum
1½ ounces lime juice
2 tsp. sugar syrup
• Garnish:
¼ slice of pineapple
1 maraschino cherry
Sprig of mint

Mix all the ingredients together in the highball glass, which should be half filled with crushed ice. Perch the fruit and the sprig of mint on the rim of the glass. Serve with a straw.

PLANTER'S PUNCH IV

Fruity drink for a summer party
• Highball/Collins glass
• Shaker

1¾ ounces orange juice
¾ ounce light rum
¾ ounce dark rum
¾ ounce lemon juice
2 tsp. grenadine
1 dash Angostura bitters
• Garnish:
½ slice of orange
½ slice of lemon
1 maraschino cherry

Shake all the ingredients together firmly, with ice, in the shaker and strain into the highball glass over ice cubes. Spear the slice of orange and the cherry on a toothpick and lay the garnish across the rim of the glass. Perch the slice of lemon on the rim of the glass. Serve with a straw.

MAI TAI

Fruity, mild drink for a party
• Large brandy snifter

1½ ounces dark rum
1½ ounces pineapple juice
¾ ounce dark rum (150 proof)
¾ ounce lemon juice
¾ ounce orange juice
2 tsp. white curaçao
2 tsp. almond syrup
• Garnish:
1 slice of lime
Sprig of mint

Half fill the brandy snifter with crushed ice. Mix all the ingredients together in the glass. Perch the slice of lime and sprig of mint on the rim of the glass. Serve with a straw.

RUM DAISY

Mild, sour drink for the evening
• Highball/Collins glass

1½ ounces dark rum
¾ ounce raspberry juice
¾ ounce lemon juice
Soda water for topping up
• Garnish:
Sprig of mint

Mix all the ingredients together, with ice cubes, in the highball glass. Top up with soda water according to taste and stir again. Perch the sprig of mint on the rim of the glass. Serve with a straw.

ZOMBIE

Fruity drink for a summer party
• Highball/Collins glass
• Shaker

1¾ ounces pineapple juice
¾ ounce light rum
¾ ounce dark rum
¾ ounce lemon or lime juice
2 tsp. apricot brandy
¾ ounce rum (150 proof)
• Garnish:
1 slice of orange
1 maraschino cherry
Sprig of mint

Shake all the ingredients, except the 150-proof rum, together, with ice, in the shaker and strain into the highball glass over crushed ice. Spear the slice of orange and cherry on a toothpick, lay the garnish across the rim of the glass, and add the sprig of mint to the glass. Pour the 150-proof rum into the glass. Serve with a stirrer and straw.

BANANA COW

Fruity, sweet drink with milk for summer days
• Highball/Collins glass
• Blender

3½ ounces milk
2 ounces dark rum
1 ounce sugar syrup
½ banana, peeled and mashed

Purée all the ingredients together, with ice cubes, in the blender and pour into the glass. Serve with a wide drinking straw.

Rum

CUBA LIBRE

Refreshing highball for every day
• Highball glass

1½ ounces light rum
2 tsp. lemon juice
Cola for topping up
• *Extra:*
½ slice of lemon

Pour all the ingredients, with ice cubes, into the highball glass and add a stirrer. Put the slice of lemon in the glass.

LUMUMBA II

Spicy long drink with cola or milk for the afternoon
• Highball/Collins glass

3½ ounces chilled cocoa or chocolate milk
1½ ounces dark rum
• *Garnish:*
1 tsp. grated chocolate

Mix the ingredients together, with ice cubes, in the highball glass and sprinkle grated chocolate on top. Serve with a straw.

A LULU

Fruity, mild drink for a party
• Rocks glass
• Shaker

1½ ounces light rum
1 ounce passion-fruit juice
1 ounce orange juice
¾ ounce nut-flavored liqueur

Shake all the ingredients together, with ice, in the shaker and pour into the glass. Serve with a straw.

CARIBBEAN CAPER

Sweet drink for the summer
• Highball/Collins glass

1¾ ounces dark rum
1½ ounces cream of coconut
Soda water for topping up

Mix the rum and cream of coconut together, with ice, in the highball glass. Top up with soda water, stir, and serve with a straw.

OCHO RIOS

Fruity, sweet drink for a party
• Large cocktail glass
• Shaker

1½ ounces dark rum
1½ ounces guava nectar
¾ ounce sugar syrup
¾ ounce lime cordial
¾ ounce light cream

Shake all the ingredients together in the shaker and strain into the cocktail glass.

PIÑA COLADA

Sweet drink for a summer party
- Highball/Collins glass
- Shaker

1¾ ounces cream of coconut
1¾ ounces pineapple juice
1½ ounces light rum
2 tsp. light cream
- *Garnish:*
¼ slice of pineapple
1 maraschino cherry

Shake all the ingredients together firmly, with ice, in the shaker and strain into the highball glass over crushed ice. Spear the slice of pineapple and cherry on a toothpick and lay the garnish across the rim of the glass.

SEPTEMBER MORNING

Fruity, mild drink for any time of year
- Large brandy snifter
- Shaker

2 ounces light rum
¾ ounce lime juice
2 tsp. grenadine
1 egg white

Shake all the ingredients together firmly in the shaker and pour carefully into the brandy snifter.

RUM TONIC

Tangy, dry drink for a summer party
- Highball/Collins glass

1½ ounces dark rum
Tonic water for topping up
- *Extra:*
1 lime quarter

Pour the rum into the highball glass with some ice cubes. Top up with tonic water and stir briefly. Squeeze the juice from the lime quarter over the drink and add the crushed lime to the glass.

BANANA DAIQUIRI

Fruity, sweet-and-sour drink for a summer party
- Balloon glass
- Blender

2 ounces light or dark rum
1 ounce lemon juice
¾ ounce sugar syrup
½ banana, peeled and sliced
- *Garnish:*
1 thick slice of banana
1 maraschino cherry

Mix all the ingredients together, with ice, in the blender, until puréed. Spear the slice of banana and the cherry on a large toothpick. Pour the drink into the balloon glass and lay the garnish across the rim of the glass. Serve with a wide straw.

YOUR HEART

Fruity, refreshing drink for a party
• Highball/Collins glass
• Shaker

2¾ ounces orange juice
¾ ounce dark rum
¾ ounce Southern Comfort
2 tsp. grenadine
Tonic water for topping up

Shake all the ingredients, except the tonic water, together, with ice, in the shaker, strain into the highball glass and top up with tonic water.

LASER

Fruity, medium-dry drink for any occasion
• Highball/Collins glass
• Shaker

2 ounces passion-fruit juice
1 ounce light rum
¾ ounce Southern Comfort
¾ ounce lemon juice
2 tsp. mandarin syrup
• Garnish:
½ slice of orange
2 maraschino cherries

Shake all the ingredients together firmly, with ice, in the shaker and strain into the highball glass over crushed ice. Spear the cherries and slice of orange on a long toothpick so they form the shape of a sail and put the garnish in the glass. Serve with an attractive stirrer.

SOUTH SEA DREAM

Sweet, long drink for a summer party
• Highball/Collins glass
• Shaker

1¾ ounces cream of coconut
1¾ ounces pineapple juice
1 ounce Pisang Ambon
¾ ounce light rum
2 tsp. light cream
• Garnish:
¼ slice of pineapple
1 maraschino cherry
Sprig of mint

Shake all the ingredients together firmly, with ice, in the shaker and strain into the highball glass over ice. Perch the piece of pineapple on the rim of the glass and fasten the cherry to it with a toothpick. Add the sprig of mint to the glass.

CHOCOLATE COCO

Mild drink for a summer party
• Large brandy snifter with a coconut-coated rim
• Shaker

2 ounces pineapple juice
1 ounce Malibu or other coconut-flavored liqueur
1 ounce light rum
¾ ounce lemon juice
¾ ounce chocolate sauce

Shake all the ingredients together, with ice, in the shaker and pour into the snifter.

RUM SOUR

Refreshing sour for the summer
- Sour glass or rocks glass
- Shaker

1¾ ounces light or dark rum
¾ ounce sugar syrup
¾ ounce lemon juice
1 shot soda water (optional)
- *Garnish:*
1 slice of lemon
1 maraschino cherry

Shake the rum, sugar syrup, and lemon juice together, with ice cubes, in the shaker and strain into the glass. Add a shot of soda water and stir briefly. Perch the fruit on the rim of the glass.

PEDRO COLLINS

Refreshing Collins for any time of day
- Collins/highball glass

1½ ounces light rum
¾ ounce lemon juice
2 tsp. sugar syrup
Soda water for topping up
- *Garnish:*
½ slice of lemon
1 maraschino cherry

Mix the rum, lemon juice, and sugar syrup together, with ice, in the Collins glass. Top up with soda water and stir. Spear the fruit on a toothpick and lay the garnish across the rim of the glass.

RUM COLLINS

Refreshing Collins for any time of day
- Collins/highball glass

1½ ounces dark rum
¾ ounce lemon juice
2 tsp. sugar syrup
Soda water for topping up
- *Garnish:*
½ slice of lemon
1 maraschino cherry

Mix the rum, lemon juice, and sugar syrup together, with ice, in the highball glass. Top up with soda water and stir. Perch the fruit on the rim of the glass.

Rum

BACARDI COOLER

Refreshing, bitter cooler for a summer party
- Highball/Collins glass
- Shaker

1½ ounces Bacardi or other light rum
¾ ounce lemon juice
2 tsp. grenadine
Tonic water for topping up
- *Garnish:*
1 lemon peel spiral

Shake all the ingredients, except the tonic water, together, with ice, in the shaker and pour into the highball glass. Top up with tonic water. Add the lemon peel spiral to the glass. Serve with a stirrer.

HEARTBREAKER

Refreshing drink for a party
- Highball/Collins glass
- Shaker

2 ounces orange juice
2 ounces pineapple juice
1 ounce dark rum
¾ ounce cherry brandy
- *Garnish:*
¼ slice of pineapple
1 maraschino cherry

Shake the ingredients together, with ice, in the shaker and strain into the Collins glass over ice cubes. Perch the fruit on the rim of the glass.

FINN DINGHY

Medium-dry drink for any occasion
- Highball/Collins glass
- Shaker

2 ounces pineapple juice
¾ ounce dark rum
¾ ounce Malibu or other coconut-flavored liqueur
2 tsp. passion-fruit syrup
1 dash lemon juice
- *Garnish:*
½ slice of orange
2 maraschino cherries

Shake all the ingredients together, with ice, in the shaker and strain into the highball glass over crushed ice. Spear the slice of orange and cherries on a long toothpick so they look like a sail and put the garnish into the glass.

BALI DREAM

Fruity drink for the evening
- Highball/Collins glass
- Shaker

2¾ ounces pineapple juice
1 ounce light rum
1 ounce Pisang Ambon
¾ ounce cream of coconut
- *Garnish:*
¼ slice of pineapple
1 maraschino cherry

Shake all the ingredients together firmly, with ice, in the shaker and strain into the highball glass over crushed ice. Perch the slice of pineapple on the rim of the glass and fasten the cherry to it with a toothpick.

PUERTO PUNCH

Fruity, refreshing drink for a summer party
- Highball/Collins glass
- Shaker

1½ ounces orange juice
1½ ounces pineapple juice
¾ ounce dark rum
¾ ounce Southern Comfort
2 tsp. lemon juice
- *Garnish:*
½ slice of orange
1 maraschino cherry

Shake the ingredients together, with ice, in the shaker and strain into the highball glass over crushed ice. Perch the slice of orange on the rim of the glass and fasten the cherry to it with a toothpick.

BARBADOS

Fruity drink for the evening
- Highball/Collins glass
- Shaker

2¾ ounces orange juice
1½ ounces dark rum
2 tsp. grenadine
2 tsp. lemon juice
1 dash orange bitters
- *Garnish:*
¼ slice of pineapple
Sprig of mint

Shake all the ingredients together, with ice, in the shaker and strain into the highball glass over ice cubes. Spear the slice of pineapple and sprig of mint on a toothpick and perch the pineapple on the rim of the glass.

CARIBBEAN NIGHT

Fruity, exotic drink for a summer party
- Highball/Collins glass
- Shaker

1½ ounces dark rum
1½ ounces pineapple juice
1 ounce orange juice
2 tsp. lemon juice
- *Garnish:*
½ slice of orange
½ slice of lemon
1 maraschino cherry

Shake the ingredients together, with ice, in the shaker and strain into the highball glass. Spear the fruit on a toothpick and lay the garnish across the rim of the glass.

COLT CRUISER

Light, long drink for hot days
- Highball/Collins glass
- Shaker

¾ ounce light rum
¾ ounce lemon juice
2 tsp. crème de banane
2 tsp. amaretto
Lemonade for topping up
- *Garnish:*
1 piece of orange peel
1 maraschino cherry

Shake all the ingredients, except the lemonade, together, with ice, in the shaker and strain into the highball glass over ice cubes. Top up with lemonade and stir. Put the orange peel and cherry in the glass and serve the drink with a stirrer.

Caribbean Night (left), Colt Cruiser (right)

RED COLADA

Sweet drink for a summer party
• Highball/Collins glass
• Shaker

1¾ ounces cream of coconut
1¾ ounces pineapple juice
1 ounce light rum
1 ounce orange curaçao
2 tsp. light cream
• Garnish:
¼ slice of pineapple
1 maraschino cherry

Shake the ingredients together firmly,
with ice, in the shaker and strain into
the highball glass over crushed ice.
Perch the fruit on the rim of the glass.

SWIMMING POOL

Sweet, fruity drink for a summer party
• Highball/Collins glass
• Shaker

1¾ ounces cream of coconut
1¾ ounces pineapple juice
1 ounce light rum
¾ ounce vodka
2 tsp. light cream
2 tsp. blue curaçao
• Garnish:
¼ slice of pineapple
1 maraschino cherry

Shake all the ingredients, except the
blue curaçao, together firmly, with ice,
in the shaker and strain into the
highball glass over crushed ice. Pour
the curaçao into the drink. Spear the
piece of pineapple and maraschino
cherry on a toothpick and lay the
garnish across the rim of the glass.

Rum

MAGIC QUEEN

Fruity drink for hot days
- Highball/Collins glass
- Shaker

1½ ounces dark rum
1 ounce orange juice
¾ ounce pineapple juice
2 tsp. triple sec
2 tsp. banana-flavored liqueur
2 tsp. lemon juice
1 tsp. grenadine
• Garnish:
½ slice of lemon
½ slice of orange
1 maraschino cherry

Shake the ingredients together, with ice, in the shaker and strain into the highball glass over crushed ice. Spear the fruit on a toothpick and lay the garnish across the rim of the glass.

EASTWARD

Fruity, sweet drink for every day
- Highball/Collins glass
- Shaker

1½ ounces cream of coconut
1½ ounces pineapple juice
1 ounce dark rum
¾ ounce amaretto
2 tsp. lime cordial
• Garnish:
¼ slice of pineapple
1 maraschino cherry
Sprig of mint

Shake the ingredients together, with ice, in the shaker and strain into the highball glass over ice cubes. Perch the slice of pineapple on the rim of the glass and fasten the cherry to it with a small toothpick. Put the sprig of mint into the glass.

COLUMBUS

Refreshing drink for hot days
• Highball/Collins glass

1 ounce dark rum
2 tsp. apricot-flavored liqueur
2 tsp. grenadine
Bitter lemon for topping up
• Garnish:
½ slice of lemon

Pour the ingredients into the highball glass, with ice cubes, and stir well. Perch the slice of lemon on the rim of the glass. Serve with a long stirrer.

RAM COOLER

Tangy, refreshing long drink for the evening
• Highball/Collins glass
• Shaker

2 ounces lime juice
1½ ounces light rum
½ ounce Galliano
• Garnish:
1 slice of lime
1 maraschino cherry

Shake the ingredients together, with ice, in the shaker and strain into the highball glass over crushed ice. Spear the fruit on a toothpick and lay the garnish across the rim of the glass.

FIREMAN'S SOUR

Refreshing drink for hot days
• Highball/Collins glass
• Shaker

¾ ounce light rum
¾ ounce lemon juice
2 tsp. grenadine
Soda water for topping up
• Garnish:
½ slice of orange
1 maraschino cherry

Shake all the ingredients, except the soda water, together, with plenty of ice, in the shaker. Pour into the glass and top up with soda water. Spear the slice of orange and cherry on a toothpick, and lay the garnish across the rim of the glass.

RUM EGGNOG

Filling after-dinner drink
• Large rocks glass
• Shaker

3½ ounces milk or light cream
1½ ounces dark rum
2 tsp. sugar syrup
1 egg yolk
• Extra:
Grated nutmeg

Shake the ingredients together firmly, with ice, in the shaker and strain into the glass. Sprinkle a little grated nutmeg on top.

Rum

JAMAICA GREEN

Delicate, tangy drink for a summer party
• Highball/Collins glass
• Shaker

1½ ounces light rum
1 ounce lemon juice
¾ ounce green crème de menthe
¾ ounce sugar syrup
• Garnish:
1 slice of lemon

Shake all the ingredients together, with ice, in the shaker and pour into the highball glass. Perch the slice of lemon on the rim of the glass.

SCORPION

Fruity drink for any time of day
• Highball/Collins glass
• Shaker

1¾ ounces passion-fruit juice
1 ounce dark rum
1 ounce lemon juice
¾ ounce light rum
2 tsp. grenadine
• Garnish:
1 piece of pineapple
2 maraschino cherries

Shake the ingredients together, with ice, in the shaker and strain into the highball glass over crushed ice. Spear the fruit on a toothpick and lay the garnish across the rim of the glass.

MOJITO

Refreshing drink for a summer party
• Highball/Collins glass

A few mint leaves
¾ ounce lemon or lime juice
2 tsp. sugar syrup
1½ ounces light rum
Soda water for topping up
• Garnish:
Sprig of mint

Put the mint leaves in the glass and crush them. Add the lemon, or lime juice, and sugar syrup and stir. Add plenty of crushed ice and the rum; stir again. Top up with soda water. Put the sprig of mint into the glass.

CORAL SEA

Creamy, sweet drink for a party
• Highball/Collins glass
• Shaker

1¾ ounces cream of coconut
1¾ ounces pineapple juice
1 ounce light rum
¾ ounce blue curaçao
2 tsp. light cream
• Garnish:
¼ slice of pineapple
1 maraschino cherry
1 mint leaf

Shake the ingredients together, with ice, in the shaker and strain into the highball glass over crushed ice. Spear the fruit and mint leaf on a toothpick, and lay the garnish across the rim of the glass.

DON FREDERICO

Fruity, refreshing long drink for a party
• Highball/Collins glass
• Shaker

1 ounce light rum
½ ounce Galliano
½ ounce grenadine
2 dashes apricot brandy
Orange juice for topping up
• *Garnish:*
1 piece of orange peel

Shake all the ingredients, except the orange juice, together, with ice, in the shaker and strain into the highball glass. Top up with orange juice and stir, then perch the orange peel on the rim of the glass.

BOTNIA 84

Fruity drink for a party
• Highball/Collins glass

1½ ounces orange juice
½ ounce light rum
½ ounce Grand Marnier
2 tsp. apricot brandy
Ginger ale for topping up
• *Garnish:*
1 piece of orange peel
1 maraschino cherry

Mix the ingredients, except the ginger ale, together, with ice cubes, in the highball glass. Top up with ginger ale. Hang the piece of orange peel over the rim of the glass and add the cherry to the drink. Serve with a stirrer.

NAVY PUNCH

Fruity drink for a party
• Highball/Collins glass
• Shaker

2 ounces dark rum
1½ ounces orange juice
¾ ounce grenadine
2 tsp. lemon juice
• *Garnish:*
½ slice of orange
½ slice of lemon
1 maraschino cherry

Shake all the ingredients together firmly, with ice, in the shaker and strain into the highball glass over crushed ice. Spear the fruit on a toothpick and lay the garnish across the rim of the glass.

BOMBAY PUNCH

Fruity drink for a party
• Highball/Collins glass
• Shaker

1½ ounces dark rum
1½ ounces orange juice
1½ ounces pineapple juice
¾ ounce lemon juice
2 tsp. orange-flavored liqueur
2 tsp. grenadine
• *Garnish:*
¼ slice of pineapple
1 green maraschino cherry

Shake the ingredients together, with ice, in the shaker and strain into the highball glass over crushed ice. Spear the fruit on a toothpick and lay the garnish across the rim of the glass.

Rum

Botnia 84 (left), Bombay Punch (right)

CON-TICO

Spicy, sweet drink for any time of year
• Highball/Collins glass
• Shaker

1¾ ounces pineapple juice
1 ounce light rum
2 tsp. Southern Comfort
2 tsp. Cointreau or other orange-
flavored liqueur
2 tsp. Cinzano (rosso antico)
• Garnish:
¼ slice of pineapple
1 slice of orange
1 maraschino cherry

Shake all the ingredients together well,
with ice cubes, in the shaker and strain
into the highball glass. Finally perch the
fruit on the rim of the glass.

TROPICAL WONDER

Fruity, mild drink for any time of year
• Highball/Collins glass
• Shaker

1½ ounces light rum
1½ ounces passion-fruit juice
1½ ounces orange juice
1½ ounces pineapple juice
• Garnish:
1 slice of orange
1 slice of lime
1 sprig of lemon balm

Shake all the ingredients together, with
ice, in the shaker and strain into the
glass. Perch the fruit and sprig of lemon
balm on the rim of the glass.

GOLDEN COLADA

Fruity, mild long drink for a summer
party
• Highball/Collins glass
• Shaker

1 ounce dark rum
¾ ounce light rum
¾ ounce cream of coconut
¾ ounce orange juice
¾ ounce pineapple juice
2 tsp. Galliano
2 tsp. light cream
• Garnish:
½ slice of pineapple
1 maraschino cherry

Shake all the ingredients together
firmly, with ice cubes, in the shaker and
strain into the highball glass, half filled
with crushed ice. Spear the slice of
pineapple and the cherry on a toothpick and lay the garnish across the rim
of the glass.

TAHITI

Fruity drink for a party
• Highball/Collins glass
• Shaker

2¾ ounces orange juice
1 ounce dark rum
1 ounce Malibu or other coconut-
flavored liqueur
¾ ounce lemon juice
• Garnish:
3 strips of coconut

Shake all the ingredients together, with
ice, in the shaker and pour into the
glass. Perch the strips of coconut on the
rim of the glass.

Rum

MONTEGO BAY

Fruity, sweet-and-sour drink for a
summer party
• Highball/Collins glass
• Shaker

1½ ounces light rum
¾ ounce lemon juice
¾ ounce lime cordial
2 tsp. blue curaçao
• Extra:
1 lime quarter

Shake all the ingredients together, with
ice, in the shaker and strain into the
glass, half filled with crushed ice. Add
the lime quarter. Serve with a straw.

FEDORA PUNCH

Slightly bitter drink for a party
• Highball/Collins glass
• Shaker

1 ounce dark rum
¾ ounce lemon juice
¾ ounce sugar syrup
2 tsp. cognac
2 tsp. bourbon
2 tsp. orange curaçao
• Garnish:
1 lemon peel spiral

Shake all the ingredients together in the
shaker and strain into the glass, half
filled with crushed ice. Perch the spiral
of peel on the rim of the glass.

SANTO DOMINGO

Fruity, mild drink for a party
• Highball/Collins glass
• Shaker

2 ounces orange juice
1½ ounces light rum
1 ounce passion-fruit juice
¾ ounce blue curaçao
• Garnish:
1 slice of star fruit
1 maraschino cherry
Sprig of mint

Shake all the ingredients together
firmly, with ice cubes, in the shaker and
pour into the glass. Perch the fruit and
the sprig of mint on the rim of the glass.
Serve with a straw.

HAWAIIAN BANGER

Spicy, mild drink for a party
• Highball/Collins glass

2¾ ounces orange juice
1½ ounces dark rum
¾ ounce Galliano
• Garnish:
½ slice of orange
1 maraschino cherry

Mix all the ingredients together, with
ice cubes, in the highball glass. Spear
the slice of orange and the cherry on a
toothpick and put it in the drink. Serve
with a straw.

BOSSA NOVA

Fruity, mild drink for a summer party
- Highball/Collins glass
- Shaker

2 ounces pineapple juice
1 ounce dark rum
¾ ounce Galliano
2 tsp. apricot brandy
• Garnish:
1 slice of orange
¼ apricot

Shake all the ingredients together, with ice, in the shaker and pour into the glass. Perch the fruit on the rim of the glass.

COCO LOCO

Fruity, mild drink for a summer party
- Large brandy snifter
- Shaker

1 ounce dark rum
1 ounce Malibu or other coconut-flavored liqueur
1 ounce passion-fruit juice
1 ounce orange juice
• Garnish:
1 slice of star fruit
1 maraschino cherry

Shake all the ingredients together, with ice, in the shaker and pour into the brandy snifter. Perch the slice of star fruit on the rim of the glass and fasten the cherry to it using a toothpick.

HAWAIIAN

Fruity, mild drink for a party
- Highball/Collins glass
- Shaker

1½ ounces dark rum
1½ ounces pineapple juice
¾ ounce grenadine
1 egg white
• Garnish:
¼ slice of pineapple

Shake all the ingredients together, with ice, in the shaker and pour into the highball glass. Perch the slice of pineapple on the rim of the glass. Serve with a straw.

MAHUKONA

Fruity, sweet-and-sour drink for a party
- Highball/Collins glass

1½ ounces light rum
1 ounce lemon juice
¾ ounce triple sec
¾ ounce sugar syrup
1 dash Angostura bitters
• Extra:
1 slice of pineapple, diced
3 maraschino cherries

Mix all the ingredients together, with ice cubes, in the highball glass. Add the fruit to the glass. Serve with a straw and a long-handled spoon.

Rum

COCONUT KISS I

Fruity, sweet drink for a summer party
• Highball/Collins glass
• Shaker

1½ ounces orange juice
1 ounce dark rum
1 ounce Malibu or other coconut-flavored liqueur
1 ounce passion-fruit syrup
• Garnish:
Sprig of mint

Shake all the ingredients together, with ice, in the shaker and pour into the highball glass. Add the sprig of mint to the glass. Serve with a drinking straw.

HULA HULA

Fruity, mild drink for a summer party
• Balloon-shaped wine glass
• Shaker

1¾ ounces passion-fruit juice
1 ounce dark rum
1 ounce light rum
1 ounce sugar syrup
1 ounce lemon juice
• Garnish:
1 slice of kiwi fruit
1 slice of star fruit

Shake all the ingredients together, with ice, in the shaker and pour into the glass. Perch the fruit on the rim of the glass. Serve with a straw.

LOOKING AT YOU

Spicy, mild drink for a summer party
• Highball/Collins glass with a sugared rim
• Shaker

3½ ounces orange juice
1 ounce Sambuca
¾ ounce light rum
2 tsp. dark rum
• Garnish:
1 slice of orange
1 maraschino cherry

Shake all the ingredients together, with ice cubes, in the shaker and strain into the glass. Top up with crushed ice. Perch the fruit on the rim of the glass.

BARBADOS SWIZZLE

Fruity, tangy drink for the summer
• Highball/Collins glass

1¾ ounces light rum
¾ ounce lime juice
2 tsp. sugar syrup
1 dash of Angostura bitters
• Garnish:
Sprig of mint
1 lime peel spiral

Pour all the ingredients together into the highball glass, top up with crushed ice, and stir. Add the sprig of mint to the glass and hang the spiral of lime peel over the rim of the glass.

PINK RUM

Fruity, mild long drink for every day
- Highball/Collins glass

1½ ounces dark rum
¾ ounce lime juice
¾ ounce grenadine
Bitter lemon for topping up
- *Extra:*
¼ lime

Mix together the rum, lime juice, and grenadine, with ice, in the highball glass. Top up with bitter lemon and stir briefly. Squeeze the juice from the lime quarter into the drink. Add the crushed lime quarter to the glass. Serve with a straw.

TIPTOP

Fruity, mild drink for a party
- Highball/Collins glass
- Shaker

1½ ounces dark rum
1½ ounces banana juice
1½ ounces passion-fruit juice
¾ ounce lemon juice
- *Garnish:*
1 slice of banana
1 maraschino cherry

Shake all the ingredients together, with ice, in the shaker and pour into the glass. Perch the slice of banana on the rim of the glass and fasten the cherry to it with a toothpick.

BAHIA I

Fruity, sweet drink for hot days
- Highball/Collins glass
- Shaker

1½ ounces mango juice
1 ounce dark rum
1 ounce light rum
1 ounce cream of coconut
- *Garnish:*
1 slice of orange
1 slice of star fruit
1 maraschino cherry

Shake all the ingredients together, with ice, in the shaker and pour into the glass. Perch the fruit on the rim of the glass.

BAHIA II

Fruity, mild drink for a summer party
- Paris goblet
- Shaker

2¾ ounces pineapple juice
2 ounces light rum
2 tsp. cream of coconut
- *Garnish:*
1 slice of orange
¾ slice of pineapple
Sprig of mint

Shake all the ingredients together, with ice, in the shaker and pour into the glass. Perch the fruit and the sprig of mint on the rim of the glass.

KIR IMPERIAL

EROTICA

KIR ROYAL

Drinks based on wine and champagne

CHAMPAGNE COCKTAIL

CHAMPENOIS

MIMOSA

KIWI-FRUIT CHAMPAGNE

KIR

Aromatic wine aperitif
• Paris goblet

2 tsp. crème de cassis
3½ ounces dry white wine
for topping up

Pour the crème de cassis into the glass,
top up with wine, and stir briefly.

KIR ROYAL

Aromatic champagne aperitif
• Champagne flute

2 tsp. crème de cassis
3½ ounces champagne or dry
sparkling wine for topping up

Pour the crème de cassis into the glass
and top up with the champagne or
sparkling wine.

KIR IMPERIAL I

Fruity champagne cocktail for a
reception
• Champagne flute

2 tsp. raspberry-flavored liqueur
3½ ounces champagne or sparkling
wine for topping up

Pour the liqueur into the glass and top
up with champagne or sparkling wine.

KIR IMPERIAL II

Sweet champagne aperitif
• Champagne flute
• Shaker

¾ ounce crème de cassis
¾ ounce vodka
Champagne for topping up

Shake the crème de cassis and vodka
together, with ice, in the shaker and
strain into the glass. Top up with
champagne.

BUCKS FIZZ

Light sparkling wine cocktail for a
reception or brunch
• Champagne flute

Orange juice
Dry sparkling wine or champagne for
topping up

Half fill the champagne flute with
orange juice and top up with sparkling
wine.

SOUTHERN TRIP

Tangy aperitif
• Champagne flute

1½ ounces Southern Comfort
Dry sparkling wine or champagne for
topping up
1 piece of orange peel

Pour the Southern Comfort into the
champagne flute and top up with
sparkling wine or champagne. Squeeze
the orange peel over the drink and add
the peel to the glass.

Champagne

KIWI FRUIT CHAMPAGNE

Fruity, sparkling cocktail for the evening
• Champagne flute
• Shaker

1½ ounces kiwi-fruit-flavored liqueur
2 tsp. lemon juice
Sparkling wine or champagne for topping up
• *Garnish:*
1 slice of kiwi fruit

Shake the kiwi-fruit liqueur and lemon juice together, with ice, in the shaker and strain into the glass. Top up with champagne. Perch the slice of kiwi fruit on the rim of the glass.

APRICOT CHAMPAGNE

Fruity cocktail for hot days
• Champagne glass
• Mixing glass

¾ ounce apricot brandy
1 ounce light rum
Champagne for topping up

Mix the apricot brandy and rum together, with ice, in the mixing glass and strain into the champagne glass. Top up with champagne.

MARGARET ROSE

Slightly bitter aperitif
• Champagne flute

¾ ounce Campari
Sparkling wine or champagne for topping up

Pour the Campari into the champagne flute and slowly top up with sparkling wine.

ORANGE CHAMPAGNE

Fruity cocktail for a party
• Champagne flute

¾ ounce orange curaçao
Sparkling wine or champagne for topping up
• *Garnish:*
1 orange peel spiral

Pour the curaçao into the champagne flute, top up with sparkling wine or champagne, and hang the peel spiral over the rim of the glass.

OVERTURE

Aromatic aperitif
• Champagne flute

½ ounce orange-flavored liqueur
1 dash orange bitters
Dry sparkling wine or champagne for topping up
• Garnish:
1 orange peel spiral

Pour the liqueur and bitters into the glass, top up with sparkling wine or champagne, and hang the orange peel spiral over the rim of the glass.

CHAMPENOIS

Refreshing cocktail for a reception
• Champagne flute

1 tsp. apricot brandy
1 dash crème de framboise
1 dash Angostura bitters
Champagne for topping up
• Garnish:
1 slice of orange
1 maraschino cherry

Mix all the ingredients, except the champagne, together, in the champagne flute. Top up with champagne. Perch the slice of orange on the rim of the glass and fasten the cherry to it with a toothpick.

Champagne

VALENCIA

Fruity champagne aperitif
- Champagne flute
- Shaker

¾ ounce apricot brandy

¾ ounce orange juice

Champagne for topping up

- *Garnish:*

1 maraschino cherry

Shake all the ingredients, except the champagne, together, with ice, in the shaker and strain into the champagne flute. Top up with champagne. Spear the maraschino cherry on a toothpick and add it to the glass.

FRANÇOIS BISE

Fruity champagne aperitif
- Champagne flute

1 tbsp. raspberry purée

Champagne for topping up

Put the raspberry purée into the glass and top up with champagne.

CHAMPAGNE COCKTAIL I

Bittersweet champagne cocktail
• Champagne glass

1 sugar cube
2 dashes Angostura bitters
Dry champagne or sparkling wine for topping up
• *Extra:*
1 piece of lemon peel

Put the sugar cube into the champagne glass and soak it in the Angostura bitters. Top up with champagne or sparkling wine. Squeeze the lemon peel over the drink and add the peel to the glass.

CHAMPAGNE COCKTAIL II

Bittersweet champagne cocktail for the evening
• Champagne flute

1 sugar cube
1 dash Angostura bitters
¾ ounce cognac
Champagne for topping up
• *Garnish:*
1 orange peel spiral

Put the sugar in the glass and soak it in the Angostura bitters. Add the cognac and top up with champagne. Hang the orange peel spiral over the rim of the glass.

LILA CRYSTAL

Light cocktail for a reception
• Champagne glass
• Mixing glass

¾ ounce Benedictine
2 tsp. gin
2 dashes orange bitters
Dry sparkling wine or champagne for topping up
1 piece of orange peel
• *Garnish:*
1 maraschino cherry

Mix the Benedictine, gin, and orange bitters together in the mixing glass and strain into the champagne glass. Top up with sparkling wine. Squeeze the orange peel over the drink and add the maraschino cherry to the glass.

EROTICA

Fruity, refreshing aperitif
• Champagne glass
• Shaker

¾ ounce passion-fruit-flavored liqueur
¾ ounce vodka
¾ ounce pineapple juice
1 dash Angostura bitters
Dry sparkling wine or champagne for topping up
• *Garnish:*
1 piece of pineapple
2 maraschino cherries

Shake all the ingredients, except the champagne, together, with ice, in the shaker. Strain into a champagne glass and top up with sparkling wine. Perch the piece of pineapple on the rim of the glass and fasten the cherry to it using a toothpick.

Champagne

Erotica (left), Champagne Cocktail II (right)

CHAMPAGNE SOUR

Fruity aperitif
• Champagne flute

1 sugar cube
1 tbsp. lemon juice
Sparkling wine or champagne for topping up
• *Garnish:*
1 slice of orange

Put the sugar cube into the glass, drizzle the lemon juice over it, and top up with sparkling wine. Perch the slice of orange on the rim of the glass.

AIR MAIL I

Sweet, fruity champagne cocktail for a party
• Champagne flute
• Shaker

1 ounce dark rum
¾ ounce lime cordial
2 tsp. honey
Champagne or sparkling wine for topping up
• *Garnish:*
1 slice of lime
1 maraschino cherry

Shake the rum, lime cordial, and honey together, with ice, in the shaker and pour into the champagne flute. Top up with champagne. Perch the fruit on the rim of the glass.

SILVER TOP

Refreshing, fruity champagne cocktail for a party
• Champagne glass
• Shaker

¾ ounce triple sec
¾ ounce gin
2 tsp. orange juice
1 tsp. grenadine
Champagne or sparkling wine for topping up
• *Garnish:*
½ slice of orange
2 maraschino cherries

Shake the triple sec, gin, orange juice, and grenadine together well, with ice, in the shaker and strain into the glass. Top up with champagne. Perch the fruit on the rim of the glass.

FEEL LIKE A HOLIDAY

Mild cocktail for a party
• Champagne flute
• Mixing glass

2 tsp. vodka
2 tsp. raspberry eau-de-vie
Sparkling wine or champagne for topping up

Mix the vodka and raspberry eau-de-vie together, with ice, in the mixing glass and strain into the champagne flute. Top up with champagne.

Champagne

MOON WALK COCKTAIL

Fruity, delicately tangy champagne cocktail for a reception
• Champagne flute
• Shaker

1 ounce orange-flavored liqueur

1 ounce grapefruit-flavored juice

1 dash rose water

Champagne or sparkling wine for topping up

Shake the liqueur, grapefruit juice, and rose water together, with ice, in the shaker and strain into the flute. Top up with champagne.

HANSEATIC

Fruity, alcoholic cocktail for the evening
• Champagne glass
• Shaker

¾ ounce bourbon

¾ ounce brandy

¾ ounce blackberry-flavored liqueur

Sparkling wine or champagne for topping up
• *Garnish:*

1 slice of lemon

Shake all the ingredients, except the sparkling wine, together, with ice, in the shaker and strain into the glass. Top up with sparkling wine. Perch the slice of lemon on the rim of the glass.

SPOTLIGHT

Fruity, slightly bitter aperitif
• Champagne glass
• Mixing glass

1 ounce cherry-flavored liqueur

2 tsp. Campari

2 tsp. dry vermouth

2 tsp. gin

Sparkling wine or champagne for topping up
• *Garnish:*

1 slice of lemon

Shake all the ingredients, except the sparkling wine, with ice, in the shaker and strain into the glass. Top up with sparkling wine. Perch the slice of lemon on the rim of the glass.

CHAMPAGNE FLIP

Fruity drink for the evening
• Champagne flute
• Shaker

1½ ounces port

1 egg yolk

1 tsp. sugar

Sparkling wine or champagne for topping up

Shake the port, egg yolk, and sugar together, with ice, in the shaker and strain into the glass. Top up with sparkling wine.

CHICAGO I

Fruity champagne cocktail for a party
• Champagne flute
• Mixing glass

¾ ounce cognac
1 tsp. Cointreau or other orange-flavored liqueur
1 dash Angostura bitters
Champagne or sparkling wine for topping up

Mix the cognac, Cointreau, and Angostura bitters together, with ice, in the mixing glass and strain into the champagne flute. Top up with champagne.

VALENCIA SMILE

Fruity cocktail for a reception
• Champagne flute
• Shaker

1 ounce apricot brandy
¾ ounce orange juice
3 dashes orange bitters
Sparkling wine or champagne for topping up
• Garnish:
1 slice of orange

Shake all the ingredients, except the sparkling wine, together, with ice, in the shaker and strain into the glass. Top up with sparkling wine. Perch the slice of orange on the rim of the glass.

CHICAGO II

Aromatic cocktail for the evening
• Champagne glass with sugared rim
• Mixing glass

¾ ounce cognac
3 dashes orange curaçao
1 dash orange bitters
Sparkling wine or champagne for topping up

Mix all the ingredients, except the sparkling wine, together, with ice, in the mixing glass and strain into the glass. Top up with sparkling wine.

CHAMPAGNE COBBLER

Fruity, mild drink for a summer party
• Cocktail glass

¾ ounce maraschino
¾ ounce triple sec
2 tsp. lemon juice
1 peach half, diced
2 maraschino cherries
2 grapes
Sparkling wine or champagne for topping up

Fill the cocktail glass one-third full with crushed ice. Mix the maraschino, triple sec, and lemon juice together in the cocktail glass. Add the fruit to the glass, top up with sparkling wine, and serve with a spoon.

Champagne

Valencia Smile (left), Champagne Cobbler (right)

AMARETTO FLIRT

Fruity cocktail for a reception
- Champagne glass
- Shaker

¾ ounce amaretto

¾ ounce orange juice

***Dry sparkling wine or champagne for
topping up***
- ***Garnish:***

½ slice of orange

1 maraschino cherry

Shake all the ingredients, except the
sparkling wine, together, with ice, in
the shaker and strain into a cocktail
glass. Top up with sparkling wine. Perch
the slice of orange on the rim of the
glass and fasten the cherry to it with a
toothpick.

CHAMPAGNE DAISY

Fruity champagne cocktail for a party
- Champagne flute
- Shaker

2 tsp. grenadine

2 tsp. lemon juice

¾ ounce yellow Chartreuse

***Sparkling wine or champagne for
topping up***
- ***Garnish:***

1 strawberry

Shake the grenadine, lemon juice, and
Chartreuse together, with ice cubes, in
the shaker and strain into the
champagne flute. Top up with sparkling
wine. Perch the strawberry on the rim
of the glass and serve the cocktail
immediately.

249

SEXY 6

Fruity aperitif
• Champagne glass
• Shaker

¾ ounce gin
¾ ounce orange juice
2 tsp. apricot brandy
2 tsp. raspberry juice
Sparkling wine or champagne for topping up
• Garnish:
1 maraschino cherry

Shake the gin, orange juice, apricot brandy, and raspberry juice together, with ice, in the shaker and strain into the glass. Top up with sparkling wine. Perch the cherry on the rim of the glass.

FRUIT CHAMPAGNE

Fruity, mild cocktail for the evening
• Champagne glass
• Shaker

1¾ ounces orange juice
¾ ounce apricot brandy
2 tsp. cognac
Sparkling wine or champagne for topping up
• Garnish:
1 maraschino cherry

Shake the orange juice, apricot brandy, and cognac together, with ice, in the shaker and strain into the glass. Top up with sparkling wine. Perch the cherry on the rim of the glass.

NORTHERN LIGHT

Aromatic cocktail for a party
• Champagne flute
• Shaker

¾ ounce light rum
¾ ounce triple sec
Sparkling wine or champagne for topping up
1 piece of orange peel
• Garnish:
½ slice of orange

Shake the rum and triple sec together, with ice, in the shaker and strain into the glass. Top up with sparkling wine and squeeze the orange peel over the drink. Perch the slice of orange on the rim of the glass.

MIRABELL

Aromatic aperitif
• Champagne flute
• Shaker

¾ ounce orange-flavored liqueur
¾ ounce gin
¾ ounce sweet red vermouth
¾ ounce orange juice
Sparkling wine or champagne for topping up

Shake all the ingredients, except the sparkling wine, together, with ice, in the shaker and strain into the glass. Top up with sparkling wine and serve immediately.

Champagne

OHIO I

Spicy aperitif
- Cocktail glass
- Mixing glass

¾ ounce Canadian whisky
2 tsp. sweet red vermouth
1 dash Angostura bitters
Sparkling wine or champagne for
topping up

Mix the whisky, vermouth, and
Angostura bitters together, with ice, in
the mixing glass and strain into the
cocktail glass. Top up with sparkling
wine.

ADRIA LOOK

Fruity cocktail for a summer party
- Champagne glass
- Mixing glass

¾ ounce gin
¾ ounce blue curaçao
2 tsp. lemon juice
Sparkling wine or champagne for
topping up
- *Garnish:*
1 maraschino cherry
½ apricot

Mix the gin, curaçao, and lemon juice
together, with ice, in the mixing glass
and strain into the champagne glass.
Top up with sparkling wine. Perch the
fruit on the rim of the glass.

OHIO II

Aromatic cocktail for a party
- Champagne glass

¾ ounce Cointreau or other orange-
flavored liqueur
¾ ounce brandy
1 dash Angostura bitters
Sparkling wine or champagne for
topping up
- *Garnish:*
1 maraschino cherry

Thoroughly mix the Cointreau, brandy,
and Angostura bitters in the champagne glass. Add 2 small ice cubes and
top up with sparkling wine. Perch the
cherry on the rim of the glass.

AMERICAN GLORY I

Fruity, mild aperitif
- Champagne flute

1½ ounces orange juice
¾ ounce grenadine
2 tsp. lemon juice
Sparkling wine or champagne for
topping up
- *Garnish:*
1 slice of orange

Fill the champagne flute one-third full
with crushed ice. Add the orange juice,
grenadine, and lemon juice and mix
well. Top up with sparkling wine. Perch
the slice of orange on the rim of the
glass.

STRAWBERRY FIELDS

Fruity, pink aperitif
• Champagne glass

5 strawberries, diced
1 tsp. orange-flavored liqueur
Pink sparkling wine or champagne
for topping up

Put the diced strawberries in the glass.
Pour the liqueur over them and top up
with sparkling wine. Serve with a
teaspoon.

ROGER VERGÉ

Fruity aperitif
• Champagne flute

1 tsp. crème de cassis
1 tsp. orange-flavored liqueur
Sparkling wine or champagne for
topping up
• *Garnish:*
1 slice of lemon

Pour the crème de cassis and orange
liqueur into the glass and top up with
sparkling wine. Perch the slice of lemon
on the rim of the glass.

HARRY'S PICK-ME-UP

Fruity, delicately tangy cocktail for a
party or as a pick-me-up
• Champagne flute
• Shaker

1 ounce cognac
2 tsp. lemon juice
2 dashes grenadine
Sparkling wine or champagne for
topping up

Shake the cognac, lemon juice, and
grenadine together, with ice, in the
shaker and strain into the champagne
flute. Top up with sparkling wine.

FLYING II

Refreshing, tangy cocktail for a party
• Champagne flute
• Shaker

¾ ounce gin
¾ ounce triple sec
¾ ounce lemon juice
Sparkling wine or champagne for
topping up

Shake the gin, triple sec, and lemon
juice together, with ice, in the shaker
and strain into the glass. Top up with
sparkling wine.

Champagne

Strawberry Fields (left), Roger Vergé (middle), Flying II (right)

JAMES BOND

Slightly bitter cocktail for a party
• Champagne glass

1½ ounces vodka
1 dash Angostura bitters
Sparkling wine or champagne for topping up

Thoroughly mix the vodka and Angostura bitters in the champagne glass. Top up with the sparkling wine.

COLD DUCK COCKTAIL

Tangy, fresh aperitif
• Champagne glass

1¾ ounces white wine
Sparkling wine or champagne for topping up
• Extra:
1 piece of lemon peel

Pour all the ingredients into the glass together. Add the piece of lemon peel to the glass.

FRENCH 76

Fruity cocktail for a party
• Champagne flute
• Shaker

1 ounce vodka
2 tsp. lemon juice
1 tsp. sugar syrup
Sparkling wine or champagne for topping up

Shake the vodka, lemon juice, and sugar syrup together, with ice, in the shaker and strain into the glass. Top up with sparkling wine.

JACQUES LAMELOISE

Sweet, mild cocktail
• Champagne flute

1 tbsp. plum-flavored liqueur
2 tsp. raspberry-flavored liqueur
Sparkling wine or champagne for topping up
• Garnish:
1 raspberry

Pour the liqueurs into the glass and top up with sparkling wine. Perch the raspberry on the rim of the glass.

Champagne

French 76 (back left), Jacques Lameloise (back right), James Bond (front left), Cold Duck Cocktail (front right)

FECAMP

Medium-dry, refreshing aperitif
• Highball/Collins glass
• Shaker

1 ounce Benedictine
¾ ounce lemon juice
2 tsp. sherry
2 tsp. Pimm's No. 1
Dry sparkling wine or champagne for topping up
• *Garnish:*
½ slice of orange
½ slice of lemon
2 maraschino cherries

Shake all the ingredients, except the sparkling wine, together, with ice, in the shaker and strain into the highball glass over ice. Then top up with sparkling wine. Spear the slices of orange and lemon, and the cherries, on a toothpick and lay the garnish across the rim of the glass.

MELODY

Fruity, long drink for the evening
• Highball/Collins glass

¾ ounce apricot brandy
¾ ounce gin
2 tsp. triple sec
Sparkling wine or champagne for topping up
• *Garnish:*
1 slice of orange

Mix all the ingredients, except the sparkling wine, together, with ice cubes, in the glass. Top up with sparkling wine. Perch the slice of orange on the rim of the glass.

ROSIE'S

Fruity, tangy aperitif
• Highball/Collins glass
• Shaker

2¾ ounces grapefruit juice
1½ ounces Campari
2 tsp. orange-flavored liqueur
Sparkling wine or champagne for topping up
• *Garnish:*
1 slice of orange

Shake the grapefruit juice, Campari, and orange-flavored liqueur together, with ice, in the shaker and strain into the glass. Top up with sparkling wine. Perch the slice of orange on the rim of the glass.

FLYING DUTCHMAN

Refreshing, medium-dry drink for any time of day
• Highball/Collins glass
• Mixing glass

¾ ounce Pisang Ambon
¾ ounce vodka
2 tsp. Malibu or other coconut-flavored liqueur
1 dash lime juice
Sparkling wine or champagne for topping up
• *Garnish:*
1 piece of lemon peel
Slice of lemon or lime
Sprig of mint

Mix all the ingredients, except the sparkling wine, together, with ice, in the mixing glass and strain into the highball glass over crushed ice. Top up with sparkling wine and squeeze the lemon peel over the drink. Perch the fruit on the rim of the glass and add the mint to the glass.

Champagne

BLUE SPLASH

Fruity, sparkling drink for a party
• Large rocks glass
• Mixing glass

¾ ounce gin
¾ ounce blue curaçao
¾ ounce lemon juice
2 tsp. dry vermouth
1 dash Angostura bitters
Sparkling wine or champagne for topping up
• *Garnish:*
1 slice of orange

Mix all the ingredients, except the sparkling wine, together, with ice, in the mixing glass and strain into the glass. Top up with sparkling wine. Perch the slice of orange on the rim of the glass.

LIME CHAMPAGNE

Fruity cocktail for the summer
• Champagne flute

1 ounce lime cordial
1 ounce bitter lemon
Sparkling wine or champagne for topping up
• *Garnish:*
1 slice of lime

Pour the cordial and bitter lemon into the champagne flute. Top up with sparkling wine. Perch the slice of lime on the rim of the glass.

PROFESSIONAL

Fruity, bitter aperitif
• Highball/Collins glass
• Shaker

1½ ounces orange juice
1 ounce Campari
1 ounce dry vermouth
3½ ounces sparkling wine or champagne for topping up
• *Garnish:*
1 slice of orange

Shake the orange juice, Campari, and vermouth together, with ice, in the shaker and strain into the glass. Top up with champagne. Perch the slice of orange on the rim of the glass.

PEPPERMINT FRESH

Spicy after-dinner drink
• Rock glass
• Shaker

1½ ounces peppermint-flavored liqueur
2 tsp. lemon juice
Sparkling wine or champagne for topping up
• *Garnish:*
Sprig of mint

Shake the liqueur and lemon juice together, with ice, in the shaker and pour into the glass. Top up with sparkling wine. Hang the sprig of mint over the rim of the glass.

JAMAICA COOLER

Fruity cooler for a party
• Long-stemmed glass

3½ ounces dry red wine
1½ ounces light rum
1 ounce sugar syrup
2 tsp. lemon juice
2 tsp. orange juice
• Garnish:
½ slice of lemon

Mix all the ingredients together, with ice cubes, in the stemmed glass. Perch the slice of lemon on the rim of the glass. Serve with a straw.

RED SIN

Fruity aperitif
• Highball/Collins glass

1½ ounces crème de cassis
2 tsp. orange juice
Red sparkling wine for topping up
• Garnish:
1 sprig of red currants

Mix the crème de cassis and orange juice together in the highball glass with ice cubes. Top up with red sparkling wine. Hang the sprig of red currants over the rim of the glass.

RED-WINE FLIP

Mild, spicy drink for the evening
• Goblet or flip glass
• Shaker

2¾ ounces red wine
1 egg yolk
2 tsp. sugar
• Extra:
Grated nutmeg

Shake all the ingredients together, with ice, in the shaker and strain into the goblet or flip glass. Sprinkle grated nutmeg on top.

SPRITZER

Refreshing drink for every day
• Large rocks glass

4 ounces white wine
Soda water for topping up
½ slice of lemon

Pour the wine into the glass and top up with soda water. Add the slice of lemon to the glass.

UNION JACK

POUSSE-CAFÉ I

Liqueur-based drinks

SMITH & WESSON

SUNNY DREAM

AURELIA

FLUFFY F

MUDDY RIVER

GOLDEN CADILLAC

POUSSE-CAFÉ I

Spicy, sweet after-dinner drink
• Pousse-café glass or tulip-shaped wine glass

Blue curaçao
Galliano

Using a measure, pour a little curaçao into the glass. Carefully pour the Galliano over an inverted bar spoon, held inside the glass with the tip touching the wall, so that it floats on top of the layer of curaçao. The layers should not mix.

POUSSE-CAFÉ II

Sweet after-dinner drink
• Pousse-café glass or tulip-shaped wine glass

Grenadine
Maraschino
Blue curaçao

In the above sequence, layer the ingredients in the glass, following the method for Pousse-Café I.

POUSSE-CAFÉ III

Sweet after-dinner drink
• Pousse-café glass or tulip-shaped wine glass

Maraschino
Blue curaçao
Grand Marnier

Layer the ingredients in the glass, following the method for Pousse-Café I.

POUSSE-CAFÉ IV

Spicy, sweet after-dinner drink
• Pousse-café glass or tulip-shaped wine glass

Green crème de menthe
Blue curaçao
Green Chartreuse

Layer the ingredients in the glass, following the method for Pousse-Café I.

POUSSE-CAFÉ V

Spicy, sweet after-dinner drink
• Pousse-café glass or tulip-shaped wine glass

Grenadine
Green crème de menthe
Cherry brandy
Yellow Chartreuse

Layer the ingredients in the glass, following the method for Pousse-Café I.

Liqueurs

Pousse-Café II (left), Pousse-Café V (middle), Pousse-Café VII (right)

POUSSE-CAFÉ VI

Fruity, sweet after-dinner drink
• Pousse-café glass or tulip-shaped
wine glass

Kahlúa
Grand Marnier
Whipped cream

Layer the ingredients in the glass,
following the method for Pousse-Café I.

POUSSE-CAFÉ VII

Spicy, sweet after-dinner drink
• Pousse-café glass or tulip-shaped
wine glass

Grenadine
Green crème de menthe
Blue curaçao
Escorial or other herb-flavored
liqueur

Layer the ingredients in the glass,
following the method for Pousse-Café I.

LAYER CAKE

Sweet after-dinner drink
• Rocks glass

¾ ounce white crème de cacao
¾ ounce apricot brandy
¾ ounce light cream

Layer the ingredients in the glass,
following the method for Pousse-Café I.

UNION JACK

Sweet pousse-café to accompany an
afternoon coffee
• Pousse-café glass or tulip-shaped
wine glass

¾ ounce grenadine
¾ ounce maraschino
¾ ounce green Chartreuse

Layer the ingredients in the glass,
following the method for Pousse-Café I.

FRENCH CONNECTION II

Aromatic after-dinner drink
• Rocks glass

1 ounce brandy
¾ ounce amaretto

Mix the ingredients together, with ice,
in the glass.

ITALIAN MELODY

Sweet after-dinner drink
• Cocktail glass
• Shaker

1 ounce amaretto
¾ ounce light cream
2 tsp. Barack liqueur (or other
apricot liqueur)
2 tsp. orange juice
• Garnish:
1 maraschino cherry

Shake all the ingredients together, with
ice, in the shaker and strain into the
cocktail glass. Perch the cherry on the
rim of the glass.

EUROPEAN FRIENDSHIP

Fruity, mild drink for a party
• Cocktail glass
• Shaker

½ ounce amaretto
½ ounce banana-flavored liqueur
½ ounce scotch
½ ounce sweet white vermouth
• Garnish:
1 maraschino cherry

Shake all the ingredients together, with
ice, in the shaker and strain into the
cocktail glass. Perch the cherry on the
rim of the glass.

Liqueurs

CHRISTMAS

Sweet drink for a party
• Highball/Collins glass
• Shaker

1¾ ounces passion-fruit juice
1¾ ounces cream of coconut
1 ounce amaretto
2 tsp. light cream
• Garnish:
2 maraschino cherries

Shake the ingredients together firmly, with ice, in the shaker and strain into the highball glass over crushed ice. Spear the maraschino cherries on a toothpick and lay the garnish across the rim of the glass.

BOCCIE BALL

Fruity, mild drink for any time of year
• Highball/Collins glass

1¾ ounces amaretto
1¾ ounces orange juice
3½ ounces soda water for topping up
• Garnish:
1 slice of orange

Mix the amaretto and orange juice together, with ice cubes, in the highball glass. Top up with soda water and stir again briefly. Perch the slice of orange on the rim of the glass.

AMAROS

Fruity, sweet short drink for the evening
• Cocktail glass
• Shaker

1½ ounces amaretto
¾ ounce Calvados
1 dash lemon juice

Shake all the ingredients together, with ice, in the shaker and strain into the glass.

ORIENT EXPRESS

Delicately spicy drink for any time of year
• Highball/Collins glass with ground almond-coated rim
• Blender

¾ ounce amaretto
7 ounces ice-cold milk
1 tbsp. instant cocoa powder

Mix all the ingredients together, in the blender, and pour into the glass. Serve with a straw.

ITALIAN CHERRY

Fruity, sweet after-dinner drink
• Cocktail glass
• Shaker

1 ounce amaretto
1 ounce cherry brandy

Shake the ingredients together, with ice, in the shaker and strain into the glass.

VICTORIA

Tangy, mild after-dinner drink
• Rocks glass
• Shaker

1 ounce amaretto
½ ounce Campari
½ ounce vodka
• Garnish:
1 maraschino cherry

Shake all the ingredients together well, with ice, in the shaker and strain into the glass filled one-third full with crushed ice. Perch the maraschino cherry on the rim of the glass.

SMITH & WESSON

Fruity, sweet drink for a party
• Highball/Collins glass
• Shaker

4 ounces apricot nectar
1½ ounces amaretto
¾ ounce tequila
• Garnish:
Apricot half

Shake all the ingredients together, with ice cubes, in the shaker and strain into the highball glass. Add 2 ice cubes. Perch the apricot half on the rim of the glass.

Liqueurs

APRICOT SOUR

Fruity after-dinner drink
• Rocks glass
• Shaker

1 ounce apricot brandy
1 ounce lemon juice
1 ounce orange juice
• Garnish:
½ slice of orange
1 maraschino cherry

Shake the ingredients together firmly, with ice cubes, in the shaker and strain into the glass. Perch the slice of orange and the cherry on the rim of the glass.

SUNNY DREAM

Sweet after-dinner drink
• Cocktail glass
• Shaker

¾ ounce apricot brandy
½ ounce orange juice
2 tsp. Cointreau or other orange-flavored liqueur
1 scoop vanilla ice cream
• Garnish:
½ slice of orange

Shake all the ingredients together firmly, without ice, in the shaker and pour into the glass. Perch the slice of orange on the rim of the glass.

LOUISIANA

Fruity, slightly tangy drink for the evening
- Cocktail glass
- Shaker

1½ ounces apricot brandy
¾ ounce gin
¾ ounce apricot juice

Shake all the ingredients together, with ice, in the shaker and strain into the glass.

PRINCESS

Sweet drink for the afternoon
- Cocktail glass

1 ounce apricot brandy
¾ ounce light cream

Pour the apricot brandy into the cocktail glass. Spoon the cream on top.

FESTIVAL

Creamy after-dinner drink
- Cocktail glass
- Shaker

¾ ounce apricot brandy
¾ ounce white crème de cacao
¾ ounce light cream
1 tsp. grenadine

Shake the ingredients together, with ice, in the shaker and strain into the glass.

BREAKFAST

Sweet eggnog for any time of day
- Rocks glass
- Shaker

2 ounces milk
¾ ounce apricot brandy
2 tsp. triple sec
2 tsp. light cream
1 tsp. confectioners' sugar
1 egg
- *Extra:*
Grated nutmeg

Shake the ingredients together firmly, with ice, in the shaker and strain into the glass. Sprinkle with a little grated nutmeg.

APRICOT COOLER

Very refreshing drink for a summer party
- Highball/Collins glass

1½ ounces apricot brandy
1 ounce lemon juice
1 tsp. grenadine
Sparkling mineral water for topping up
- *Garnish:*
1 slice of lemon

Shake all the ingredients except the mineral water together, with shaved ice, in the shaker and strain into the highball glass over ice. Top up with mineral water. Perch the slice of lemon on the rim of the glass. Serve with a long stirrer.

Liqueurs

Louisiana (top left), Festival (top right), Princess (bottom left), Apricot Cooler (bottom right)

AURELIA

Creamy drink for a party
• Cocktail glass
• Mixing glass

¾ ounce Batida de Coco
¾ ounce blue curaçao
¾ ounce grenadine
• Garnish:
1 maraschino cherry

Mix the ingredients together, with ice, in the mixing glass and strain into the cocktail glass. Spear the maraschino cherry on a toothpick and add it to the glass.

APRICOT ORANGE

Sweet drink for a party
• Large cocktail glass
• Shaker

1½ ounces Cointreau or other orange-flavored liqueur
1 ounce orange juice
1 ounce apricot juice
2 tsp. apricot brandy
• Garnish:
1 maraschino cherry

Shake all the ingredients together, with ice cubes, in the shaker and strain into the glass. Perch the cherry on the rim of the glass.

JIMMY'S DREAM

Sweet, fruity drink for a party
• Highball/Collins glass
• Shaker

2 ounces orange juice
¾ ounce Batida de Coco
¾ ounce amaretto
¾ ounce passion-fruit-flavored liqueur
¾ ounce lemon juice
• Garnish:
½ slice of orange

Shake the ingredients together, with ice, in the shaker and strain into the highball glass over crushed ice. Perch the slice of orange on the rim of the glass.

FLUFFY F

Sweet drink for the afternoon
• Cocktail glass
• Shaker

¾ ounce crème de banane
¾ ounce white crème de cacao
¾ ounce Frangelico
¾ ounce light cream
• Garnish:
1 maraschino cherry

Shake the ingredients together, with ice, in the shaker and strain into the cocktail glass. Perch the cherry on the rim of the glass.

Liqueurs

GOLDEN COCONUT

Sweet after-dinner drink
• Rocks glass
• Shaker

1 ounce light cream
¾ ounce banana-flavored liqueur
¾ ounce white crème de cacao
¾ ounce cream of coconut
• Garnish:
1 maraschino cherry

Shake all the ingredients together firmly, with ice cubes, in the shaker, and strain into the glass. Perch the cherry on the rim of the glass.

DALLAS

Creamy drink for a party
• Highball/Collins glass
• Shaker

¾ ounce crème de banane
¾ ounce blue curaçao
¾ ounce Batida de Coco
Pineapple juice for topping up
• Garnish:
1 strawberry
Sprig of mint

Shake all the ingredients, except the pineapple juice, together, with ice, in the shaker and strain into the highball glass over ice. Top up with pineapple juice and stir. Perch the strawberry on the rim of the glass. Add the sprig of mint to the glass. Serve with a stirrer.

GREEN BANANAS

Fruity, mild drink for any time of year
• Highball/Collins glass
• Shaker

⅔ cup orange juice
1½ ounces green banana-flavored liqueur
¾ ounce lemon juice
• Garnish:
1 slice of orange

Shake all the ingredients together, with ice, in the shaker, and strain into the glass. Perch the slice of orange on the rim of the glass.

COCONUT FRUIT

Fruity, sweet drink for a party
• Highball/Collins glass
• Shaker

3½ ounces pineapple juice
1 ounce green banana-flavored liqueur
1 ounce Malibu or other coconut-flavored liqueur
• Garnish:
1 slice of pineapple

Shake all the ingredients together, with ice cubes, in the shaker and strain into the highball glass. Add 1 tablespoon crushed ice. Perch the slice of pineapple on the rim of the glass.

GRASSHOPPER

Creamy after-dinner drink
• Cocktail glass
• Shaker

¾ ounce white crème de cacao
¾ ounce green crème de menthe
¾ ounce light cream

Shake the ingredients together, with ice, in the shaker, and strain into the glass.

CONNECTION

Sweet after-dinner drink
• Rocks glass

¾ ounce Bailey's Irish Cream
¾ ounce vodka

Mix the ingredients together in the glass. The addition of 2 or 3 ice cubes is optional.

CHOCO FLIP

Sweet, creamy drink for a party
• Cocktail glass
• Shaker

1 ounce chocolate-flavored liqueur
¾ ounce scotch
¾ ounce light cream
1 egg yolk

Shake all the ingredients together firmly, with ice, in the shaker, and pour into the glass.

TROPICAL

Sweet aperitif
• Cocktail glass
• Mixing glass

¾ ounce white crème de cacao
¾ ounce maraschino
¾ ounce dry vermouth
1 dash Angostura bitters
• Garnish:
1 maraschino cherry

Mix the ingredients together, with ice, in the mixing glass and strain into the cocktail glass. Spear the cherry on a toothpick and add it to the glass.

ANGEL'S KISS

Spicy, sweet drink for the afternoon
• Champagne flute

1½ ounces brown crème de cacao
Lightly whipped cream for topping up
• Garnish:
1 maraschino cherry

Pour the liqueur into the champagne flute. Spoon the cream over the liqueur to form a layer about ¾ inch thick. Perch the cherry on the rim of the glass.

Liqueurs

GOLDEN CADILLAC

Creamy after-dinner drink
• Cocktail glass
• Shaker

¾ ounce white crème de cacao
¾ ounce light cream
¾ ounce Galliano
¾ ounce orange juice

Shake the ingredients together, with ice, in the shaker and strain into the glass.

LUMUMBA III

Sweet, refreshing long drink for hot days
• Large rocks glass

1 ounce brown crème de cacao
¾ ounce brandy
Ice-cold milk for topping up
• Garnish:
Grated chocolate

Pour the crème de cacao and brandy into the glass, top up with milk, and stir. Sprinkle with a little grated chocolate.

NICOLA

Spicy, sweet after-dinner drink
• Cocktail glass
• Shaker

1 dash grenadine
¾ ounce light cream
¾ ounce brown crème de cacao
¾ ounce amaretto

Pour the grenadine into the cocktail glass. Shake the remaining ingredients together, with ice cubes, in the shaker and strain into the glass.

KING ALFONSO

Creamy drink for the afternoon
• Cocktail glass

1½ ounces crème de café
¾ ounce lightly whipped cream

Pour the liqueur into the glass. Carefully pour the cream on top of the liqueur.

COCOA CREAM

Spicy, sweet after-dinner drink
• Cocktail glass
• Shaker

1½ ounces brown crème de cacao
1½ ounces light cream

Shake the ingredients together, with ice, in the shaker and strain into the glass.

MUDDY RIVER

Sweet after-dinner drink
• Rocks glass

1½ ounces Kahlúa
1½ ounces light cream

Mix the ingredients together, with ice, in the glass.

MOCHA FLIP

Sweet flip for the evening
• Tulip-shaped glass or champagne flute
• Shaker

1¾ ounces Kahlúa
2 tsp. light cream
1 egg yolk
• *Extra:*
Grated nutmeg

Shake the Kahlúa, cream, and egg yolk together firmly, with ice cubes, in the shaker and strain into the flip glass. Sprinkle a pinch of nutmeg on top.

CARIBBEAN CASSIS

Fruity, long drink for a party
• Highball/Collins glass
• Shaker

4 ounces orange juice
1½ ounces crème de cassis
¾ ounce light rum
¾ ounce lemon juice
• *Garnish:*
1 slice of lemon

Shake all the ingredients together well, with ice, in the shaker, and strain into the glass over ice cubes. Perch the slice of lemon on the rim of the glass.

REVERIE

Sweet, creamy drink
• Cocktail glass
• Shaker

¾ ounce cassis
¾ ounce white crème de cacao
¾ ounce light cream

Shake the ingredients together, with ice, in the shaker and strain into the cocktail glass.

WHITE SPIDER

Short drink for the evening
• Rocks glass

1 ounce white crème de menthe
1 ounce vodka

Pour the ingredients into the glass over ice cubes and serve the drink with a stirrer.

CRÈME DE MENTHE FRAPPÉ

Sweet frappé to accompany afternoon coffee
• Small balloon-shaped wine glass

1½ ounces green or white crème de menthe

Half fill the glass with crushed ice. Pour the crème de menthe into the glass and stir gently. Serve immediately with 2 short drinking straws.

Liqueurs

Mocha Flip (left), Caribbean Cassis (middle), Crème de Menthe Frappé (right)

DIANA

Sweet after-dinner frappé
• Small white wine glass

1 ounce white crème de menthe
2 tsp. brandy

Half fill the glass with crushed ice. Pour the crème de menthe over the ice and then carefully add the brandy. Do not stir.

DUCE HOPE

Aromatic drink for a party
• Cocktail glass
• Shaker

¾ ounce green crème de menthe
¾ ounce amaretto
¾ ounce Grand Marnier

Shake the ingredients together, with ice, in the shaker and strain into the cocktail glass.

PEPPERMINT COCKTAIL

Fresh, medium-dry after-dinner drink
• Cocktail glass
• Shaker

1½ ounces green crème de menthe
¾ ounce dry vermouth
1 tsp. cognac

Shake all the ingredients together, with ice cubes, in the shaker, and strain into the cocktail glass.

AFTERWARDS I

Fruity, mild after-dinner or party drink
• Cocktail glass
• Shaker

1 ounce blue curaçao
1 ounce apricot brandy
2 tsp. lemon juice
• Garnish:
1 slice of lemon

Shake all the ingredients together, with ice cubes, in the shaker and strain into the cocktail glass. Perch the slice of lemon on the rim of the glass.

Liqueurs

CURAÇAO FLIP

Fruity, sweet flip for the evening
- Cocktail glass
- Shaker

1½ ounces blue curaçao
1½ ounces orange juice
1 egg yolk

Shake all the ingredients together firmly, with ice cubes, in the shaker, and strain into the cocktail glass.

PARIS OPERA

Fruity, mild drink for a party
- Rocks glass
- Shaker

1 ounce blue curaçao
1 ounce grapefruit juice
¾ ounce light rum
• Garnish:
1 maraschino cherry

Shake all the ingredients together, with ice cubes, in the shaker, and strain into the glass over ice cubes. Perch the cherry on the rim of the glass.

LAMBADA

Fruity, long drink for a summer party
- Highball/Collins glass
- Shaker

¾ ounce blue curaçao
¾ ounce Malibu or other coconut-flavored liqueur
¾ ounce peach juice
2 tsp. peach-flavored liqueur
2 tsp. pineapple juice
• Garnish:
1 maraschino cherry

Shake the ingredients together, with ice, in the shaker and strain into the highball glass over ice. Perch the cherry on the rim of the glass.

BLUE KONTIKI

Fruity, mild drink for a party
- Cocktail glass
- Shaker

2 tsp. blue curaçao
Sugar
1 ounce Kontiki or other tropical-fruit-flavored liqueur
¾ ounce grapefruit juice

Dip the rim of the cocktail glass first in curaçao, then in sugar. Shake the liqueur and grapefruit juice together well, with ice cubes, in the shaker and strain into the glass.

CHAMELEON

Fruity, mild drink for the evening
• Highball/Collins glass

1½ ounces blue curaçao

Orange juice for topping up

• Garnish:

½ slice of orange

1 maraschino cherry

Pour the curaçao into the glass over ice cubes, top up with orange juice, and stir briefly. Perch the slice of orange on the rim of the glass and fasten the cherry to it with a toothpick. Serve with a straw.

OKENNATT

Refreshing, long drink for a party
• Highball/Collins glass

¾ ounce blue curaçao

¾ ounce Parfait Amour

Bitter lemon and soda water for topping up

• Garnish:

1 slice of lemon

1 maraschino cherry

Pour the curaçao and Parfait Amour into the highball glass together over shaved ice. Top up with bitter lemon to two-thirds full, and top up the final third with soda water. Spear the slice of lemon and maraschino cherry on a toothpick, and lay the garnish across the rim of the glass. Serve with a stirrer.

Liqueurs

GREEN WIDOW I

Fruity, sweet drink for any time of year
• Highball/Collins glass with sugared rim

⅔ cup orange juice

¾ ounce blue curaçao

2 tsp. banana-flavored liqueur

• Garnish:

1 slice of orange

Pour the curaçao into the highball glass, add a few ice cubes, and top up with orange juice. Float the banana liqueur on top of the drink. Perch the slice of orange on the rim of the glass and serve with a straw.

CARIBBEAN WONDER

Fruity, sweet drink for hot days
• Highball/Collins glass
• Shaker

1½ ounces blue curaçao

1½ ounces banana juice

1½ ounces pineapple juice

1½ ounces buttermilk

2 tsp. light rum

• Garnish:

¼ slice of pineapple

Shake all the ingredients together firmly, with ice cubes, in the shaker and strain into the highball glass. Perch the piece of pineapple on the rim of the glass.

CURAÇAO TONIC

Tangy, sweet drink for hot days
• Highball/Collins glass

1 ounce blue curaçao
Tonic water for topping up
• Garnish:
1 slice of lemon

Fill the highball glass one-third full with ice cubes and pour the liqueur over them. Top up with tonic water and stir slowly. Perch the slice of lemon on the rim of the glass.

BLUE CHANGE

Fruity, mild drink for any time of year
• Highball/Collins glass

1½ ounces blue curaçao
2¾ ounces pineapple juice
2¾ ounces grapefruit juice
• Garnish:
¼ slice of pineapple

Put 3 ice cubes in the highball glass, pour the liquids into the glass one after the other and stir briefly. Perch the slice of pineapple on the rim of the glass.

PINEAPPLE-CURAÇAO

Fruity, mild drink for any time of year
• Highball/Collins glass
• Shaker

4 ounces pineapple juice
1½ ounces blue curaçao
¾ ounce lemon juice
• Garnish:
¼ slice of pineapple

Shake all the ingredients together, with ice, in the shaker and strain into the glass. Perch the slice of pineapple on the rim of the glass.

RED DREAMS II

Fruity, mild drink for the evening
• Large cocktail glass
• Shaker

¾ ounce orange curaçao
¾ ounce apple-flavored liqueur
¾ ounce vodka
¾ ounce orange juice
• Garnish:
1 maraschino cherry

Shake all the ingredients together, with ice cubes, in the shaker and strain into the chilled glass. Perch the cherry on the rim of the glass.

Liqueurs

RED DEVIL

Light, bitter after-dinner drink
- Cocktail glass
- Shaker

¾ ounce triple sec
¾ ounce Campari
¾ ounce orange juice

Shake the ingredients together, with ice, in the shaker and strain into the glass.

BABY

Sweet drink for a party
- Cocktail glass
- Shaker

1½ ounces triple sec
¾ ounce light cream
1 dash Angostura bitters

Shake all the ingredients together firmly, with ice, in the shaker and strain into the glass.

GOLDEN DREAM

Creamy, sweet drink
- Cocktail glass
- Shaker

¾ ounce triple sec
¾ ounce orange juice
¾ ounce light cream
2 tsp. Galliano

Shake the ingredients together, with ice, in the shaker and strain into the glass.

SWEET MURIELLE

Creamy drink for the afternoon
- Cocktail glass
- Shaker

¾ ounce triple sec
¾ ounce brown crème de cacao
¾ ounce light cream
• Garnish:
Cocoa powder

Shake all the ingredients together firmly, with ice, in the shaker and strain into the cocktail glass. Sprinkle a little cocoa powder on top.

REGATTA

Medium-dry drink for a party
- Cocktail glass
- Shaker

¾ ounce triple sec
¾ ounce Galliano
¾ ounce lemon juice
1 dash vodka
Dry sparkling wine or champagne

Shake all the ingredients, except the sparkling wine or champagne, together, with ice, in the shaker and strain into the glass. Add a little sparkling wine or champagne to the cocktail.

SWEET ORANGE

Fruity, sweet drink for any time of year
• Highball/Collins glass
• Shaker

2 ounces orange-flavored liqueur

2 ounces orange juice

2 ounces apricot nectar

• Garnish:

1 orange segment

Shake all the ingredients together, with ice, in the shaker and strain into the highball glass over ice cubes. Add the orange segment to the glass.

SHADES OF BHOK

Aromatic, short drink for the afternoon
• Cocktail glass
• Shaker

¾ ounce Drambuie

¾ ounce apricot brandy

¾ ounce lemon juice

2 tsp. Parfait Amour

• Extra:

1 piece of lemon peel

Shake all the ingredients together, with ice, in the shaker and strain into the cocktail glass. Add the piece of lemon peel to the glass.

LOVELY RAINBOW

Fruity, mild drink for any time of year
• Rocks glass

1½ ounces Drambuie

¾ ounce orange juice

1 dash lemon juice

1 dash grenadine

• Garnish:

1 slice of orange

1 slice of lemon

Half fill the glass with ice cubes and pour the ingredients, in the above order, into the glass. Perch the slices of lemon and orange on the rim of the glass. Serve with a straw.

MISTY MARIE

Creamy, short drink for the afternoon
• Cocktail glass
• Shaker

¾ ounce Drambuie

½ ounce light cream

2 tsp. anisette

Shake the ingredients together firmly, with ice, in the shaker and strain into the cocktail glass.

Liqueurs

SCOTTISH HEART

Fruity, mild drink for a party
• Highball/Collins glass
• Shaker

2 ounces orange juice
2 ounces apricot nectar
1½ ounces Drambuie
¾ ounce scotch
• *Garnish:*
2 maraschino cherries

Shake all the ingredients together, with ice, in the shaker and strain into the highball glass over ice cubes. Spear the cherries on a toothpick and lay the garnish across the rim of the glass.

FOR THE DUKE

Fruity, spicy drink for the evening
• Large champagne glass
• Shaker

1¾ ounces Drambuie
1¾ ounces orange juice
White of 1 egg
• *Garnish:*
1 slice of orange
1 maraschino cherry

Shake all the ingredients together firmly, with ice cubes, in the shaker and strain into the champagne glass. Perch the fruit on the rim of the glass.

SCOTTISH DREAMS

Fruity, mild drink for a party
• Highball/Collins glass
• Shaker

2 ounces orange juice
2 ounces apricot nectar
1½ ounces Drambuie
1 tsp. lemon juice
• *Garnish:*
½ slice of orange
1 maraschino cherry

Shake all the ingredients together, with ice, in the shaker and strain into the highball glass over ice cubes. Spear the fruit on a toothpick and lay the garnish across the rim of the glass.

GREAT BRITAIN

Fruity, tangy drink for a party
• Highball/Collins glass
• Shaker

1½ ounces Drambuie
¾ ounce gin
1 ounce lemon juice
Soda water for topping up
• *Garnish:*
1 maraschino cherry

Shake the Drambuie, gin, and lemon juice together, with ice cubes, in the shaker and strain into the glass. Top up with soda water and stir. Perch the cherry on the rim of the glass.

TROPICAL DRAMBUIE

Fruity, long drink for a party
• Highball/Collins glass

1½ ounces Drambuie
¾ ounce light rum
2¾ ounces passion-fruit juice
• Garnish:
1 slice of lemon

Mix the Drambuie and rum together, with ice cubes, in the glass. Top up with passion-fruit juice and stir. Perch the slice of lemon on the rim of the glass.

APRICOT DRAMBUIE

Fruity, mild drink for a party
• Highball/Collins glass

2¾ ounces apricot nectar
1½ ounces Drambuie
2 tsp. lemon juice
• Garnish:
1 slice of lemon

Mix the ingredients together, with ice cubes, in the highball glass. Perch the slice of lemon on the rim of the glass.

SNOWBALL

Refreshing drink for a party
• Highball/Collins glass

1½ ounces advocaat
Lemonade for topping up

Pour the advocaat into the highball glass over ice and carefully top up with lemonade. Serve with a long stirrer.

SPIRIT OF MUNICH

Refreshing, fruity drink for a party
• Highball/Collins glass
• Shaker

1¾ ounces orange juice
1½ ounces Escorial or other herb-flavored liqueur
1½ ounces passion-fruit juice
2 tsp. lemon juice
• Garnish:
½ slice of orange
1 mint leaf

Shake all the ingredients together, with ice, in the shaker and strain into the highball glass over crushed ice. Perch the slice of orange on the rim of the glass. Float the mint leaf on top of the drink.

Liqueurs

Apricot Drambuie (top left), Spirit of Munich (top right), Tropical Drambuie (bottom left), Snowball (bottom right)

283

EURO CUP

Creamy, short drink for a party
• Cocktail glass
• Shaker

¾ ounce Galliano
½ ounce light cream
2 tsp. triple sec
1 tsp. blue curaçao
1 tsp. lemon juice
• Garnish:
1 maraschino cherry

Shake all the ingredients together firmly, with ice, in the shaker and strain into the glass. Perch the cherry on the rim of the glass.

WHITE SNOW

Sweet drink for the afternoon
• Cocktail glass
• Shaker

¾ ounce Galliano
¾ ounce passion-fruit juice
¾ ounce light cream
2 tsp. white crème de cacao
• Garnish:
Ground cinnamon
1 slice of star fruit

Shake the ingredients together firmly, with ice, in the shaker and strain into the glass. Sprinkle a little ground cinnamon on top. Perch the slice of star fruit on the rim of the glass.

COBRA

Spicy, sweet after-dinner drink
• Cocktail glass
• Shaker

1 ounce Galliano
2 tsp. amaretto

Shake all the ingredients together well, with ice cubes, in the shaker and strain into the cocktail glass.

GOLDEN TORPEDO

Creamy, sweet after-dinner drink
• Cocktail glass
• Shaker

¾ ounce Galliano
¾ ounce light cream
¾ ounce amaretto

Shake all the ingredients together, with ice cubes, in the shaker and strain into the cocktail glass.

GALLIANO STINGER

Refreshing, spicy drink for any time of year
• Cocktail glass
• Shaker

1½ ounces Galliano
¾ ounce white crème de menthe

Shake all the ingredients together, with ice, in the shaker and strain into the chilled cocktail glass.

Liqueurs

Euro Cup (left), White Snow (right)

GALLIANO SOUR

Fruity, spicy drink for any time of year
• Rocks glass
• Shaker

¾ ounce Galliano

¾ ounce scotch

¾ ounce lemon juice

2 tsp. sugar syrup

Shake all the ingredients together, with ice, in the shaker and strain into the chilled glass.

GALLIANO MIST

Fruity, spicy drink for hot days
• Rocks glass

2 ounces Galliano

Lemon wedge

Fill the glass two-thirds full with crushed ice. Pour the Galliano into the glass, squeeze the juice from the lemon wedge into the drink, add the lemon to the glass, and stir the drink briefly.

285

KING'S CUP

Spicy, mild after-dinner drink
• Rocks glass

1½ ounces Galliano
¾ ounce light cream

Fill the glass one-third full with crushed ice. Pour the Galliano into the glass, add the cream, and stir briefly.

ORANGE GRAPEFRUIT

Fruity, mild drink for the evening
• Highball/Collins glass
• Shaker

1¾ ounces Grand Marnier
2 tsp. grenadine
Grapefruit juice for topping up
• *Garnish:*
1 maraschino cherry

Shake the Grand Marnier and grenadine together, with ice cubes, in the shaker and strain into the glass. Top up with grapefruit juice. Perch the cherry on the rim of the glass.

PEACHNUTS

Sweet, creamy drink for a party
• Champagne glass
• Shaker

1 ounce hazelnut-flavored liqueur
¾ ounce light cream
2 tsp. peach-flavored liqueur
2 tsp. light rum

Shake the ingredients together, with ice, in the shaker and strain into the champagne glass.

GREEN CAT

Sour short drink for a party
• Cocktail glass
• Shaker

1½ ounces kiwi-fruit-flavored liqueur
¾ ounce light rum
2 dashes lemon juice
1 dash Frothee
• *Garnish:*
1 maraschino cherry

Shake all the ingredients together, with ice, in the shaker and strain into the cocktail glass. Spear the cherry on a toothpick and add it to the glass.

Liqueurs

BODIL

Creamy, sweet drink for the afternoon
- Cocktail glass
- Shaker

¾ ounce Parfait Amour
¾ ounce green crème de menthe
2 tsp. cocoa-flavored liqueur
2 tsp. light cream
• Extra:
Grated nutmeg

Shake the ingredients together, with ice, in the shaker and strain into the glass. Sprinkle a little nutmeg on top.

NEW WAVE

Sweet after-dinner drink
- Cocktail glass
- Shaker

1 ounce peach-flavored liqueur
½ ounce pineapple juice
½ ounce light cream
2 tsp. Galliano
• Garnish:
1 piece of pineapple
1 strawberry

Shake all the ingredients together firmly, with ice, in the shaker and strain into the glass. Spear the fruit on a toothpick and lay the garnish across the rim of the glass.

BONN 2000

Medium-dry aperitif
- Cocktail glass
- Mixing glass

¾ ounce peach-flavored liqueur
¾ ounce Noilly Prat or other dry vermouth
2 tsp. Poire William
• Garnish:
1 mini pear

Mix the ingredients together, with ice, in the mixing glass and strain into the cocktail glass. Spear the mini pear on a toothpick and add it to the glass.

HAITI NIGHT

Fruity, low-alcohol drink for a party
- Highball/Collins glass
- Shaker

1½ ounces peach-flavored liqueur
¾ ounce mandarin-flavored syrup
2¾ ounces passion-fruit juice
2 tsp. lemon juice
• Garnish:
½ slice of lemon
½ slice of orange

Shake all the ingredients together, with ice, in the shaker and strain into the highball glass over crushed ice. Spear the slices of orange and lemon on a toothpick and lay the garnish across the rim of the glass.

DREAM OF LOVE

Fruity, long drink for a party
• Highball/Collins glass
• Shaker

2¾ ounces pineapple juice
1 ounce peach-flavored liqueur
¾ ounce Malibu or other coconut-flavored liqueur
2 tsp. blue curaçao
2 tsp. lemon juice
• Garnish:
1 small slice of melon
1 maraschino cherry
1 orchid

Shake the ingredients together, with ice, in the shaker and strain into the highball glass over crushed ice or ice cubes. Perch the slice of melon and maraschino cherry on the rim of the glass. Garnish the rim of the glass with the orchid.

SPRINGTIME

Sweet, long drink for a summer party
• Highball/Collins glass
• Shaker

2¾ ounces pineapple juice
1½ ounces peach-flavored liqueur
¾ ounce cream of coconut
2 tsp. lemon juice
• Garnish:
1 piece of pineapple
1 maraschino cherry

Shake all the ingredients together firmly, with ice, in the shaker and strain into the highball glass over crushed ice. Spear the piece of pineapple and maraschino cherry on a toothpick and perch on the rim of the glass.

Liqueurs

STAR

Sweet, refreshing drink for a party
- Highball/Collins glass
- Shaker

1½ ounces cream of coconut
1 ounce peach liqueur
1 ounce passion-fruit juice
¾ ounce brandy
2 tsp. lemon juice
- *Garnish:*
½ slice of orange
2 maraschino cherries

Fill the highball glass one-quarter full with crushed ice. Shake the ingredients together, with ice, in the shaker and strain into the highball glass. Spear the orange and cherries on a long wooden skewer, so they look like a sail, and add to the glass with a stirrer.

HAZEL

Sweet, long drink for a party
- Highball/Collins glass
- Shaker

1½ ounces pineapple juice
1 ounce peach liqueur
1 ounce cream of coconut
¾ ounce vodka
2 tsp. blue curaçao
- *Garnish:*
2 maraschino cherries
1 piece of pineapple

Shake all the ingredients, except the blue curaçao, together, with ice, in the shaker. Half fill the highball glass with crushed ice. Strain the drink into the highball glass, then float the curaçao on top of the prepared drink. Spear the cherries and piece of pineapple on a toothpick and lay the garnish across the rim of the glass.

PISTACHIO PISANG

Sweet after-dinner drink
• Cocktail glass
• Shaker

1 ounce Pisang Ambon
¾ ounce light cream
2 tsp. amaretto

Shake the ingredients together, with ice cubes, in the shaker and strain into the cocktail glass.

JUNGLE JUICE

Fruity, sweet drink for a party
• Highball/Collins glass
• Shaker

1¾ ounces orange juice
¾ ounce Pisang Ambon
¾ ounce lemon juice
2 tsp. apricot brandy
2 tsp. gin
• Garnish:
1 piece of pineapple
1 maraschino cherry

Shake all the ingredients together, with ice, in the shaker and strain into the highball glass over crushed ice. Perch the piece of pineapple on the rim of the glass and fasten the maraschino cherry to it with a small toothpick.

AZZURO

Fruity, long drink for a party
• Highball/Collins glass
• Shaker

1½ ounces passion-fruit juice
¾ ounce Pisang Ambon
¾ ounce blue curaçao
¾ ounce orange juice
1 dash Frothee
• Garnish:
Small pieces of fruit

Shake the ingredients together, with ice, in the shaker and strain into the highball glass over crushed ice. Spear the fruit on a toothpick and lay the garnish across the rim of the glass.

TROPICAL MAGIC I

Fruity, mild drink for a party
• Large rocks glass

1½ ounces Pisang Ambon
Passion-fruit juice for topping up
• Garnish:
1 slice of banana
1 maraschino cherry

Half fill the glass with ice cubes and pour the Pisang Ambon over the ice. Top up with passion-fruit juice and stir briefly. Spear the fruit on a toothpick and lay the garnish across the rim of the glass.

Liqueurs

GREEN ORANGE

Fruity, mild drink for the evening
• Highball/Collins glass

2¾ ounces orange juice

1½ ounces Pisang Ambon

• *Garnish:*

1 slice of orange

Pour the ingredients into the highball glass over ice cubes and stir well. Perch the slice of orange on the rim of the glass.

SOUTHERN COMFORT SOUR

Refreshing sour for a party
• Rocks glass
• Shaker

1½ ounces Southern Comfort

1½ ounces lemon juice

¾ ounce orange juice

2 tsp. sugar syrup

• *Garnish:*

½ slice of orange

1 maraschino cherry

Shake the ingredients together, with ice, in the shaker and strain into the glass over shaved ice. Spear the slice of orange and maraschino cherry on a toothpick and lay the garnish across the rim of the glass.

PINK SOUTHERN COMFORT

Spicy, mild drink for a party
• Rocks glass
• Shaker

¾ ounce Southern Comfort

¾ ounce light rum

2 tsp. grapefruit juice

2 dashes grenadine

Shake all the ingredients together, with ice cubes, in the shaker and strain into the rocks glass over ice cubes.

WHISKEY CREAM

Spicy, sweet after-dinner drink
• Cocktail glass
• Shaker

¾ ounce Southern Comfort

¾ ounce light cream

¾ ounce white crème de cacao

Shake all the ingredients together firmly, with ice cubes, in the shaker and strain into the cocktail glass.

STEAMBOAT

Refreshing, long drink for a party
• Highball/Collins glass

1½ ounces Southern Comfort
3½ ounces soda water
• Garnish:
1 slice of lemon

Pour the Southern Comfort into the
highball glass over ice, top up with soda
water, and stir. Add the slice of lemon
to the glass. Serve with a long stirrer.

HONOLULU JUICER

Fruity, mild drink for a summer party
• Highball/Collins glass
• Shaker

2 ounces pineapple juice
1½ ounces Southern Comfort
¾ ounce dark rum
¾ ounce lemon juice
¾ ounce lime juice
• Garnish:
½ slice of pineapple
1 maraschino cherry

Shake all the ingredients together
firmly, with ice, in the shaker. Fill the
highball glass one-third full with
crushed ice and strain the cocktail into
the glass. Perch the slice of pineapple
on the rim of the glass and fasten the
cherry to it with a toothpick.

NEW ORLEANS

Fruity, mild drink for a summer party
• Highball/Collins glass
• Shaker

1½ ounces orange juice
1 ounce Southern Comfort
¾ ounce bourbon
¾ ounce lemon juice
2 tsp. almond-flavored liqueur

Shake all the ingredients together, with
ice cubes, in the shaker and strain into
the highball glass over crushed ice.
Serve with a straw.

TONIC OF THE SOUTH

Bittersweet, long drink for the evening
• Highball/Collins glass

1½ ounces Southern Comfort
Tonic water for topping up
• Garnish:
1 slice of lime

Pour the Southern Comfort into the
highball glass over ice cubes. Top up
with tonic water and stir briefly. Perch
the slice of lime on the rim of the glass.
Serve with a stirrer.

Liqueurs

SOUTHERN COLA

Sweet, long drink for the evening
• Highball/Collins glass

1½ ounces Southern Comfort
Cola for topping up
• Garnish:
1 slice of lemon

Pour the Southern Comfort into the highball glass over ice cubes. Top up with cola and stir briefly. Perch the slice of lemon on the rim of the glass. Serve with a straw.

MISSISSIPPI II

Alcoholic, short drink for any occasion
• Rocks glass

1 ounce Southern Comfort
2 tsp. bourbon
2 tsp. dry vermouth
• Garnish:
¼ slice of orange

Mix the ingredients together, with ice, in the glass. Add the slice of orange to the glass. Serve with a stirrer.

SOUTHERN SUMMER

Fruity, mild drink for a summer party
• Highball/Collins glass
• Shaker

1½ ounces Southern Comfort
1½ ounces peach juice
¾ ounce Canadian whisky
2 tsp. lemon juice
Ginger ale for topping up
• Garnish:
1 slice of lemon
1 maraschino cherry

Shake all the ingredients, except the ginger ale, together, with ice cubes, in the shaker and strain into the highball glass over ice cubes. Top up with ginger ale and stir briefly. Perch the slice of lemon on the rim of the glass and fasten the cherry to it with a toothpick.

VELVET HAMMER

Sweet after-dinner drink
• Cocktail glass
• Shaker

¾ ounce Tia Maria or other coffee-flavored liqueur

¾ ounce Cointreau or other orange-flavored liqueur

¾ ounce light cream

Shake the ingredients together, with ice, in the shaker and strain into the cocktail glass.

CREAM DREAM

Creamy, sweet drink for a party
• Cocktail glass
• Shaker

1 ounce Tia Maria or other coffee-flavored liqueur

¾ ounce amaretto

¾ ounce light cream

2 tsp. Galliano

• Garnish:

1 maraschino cherry

Shake the ingredients together firmly, with ice, in the shaker and strain into the glass. Perch the maraschino cherry on the rim of the glass.

V. W.

Aromatic, pear-flavored aperitif
• Cocktail glass
• Mixing glass

1 ounce Poire William

1 ounce sweet white vermouth

• Garnish:

1 maraschino cherry

Mix the ingredients, with ice, in the mixing glass and strain into the cocktail glass. Spear the cherry on a toothpick and add it to the glass.

SWEET PEAR

Sweet, long drink for a party
• Highball/Collins glass
• Shaker

2¾ ounces orange juice

1 ounce Poire William

2 tsp. orange curaçao

¾ ounce cream of coconut

• Garnish:

1 mini pear

Shake the ingredients together, with ice, in the shaker and strain into the highball glass over crushed ice. Perch the mini pear on the rim of the glass.

BOSTON

JERSEY

Calvados-based drinks

DIKI DIKI

CALVADOS SOUR

APPLE BLOSSOM

GREENWICH

CALVADOS COCKTAIL

BOSTON

Tangy aperitif
- Champagne or cocktail glass
- Mixing glass

1 ounce Calvados
2 tsp. gin
2 tsp. scotch

Mix the ingredients together, with ice, in the mixing glass and strain into the champagne or cocktail glass.

JACK ROSE

Fruity, short aperitif
- Champagne or cocktail glass
- Shaker

1 ounce Calvados
¾ ounce lemon juice
2 tsp. grenadine

Shake the ingredients together, with ice, in the shaker and strain into the glass.

ANGEL'S HOPE

Medium-dry aperitif
- Cocktail glass
- Shaker

¾ ounce Calvados
¾ ounce gin
¾ ounce orange-flavored liqueur

Shake the ingredients, with ice, in the shaker and strain into the cocktail glass.

DIKI DIKI

Tangy aperitif
- Champagne or cocktail glass
- Shaker

1½ ounces Calvados
2 tsp. Swedish Punch
2 tsp. grapefruit juice

Shake the ingredients together, with ice, in the shaker and strain into the cocktail glass.

JERSEY

Tangy, short aperitif
- Cocktail glass
- Shaker

1 ounce Calvados
¾ ounce lemon juice
2 tsp. sugar syrup
1 dash Angostura bitters

Shake the ingredients together, with ice, in the shaker and strain into the cocktail glass.

LIBERTY

Aromatic aperitif
- Cocktail glass
- Mixing glass

1½ ounces Calvados
¾ ounce rum
1 dash sugar syrup

Mix the ingredients together, with ice, in the mixing glass and strain into the cocktail glass.

Calvados

Boston (left), Jack Rose (top right), Diki Diki (bottom right)

BENTLEY

Medium-dry aperitif
• Cocktail glass
• Mixing glass

1 ounce Calvados
1 ounce Dubonnet

Mix the ingredients together, with ice, in the mixing glass and strain into the cocktail glass. Add ice to taste.

BIG APPLE I

Aromatic drink for any time of day
• Cocktail glass
• Mixing glass

1 ounce Calvados
2 tsp. brandy
1 ounce apple juice

Mix the ingredients together, with ice, in the mixing glass and strain into the cocktail glass.

WHITE WING

Spicy, fresh after-dinner drink
• Cocktail glass
• Shaker

1 ounce Calvados
1 ounce white peppermint-flavored liqueur

Shake all the ingredients together, with ice, in the shaker and strain into the cocktail glass.

CALVADOS SOUR

Refreshing sour for the summer
• Rocks glass
• Shaker

1½ ounces Calvados
¾ ounce lemon juice
2 tsp. sugar syrup
• Garnish:
½ slice of orange
1 maraschino cherry

Shake the ingredients together, with ice, in the shaker and strain into the glass. Perch the slice of orange and the cherry on the rim of the glass. The addition of a little mineral water is optional.

NORMANDY I

Fruity, medium-dry aperitif
• Paris goblet with a sugared rim
• Shaker

1 ounce Calvados
¾ ounce orange juice
2 tsp. sugar syrup
• Garnish:
1 lemon peel spiral

Shake the ingredients together, with ice, in the shaker and strain into the balloon glass with the sugared rim. Add the lemon peel spiral to the glass.

Calvados

CALVA JULEP

Spicy, fruity julep for the summer months
- Rocks glass

3 mint leaves	
1 tsp. sugar	
1½ ounces Calvados	
1 tsp. lemon juice	
• Garnish:	
Sprig of mint	

Crush the mint leaves with the sugar in the glass. Add the Calvados and lemon juice, stir, and leave to infuse for a few minutes. Add 2 ice cubes to the drink. Hang the sprig of mint on the rim of the glass.

APPLEJACK RABBIT

Fruity, delicately tangy drink for the evening
- Cocktail glass
- Shaker

¾ ounce Calvados or applejack	
¾ ounce orange juice	
¾ ounce lemon juice	
¾ ounce maple syrup	
• Garnish:	
½ slice of orange	

Shake all the ingredients together firmly, with ice, in the shaker and strain into the glass. Perch the slice of orange on the rim of the glass.

VERMONT

Mild, fruity after-dinner drink
- Cocktail glass
- Shaker

1½ ounces Calvados	
2 tsp. grenadine	
2 tsp. lemon juice	

Shake all the ingredients together, with ice, in the shaker and strain into the glass.

LUGGER

Medium-dry aperitif
- Cocktail glass
- Mixing glass

¾ ounce Calvados	
¾ ounce brandy	
2 tsp. apricot brandy	

Mix the ingredients together, with ice, in the mixing glass and strain into the cocktail glass.

B AND C

Fruity, spicy after-dinner drink
- Rocks glass

¾ ounce Benedictine	
¾ ounce Calvados	

Mix the ingredients together, with ice cubes, in the glass.

FUN APPLE

Fruity, delicately tangy drink for a party
• Cocktail glass
• Shaker

¾ ounce Calvados
¾ ounce of your favorite cider
2 tsp. brandy
2 tsp. gin

Shake all the ingredients together in the shaker and strain into the glass.

GREENWICH

Mild, spicy after-dinner drink
• Cocktail glass
• Shaker

¾ ounce Calvados
¾ ounce gin
¾ ounce white crème de cacao

Shake all the ingredients together, with ice, in the shaker and strain into the glass.

NICE ADVENTURE

Tangy, fruity drink for any time of year
• Cocktail glass
• Shaker

1½ ounces Calvados
¾ ounce gin
¾ ounce grapefruit juice

Shake all the ingredients together, with ice, in the shaker and strain into the glass.

APPLE BLOSSOM

Fruity, delicately tangy drink for a summer party
• Champagne glass
• Blender

1 ounce Calvados
¾ ounce apple juice
1 tbsp. maple syrup
2 tsp. lemon juice
• Garnish:
1 slice of lemon

Mix all the ingredients together briefly, with a scoop of crushed ice, in the blender and pour into the champagne glass. Perch the slice of lemon on the rim.

LUMBERJACK

Fruity, aromatic after-dinner drink
• Rocks glass
• Mixing glass

1 ounce Calvados
2 tsp. scotch
2 tsp. gin
• Extra:
1 piece of lemon peel

Mix all the ingredients together, with ice cubes, in the mixing glass and strain into the glass. Squeeze the lemon peel over the drink and add the peel to the glass.

Calvados

Calvados Cocktail I (left), Calvados Cocktail II (right)

CALVADOS COCKTAIL I

Fruity, sweet drink for the evening
• Cocktail glass
• Shaker

1½ ounces Calvados
¾ ounce grenadine
¾ ounce orange juice
1 dash orange bitters

Shake all the ingredients together, with ice, in the shaker and strain into the glass.

CALVADOS COCKTAIL II

Fruity, mild drink for the evening or as an after-dinner drink
• Cocktail glass
• Shaker

¾ ounce Calvados
¾ ounce orange-flavored liqueur
¾ ounce orange juice
• Garnish:
½ slice of orange

Shake all the ingredients together, with ice, in the shaker and strain into the glass. Perch the slice of orange on the rim of the glass.

STAR COCKTAIL

Fruity, spicy, tangy aperitif
- Cocktail glass
- Mixing glass

1½ ounces Calvados
¾ ounce dry vermouth
1 dash Angostura bitters
- *Garnish:*
1 green olive

Mix all the ingredients together in the mixing glass and strain into the cocktail glass over ice cubes. Spear the olive on a toothpick and add it to the glass.

KIDDY CAR

Tangy, fruity after-dinner drink
- Cocktail glass
- Shaker

1¾ ounces Calvados
2 tsp. lemon juice
2 dashes orange-flavored liqueur
- *Garnish:*
1 maraschino cherry

Shake all the ingredients together, with ice, in the shaker and strain into the glass. Perch the cherry on the rim of the glass.

NEW YORKER APPLE

Fruity, delicately tangy aperitif
- Cocktail glass
- Mixing glass

1½ ounces Calvados
¾ ounce sweet red vermouth
1 dash orange bitters
- *Garnish:*
1 maraschino cherry

Mix all the ingredients together, with ice, in the mixing glass and strain into the glass. Perch the cherry on the rim of the glass.

FROZEN FRUITS

Fruity, delicately dry drink for a summer party
- Cocktail glass
- Blender

1 ounce Calvados
2 tsp. banana-flavored liqueur
2 tsp. lime juice
- *Garnish:*
1 slice of banana

Mix all the ingredients together, with a scoop full of crushed ice, in the blender and pour into the glass. Spear the slice of banana on a toothpick and lay the garnish across the rim of the glass.

Calvados

APPLEHAWK

Fruity, tangy drink for any time of year
• Cocktail glass
• Shaker

1 ounce Calvados

1 ounce grapefruit juice

1 tbsp. sugar syrup

• Garnish:

1 maraschino cherry

Shake all the ingredients together firmly, with ice, in the shaker and strain into the glass. Perch the cherry on the rim of the glass.

FINE APPLE

Fruity, delicately tangy drink for the evening
• Rocks glass
• Mixing glass

¾ ounce Calvados

2 tsp. cognac

2 tsp. orange-flavored liqueur

• Extra:

1 piece of orange peel

1 piece of lemon peel

Mix all the ingredients together, with ice, in the mixing glass and strain into the glass over ice cubes. Squeeze the lemon and orange peels over the drink and add both peels to the glass.

KICKER

Spicy, rather sweet after-dinner drink
• Cocktail glass
• Mixing glass

¾ ounce Calvados

¾ ounce dark rum

¾ ounce sweet red vermouth

• Garnish:

1 maraschino cherry

Mix all the ingredients together, with ice, in the mixing glass and strain into the cocktail glass. Add the cherry to the glass.

APPLE FIZZ

Fruity, slightly tangy drink for any time of year
• Rocks glass
• Shaker

1 ounce Calvados

1 ounce lemon juice

1 ounce maple syrup

Soda water for topping up

• Garnish:

1 slice of lemon

Shake all the ingredients, except the soda water, together, with ice, in the shaker and strain into the glass. Top up with soda water and stir. Perch the slice of lemon on the rim of the glass.

GOLDEN HEATH

Fruity, tangy after-dinner drink
• Cocktail glass
• Shaker

¾ ounce Calvados

¾ ounce Drambuie

¾ ounce lemon juice

Shake all the ingredients together, with ice, in the shaker and strain into the glass.

NEWTON'S APPLE

Fruity, slightly bitter after-dinner drink
• Cocktail glass
• Mixing glass

1½ ounces Calvados

2 tsp. triple sec

2 dashes Angostura bitters

Mix all the ingredients together, with ice cubes, in the mixing glass and strain into the cocktail glass.

JACK CARNATION

Fruity, delicately tangy drink for a party
• Cocktail glass
• Shaker

1½ ounces Calvados

1 ounce lemon juice

2 tsp. grenadine

2 tsp. sugar syrup

Shake all the ingredients together, with ice, in the shaker and strain into the glass.

CALVADOS COBBLER

Fruity cobbler for hot days
• Tulip-shaped wine glass

2 ounces hard apple cider

1 ounce Calvados

2 tsp. lemon juice

2 tsp. sugar syrup

• Garnish:

1 mini apple

1 slice of lemon

Fill the glass half full with crushed ice. Add the Calvados, lemon juice, and sugar syrup and stir briefly. Top up with cider and stir again. Perch the fruit on the rim of the glass.

APPLES AND MORE

Fruity, delicately tangy drink for a party
• Cocktail glass with sugared rim
• Shaker

¾ ounce Calvados

½ ounce apricot brandy

¾ ounce lemon juice

2 tsp. grenadine

1 dash orange bitters

Shake all the ingredients together, with ice, in the shaker and strain into the glass with the sugared rim.

Calvados

Calvados Cobbler (back left), Apples and More (back right), Golden Heath (front)

CIDER COCKTAIL

Fruity, short drink for any time of year
• Small Paris goblet

¾ ounce Calvados
Cider for topping up
• Garnish:
1 apple peel spiral

Pour the Calvados into the goblet, top up with cider, and stir briefly. Hang the apple peel spiral over the rim of the glass.

APPLE

Fruity, delicately tangy drink for the evening
• Rocks glass
• Mixing glass

1½ ounces apple juice
1 ounce Calvados
¾ ounce gin
1 tsp. lemon juice

Mix all the ingredients together, with ice, in the mixing glass and strain into the rocks glass.

HAWAIIAN APPLE

Fruity drink for any time of year
• Rocks glass
• Shaker

1½ ounces Calvados
½ ounce brandy
¾ ounce pineapple juice
• Extra:
1 slice of pineapple, diced

Shake all the ingredients together, with ice, in the shaker and strain into the glass over ice cubes. Add the diced pineapple. Serve with a toothpick.

FROZEN APPLE

Fruity, delicately tangy drink for a summer party
• Cocktail glass
• Blender

1 ounce Calvados
1 tbsp. sugar
2 tsp. lime juice
½ white of an egg

Mix all the ingredients together, with a bar scoop full of crushed ice, in the blender. Pour into the glass.

Calvados

APPLE SUNSET

Fruity, sweet drink for any time of year
• Highball/Collins glass

1½ ounces Calvados
2 tsp. crème de cassis
2 tsp. grenadine
3½ ounces orange juice
• Garnish:
1 maraschino cherry

Mix the Calvados, crème de cassis, and grenadine together, with ice cubes, in the highball glass. Slowly top up with orange juice. Perch the cherry on the rim of the glass. Serve with a straw.

MOONLIGHT CUP

Mild, fruity drink for the evening
• Highball/Collins glass
• Shaker

2 ounces apple juice
1½ ounces Calvados
½ tsp. sugar
Ginger ale for topping up
• Garnish:
1 slice of lemon

Shake all the ingredients, except the ginger ale, together, with ice, in the shaker and strain into the glass. Top up with ginger ale and stir briefly. Add the slice of lemon to the glass.

KENNY

Tangy, spicy drink for the evening
• Highball/Collins glass

1½ ounces Calvados
¾ ounce sweet red vermouth
Tonic water for topping up
• Garnish:
1 slice of lemon

Mix all the ingredients together slowly, with ice cubes, in the highball glass. Perch the slice of lemon on the rim of the glass.

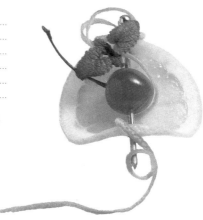

JACK COLLINS

Refreshing Collins for any time of day
• Collins/highball glass

1½ ounces Calvados
¾ ounce lemon juice
2 tsp. sugar syrup
Soda water for topping up
• Garnish:
½ slice of lemon
1 maraschino cherry

Mix all the ingredients, except the soda water, together, with ice, in the glass. Top up with soda water and stir well. Perch the slice of lemon on the rim of the glass and add the cherry to the glass. Serve with a long stirrer.

BITTER APPLE

Fruity, tangy drink for a summer party
• Large rocks glass

1½ ounces Calvados
2 dashes Angostura bitters
Soda water for topping up
• Extra:
1 piece of lemon peel

Half fill the glass with crushed ice. Pour the Calvados and Angostura bitters over the ice, top up with soda water, and stir carefully. Squeeze the lemon peel over the drink.

TROPICAL APPLE

Fruity, delicately tangy drink for a summer party
• Highball/Collins glass
• Shaker

1¾ ounces Calvados
¾ ounce light rum
¾ ounce lime juice
2 tsp. almond syrup
• Extra:
1 lime quarter

Shake all the ingredients together firmly, with ice, in the shaker. Half fill the glass with crushed ice and strain the cocktail into the glass. Add the lime quarter to the glass.

APPLE SUNRISE

Mild, fruity drink for any time of year
• Highball/Collins glass

1½ ounces Calvados
1 dash lemon juice
2¾ ounces orange juice
¾ ounce crème de cassis

Half fill the highball glass with crushed ice. Pour the Calvados, lemon juice, and orange juice into the glass and stir. Slowly pour the crème de cassis into the glass so it floats on top of the drink. Serve with a straw.

DRUGSTORE

CAMPUS

PATHETIC

D.B.U.

Bitters-based drinks

CAMPANILE

CAMPARI TONIC

APRICAMP

COLUMBO

DRUGSTORE

Bitter after-dinner drink
• Cocktail glass

1 ounce Fernet Branca or other herbal bitters
¾ ounce sweet red vermouth
2 tsp. white crème de menthe

Mix the ingredients together in the glass.

PATHETIC

Slightly bitter, short drink
• Cocktail glass
• Mixing glass

¾ ounce orange curaçao
¾ ounce dry vermouth
½ ounce Campari

Mix the ingredients together, with ice, in the mixing glass and strain into the cocktail glass.

CABALLERO

Fruity, delicately tangy drink for the evening
• Cocktail glass
• Mixing glass

¾ ounce Campari
1 ounce banana-flavored liqueur

Mix the ingredients together, with ice, in the mixing glass and strain into the cocktail glass.

CAMPARI FLIP

Fruity, tangy flip for the evening
• Champagne flute
• Shaker

1½ ounces Campari
1½ ounces orange juice
2 tsp. gin
1 egg yolk

Shake all the ingredients together firmly, with ice, in the shaker and strain into the champagne flute.

SHAKERATO

Bitter aperitif
• Cocktail glass
• Shaker

1¾ ounces Campari
3 dashes lemon juice
• Extra:
1 piece of lemon peel

Shake the ingredients together, with ice, in the shaker and strain into the glass. Squeeze the lemon peel over the drink and add the peel to the glass.

Bitters

Drugstore (back left), Campari Flip (back right), Pathetic (front)

COCONUT BITTER

Aromatic, fruity drink for a party
• Rocks glass
• Shaker

1½ ounces orange juice
¾ ounce Campari
¾ ounce vodka
2 tsp. cream of coconut
• Garnish:
1 slice of orange

Shake all the ingredients together, with ice, in the shaker and strain into the glass. Perch the slice of orange on the rim of the glass.

H. S. V.

Refreshing, bitter sparkling-wine aperitif
• Champagne flute

1½ ounces Campari
Dry champagne or sparkling wine for topping up
• Extra:
1 piece of orange peel

Pour the Campari into the champagne flute and top up with champagne. Add the piece of orange peel to the glass.

FANCY CAMPARI

Tangy, short aperitif
• Cocktail glass
• Mixing glass

1½ ounces Campari
¾ ounce vodka
2 dashes Angostura bitters

Mix all the ingredients together, with ice, in the mixing glass and strain into the cocktail glass.

SILVER CAMPARI

Dry, tangy champagne aperitif
• Champagne glass
• Shaker

¾ ounce Campari
¾ ounce gin
1 ounce lemon juice
2 tsp. sugar syrup
Dry champagne or sparkling wine for topping up
• Extra:
1 piece of lemon peel

Shake all the ingredients, except the champagne, together, with ice, in the shaker and strain into the champagne glass. Top up with champagne and squeeze the lemon peel over the drink.

Bitters

FERNANDO I

Fruity, delicately tangy drink for the
evening
• Cocktail glass
• Shaker

1 ounce banana-flavored liqueur

¾ ounce Campari

*2 tsp. Escorial or other herb-flavored
liqueur*

Shake all the ingredients together, with
ice, in the shaker and strain into the
glass.

CAMPANILE

Fruity, tangy drink for the evening
• Large cocktail glass
• Shaker

1½ ounces orange juice

¾ ounce Campari

¾ ounce gin

¾ ounce apricot brandy

Shake all the ingredients together, with
ice cubes, in the shaker and strain into
the cocktail glass.

CAMPUS

Tangy, spicy drink for the evening
• Rocks glass
• Mixing glass

1¾ ounces Campari

¾ ounce scotch

2 tsp. gin

• Extra:

1 orange segment

Mix all the ingredients together, with
ice, in the mixing glass and strain into
the rocks glass over ice cubes. Add the
orange segment to the glass.

AMERICANO II

Light, long aperitif
• Highball/Collins glass

1½ ounces Campari

¾ ounce sweet red vermouth

*Sparkling mineral water for topping
up*

• Garnish:

½ slice of orange

Pour the Campari and vermouth into
the highball glass over ice cubes and
stir. Add the slice of orange to the glass
and top up the drink with mineral
water. Serve with a stirrer.

D. B. U.

Refreshing champagne aperitif or after-dinner drink
- Champagne glass or flute
- Shaker

¾ ounce Campari
¾ ounce Cointreau or other orange-flavored liqueur
¾ ounce grapefruit juice
Dry champagne or sparkling wine for topping up

Shake all the ingredients, except the champagne, together, with plenty of ice, in the shaker and strain into the champagne flute. Top up with champagne.

CAMPARI AND LEMON

Tangy, fruity aperitif
- Highball/Collins glass

1¾ ounces Campari
Bitter lemon for topping up

Pour the Campari into the highball glass over ice cubes. Top up with bitter lemon and stir briefly.

ROSEMIE

Tangy, fruity aperitif
- Highball/Collins glass

2¾ ounces grapefruit juice
1½ ounces Campari
Champagne for topping up
- *Extra:*
1 slice of orange

Pour the grapefruit juice and Campari into the highball glass over ice cubes and stir. Top up with champagne. Add the slice of orange to the glass.

CAMPARI AND TONIC

Refreshing, long drink for hot days
- Highball/Collins glass

1½ ounces Campari
Tonic water for topping up
- *Extra:*
1 lemon wedge

Pour the Campari into the highball glass over ice cubes and top up with tonic water. Add the wedge of lemon to the glass. Serve with a stirrer.

Bitters

CAMPARI AND ORANGE

Refreshing, long drink for hot days
• Highball/Collins glass

1½ ounces Campari
Orange juice for topping up
• *Garnish:*
½ slice of orange

Pour the Campari into the highball glass over ice and top up with orange juice. Add the slice of orange to the glass and serve the drink with a stirrer.

CAMPARI AND SODA

Tangy, long aperitif
• Highball/Collins glass

1¾ ounces Campari
½ slice of lemon
Soda water for topping up

Put the Campari and slice of lemon into the highball glass with some ice cubes. Top up with soda water and stir briefly. Serve with a stirrer.

CAMPOR

Tangy, fruity drink for the evening
• Highball/Collins glass

1½ ounces Campari
1 dash orange bitters
1 dash lemon juice
Orange juice for topping up
• *Garnish:*
1 slice of orange

Mix the Campari, orange bitters, and lemon juice together, with ice cubes, in the highball glass. Top up with the orange juice and stir briefly. Perch the slice of orange on the rim of the glass.

CAMPARI PUNCH

Tangy, fruity drink for the evening
• Balloon glass
• Shaker

1½ ounces orange juice
1½ ounces grapefruit juice
1 ounce Campari
¾ ounce Cointreau or other orange-flavored liqueur
¾ ounce lemon juice

Shake all the ingredients together, with ice, in the shaker and pour into the balloon glass.

APRICAMP

Tangy, fruity drink for a party
• Paris goblet or red wine glass
• Mixing glass

1 ounce Campari

1 ounce apricot brandy

Orange juice for topping up
• *Extra:*

1 piece of orange peel

Mix the Campari and apricot brandy together, with ice, in the mixing glass and strain into the glass. Top up with orange juice and stir again. Add the orange peel to the glass.

ADRIA

Tangy, fruity drink for a summer party
• Highball/Collins glass
• Shaker

1 ounce Campari

¾ ounce vodka

1 tbsp. orange-flavored liqueur

1 tbsp. lemon juice

Bitter orange for topping up
• *Garnish:*

2 kumquats

Shake all the ingredients, except the bitter orange, together, with ice, in the shaker and strain into the highball glass over ice cubes. Top up with bitter orange and stir briefly. Spear the kumquats on a toothpick and lay the garnish across the rim of the glass.

Bitters

LONG JEAN

Tangy, fruity drink for the evening
• Rocks glass

¾ ounce Campari

2 tsp. Grand Marnier

Orange juice for topping up

• Garnish:

1 slice of orange

1 slice of lemon

Pour the Campari and Grand Marnier into the glass over ice cubes. Top up with orange juice and stir well. Perch the slices of citrus fruit on the rim of the glass.

COLUMBO

Tangy, fruity long drink for the evening
• Highball/Collins glass

1½ ounces Campari

1½ ounces orange juice

¾ ounce lemon juice

¾ ounce lime cordial

Tonic water for topping up

• Garnish:

¼ slice of lime

Mix all the ingredients, except the tonic water, together, with ice cubes, in the highball glass. Top up with tonic water and stir briefly. Perch the slice of lime on the rim of the glass.

VELVET AND SILK

Tangy, spicy aperitif
• Rocks glass

1 ounce Cynar
¾ ounce gin
• Garnish:
1 slice of lemon

Shake the ingredients together, with 3 ice cubes, in the glass. Perch the slice of lemon on the rim of the glass.

CYNAR AND ORANGE

Elegant, tangy aperitif
• Highball/Collins glass

1½ ounces Cynar
1 dash orange bitters
Orange juice for topping up
• Garnish:
1 slice of orange

Mix the Cynar and orange bitters together, with ice cubes, in the highball glass. Top up with orange juice and stir briefly. Perch the slice of orange on the rim of the glass.

CYNAR COCKTAIL

Tangy, spicy aperitif
• Cocktail glass

1 ounce Cynar
1 ounce sweet white vermouth
• Garnish:
½ slice of orange

Mix the ingredients together, with 2 ice cubes, in the cocktail glass. Perch the slice of orange on the rim of the glass.

CYNAR AND SODA

Refined, tangy aperitif
• Highball/Collins glass

1½ ounces Cynar
1 dash orange bitters
Soda water for topping up

Mix the Cynar and orange bitters together, with ice cubes, in the highball glass. Top up with soda water and stir briefly.

Bitters

FRIENDS

Tangy, spicy drink for the evening
• Cocktail glass
• Mixing glass

¾ ounce Aperol
¾ ounce gin
¾ ounce dry vermouth
• Extra:
1 piece of lemon peel

Mix all the ingredients together, with ice, in the mixing glass and strain into the cocktail glass. Squeeze the lemon peel over the drink and add the peel to the glass.

SIENA

Spicy, refined, tangy drink for the evening
• Cocktail glass
• Mixing glass

¾ ounce Aperol
¾ ounce gin
¾ ounce sweet white vermouth
• Garnish:
1 maraschino cherry

Mix all the ingredients together, with ice, in the mixing glass and strain into the glass. Perch the cherry on the rim of the glass.

GILIA

Tangy aperitif or after-dinner drink
• Rocks glass

1½ ounces Aperol
¾ ounce scotch

Mix the ingredients together, with ice cubes, in the glass. Serve with a stirrer.

SHAFT

Dry, sparkling aperitif
• Highball/Collins glass

1 ounce Aperol
1 ounce gin
Dry sparkling wine or champagne for topping up
• Garnish:
½ slice of orange

Mix all the ingredients, except the sparkling wine, together, with ice cubes, in the highball glass. Top up with sparkling wine. Perch the slice of orange on the rim of the glass and serve the drink with a stirrer.

SUMMER IN ITALY

Tangy, spicy drink for the evening
• Highball/Collins glass

¾ ounce Amaro Siciliano
¾ ounce gin
1 orange segment
Tonic water for topping up

Mix the Amaro and gin together, with
plenty of ice, in the highball glass. Add
the orange segment to the glass, top up
with tonic water, and stir briefly.

RAMAZZOTTI LONG

Elegant, tangy after-dinner drink
• Highball/Collins glass

1½ ounces Amaro Felsina Ramazzotti
or other bitters
2 dashes orange bitters
Soda water for topping up
• Garnish:
1 slice of orange

Mix the bitters together, with ice cubes,
in the highball glass. Top up with soda
water and stir briefly. Perch the slice of
orange on the rim of the glass.

Bitters

RAMAZZOTTI SPECIAL

Spicy, elegant after-dinner drink
• Rocks glass

1¾ ounces Amaro Felsina Ramazzotti
or other bitters
1 tbsp. lemon juice
• Garnish:
1 slice of lemon

Mix the bitters and lemon juice
together, with ice cubes, in the glass.
Perch the slice of lemon on the rim of
the glass.

NATALIA

Spicy, elegant, tangy after-dinner drink
• Cocktail glass
• Mixing glass

¾ ounce Amaro Siciliano
¾ ounce gin
¾ ounce sweet white vermouth
1 dash orange-flavored liqueur
• Garnish:
½ slice of orange

Mix all the ingredients together, with
ice, in the mixing glass and strain into
the cocktail glass. Perch the slice of
orange on the rim of the glass.

PAJA

Elegant, tangy after-dinner drink
• Highball/Collins glass

1 lemon wedge
1 orange segment
1½ ounces Amaro Siciliano
4 ounces carbonated orange drink

Put the citrus fruit in the highball glass. Pour the bitters and orange drink over the fruit, stir briefly, and add a few ice cubes.

PINKY

Medium-dry, creamy drink for a party
• Highball/Collins glass
• Shaker

2 ounces pineapple juice
1½ ounces cream of coconut
1 ounce Aperol
¾ ounce gin
• Garnish:
1 piece of pineapple
1 maraschino cherry
Sprig of mint

Shake the ingredients together firmly, with ice, in the shaker and strain into the highball glass. Spear the piece of pineapple, the cherry, and the sprig of mint on a toothpick, and perch the fruit on the rim of the glass.

AMARO SOUR

Spicy, tangy sour for the evening
• Rocks glass
• Shaker

1½ ounces Amaro Siciliano
¾ ounce lemon juice
2 tsp. sugar syrup
Soda water for topping up
• Garnish:
1 slice of orange
1 slice of lemon
1 maraschino cherry

Shake all the ingredients, except the soda water, together firmly, with ice, in the shaker and strain into the glass over ice cubes. Spear the fruit on a toothpick and add it to the glass. Top up the drink with soda water and stir briefly.

RED LIGHTNING

Tangy, spicy after-dinner drink
• Highball/Collins glass

1½ ounces Amaro Siciliano
¾ ounce Campari
Soda water for topping up
• Garnish:
1 lemon peel spiral
1 maraschino cherry

Mix the Amaro and Campari together, with plenty of ice, in the highball glass. Top up with soda water and stir briefly. Hang the spiral of peel over the rim of the glass. Perch the cherry on the rim of the glass.

RIDLEY   DORADO

JALAPA

Tequila-based
drinks

TAMPICO

LA CONGA

MEXICAN DREAM   DEBUTANTE

TEQUILA SOUR

TEQUILA GIMLET

TEQUILA SOUR SPECIAL

Fruity, tangy sour for the summer
• Rocks glass
• Shaker

1 ounce tequila
½ ounce apricot brandy
2 tsp. lemon juice

Shake all the ingredients together firmly, with ice, in the shaker and strain into the glass.

SIERRA MARGARITA

Aromatic aperitif
• Cocktail glass with salt-coated rim
• Shaker

1½ ounces Sierra or other white tequila
¾ ounce lemon or lime juice
2 tsp. orange-flavored liqueur

Shake the ingredients together, with ice, in the shaker and strain into the glass.

JALAPA

Fruity, mildly tangy drink for the evening
• Cocktail glass
• Shaker

1 ounce tequila
1 ounce lime juice
1 ounce passion-fruit nectar

Shake all the ingredients together well, with ice, in the shaker and strain into the glass.

DORADO

Delicately tangy drink for any time of year
• Cocktail glass
• Shaker

1¼ ounces tequila
¾ ounce lemon juice
2 tsp. honey

Shake all the ingredients together, with ice, in the shaker and strain into the glass.

RIDLEY

Spicy after-dinner drink
• Rocks glass

1 ounce tequila
1 ounce gin
1 dash Galliano

Half fill the glass with crushed ice. Pour the tequila, gin, and finally the Galliano into the glass. Stir briefly.

BRAVE BULL

Mild, spicy drink for the evening
• Sherry glass
• Mixing glass

1 ounce tequila
1 ounce Kahlúa

Mix all the ingredients together, with ice, in the mixing glass and strain into the sherry glass.

Tequila

Sierra Margarita (back), Brave Bull (middle), Jalapa (front)

TOREADOR

Sweet after-dinner drink
• Cocktail glass
• Shaker

1 ounce tequila
2 tsp. brown crème de cacao
2 tsp. light cream
• Garnish:
Whipped cream
Cocoa powder

Shake all the ingredients together, with ice, in the shaker and strain into the glass. Pile whipped cream on top of the drink and sprinkle a little cocoa on top.

LA CONGA

Fruity, slightly bitter drink for any time of year
• Rocks glass

1½ ounces tequila
2 tsp. pineapple juice
2 dashes Angostura bitters
Soda water for topping up
• Garnish:
1 slice of lemon

Mix all the ingredients, except the soda water, together, with ice cubes, in the glass. Add soda water to taste and stir briefly. Perch the slice of lemon on the rim of the glass.

BITTERSWEET TEQUILA

Fruity, bittersweet drink for a summer party
• Rocks glass
• Shaker

1 ounce tequila
½ ounce strawberry-flavored liqueur
2 tsp. lemon juice
2 dashes orange bitters
• Garnish:
2 strawberries
1 lime quarter

Shake all the ingredients together firmly, with ice, in the shaker and strain into the glass. Add a few ice cubes and the fruit to the glass.

COCONUT TEQUILA

Fruity, delicately tangy drink for a summer party
• Cocktail glass
• Shaker

1 ounce tequila
2 tsp. cream of coconut
2 tsp. lemon juice
1 tbsp. maraschino
• Garnish:
½ slice of pineapple
½ slice of kiwi fruit

Shake all the ingredients together firmly, with crushed ice, in the shaker and strain into the glass. Perch the fruit on the rim of the glass.

Tequila

TAMPICO

Fruity, slightly tangy drink for the evening
• Cocktail glass
• Shaker

1½ ounces tequila
¾ ounce papaya juice
2 dashes orange bitters
• Garnish:
1 piece of papaya

Shake all the ingredients together, with ice, in the shaker and strain into the glass. Perch the piece of papaya on the rim of the glass.

MEXICAN DREAM

Tangy, fruity drink for the evening
• Cocktail glass
• Shaker

¾ ounce tequila
¾ ounce brandy
¾ ounce lemon juice
1 tsp. grenadine
• Extra:
1 piece of lemon peel

Shake all the ingredients together, with ice, in the shaker and strain into the glass. Squeeze the lemon peel over the drink and add the peel to the glass.

PRADO

Fruity, delicately tangy drink for the evening
• Rocks glass
• Shaker

1 ounce tequila
2 tsp. maraschino
½ ounce lime juice
1 tbsp. grenadine
1 egg white
• Extra:
1 maraschino cherry
1 lime quarter

Shake all the ingredients together firmly, with ice, in the shaker and strain into the glass. Add the fruit to the glass.

TEBONNET

Spicy, elegant, dry drink for the evening
• Rocks glass

1 ounce tequila
1 ounce Dubonnet
• Garnish:
1 slice of lemon

Mix the ingredients together in the glass. Add crushed ice to taste. Perch the slice of lemon on the rim of the glass.

GRACE OF MONACO

Aromatic, short drink for the afternoon
• Cocktail glass
• Mixing glass

¾ ounce white tequila
¾ ounce apricot brandy
¾ ounce mandarin-flavored liqueur
• *Extra:*
1 piece of lemon peel

Mix the ingredients together, with ice, in the mixing glass and strain into the cocktail glass. Add the piece of lemon peel to the glass.

OLÉ

Sweet after-dinner drink
• Rocks glass
• Mixing glass

1 ounce white tequila
1 ounce crème de banane
1 dash blue curaçao
• *Extra:*
1 piece of lemon peel
1 slice of lime

Mix the ingredients together, with ice, in the mixing glass and strain into the rocks glass over ice cubes. Squeeze the lemon peel over the drink and add the slice of lime to the glass.

DEBUTANTE

Medium-dry aperitif
• Cocktail glass
• Shaker

1 ounce tequila
¾ ounce peach-flavored liqueur
1 tsp. peppermint-flavored liqueur
1 tsp. lemon juice
• *Garnish:*
1 maraschino cherry

Shake the ingredients together, with ice, in the shaker and strain into the glass. Add the cherry to the glass.

TEQUILA SOUR

Fruity sour for any time of year
• Rocks glass
• Shaker

1 ounce lemon juice
¾ ounce tequila
¾ ounce sugar syrup
• *Garnish:*
1 maraschino cherry

Shake all the ingredients together, with ice, in the shaker and strain into the glass. Perch the cherry on the rim of the glass. The drink may be topped up with sparkling mineral water, if desired.

Tequila

TEQUILA GIMLET

Slightly sour drink for the evening
• Cocktail glass
• Shaker

1½ ounces tequila
¾ ounce lemon juice
¾ ounce lime juice

Shake all the ingredients together well, with ice cubes, in the shaker and strain into the cocktail glass.

MARTINI MAYADOR

Tangy, short drink for the evening
• Cocktail glass
• Mixing glass

1½ ounces tequila
¾ ounce dry vermouth
• Garnish:
1 olive

Mix the ingredients together, with ice, in the mixing glass and strain into the cocktail glass. Spear the olive on a toothpick and add it to the glass.

BLUE MOON II

Spicy, sweet after-dinner drink
• Cocktail glass
• Shaker

1½ ounces light cream
1 ounce tequila
¾ ounce Galliano
2 tsp. blue curaçao

Shake all the ingredients together well, with ice cubes, in the shaker and strain into the glass.

KNOCK OUT I

Tangy, fruity drink for the evening
• Cocktail glass
• Shaker

¾ ounce tequila
¾ ounce lemon juice
2 tsp. Galliano
2 tsp. orange juice

Shake all the ingredients together well, with ice, in the shaker and strain into the glass.

PINK MARGARITA

Fruity, delicately tangy drink for the
evening
• Cocktail glass
• Shaker

1 ounce tequila
1 tbsp. grenadine
2 tsp. raspberry-flavored liqueur
2 tsp. lemon juice
• Garnish:
1 maraschino cherry

Shake all the ingredients together
firmly, with ice, in the shaker and strain
into the glass. Perch the cherry on the
rim of the glass.

GOLDEN VOLCANO

Creamy drink for the evening
• Cocktail glass
• Shaker

½ ounce tequila
½ ounce Galliano
2 tsp. light cream
2 tsp. lime juice
2 tsp. orange juice
1 tsp. triple sec
• Garnish:
1 maraschino cherry

Shake the ingredients together firmly,
with ice, in the shaker and strain into
the glass. Perch the cherry on the rim of
the glass, or spear it on a toothpick and
lay the garnish across the rim of the
glass.

JULIET

Sweet drink for the evening
- Cocktail glass
- Shaker

¾ ounce gold tequila

¾ ounce Pisang Ambon

1 ounce pineapple juice

1 dash grenadine

- *Garnish:*

1 slice of star fruit

1 maraschino cherry

Shake the ingredients together, with ice, in the shaker and strain into the glass. Spear the slice of star fruit and the cherry on a toothpick and perch the fruit on the rim of the glass.

PACIFICO

Fruity, delicately tangy drink for a summer party
- Cocktail glass
- Blender

1½ ounces tequila

¾ ounce passion-fruit syrup

2 tsp. lemon juice

- *Garnish:*

1 slice of lemon

Mix all the ingredients together, with a bar scoop full of crushed ice, in the blender and pour into the glass. Perch the slice of lemon on the rim of the glass.

TEQUIN

Fruity, tangy drink for the evening
• Cocktail glass
• Shaker

¾ ounce tequila
2 tsp. gin
2 tsp. lime juice
• Garnish:
1 slice of lime

Shake all the ingredients together firmly, with ice, in the shaker and strain into the glass. Perch the slice of lime on the rim of the glass.

MEXICANA

Fruity, tangy drink for a party
• Cocktail glass
• Shaker

1½ ounces tequila
¾ ounce lemon juice
1 tbsp. grenadine
2 tsp. pineapple juice
• Garnish:
1 maraschino cherry

Shake all the ingredients together firmly, with ice, in the shaker and strain into the glass. Perch the cherry on the rim of the glass.

MARLON BRANDO'S PUEBLA FLIP

Spicy, sweet drink for the evening
• Flip glass or tulip-shaped glass
• Shaker

1 ounce tequila
1 tsp. dark rum
1 tsp. brown crème de cacao
Heaping ½ tbsp. vanilla-flavored sugar
1 egg yolk
• Garnish:
Ground cinnamon

Shake all the ingredients together firmly, with ice, in the shaker and strain into the glass. Sprinkle a little cinnamon on top.

TEQUILA MARTINI

Dry, spicy aperitif
• Cocktail glass
• Mixing glass

1½ ounces tequila
¾ ounce dry vermouth
• Garnish:
1 green olive

Mix all the ingredients together, with ice, in the mixing glass and strain into the cocktail glass. Add the olive to the glass.

Tequila

MEXICAN GUAYABA

Fruity, elegant, tangy drink for a party
- Cocktail glass
- Shaker

1 ounce tequila
2 tsp. orange juice
2 tsp. lime juice
2 tsp. guava syrup
- *Extra:*
1 piece of orange peel

Shake all the ingredients together firmly, with ice, in the shaker and strain into the glass. Squeeze the orange peel over the drink and add the peel to the glass.

FROZEN TEQUILA

Fruity, delicately tangy drink for a summer party
- Cocktail glass
- Blender

1½ ounces pineapple juice
1 ounce tequila
2 tsp. lemon juice

Mix all the ingredients together well, with a bar scoop of crushed ice, in the blender and pour into the glass.

COPA DE ORO

Fruity, sweet flip for any time of year
- Tulip-shaped glass
- Shaker

¾ ounce tequila
2 tsp. Grand Marnier
2 tsp. sugar syrup
1 egg yolk

Shake all the ingredients together firmly, with plenty of ice, in the shaker and strain into the glass.

FROZEN BLACKBERRY TEQUILA

Dry, fruity drink for a summer party
- Cocktail glass
- Blender

1½ ounces tequila
¾ ounce blackberry-flavored liqueur
2 tsp. lemon juice
- *Garnish:*
1 slice of lemon

Mix all the ingredients together, with a bar scoop full of crushed ice, in the blender and pour into the glass. Perch the slice of lemon on the rim of the glass.

NORTH AMERICANO

Fruity, dry aperitif
• Cocktail glass
• Mixing glass

1½ ounces tequila
2 tsp. dry sherry
• Garnish:
1 slice of lemon

Mix all the ingredients together, with ice, in the mixing glass and strain into the cocktail glass. Perch the slice of lemon on the rim of the glass.

TORNADO

Medium-dry drink for any occasion
• Highball/Collins glass
• Shaker

1½ ounces grapefruit juice
1½ ounces passion-fruit juice
1 ounce tequila
¾ ounce peach-flavored liqueur
2 tsp. lime cordial
• Garnish:
½ slice of orange
2 maraschino cherries

Shake the ingredients together firmly, with ice, in the shaker and strain into the highball glass over crushed ice. Spear the cherries and the slice of orange on a long wooden skewer, so they look like a sail, and put it in the glass. Serve with a stirrer.

VIVA

Fruity, long drink for a party
• Highball/Collins glass

2 ounces passion-fruit juice
2 ounces orange juice
1½ ounces white tequila
¾ ounce orange curaçao
2 tsp. lime juice
• Garnish:
1 strawberry
1 slice of star fruit

Mix the ingredients together, with ice cubes, in the highball glass. Spear the slice of star fruit and the strawberry on a toothpick and perch the fruit on the rim of the glass. Serve with a stirrer.

TEMPEST

Fruity, medium-dry drink for any occasion
• Highball/Collins glass
• Shaker

1 ounce tequila
2 tsp. mandarin-flavored syrup
1½ ounces passion-fruit juice
1½ ounces orange juice
2 tsp. lemon juice
• Garnish:
1 slice of star fruit
1 maraschino cherry

Shake the ingredients together, with ice, in the shaker and strain into the highball glass over crushed ice. Perch the slice of star fruit on the rim of the glass and fasten the cherry to the star fruit with a toothpick.

Tequila

Sierra Sunrise (left), Sierra Gringo (right)

SIERRA SUNRISE

Fruity, refreshing drink for a summer party
• Highball/Collins glass
• Shaker

3½ ounces orange juice
1¾ ounces Sierra or other white tequila
¾ ounce grenadine

Shake the orange juice and tequila together, with ice, in the shaker and strain into the highball glass over ice cubes. Slowly pour the grenadine into the drink and leave it to settle. Stir before drinking.

SIERRA GRINGO

Fruity, long drink for the summer
• Highball/Collins glass
• Shaker

¾ ounce Sierra or other gold tequila
2 tsp. bourbon
2 tsp. lemon juice
1¾ ounces passion-fruit juice
• Garnish:
1 slice of lemon
1 cherry

Shake all the ingredients together, with ice, in the shaker and pour into the glass. Spear the fruit on a toothpick and lay the garnish across the rim of the glass.

ACAPULCO DREAM

Mild, fruity drink for a party
- Highball/Collins glass
- Shaker

3½ ounces pineapple juice
1½ ounces grapefruit juice
1 ounce tequila
2 tsp. dark rum
- *Garnish:*
1 slice of pineapple

Shake all the ingredients together, with ice, in the shaker and strain into the glass over ice cubes. Finally, perch the slice of pineapple on the rim of the glass.

MEXICAN NIGHT

Fruity, tangy drink for a party
- Highball/Collins glass

1½ ounces tequila
2 dashes lime cordial
1 lemon quarter
Bitter lemon for topping up

Mix the tequila, lime cordial, and lemon quarter together, with ice, in the glass. Top up with bitter lemon and stir briefly.

JUNGLE BIRD

Fruity, medium-dry drink for a summer party
- Highball/Collins glass
- Shaker

1½ ounces tequila
1½ ounces papaya juice
1½ ounces lemon juice
2 tsp. passion-fruit syrup
- *Garnish:*
¼ slice of pineapple
1 maraschino cherry

Shake the ingredients together, with ice, in the shaker and strain into the highball glass over crushed ice. Spear the fruit on a toothpick and lay the garnish across the rim of the glass.

MEXICAN OLD-FASHIONED

Bittersweet long drink for a summer party
- Rocks glass

1 sugar cube
1 dash Angostura bitters
1 lemon quarter
1 orange segment
1 maraschino cherry
1¾ ounces tequila
Soda water for topping up

Put the sugar cube in the glass and soak it in the Angostura bitters, then crush it in a mortar or with a bar spoon. Add the fruit to the glass, pour tequila over the fruit and sugar, and add 4 ice cubes. Stir well. Top up with soda water and stir again carefully. Serve with a spoon.

Tequila

TEQUILA FEVER

Refreshing long drink for hot days
- Highball/Collins glass
- Shaker

1½ ounces gold tequila
1½ ounces combined mango and
lemon juices
2 tsp. orange curaçao
2 ounces passion-fruit juice
2 tsp. lemon juice
• Garnish:
1 slice of star fruit
1 maraschino cherry
Sprig of mint

Shake the ingredients together, with ice, in the shaker and strain into the highball glass over ice cubes. Spear the slice of star fruit and the cherry on a toothpick and lay the garnish across the rim of the glass. Add the sprig of mint to the glass.

TEQUILA SUNRISE

Fruity, long drink for hot days
- Highball/Collins glass

1½ ounces white tequila
Orange juice for topping up
½ slice of orange
¾ ounce grenadine

Pour the tequila and orange juice together into the highball glass over ice cubes. Float the slice of orange on top of the drink and pour the grenadine on top. Serve with a stirrer.

FROZEN SUN

Fruity, delicately tangy drink for a summer party
- Cocktail glass
- Blender

1½ ounces tequila
2 tsp. lime juice
2 tsp. grenadine
• Garnish:
1 slice of orange

Mix all the ingredients together, with a bar scoop full of crushed ice, in the blender and pour into the chilled glass. Perch the slice of orange on the rim of the glass.

CARABINIERI

Fruity, delicately tangy drink for a summer party
- Highball/Collins glass
- Shaker

2¾ ounces orange juice
1 ounce tequila
¾ ounce Galliano
¾ ounce lime juice
1 egg yolk

Shake all the ingredients together well, with ice cubes, in the shaker. Half fill the highball glass with crushed ice and strain the drink into the glass.

MEXICAN MOCKINGBIRD

Spicy, delicately tangy drink for a summer party
• Highball/Collins glass
• Shaker

1½ ounces tequila
¾ ounce green crème de menthe
2 tsp. lime juice
Soda water for topping up
• Garnish:
Sprig of mint

Shake all the ingredients, except the soda water, together, with ice, in the shaker. Fill the highball glass one-third full with ice cubes and strain the drink into the glass. Top up with soda water and stir briefly. Perch the sprig of mint on the rim of the glass.

TAPICO

Refreshing, bitter drink for a party
• Highball/Collins glass
• Shaker

1½ ounces white tequila
¾ ounce crème de cassis
¾ ounce banana juice
Tonic water for topping up
• Garnish:
½ slice of orange
1 maraschino cherry

Shake all the ingredients, except the tonic water, together, with ice, in the shaker and strain into the highball glass over ice cubes. Top up with tonic water. Spear the slice of orange and the cherry on a toothpick and perch it on the rim of the glass.

Tequila

MEXICAN SCREWDRIVER

Fruity drink for a summer party
• Highball/Collins glass

3½ ounces orange juice

1½ ounces tequila

• *Extra:*

1 slice of orange

Mix the ingredients together, with ice cubes, in the glass. Add the slice of orange to the glass. Serve with a stirrer.

DESPERTADOR

Fruity, slightly tangy drink for any time of year
• Highball/Collins glass
• Shaker

1 ounce tequila

¾ ounce grenadine

2 tsp. Cointreau or other orange-flavored liqueur

1 tsp. honey

Grapefruit juice for topping up

• *Garnish:*

1 slice of lemon

1 maraschino cherry

Shake all the ingredients, except the grapefruit juice, together, with ice, in the shaker and strain into the glass. Top up with grapefruit juice and stir briefly. Spear the fruit on a toothpick and lay the garnish across the rim of the glass.

TEQUAS

Fruity, elegant, tangy drink for a party
- Rocks glass
- Shaker

1½ ounces lemon juice
1 ounce tequila
¾ ounce pineapple syrup
- *Garnish:*
1 slice of lemon

Shake all the ingredients together firmly, with ice, in the shaker. Half fill the glass with ice cubes and strain the drink into the glass. Perch the slice of lemon on the rim of the glass.

CARAMBA I

Fruity, delicately tangy drink for the summer
- Highball/Collins glass
- Shaker

1½ ounces tequila
¾ ounce grapefruit juice
2 tsp. sugar syrup
Soda water for topping up

Shake the tequila, grapefruit juice, and sugar syrup together, with crushed ice, in the shaker and pour into the glass. Top up with soda water and stir briefly.

ALLELUIA

Refreshing, fruity drink for a summer party
- Highball/Collins glass
- Shaker

¾ ounce white tequila
½ ounce maraschino
½ ounce blue curaçao
½ ounce lemon juice
1 dash of egg white
Bitter lemon for topping up
- *Garnish:*
1 slice of lemon
2 maraschino cherries
1 piece of orange peel
Sprig of mint

Shake all the ingredients, except the bitter lemon, together, with ice, in the shaker and strain into the highball glass. Top up with bitter lemon and stir. Spear the slice of lemon and maraschino cherries on a toothpick and perch the fruit on the rim of the glass. Add the orange peel and sprig of mint to the glass.

BLOODY JUANITA

Piquant, long drink for the evening
- Rocks glass

3½ ounces tomato juice
1½ ounces tequila
Ground black pepper
Celery salt
Worcestershire sauce
Hot-pepper sauce

Mix the tomato juice and tequila together, with ice, in the glass. Season to taste with the seasonings.

FERRARI COCKTAIL

Drinks based on fortified wine

FIVE O'CLOCK

TROCADERO

ALADDIN

SOUTHERN STAR

DANIELLE

VERMOUTH TONIC

ADMIRAL

AIR MAIL II

Elegant, tangy aperitif
- Cocktail glass
- Shaker

1½ ounces sweet red vermouth
¾ ounce grappa
2 dashes Angostura bitters

Shake all the ingredients together, with ice, in the shaker and strain into the glass.

STREGA COMET

Elegant, tangy aperitif
- Cocktail glass
- Shaker

2 ounces dry vermouth
¾ ounce Strega

Shake all the ingredients together, with ice, in the shaker and strain into the glass.

FIVE O'CLOCK

Fruity, spicy drink for the evening
- Cocktail glass
- Shaker

¾ ounce sweet red vermouth
¾ ounce gin
¾ ounce light rum
¾ ounce orange juice

Shake all the ingredients together firmly, with ice cubes, in the shaker and strain into the glass.

FERRARI COCKTAIL

Spicy, elegant, tangy drink for the evening
- Cocktail glass
- Mixing glass

1½ ounces dry vermouth
¾ ounce amaretto
Grated peel of ½ lemon

Mix all the ingredients together, with ice cubes, in the mixing glass and strain into the cocktail glass.

PERFECTION

Elegant, tangy aperitif
- Cocktail glass
- Mixing glass

¾ ounce dry vermouth
¾ ounce sweet red vermouth
¾ ounce gin

Mix all the ingredients together, with ice, in the mixing glass and strain into the glass.

SWEPT AWAY

Spicy, elegant, tangy drink for the evening
- Rocks glass

1 ounce Cinzano (rosso antico)
¾ ounce light rum

Mix the ingredients together, with crushed ice, in the glass and serve immediately.

Fortified Wine

Air Mail (back), Five O'clock (middle), Strega Comet (front)

MASCOT

Tangy, spicy drink for the evening
- Cocktail glass
- Shaker

....
1½ ounces dry vermouth
2 tsp. anisette
2 tsp. Benedictine
....

Shake all the ingredients together firmly, with ice, in the shaker and strain into the glass.

LOVELY BUTTERFLY

Spicy, elegant, tangy aperitif
- Cocktail glass
- Shaker

....
¾ ounce dry vermouth
¾ ounce sweet white vermouth
2 tsp. Dubonnet
2 tsp. orange juice
....

Shake all the ingredients together, with ice, in the shaker and strain into the glass.

ADONIS

Spicy, mild aperitif
- Cocktail glass
- Mixing glass

....
¾ ounce sweet white vermouth
¾ ounce sherry
2 tsp. sweet red vermouth
1 dash orange bitters
....

Mix all the ingredients together, with ice, in the mixing glass and strain into the cocktail glass.

TOP OF THE HILL

Fruity, elegant, tangy short drink for the afternoon
- Cocktail glass
- Shaker

....
1½ ounces sweet red vermouth
1½ ounces orange juice
2 dashes pineapple juice
1 dash orange bitters
• Garnish:
½ slice of orange
....

Shake all the ingredients together firmly, with ice, in the shaker and strain into the glass. Perch the slice of orange on the rim of the glass.

TROCADERO

Medium-dry aperitif
- Cocktail glass
- Mixing glass

....
1 ounce dry vermouth
1 ounce sweet red vermouth
1 dash grenadine
1 dash orange bitters
• Garnish:
1 maraschino cherry
....

Mix the ingredients together, with ice, in the mixing glass and strain into the cocktail glass. Spear the cherry on a toothpick and add it to the glass.

CHORUS GIRL

Fruity, elegant, tangy drink for a party
- Cocktail glass
- Shaker

¾ ounce sweet red vermouth

¾ ounce dry vermouth

¾ ounce gin

¾ ounce orange juice

- Garnish:

1 maraschino cherry

Shake all the ingredients together firmly, with ice, in the shaker and strain into the glass. Perch the cherry on the rim of the glass.

DELMONICO

Spicy, elegant, tangy drink for the evening
- Rocks glass
- Shaker

¾ ounce dry vermouth

¾ ounce sweet red vermouth

¾ ounce cognac

¾ ounce gin

1 dash Angostura bitters

- Extra:

1 piece of orange peel

1 piece of cucumber peel

1 maraschino cherry

Shake all the ingredients together, with ice, in the shaker and strain into the glass. Add the pieces of peel and the cherry to the glass.

GREEN WIDOW II

Spicy, elegant, tangy drink for the evening
- Rocks glass

¾ ounce dry vermouth

¾ ounce gin

¾ ounce green peppermint-flavored liqueur

- Garnish:

Sprig of mint

Fill the glass half full with crushed ice. Pour the vermouth, gin, and peppermint liqueur over the ice. Perch the sprig of mint on the rim of the glass.

AFFINITY COCKTAIL

Spicy, elegant, tangy drink for the evening
- Cocktail glass
- Mixing glass

¾ ounce sweet red vermouth

¾ ounce dry vermouth

¾ ounce scotch

2 dashes Angostura bitters

- Extra:

1 piece of lemon peel

Mix all the ingredients together, with ice, in the mixing glass and strain into the cocktail glass. Squeeze the lemon peel over the drink.

ALADDIN

Spicy, sweet drink for the evening
• Champagne or cocktail glass
• Shaker

1½ ounces sweet red vermouth
¾ ounce kirsch or cherry eau-de-vie
2 tsp. grenadine
• Garnish:
1 maraschino cherry

Shake all the ingredients together
firmly, with ice, in the shaker and strain
into the glass. Perch the cherry on the
rim of the glass.

FLORA MCDONALD

Spicy, elegant, tangy drink for the
evening
• Cocktail glass
• Shaker

1½ ounces dry vermouth
¾ ounce Drambuie
¾ ounce gin
• Garnish:
1 slice of orange

Shake all the ingredients together
firmly, with ice, in the shaker and strain
into the glass. Perch the slice of orange
on the rim of the glass.

DOLLY

Mild, fruity drink for the evening
• Champagne or cocktail glass
• Shaker

1 ounce sweet white vermouth
1 ounce passion-fruit nectar
¾ ounce gin
• Garnish:
1 slice of lemon

Shake all the ingredients together, with
ice, in the shaker and strain into the
glass. Perch the slice of lemon on the
rim of the glass.

SOUTHERN STAR

Elegant, tangy drink for the evening
• Cocktail glass
• Shaker

¾ ounce sweet red vermouth
¾ ounce light rum
1 tsp. lemon juice
1 dash orange bitters

Shake all the ingredients together, with
ice, in the shaker and strain into the
glass.

ADMIRAL

Tangy, short drink for the evening
• Cocktail glass
• Mixing glass

1½ ounces dry vermouth
¾ ounce bourbon
1 dash lemon juice
• *Garnish:*
1 slice of lemon

Shake all the ingredients together, with ice, in the shaker and strain into the glass. Perch the slice of lemon on the rim of the glass.

DIPLOMAT

Elegant, tangy aperitif
• Cocktail glass
• Shaker

1½ ounces dry vermouth
¾ ounce sweet red vermouth
1 tsp. maraschino
• *Garnish:*
1 maraschino cherry

Shake all the ingredients together firmly, with ice, in the shaker and strain into the glass. Perch the cherry on the rim of the glass.

BITTERSWEET II

Elegant, tangy aperitif
• Cocktail glass

1 ounce dry vermouth
1 ounce sweet red vermouth
1 dash Angostura bitters
• *Extra:*
1 piece of orange peel

Mix all the ingredients together, with ice cubes, in the cocktail glass. Squeeze the orange peel over the drink and add the peel to the glass.

DANIELLE

Elegant, tangy aperitif
• Cocktail glass
• Mixing glass

1½ ounces sweet red vermouth
¾ ounce brandy
1 dash Angostura bitters
• *Garnish:*
1 slice of lemon

Shake all the ingredients together firmly, with ice, in the shaker and strain into the glass. Perch the slice of lemon on the rim of the glass.

Fortified Wine

MERMAID

Fruity, delicately tangy drink for a summer party
• Highball/Collins glass

¾ *ounce sweet white vermouth*
¾ *ounce gin*
¾ *ounce blue curaçao*
Bitter orange for topping up
• *Garnish:*
1 lemon peel spiral
1 slice of orange

Mix all the ingredients, except the bitter orange, together, with ice cubes, in the highball glass. Top up with bitter orange and stir briefly. Hang the spiral of peel over the rim of the glass and perch the slice of orange on the rim also.

ONE TIMES ONE

Spicy, elegant, tangy drink for the evening
• Highball/Collins glass
• Shaker

1 ounce dry vermouth
1 ounce gin
1 ounce lime cordial
1 tsp. lemon juice
Soda water for topping up

Shake all the ingredients, except the soda water, together, with ice, in the shaker and strain into the glass. Top up with soda water and stir briefly.

AMERICANO I

Rather sweet drink for a hot day
• Rocks glass

1 ounce sweet red vermouth
1 ounce Campari
Soda water for topping up
• *Extra:*
1 piece of lemon peel

Mix the vermouth and Campari together, with ice, in the glass. Top up with soda water and stir. Squeeze the lemon peel over the drink.

VERMOUTH TONIC

Tangy, spicy drink for the evening
• Highball/Collins glass

1¾ ounces dry vermouth
1 tsp. lemon juice
Tonic water for topping up
• *Garnish:*
1 slice of lemon

Mix the vermouth and lemon juice together, with ice cubes, in the highball glass. Top up with tonic water and stir briefly. Perch the slice of lemon on the rim of the glass.

CATCH ME

Fruity, bittersweet drink for the evening
• Champagne glass
• Shaker

1½ ounces sweet red vermouth
1½ ounces Grand Marnier
¾ ounce lemon juice
¾ ounce mixed fruit juice
Tonic water for topping up

Shake all the ingredients, except the tonic water, together, with ice, in the shaker and strain into the champagne glass. Top up with tonic water and stir briefly.

MEZZ'E MEZZ'

Fruity, tangy drink for the evening
• Rocks glass
• Shaker

2 ounces sweet white vermouth
2 ounces grapefruit juice
2 tsp. Campari
• Extra:
1 hazelnut

Shake all the ingredients together, with ice cubes, in the shaker and strain into the glass. Add the nut to the glass.

EXOTIC HOUR

Fruity, delicately tangy drink for the evening
• Highball/Collins glass

1½ ounces sweet red vermouth
1½ ounces pineapple juice
Carbonated orange drink for topping up
• Garnish:
½ slice of pineapple

Mix the vermouth and pineapple juice together well, with ice cubes, in the glass. Top up with the carbonated orange drink. Perch the slice of pineapple on the rim of the glass.

TEXAS RANCHER

Spicy, elegant, tangy drink for any time of year
• Rocks glass
• Shaker

1½ ounces grapefruit juice
1 ounce dry vermouth
¾ ounce sweet white vermouth
¾ ounce gin
1 tsp. maraschino
• Garnish:
¼ slice of grapefruit

Shake all the ingredients together, with ice, in the shaker and strain into the glass. Perch the slice of grapefruit on the rim of the glass.

Fortified Wine

Long Evening (left), Gold Lion (right)

LONG EVENING

Spicy, elegant, tangy aperitif
• Old-fashioned glass
• Mixing glass

¾ ounce dry vermouth

¾ ounce sweet red vermouth

2 tsp. brandy

2 dashes Angostura bitters

Soda water for topping up

• Garnish:

1 slice of lemon

Mix all the ingredients, except the soda water, together, with ice, in the mixing glass and strain into the glass over ice cubes. Top up with soda water. Perch the slice of lemon on the rim of the glass.

GOLD LION

Fruity, elegant, tangy drink for the evening
• Highball/Collins glass

4 ounces orange juice

1½ ounces sweet red vermouth

¾ ounce vodka

¾ ounce lemon juice

• Garnish:

1 slice of orange

Sprig of mint

Mix all the ingredients together well, with ice cubes, in the highball glass. Perch the slice of orange and sprig of mint on the rim of the glass. Serve with a stirrer and straw.

PORTO

Fruity, elegant, tangy aperitif
• Cocktail glass
• Mixing glass

1½ ounces port
¾ ounce brandy

Mix the ingredients together, with ice
cubes, in the mixing glass and strain
into the cocktail glass.

BETSY ROSS COCKTAIL

Fruity, elegant, tangy aperitif
• Cocktail glass
• Shaker

1 ounce port
1 ounce cognac
1 dash orange-flavored liqueur
1 dash Angostura bitters
• Extra:
1 piece of lemon peel

Shake all the ingredients together, with
ice, and strain into the glass. Squeeze
the lemon peel over the drink.

PORT FLIP

Creamy after-dinner drink
• Flip glass or champagne flute
• Shaker

1½ ounces port
2 tsp. cognac
1 tsp. sugar syrup
1 egg yolk
• Extra:
Grated nutmeg

Shake the ingredients together firmly,
with ice, in the shaker and strain into
the glass. Sprinkle a little nutmeg on
top.

TAYLOR MADE

Fruity drink for hot days
• Cobbler glass

1¾ ounces port
¾ ounce B&B liqueur
2 dashes orange bitters
• Extra:
2 peach quarters
2 strawberries, halved
4 small balls of honeydew melon

Fill the glass half full with crushed ice
and mix the ingredients together in the
glass. Add the fruit to the glass.

Fortified Wine

PORT SANGAREE

Fruity, sweet drink for the evening
- Cocktail glass
- Shaker

1½ ounces port
2 tsp. blue curaçao
2 tsp. sugar syrup
• Extra:
Grated nutmeg

Shake all the ingredients together, with ice, in the shaker and strain into the glass. Sprinkle a little nutmeg on top.

BERLENGA

Refined, spicy aperitif
- Cocktail glass
- Mixing glass

---

2 ounces white port
¾ ounce gin
• Garnish:
½ slice of lemon

Mix all the ingredients together, with ice, in the mixing glass and strain into the cocktail glass. Perch the slice of lemon on the rim of the glass.

EXTRAVAGANT PORT

Fruity, elegant, tangy drink for a summer party
- Highball/Collins glass
- Shaker

1½ ounces port
¾ ounce brandy
2 tsp. orange-flavored liqueur
Bitter lemon for topping up
• Garnish:
1 slice of orange

Shake all the ingredients, except the bitter lemon, together, with ice, in the shaker and strain into the glass over ice cubes. Top up with bitter lemon and stir briefly. Perch the slice of orange on the rim of the glass.

PORTO RICO

Fruity, tangy drink for the evening
- Cocktail glass
- Shaker

1½ ounces port
¾ ounce scotch
2 tsp. lemon juice
• Garnish:
1 slice of orange

Shake all the ingredients together, with ice, in the shaker and strain into the glass. Perch the slice of orange on the rim of the glass.

MOSS ROSE COCKTAIL

Fruity, elegant, tangy drink for a party
• Champagne or cocktail glass
• Shaker

1½ ounces cream sherry
¾ ounce grapefruit juice
1 dash gin

Shake all the ingredients together, with ice, in the shaker and strain into the glass.

P.J. (PERRIER JOUET)

Dry champagne aperitif
• Champagne flute

¾ ounce dry sherry
1 tsp. B&B liqueur
Champagne for topping up, such as Perrier Jouet

Mix the sherry and liqueur together in the champagne flute and top up with champagne.

GORDON'S

Fruity, delicately tangy aperitif
• Cocktail glass
• Mixing glass

1½ ounces medium sherry
2 tsp. gin

Mix the ingredients together, with ice, in the mixing glass and strain into the cocktail glass.

ARENA

Elegant, tangy aperitif
• Champagne or cocktail glass
• Mixing glass

¾ ounce dry sherry
¾ ounce dry vermouth
¾ ounce sweet red vermouth
1 dash orange bitters
• Garnish:
1 piece of crystallized ginger

Mix all the ingredients together, with ice, in the mixing glass and strain into the glass. Spear the piece of crystallized ginger on a toothpick and add it to the glass.

INCA

Spicy, elegant, tangy aperitif
• Cocktail glass
• Mixing glass

¾ ounce medium sherry
¾ ounce dry vermouth
¾ ounce sweet red vermouth
¾ ounce gin
1 dash orange bitters
• Extra:
1 piece of lemon peel

Mix all the ingredients together, with ice, in the mixing glass and strain into the cocktail glass. Squeeze the lemon peel over the drink.

Fortified Wine

Moss Rose Cocktail (front), P.J. (back left), Arena (back right)

BAHIA COCKTAIL

Spicy, elegant, tangy aperitif
• Cocktail glass
• Mixing glass

1 ounce medium sherry
1 ounce dry vermouth
2 dashes pastis
1 dash orange bitters
• Garnish:
1 piece of lemon peel

Mix all the ingredients together, with plenty of ice, in the mixing glass and strain into the cocktail glass. Squeeze the lemon peel over the drink.

COPACABANA PALACE

Fruity, spicy, delicately tangy aperitif
• Cocktail glass
• Mixing glass

1 ounce dry sherry
1 ounce sweet red vermouth
2 dashes green Chartreuse

Mix all the ingredients together, with ice, in the mixing glass and strain into the cocktail glass.

BAMBOO

Elegant, tangy aperitif
• Cocktail glass
• Mixing glass

1 ounce fino sherry
1 ounce dry vermouth
1 dash orange bitters
• Garnish:
1 slice of lemon

Mix all the ingredients together, with ice, in the mixing glass and strain into the cocktail glass. Perch the slice of lemon on the rim of the glass.

SHERRY FLIP

Creamy after-dinner drink
• Champagne flute
• Shaker

1½ ounces medium sherry
¾ ounce brandy or cognac
¾ ounce sugar syrup
1 egg yolk
• Extra:
Grated nutmeg

Shake all the ingredients together firmly, with ice, in the shaker and strain into the champagne flute. Sprinkle a little grated nutmeg on top.

Fortified Wine

BELLE EPOQUE

Dry champagne aperitif
• Champagne flute

2 tsp. dry sherry
1 tsp. vieux marc de champagne
Champagne for topping up
• Garnish:
½ slice of orange
1 maraschino cherry

Pour all the ingredients, except the champagne, into the flute and then top up with champagne. Spear the fruit on a toothpick and lay the garnish across the rim of the glass.

DUBONNET CARIBIENNE

Medium-dry drink for any time of day
• Rocks glass

1 ounce Dubonnet
1 ounce dark rum
Mineral water for topping up
• Extra:
½ slice of lemon
1 maraschino cherry

Pour the Dubonnet and rum into the glass over ice cubes and top up with mineral water. Add the fruit to the glass. Serve with a stirrer.

DUBONNET ON THE ROCKS

Aromatic, short aperitif
• Rocks glass

1¼ ounces Dubonnet
• Extra:
1 piece of lemon peel

Pour the Dubonnet into the glass over ice cubes. Add the lemon peel to the glass.

ALFONSO I

Medium-dry champagne aperitif
• Champagne flute

1 sugar cube
1 dash Angostura bitters
1½ ounces Dubonnet
Champagne or sparkling wine for topping up
• *Extra:*
1 piece of lemon peel

Put the sugar cube in the champagne flute and soak it in the Angostura bitters. Add the ice cubes. Pour the Dubonnet over the sugar and top up with champagne or sparkling wine. Squeeze the lemon peel over the drink and add the peel to the glass.

ALFONSO II

Mild, short aperitif
• Cocktail glass
• Shaker

1 ounce Dubonnet
1 ounce medium sherry

Shake the ingredients together, with ice, in the shaker and strain into the glass.

CAT'S

Fruity, elegant, tangy drink for the evening
• Champagne or cocktail glass
• Shaker

1½ ounces Dubonnet

2 tsp. Armagnac

2 tsp. maraschino

• Garnish:

1 maraschino cherry

Shake all the ingredients together, with ice, in the shaker and strain into the glass. Perch the cherry on the rim of the glass.

APPETIZER

Tangy aperitif
• Champagne or cocktail glass
• Shaker

¾ ounce Dubonnet

¾ ounce gin

¾ ounce orange juice

3 dashes Angostura bitters

Shake all the ingredients together, with ice, in the shaker and strain into the glass.

BOB DANDY

Medium-dry aperitif
- Cocktail glass
- Mixing glass

1½ ounces Dubonnet
¾ ounce brandy

Mix the ingredients together, with ice, in the mixing glass and strain into the cocktail glass. The addition of a few ice cubes is optional.

CORONATION

Tangy aperitif
- Cocktail glass
- Mixing glass

¾ ounce Dubonnet
¾ ounce dry vermouth
¾ ounce gin

Mix the ingredients together, with ice, in the mixing glass and strain into the cocktail glass.

BULL'S EYE

Sweet drink for a party
- Cocktail glass

1 egg yolk
Malaga wine for topping up

Carefully put the egg yolk into the glass so it remains whole and top up with Malaga.

BUSHRANGER

Tangy drink for the evening
- Cocktail glass
- Mixing glass

1 ounce Dubonnet
1 ounce light rum
2 dashes Angostura bitters
• Garnish:
1 maraschino cherry

Mix all the ingredients together, with ice, in the mixing glass and strain into the cocktail glass. Spear the cherry on a toothpick and add it to the glass.

DUBONNET CREAM

Fruity, bittersweet aperitif
- Highball/Collins glass

2 ounces Dubonnet
1 ounce crème de cassis
Soda water for topping up
2 dashes lemon juice
1 slice of lemon

Mix the Dubonnet and crème de cassis together, with ice cubes, in the highball glass. Top up with soda water. Add the lemon juice and slice of lemon and stir briefly.

BRASILIA

CAIPIRINHA

BATIDA DEL SOL

BATIDA RIO

*Drinks
based on
cachaça*

TELENOVELA

CARNEVAL

BRAZILIAN SUNRISE

SURF

BEST WISHES

BATIDA DE MARACUJA

CHAÇINI

Spicy, dry aperitif
- Cocktail glass
- Mixing glass

1½ ounces cachaça

2 tsp. light rum

2 tsp. dry vermouth

1 dash Angostura bitters

• Extra:

1 piece of lemon peel

Mix all the ingredients together, with ice, in the mixing glass and strain into the cocktail glass. Squeeze the lemon peel over the drink and add the peel to the glass.

CAIPIRINHA

Sour, tangy aperitif
- Rocks glass

1 lime, cut into quarters

2-3 tsp. brown sugar

1¾ ounces cachaça

Put the lime quarters into the glass and crush them with the end of the bar spoon. Add the brown sugar and cachaça, top up with crushed ice, and stir well.

BRASILIA

Fruity, sweet drink for a summer party
- Highball/Collins glass
- Shaker

1¾ ounces orange juice

1¾ ounces pineapple juice

1½ ounces cachaça

¾ ounce cream of coconut

2 tsp. blue curaçao

• Garnish:

1 piece of melon

Shake all the ingredients together, with ice, in the shaker and strain into the highball glass over crushed ice. Perch the piece of melon on the rim of the glass. Serve with a stirrer.

BATIDA DE MARACUJA

Fruity, fresh drink for a summer party
- Highball/Collins glass
- Shaker

2 ounces passion-fruit juice

1 ounce cachaça

2 tsp. lemon juice

• Garnish:

1 slice of star fruit

Shake the ingredients together, with ice, in the shaker and strain into the highball glass over crushed ice. Perch the slice of star fruit on the rim of the glass.

Cachaça

Brasilia (back left), Batida de Maracuja (back right), Chaçini (front left), Caipirinha (front right)

SURF

Sweetish drink for all occasions
- Highball/Collins glass
- Shaker

1½ ounces banana juice
1½ ounces passion-fruit juice
1 ounce cachaça
¾ ounce peach-flavored liqueur
3 dashes blue curaçao
• Garnish:
½ slice of orange
2 maraschino cherries

Shake the ingredients together, with ice, in the shaker and strain into the highball glass over crushed ice. Perch the slice of orange on the rim of the glass and fasten the cherries to it with a toothpick. Serve with a stirrer.

BATIDA

Fruity, mild drink for a summer party
- Highball/Collins glass
- Blender

1¾ ounces cachaça
1½ ounces lime juice
2 tsp. honey
• Extra:
2 lime quarters

Mix all the ingredients together in the blender. Add about 4 ice cubes, and continue blending. Pour into the glass. Squeeze the juice from the pieces of lime into the drink and add the crushed lime quarters to the glass.

CARAMBA II

Fruity, tangy drink for the summer
- Highball/Collins glass
- Shaker

1½ ounces cachaça
¾ ounce grapefruit juice
2 tsp. sugar syrup
Soda water for topping up
• Garnish:
½ slice of grapefruit

Shake all the ingredients, except the soda water, together, with crushed ice, in the shaker and pour into the glass. Top up with soda water and stir briefly. Perch the slice of grapefruit on the rim of the glass.

BATIDA DEL SOL

Fruity, sweet drink for a summer party
- Highball/Collins glass
- Shaker

1¾ ounces pineapple juice
1 ounce cachaça
¾ ounce coconut-flavored liqueur
2 tsp. dark rum
2 tsp. cream of coconut
• Garnish:
½ slice of pineapple
1 maraschino cherry

Shake all the ingredients together firmly, with ice, in the shaker and strain into the glass. Top up with crushed ice. Perch the slice of pineapple on the rim of the glass and fasten the cherry to it with a toothpick.

Cachaça

RECIFE

Fruity, elegant, tangy drink for a summer party
- Highball/Collins glass
- Shaker

2¾ ounces pineapple juice
1 ounce cachaça
¾ ounce dark rum
2 tsp. tequila
1 dash orange bitters
- Garnish:
¼ slice of pineapple
1 maraschino cherry

Shake all the ingredients together firmly, with ice, in the shaker and strain into the glass. Top up with crushed ice. Perch the fruit on the rim of the glass.

BATIDA RIO

Fruity, sweet drink for a summer party
- Highball/Collins glass
- Blender

2 ounces pineapple juice
¾ ounce cachaça
2 tsp. light rum
2 tsp. banana-flavored liqueur
2 tsp. light cream
2 tsp. cream of coconut
½ banana, peeled and sliced
- Garnish:
¼ slice of pineapple

Blend all the ingredients in the blender, with a bar scoop full of crushed ice, until foaming and pour into the glass. Perch the slice of pineapple on the rim of the glass.

BRAZILIAN SUNRISE

Fruity, sweet drink for a party
• Highball/Collins glass

1½ ounces cachaça

3½ ounces orange juice

2 tsp. lemon juice

¾ ounce grenadine

• Garnish:

1 slice of orange

Mix the cachaça and the juices
together, with ice cubes, in the glass.
Slowly add the grenadine. Perch the
slice of orange on the rim of the glass.
Serve with a straw.

BEST WISHES

Fruity, tangy long drink for a summer
party
• Highball/Collins glass
• Shaker

2¾ ounces grapefruit juice

1 ounce cachaça

¾ ounce light rum

2 tsp. tequila

2 tsp. sugar syrup

• Garnish:

1 slice of lime

Shake all the ingredients together
firmly, with ice, in the shaker and strain
into the glass. Add some crushed ice
and perch the slice of lime on the rim
of the glass.

CARNIVAL

Fruity, sweet drink for a summer party
• Highball/Collins glass
• Shaker

2 ounces pineapple juice

1 ounce coconut-flavored liqueur

1½ ounces cachaça

¾ ounce light cream

2 tsp. dark rum

• Garnish:

¼ slice of pineapple

Shake all the ingredients together
firmly, with ice, in the shaker and strain
into the glass. Add a little crushed ice.
Perch the slice of pineapple on the rim
of the glass.

TELENOVELA

Fruity, elegant, tangy drink for a
summer party
• Highball/Collins glass
• Shaker

2 ounces passion-fruit nectar

1 ounce cachaça

¾ ounce coconut-flavored liqueur

2 tsp. dark rum

2 tsp. cream of coconut

• Garnish:

1 slice of lime

Shake all the ingredients together
firmly, with ice, in the shaker and strain
into the glass. Add some crushed ice.
Perch the slice of lime on the rim of the
glass.

WALDORF

TEMPTATION

BLANCHE

Drinks

**based on
aniseed-flavored
spirits**

GREEN MONKEY

PERNOD FIZZ

DR. FUNK

PINK PERNOD

BUNNY HUG

GLAD EYE

GANGADINE COCKTAIL

WALDORF

Spicy aperitif
• Cocktail glass
• Shaker

¾ ounce Pernod
¾ ounce Irish whiskey
2 dashes Angostura bitters

Shake all the ingredients together, with ice, in the shaker and strain into the cocktail glass.

HURRICANE II

Spicy drink for the evening
• Cocktail glass
• Shaker

¾ ounce cognac
2 tsp. Pernod
2 tsp. vodka

Shake all the ingredients together, with ice, in the shaker and strain into the glass.

TEMPTATION

Spicy aperitif
• Cocktail glass
• Shaker

¾ ounce Pernod
¾ ounce bourbon
¾ ounce gin

Shake all the ingredients together, with ice, in the shaker and strain into the cocktail glass.

ZAZARAC II

Mild, spicy drink for the evening
• Rocks glass
• Shaker

¾ ounce Pernod
¾ ounce light rum
¾ ounce whiskey
¾ ounce sugar syrup
2 dashes Angostura bitters
• Extra:
1 piece of lemon peel

Shake all the ingredients together, with ice cubes, in the shaker and pour into the glass. Squeeze the lemon peel over the drink and add the peel to the glass.

GREEN MONKEY

Spicy, sweet drink for a party
• Rocks glass

1½ ounces Galliano
2 tsp. Pernod

First pour the Galliano into the glass, over ice, then pour the Pernod on top and stir.

Aniseed

Temptation (top left), Zazarac II (top right), Green Monkey (bottom)

PERNOD FIZZ

Spicy, fruity drink for the evening
• Highball/Collins glass
• Shaker

1 ounce Pernod
2 tsp. brandy
2 tsp. grenadine
¾ ounce lemon juice
¾ ounce orange juice
1 egg white
Soda water for topping up

Shake all the ingredients, except the soda water, together, with ice, in the shaker and strain into the glass. Top up with soda water and stir briefly.

DR. FUNK

Mild, spicy drink for the evening
• Highball/Collins glass
• Shaker

1½ ounces dark rum
¾ ounce Pernod
¾ ounce lemon juice
¾ ounce lime juice
1 ounce grenadine
Soda water for topping up

Shake all the ingredients, except the soda water, together, with ice, in the shaker and pour into the highball glass. Top up with soda water and stir briefly. Serve with a straw.

MARTINIQUE I

Fruity, spicy drink for the summer months
• Highball/Collins glass

1½ ounces dark rum
¾ ounce lemon juice
¾ ounce sugar syrup
2 tsp. Pernod
1 dash Angostura bitters

Fill the highball glass half full with crushed ice. Pour all the ingredients into the glass and stir until the glass mists over. Serve with a straw.

PINK PERNOD

Mild, spicy drink for the evening
• Highball/Collins glass

¾ ounce Pernod
¾ ounce grenadine
Ginger ale for topping up

Mix the Pernod and grenadine together well, with ice, in the highball glass. Top up with ginger ale and stir briefly.

Aniseed

Pink Pernod (left), Dixie (middle), Classic Pernod (right)

DIXIE

Spicy, fruity, tangy aperitif
• Cocktail glass
• Shaker

¾ ounce gin
2 tsp. Pernod
2 tsp. dry vermouth
2 tsp. lemon juice
2 dashes grenadine

Shake all the ingredients together, with ice, in the shaker and strain into the cocktail glass.

CLASSIC PERNOD

Spicy, refreshing aperitif
• Highball/Collins glass

1¾ ounces Pernod
7 ounces still mineral water for
topping up

Pour the Pernod into the highball glass. Top up with the mineral water and stir briefly. A few ice cubes may be added, if desired.

371

BUNNY HUG

Spicy, elegant, tangy aperitif
- Cocktail glass
- Shaker

¾ ounce pastis
¾ ounce gin
¾ ounce whiskey

Shake all the ingredients together, with ice, in the shaker and strain into the cocktail glass.

YELLOW PARROT

Sweet aperitif
- Cocktail glass
- Mixing glass

¾ ounce pastis
¾ ounce yellow Chartreuse
¾ ounce apricot brandy

Mix all the ingredients together, with ice, in the mixing glass and strain into the cocktail glass.

ATOMIC

Spicy, elegant, tangy drink for the evening
- Cocktail glass
- Shaker

¾ ounce pastis
¾ ounce brandy
1 dash orange bitters

Shake all the ingredients together firmly, with plenty of ice, in the shaker and strain into the glass.

DUCHESS

Spicy, elegant, tangy aperitif
- Rocks glass
- Mixing glass

¾ ounce pastis
¾ ounce sweet red vermouth
¾ ounce dry vermouth

Mix all the ingredients together well, with ice, in the mixing glass and strain into the glass over ice.

GLAD EYE

Spicy, elegant, tangy aperitif or after-dinner drink
- Cocktail glass
- Shaker

1½ ounces pastis
¾ ounce green crème de menthe

Shake all the ingredients together well, with plenty of ice, in the shaker and strain into the glass.

BALTIMORE

Tangy, spicy aperitif
- Cocktail glass
- Shaker

¾ ounce pastis
¾ ounce brandy
1 tsp. egg white

Shake all the ingredients together firmly, with ice, in the shaker and strain into the glass.

Aniseed

Yellow Parrot (top left), Duchess (top right), Glad Eye (bottom)

"ABSINTHE" COCKTAIL

Spicy, delicately tangy aperitif
• Cocktail glass
• Shaker

1 ounce pastis
1 ounce still mineral water
1 tsp. sugar syrup
1 dash Angostura bitters

Shake all the ingredients together well, with ice, in the shaker and strain into the glass.

GANGADINE COCKTAIL

Spicy, elegant, tangy drink for the evening
• Cocktail glass
• Shaker

¼ ounce pastis
¼ ounce gin
¼ ounce white crème de menthe
1 tsp. grenadine

Shake all the ingredients together firmly, with ice, in the shaker and strain into the glass.

TOMATO

Spicy, sweet aperitif
• Rocks glass

¾ ounce pastis
2 tsp. grenadine
Still mineral water for topping up

Mix the pastis and grenadine together, with ice cubes, in the glass. Top up with water and stir briefly.

LONDON FOG COCKTAIL

Spicy drink for the evening
• Cocktail glass
• Shaker

¾ ounce anisette
¾ ounce white peppermint-flavored liqueur
1 dash Angostura bitters
• *Garnish:*
Sprig of mint

Shake all the ingredients together, with ice, in the shaker and strain into the glass. Perch the sprig of mint on the rim of the glass.

Aniseed

GOOD-BYE JOHNNIE

Spicy drink for the evening
- Cocktail glass
- Shaker

¾ ounce anisette
¾ ounce brandy
1 egg white
- *Garnish:*
Caraway seeds

Shake all the ingredients together, with ice, in the shaker and strain into the glass. Sprinkle a pinch of caraway seeds on top.

BLANCHE

Elegant, tangy drink for the evening
- Cocktail glass
- Shaker

¾ ounce anisette
¾ ounce Cointreau or other orange-flavored liqueur
¾ ounce triple sec

Shake all the ingredients together, with plenty of ice, in the shaker and strain into the glass.

BIONDINA

Spicy, tangy drink for the evening
- Cocktail glass
- Shaker

¾ ounce anisette
¾ ounce triple sec

Shake all the ingredients together firmly, with ice, in the shaker and strain into the glass.

KNOCK OUT II

Spicy, dry aperitif
- Cocktail glass
- Shaker

¾ ounce anisette
¾ ounce dry vermouth
¾ ounce gin
2 dashes white peppermint-flavored liqueur

Shake all the ingredients together, with ice, in the shaker and strain into the cocktail glass.

HORIZON

Tangy, spicy drink for the evening
- Cocktail glass
- Shaker

1½ ounces dark rum
¾ ounce lemon juice
2 tsp. anisette
2 tsp. grenadine

Shake all the ingredients together briefly, with ice, in the shaker and strain into the cocktail glass.

BOSPHORUS SPRING

Spicy, long drink for hot days
- Highball/Collins glass
- Shaker

¾ ounce raki
¾ ounce Pernod
2 tsp. lemon juice
1 tsp. lime cordial
Soda water for topping up
- *Garnish:*
1 lemon peel spiral

Shake all the ingredients, except the soda water, together, with crushed ice, in the shaker and strain into the glass. Top up with soda water and stir. Add the lemon peel spiral to the glass.

LION'S MILK

Spicy, long drink for the evening
- Large rocks glass

1½ ounces raki
Milk for topping up
Pinch of ground caraway

Pour the raki into the glass, top up with milk, and stir briefly. Sprinkle a pinch of ground caraway on top.

CLASSIC RAKI

Spicy drink for the evening
- Small highball/Collins glass

1½ ounces raki
Still mineral water for topping up

Pour the raki into the glass, top up with water, and stir briefly. Add ice to taste.

TIME BOMB

MIDNIGHT SUN

PINK FLIP

HELVETIA

Drinks based on eaux-de-vie and korn schnapps

NORTHERN LIGHTS

ROSE COCKTAIL

SOUTH EXPRESS

TIME BOMB

Spicy, tangy after-dinner drink or aperitif
• Cocktail glass
• Shaker

¾ ounce aquavit
¾ ounce vodka
¾ ounce lemon juice
• Extra:
1 piece of lemon peel

Shake all the ingredients together, with ice cubes, in the shaker and strain into the glass. Perch the piece of lemon peel on the rim of the glass.

FIL D'ARGENT

Fruity, elegant, tangy after-dinner drink or aperitif
• Cocktail glass
• Shaker

¾ ounce aquavit
¾ ounce vodka
2 tsp. pastis
2 tsp. orange-flavored liqueur
2 dashes lemon juice

Shake all the ingredients together firmly, with ice, in the shaker and strain into the glass.

FERNANDO II

Spicy, fruity, tangy aperitif
• Cocktail glass
• Shaker

¾ ounce aquavit
¾ ounce gin
¾ ounce lemon juice
1 dash Angostura bitters

Shake all the ingredients together briefly, with ice, in the shaker and strain into the glass.

DANISH DYNAMITE

Spicy, fruity, mild drink for the evening
• Cocktail glass
• Shaker

1½ ounces orange juice
1 ounce aquavit
2 tsp. lime juice
• Garnish:
½ slice of orange

Shake all the ingredients together, with ice, in the shaker and strain into the glass. Perch the slice of orange on the rim of the glass.

Eaux-de-vie and Korn Schnapps

Northern Lights (left), Midnight Sun (right)

NORTHERN LIGHTS

Spicy, elegant, tangy drink for a
summer party
- Rocks glass
- Shaker

¾ ounce aquavit
¾ ounce Canadian whisky
1 tsp. grenadine
1 dash Angostura bitters
Soda water for topping up
- *Extra:*
1 lemon wedge
1 orange segment

Shake all the ingredients, except the
soda water, together, with ice, in the
shaker and strain into the glass over ice
cubes. Add the fruit to the glass, top up
with soda water, and stir briefly.

MIDNIGHT SUN

Spicy, elegant, tangy aperitif
- Champagne or cocktail glass
- Shaker

1 ounce aquavit
2 tsp. grapefruit juice
2 tsp. lemon juice
2 tsp. sugar syrup
2 dashes grenadine
- *Garnish:*
½ slice of orange

Shake all the ingredients together
firmly, with ice, in the shaker and strain
into the glass. Perch the slice of orange
on the rim of the glass.

ROSE COCKTAIL

Aromatic aperitif
• Cocktail glass
• Mixing glass

1 ounce kirsch
¾ ounce dry vermouth
2 tsp. grenadine
• Garnish:
1 maraschino cherry

Mix the ingredients together, with ice, in the mixing glass and strain into the cocktail glass. Perch the cherry on the rim of the glass.

DR. SACK

Strong aperitif
• Cocktail glass
• Mixing glass

¾ ounce kirsch
¾ ounce cherry brandy
¾ ounce gin
• Garnish:
1 maraschino cherry

Mix the ingredients together, with ice, in the mixing glass and strain into the cocktail glass. Add the cherry to the glass.

KIRSCH COCKTAIL

Strong, short drink for the evening
• Cocktail glass
• Mixing glass

1¾ ounces kirsch
2 tsp. grenadine
1 dash triple sec
• Garnish:
1 maraschino cherry

Mix all the ingredients together, with ice, in the mixing glass and strain into the cocktail glass. Spear the cherry on a toothpick and lay the garnish across the rim of the glass.

CHERRY CREAM

Fruity, sweet after-dinner drink
• Cocktail glass
• Shaker

1 ounce kirsch
¾ ounce cherry brandy
¾ ounce light cream
• Garnish:
1 maraschino cherry

Shake all the ingredients together firmly, with ice, in the shaker and strain into the glass. Perch the cherry on the rim of the glass.

Eaux-de-vie and Korn Schnapps

WESTERN COCKTAIL

Spicy aperitif
- Cocktail glass
- Mixing glass

¾ ounce sweet red vermouth
2 tsp. kirsch
2 tsp. dry vermouth
• Garnish:
1 maraschino cherry

Mix all the ingredients together, with ice, in the mixing glass and strain into the cocktail glass. Spear the cherry on a toothpick and add it to the glass.

PINK FLIP

Fruity, sweet drink for the evening
- Cocktail glass
- Shaker

¾ ounce kirsch
¾ ounce cherry-flavored liqueur
1 egg yolk
• Extra:
Grated nutmeg

Shake all the ingredients together firmly, with ice, in the shaker and strain into the cocktail glass. Sprinkle a little grated nutmeg on top.

HELVETIA

Sweet after-dinner drink
- Cocktail glass
- Shaker

¾ ounce kirsch
¾ ounce cherry brandy
¾ ounce light cream
2 tsp. grenadine
• Garnish:
1 maraschino cherry

Shake all the ingredients together firmly, with ice, in the shaker and strain into the glass. Then spear the cherry on a toothpick and lay the garnish across the rim of the glass.

COLORADO

Mild, fruity after-dinner drink
- Cocktail glass
- Shaker

¾ ounce kirsch
¾ ounce cherry-flavored liqueur
¾ ounce light cream
2 tsp. cherry juice

Shake all the ingredients together firmly, with ice, in the shaker and strain into the glass.

SOUTH EXPRESS

Spicy aperitif
• Champagne or cocktail glass
• Mixing glass

¾ ounce kirsch
¾ ounce dry vermouth
¾ ounce sweet red vermouth

Mix all the ingredients together, with ice, in the mixing glass and strain into the cocktail glass.

NORMANDY II

Fruity, short drink for the evening
• Cocktail glass
• Shaker

¾ ounce kirsch
¾ ounce sweet red vermouth
2 tsp. orange-flavored liqueur
2 tsp. grenadine

Shake all the ingredients together, with ice, in the shaker and strain into the glass.

T. E. E.

Fruity, delicately tangy drink for a party
• Cocktail glass
• Mixing glass

½ ounce cognac
½ ounce peach-flavored liqueur
2 tsp. kirsch
2 tsp. Campari

Mix all the ingredients together, with ice, in the mixing glass and strain into the cocktail glass.

AFTERWARDS II

Sweet, short drink for the summer
• Rocks glass

½ ounce kirsch
½ ounce vodka
½ ounce green peppermint-flavored liqueur

Half fill the glass with crushed ice and mix all the ingredients together in the glass. Serve with a straw.

GOAT'S COCKTAIL

Elegant, tangy drink for the evening
• Champagne or cocktail glass
• Shaker

1 ounce kirsch
1 ounce brandy
2 tsp. light cream
1 dash pastis

Shake all the ingredients together firmly, with ice, in the shaker and strain into the glass.

Eaux-de-vie and Korn Schnapps

South Express (left), Goat's Cocktail (middle), Afterwards (right)

ROSEBUD MOUTH

Fruity, long drink for a party
- Champagne glass
- Shaker

1½ ounces orange juice
¾ ounce kirsch
¾ ounce cherry-flavored liqueur
2¾ ounces sparkling wine or
champagne
- Garnish:
2 maraschino cherries

Shake all the ingredients, except the
champagne, together, with ice, in the
shaker and strain into the champagne
glass. Top up with champagne. Spear
the cherries on a toothpick and lay the
garnish across the rim of the glass.

KIRSCH CASSIS

Very fruity drink for the evening
- Rocks glass

1 ounce kirsch
2 ounces black-currant juice
Soda water for topping up

Mix the kirsch and black-currant juice
together in the glass. Top up with soda
water and stir briefly.

ICE KIR

Fruity, long drink for the evening
- Highball/Collins glass
- Mixing glass

1 scoop cherry ice cream
1 ounce kirsch
1 ounce crème de cassis
Sparkling wine or champagne for
topping up
- Garnish:
1 maraschino cherry

Put the cherry ice cream in the highball
glass. Mix the kirsch and crème de
cassis together, with ice, in the mixing
glass and strain into the highball glass.
Top up with sparkling wine. Add the
cherry to the glass. Serve with a spoon.

MARASCHINO DAISY

Fruity, mild drink for a party
- Champagne glass
- Shaker

1½ ounces cherry juice
¾ ounce kirsch
¾ ounce maraschino
¾ ounce cherry-flavored liqueur
Champagne or sparkling wine for
topping up
- Garnish:
3 maraschino cherries

Shake all the ingredients, except the
champagne, together, with crushed
ice, in the shaker and strain into the
champagne glass. Top up with champagne and add the cherries to the glass.

Eaux-de-vie and Korn Schnapps

OMNIBUS

Fruity, sweet drink for a summer party
• Highball/Collins glass

1½ ounces kirsch
1½ ounces raspberry syrup
Soda water for topping up
• Garnish:
2 raspberries

Put the kirsch and raspberry syrup into the glass, add a bar scoop full of crushed ice, top up with soda water, and stir briefly. Spear the raspberries on a toothpick and lay the garnish across the rim of the glass.

GRAPPON

Fruity, elegant, tangy drink for the evening
• Cocktail glass
• Shaker

1½ ounces grappa
¾ ounce peach brandy
¾ ounce lemon juice
• Extra:
1 piece of lemon peel

Shake all the ingredients together, with ice, in the shaker and strain into the glass. Squeeze the lemon peel over the drink and add it to the glass.

ART

Mild, fruity drink for any time of year
• Highball/Collins glass

1 ounce kirsch
¾ ounce grenadine
Soda water for topping up
• Extra:
4 maraschino cherries

Mix the kirsch and grenadine together, with ice cubes, in the highball glass. Top up with soda water and stir briefly. Add the cherries to the glass. Serve with a stirrer.

GRAPEMINT

Spicy after-dinner drink
• Cocktail glass
• Shaker

1½ ounces grappa
¾ ounce peppermint syrup
• Garnish:
1 maraschino cherry

Shake all the ingredients together firmly, with ice, in the shaker and strain into the glass. Perch the cherry on the rim of the glass.

GRAPPATO

Bittersweet after-dinner drink
• Cocktail glass
• Mixing glass

1 ounce grappa
2 tsp. amaretto
• Garnish:
1 maraschino cherry

Mix all the ingredients together, with ice, in the mixing glass and strain into the cocktail glass. Perch the cherry on the rim of the glass.

CLOVER

Elegant, tangy drink for a summer party
• Rocks glass
• Shaker

1 ounce grappa
¾ ounce lemon juice
2 tsp. strawberry syrup
1 egg white
• Extra:
1 lemon wedge

Shake all the ingredients together firmly, with ice, in the shaker and strain into the glass. Add a few ice cubes and the lemon wedge to the glass.

Eaux-de-vie and Korn Schnapps

KORN KIR

Mild, fruity drink for the evening
• Rocks glass
• Mixing glass

¾ ounce korn schnapps
¾ ounce crème de cassis
¾ ounce black-currant juice
Soda water for topping up

Shake all the ingredients, except the soda water, together, with ice cubes, in the shaker and strain into the glass. Top up with soda water.

CURAKO

Fruity, spicy drink for the evening
• Cocktail glass
• Mixing glass

1 ounce korn or other flavorless schnapps
¾ ounce blue curaçao
2 dashes Angostura bitters
• *Garnish:*
1 maraschino cherry

Mix all the ingredients together, with ice cubes, in the mixing glass and strain into the cocktail glass. Add the cherry to the glass.

KORN SOUR

Refreshing, tangy drink for the summer
- Rocks glass
- Shaker

1½ ounces korn or other flavorless schnapps
¾ ounce lemon juice
2 tsp. sugar syrup
- *Garnish:*
1 maraschino cherry

Shake the ingredients together, with ice, in the shaker and strain into the glass. Add the cherry to the glass. Add a little sparkling mineral water, if desired.

KORNELIUS

Spicy, sweet after-dinner drink or aperitif
- Cocktail glass
- Shaker

1 ounce doppelkorn or other flavorless schnapps
2 tsp. dry vermouth
2 tsp. sweet red vermouth
2 tsp. grenadine
- *Garnish:*
1 slice of orange

Shake all the ingredients together, with ice, in the shaker and strain into the glass. Perch the slice of orange on the rim of the glass.

JUMPING JACK

Fruity, sweet drink for a party
- Highball/Collins glass
- Shaker

2¾ ounces orange juice
1½ ounces korn or other flavorless schnapps
¾ ounce strawberry syrup
2 tsp. lemon juice
- *Garnish:*
1 strawberry

Shake the ingredients together, with ice, in the shaker and strain into the highball glass over ice cubes. Perch the strawberry on the rim of the glass.

GERMAN MARY

Piquant, spicy drink for the evening
- Highball/Collins glass
- Shaker

3½ ounces tomato juice
¾ ounce korn or other flavorless schnapps
2 tsp. lemon juice
Freshly ground black pepper
Celery salt
Hot-pepper sauce
Worcestershire sauce

Shake all the liquid ingredients together firmly, with ice, in the shaker, season to taste and strain into the glass.

Eaux-de-vie and Korn Schnapps

POIRE WILLIAM & BITTER LEMON

Fruity, tangy drink for the evening
• Highball/Collins glass

1½ ounces Poire William
Bitter lemon for topping up
• Garnish:
1 wedge of pear

Pour the Poire William into the highball glass over ice cubes. Top up with bitter lemon and stir briefly. Perch the wedge of pear on the rim of the glass.

WILLIAM'S MAGIC

Fruity, short drink for a party
• Champagne glass
• Shaker

¾ ounce Poire William
2 tsp. light rum
1 tsp. lemon juice
2 tsp. champagne or sparkling wine for topping up
• Garnish:
1 maraschino cherry

Shake all the ingredients, except the champagne, together, with ice, in the shaker and strain into the champagne glass. Add the champagne and the cherry to the glass.

CORSAIR

Fruity, tangy champagne cocktail for any occasion
• Large champagne glass
• Mixing glass

¾ ounce banana eau-de-vie
1 tsp. Campari
2 tsp. grenadine
1½ ounces black-currant juice
Champagne or dry sparkling wine for topping up
• Garnish:
1 maraschino cherry
1 piece of lemon peel

Mix all the ingredients, except the champagne, together, with ice, in the mixing glass, strain into the champagne glass, and top up with champagne. Perch the cherry on the rim of the glass. Squeeze the lemon peel over the drink.

SWEET WILLIAM

Mild, fruity after-dinner drink
• Cocktail glass
• Shaker

¾ ounce Poire William
¾ ounce apricot brandy
¾ ounce light cream
• Garnish:
1 maraschino cherry

Shake all the ingredients together firmly, with ice, in the shaker and strain into the glass. Perch the cherry on the rim of the glass.

VOLCANO

Tangy champagne cocktail for a
reception
• Heatproof champagne glass

1 ounce raspberry eau-de-vie
¾ ounce blue curaçao
Champagne or sparkling wine for
topping up
• *Extra:*
1 piece of orange peel

Pour all the ingredients, except the
champagne, into the champagne glass
and ignite them. Extinguish the flames
with the champagne or sparkling wine.
Squeeze the orange peel over the drink
and add the peel to the glass.

STRAWBERRY CREAM

Fruity, sweet after-dinner drink
• Cocktail glass
• Shaker

¾ ounce raspberry eau-de-vie
¾ ounce strawberry-flavored liqueur
¾ ounce light cream
• *Garnish:*
1 slice of kiwi fruit
2 small strawberries

Shake all the ingredients together
firmly, with ice cubes, in the shaker and
strain into the glass. Perch the fruit on
the rim of the glass.

KIWO 81

Medium-dry, refreshing drink for a
party
• Highball/Collins glass
• Shaker

1½ ounces pineapple juice
1 ounce banana eau-de-vie
¾ ounce banana syrup
2 tsp. orange juice
2 tsp. lemon juice
1 dash grenadine
• *Garnish:*
1 slice of banana
1 cherry

Shake all the ingredients, except the
grenadine, together, with ice, in the
shaker. Half fill the highball glass with
crushed ice and strain the drink into it.
Float the grenadine on top of the drink.
Spear the slice of banana and the
cherry on a toothpick and lay the
garnish across the rim of the glass.

BERRY DRINK

Fruity, elegant, tangy long drink for a
party
• Highball/Collins glass

1½ ounces raspberry eau-de-vie
¾ ounce lemon juice
Red-currant nectar for topping up
• *Extra:*
Fresh raspberries

Mix the raspberry eau-de-vie and
lemon juice together, with some ice
cubes, in the highball glass. Top up with
red-currant nectar, stir, and add the
raspberries. Serve with a stirrer.

Eaux-de-vie and Korn Schnapps

PINKY RASPBERRY

Fruity, tangy drink for the evening
• Highball/Collins glass
• Shaker

2 ounces grapefruit juice
¾ ounce raspberry-flavored liqueur
¾ ounce Campari
Tonic water for topping up
• *Garnish:*
3 fresh raspberries

Shake all the ingredients, except the tonic water, together, with ice, in the shaker and strain into the glass over ice cubes. Top up with tonic water and stir briefly. Perch the raspberries on the rim of the glass.

LOOPING

Fruity, tangy drink for the evening
• Highball/Collins glass

1 ounce raspberry eau-de-vie
2 tsp. coconut-flavored liqueur
Carbonated grapefruit drink
• *Garnish:*
1 lemon wedge

Mix the raspberry eau-de-vie and coconut liqueur together, with ice cubes, in the highball glass. Top up with the grapefruit drink and stir briefly. Perch the wedge of lemon on the rim of the glass.

SUMMER LIGHT

Fruity, elegant, tangy drink for a party
• Highball/Collins glass

1 ounce raspberry eau-de-vie
2 tsp. grenadine
Bitter lemon for topping up
• *Garnish:*
1 slice of lemon

Mix all the ingredients, except the bitter lemon, together, with ice cubes, in the highball glass. Top up with bitter lemon and stir briefly. Perch the slice of lemon on the rim of the glass.

WILD ROSE

Fruity, tangy drink for a party
- Highball/Collins glass
- Shaker

1½ ounces apricot eau-de-vie

1½ ounces orange juice

¾ ounce lemon juice

¾ ounce lime juice

Tonic water for topping up

- *Garnish:*

1 slice of orange

Shake all the ingredients, except the tonic water, together firmly, with ice, in the shaker and strain into the glass over ice cubes. Top up with tonic water and stir briefly. Perch the slice of orange on the rim of the glass.

ANGEL'S WING

Mild, spicy drink for the evening
- Cocktail glass
- Shaker

1 ounce plum brandy

1 ounce white crème de cacao

1 dash light cream

- *Garnish:*

1 maraschino cherry

Shake all the ingredients together well, with ice, in the shaker and strain into the cocktail glass. Perch the cherry on the rim of the glass.

ALICE MINE

Mild, spicy drink for the evening
- Cocktail glass
- Shaker

1 ounce kümmel

1 ounce sweet red vermouth

2 dashes whiskey

Shake all the ingredients together, with ice, in the shaker and strain into the glass.

YELLOW PLUM

Fruity, elegant, tangy drink for the evening
- Cocktail glass
- Shaker

1 ounce blue plum eau-de-vie

2 tsp. orange juice

2 tsp. lemon juice

2 tsp. sugar syrup

1 tsp. maraschino

Shake all the ingredients together, with ice, in the shaker and strain into the glass.

CHERRY ALE

LIGHT BANANA

Nonalcoholic drinks

BREAKFAST DRINK

ZERO PERCENT

GREENY

CABRIOLET 911

AVALANCHE

LEMON SQUASH

SWEETY

Fruity, sweet drink for any occasion
• Cocktail glass
• Shaker

1½ ounces pineapple juice
1½ ounces orange juice
2 tsp. nonalcoholic grenadine
• *Garnish:*
1 maraschino cherry

Shake all the ingredients together well, with ice cubes, in the shaker and strain into the cocktail glass. Perch the cherry on the rim of the glass.

LIGHT RED

Sweet, refreshing cocktail for a reception
• Champagne flute
• Shaker

2 ounces red grape juice
¾ ounce cherry juice
2 tsp. sugar syrup
Nonalcoholic sparkling wine for topping up
• *Garnish*
1 small cluster of grapes

Shake all the ingredients, except the sparkling wine, together, with ice, in the shaker and strain into the champagne flute. Top up with sparkling wine. Hang the cluster of grapes over the rim of the glass.

LIGHT BANANA

Fruity cocktail for a reception
• Highball/Collins glass
• Shaker

1½ ounces orange juice
1½ ounces pineapple juice
¾ ounce banana syrup
2 tsp. lemon juice
½ banana, peeled and sliced
Nonalcoholic sparkling wine for topping up
• *Garnish:*
1 slice of star fruit
1 mint sprig

Shake all the ingredients, except the sparkling wine, together firmly, with ice, in the shaker and strain into the highball glass over crushed ice. Top up with sparkling wine. Perch the slice of star fruit and mint sprig on the rim of the glass.

CHERRY ALE

Fruity drink for a party
• Rocks glass

¾ ounce cherry juice
1 dash lime juice
2 ounces ginger ale
• *Garnish:*
1 maraschino cherry

Mix the cherry and lime juice together, with ice cubes, in the glass. Top up with ginger ale and stir. Perch the cherry on the rim of the glass.

Sweety (back left), **Light Red** (back right), **Cherry Ale** (front left), **Light Banana** (front right)

RED SKY

Fruity, sweet drink for a party
• Large cocktail glass
• Shaker

1½ ounces pineapple juice
1½ ounces lime cordial
¾ ounce light cream
2 tsp. nonalcoholic grenadine

Shake all the ingredients together well, with ice cubes, in the shaker and strain into the glass.

EVENING SUN

Fruity, sweet drink for any time of year
• Cocktail glass
• Shaker

1½ ounces light cream
¾ ounce banana juice
2 tsp. nonalcoholic grenadine

Shake all the ingredients together, with ice, in the shaker and strain into the glass.

PINEAPPLE SOUR

Fruity sour for hot days
• Cocktail glass
• Shaker

2 ounces pineapple juice
¾ ounce lemon juice
2 tsp. sugar syrup

Shake all the ingredients together, with ice, in the shaker and strain into the glass.

GRENADINE FRAPPÉ

Fruity, tangy, mild drink for hot days
• Large cocktail glass
• Shaker

1 scoop lemon sorbet
1½ ounces lime juice
¾ ounce nonalcoholic grenadine
• *Garnish:*
1 lime quarter
1 sprig lemon balm

Put the sorbet into the cocktail glass. Shake the lime juice and grenadine together in the shaker and pour over the sorbet. Perch the lime quarter and sprig of lemon balm on the rim of the glass.

SPORTSMAN

Fruity, sweet drink for any time of year
• Large rocks glass
• Shaker

1½ ounces orange juice
¾ ounce lemon juice
¾ ounce nonalcoholic grenadine
1 egg yolk
• *Garnish:*
1 slice of orange

Shake all the ingredients together, with ice cubes, in the shaker and strain into the glass. Perch the slice of orange on the rim of the glass.

Nonalcoholic

CANARIA

Fruity, tangy drink for a party
• Cocktail glass
• Shaker

2 ounces grapefruit juice
2 tsp. lime juice
2 tsp. orange syrup
• Garnish:
1 slice of lime

Shake all the ingredients together, with
ice cubes, in the shaker and strain into
the cocktail glass. Perch the slice of
lime on the rim of the glass.

LIGHT LIMARA

Refreshing sparkling cocktail for a party
• Champagne flute
• Shaker

½ ounce passion-fruit syrup
1½ ounces passion-fruit juice
¾ ounce orange juice
2 tsp. lemon juice
Nonalcoholic sparkling wine for
topping up
• Garnish:
1 slice of lemon

Shake all the ingredients, except the
sparkling wine, together, with ice, in
the shaker. Strain into the champagne
flute and top up with sparkling wine.
Perch the slice of lemon on the rim of
the glass.

LIGHT STRAWBERRY

Fruity, refreshing, sparkling cocktail
• Champagne glass
• Shaker

1 tbsp. puréed strawberries
2 tsp. strawberry syrup
2 tsp. pineapple juice
2 tsp. lemon juice
2 tsp. grapefruit juice
Nonalcoholic sparkling wine for
topping up
• Garnish:
½ strawberry

Shake all the ingredients, except the
sparkling wine, together firmly, with
ice, in the shaker. Strain into the
champagne glass and top up with
sparkling wine. Perch the strawberry on
the rim of the glass.

PINEAPPLE COCKTAIL

Fruity, sweet drink for a party
• Cocktail glass
• Shaker

1½ ounces pineapple juice
1 ounce orange juice
• Garnish:
Pineapple segment

Shake the ingredients together, with ice
cubes, in the shaker and strain into the
cocktail glass. Perch the pineapple
segment on the rim of the glass.

BREAKFAST DRINK

Fruity, sweet drink for mornings
• Cocktail glass
• Shaker

2 ounces orange juice
2 tsp. nonalcoholic grenadine
1 tbsp. egg white

Shake all the ingredients together well, with ice cubes, in the shaker and strain into the glass.

OFFENBURG FLIP

Fruity, sweet drink for any time of year
• Highball/Collins glass
• Blender

1½ ounces orange juice
1½ ounces banana syrup
¾ ounce lemon juice
1 egg yolk
½ banana, peeled and diced
• Garnish:
2 slices of banana

Mix all the ingredients together well, with ice cubes, in the blender and strain into the highball glass. Spear the slices of banana on a toothpick and lay the garnish across the rim of the glass.

BLACK FOREST FLIP

Fruity, tangy drink for any time of year
• Tulip-shaped glass
• Shaker

2 ounces cherry juice
¾ ounce lime cordial
2 tsp. lemon juice
1 egg yolk
• Garnish:
1 small sprig lemon balm

Shake all the ingredients together, with ice cubes, in the shaker and strain into the glass. Perch the sprig of lemon balm on the rim of the glass.

BIG APPLE II

Refreshing, medium-dry drink for the summer
• Highball/Collins glass
• Mixing glass

2 ounces apple juice
¾ ounce nonalcoholic grenadine
Sparkling mineral water for topping up
• Garnish:
1 slice of apple
1 apple peel spiral

Mix the ingredients, except the mineral water, together, with ice, in the mixing glass and strain into the highball glass over ice cubes. Top up with mineral water and stir. Perch the slice of apple on the rim of the glass and hang the apple peel spiral over the rim of the glass. Put a stirrer in the glass.

BIG APPLE III

Fruity drink for any time of year
• Highball/Collins glass
• Shaker

2 ounces orange juice
2 ounces apple juice
1 ounce nonalcoholic grenadine
Soda water for topping up
• *Garnish:*
1 slice of apple

Shake the fruit juices and grenadine together in the shaker and pour into the highball glass over ice cubes. Top up with soda water and stir briefly. Perch the slice of apple on the rim of the glass.

ZERO PERCENT

Refreshing, fruity drink for the summer
• Highball/Collins glass
• Shaker

1½ ounces pineapple juice
1½ ounces orange juice
¾ ounce lemon juice
¾ ounce mandarin syrup
2 tsp. nonalcoholic grenadine
• *Garnish:*
Small pieces of fruit

Shake all the ingredients, except the grenadine, together, with ice cubes, in the shaker and strain into the highball glass over crushed ice. Pour the grenadine onto the drink. Spear the pieces of fruit on a toothpick and lay the garnish across the rim of the glass.

GREEN WAVE

Refreshing drink for the summer
• Highball/Collins glass

1½ ounces peppermint syrup
Tonic water for topping up
• *Garnish:*
1 sprig of mint

Put the peppermint syrup in the highball glass with shaved ice, top up with tonic water, and stir. Add the sprig of mint and a stirrer to the glass.

GREENY

Sweet, long drink for every day
• Highball/Collins glass
• Shaker

¾ ounce almond syrup
1½ ounces orange juice
¾ ounce lemon juice
Ginger ale for topping up
3 dashes nonalcoholic blue curaçao
• *Garnish:*
1 sprig of mint

Shake all the ingredients, except the ginger ale and curaçao, together, with ice, in the shaker and strain into the highball glass over crushed ice. Top up with ginger ale and add the curaçao to the drink. Put the sprig of mint in the glass.

CABRIOLET 911

Refreshing, rather bitter drink for the evening
• Highball/Collins glass
• Shaker

¾ ounce nonalcoholic blue curaçao
¾ ounce grapefruit juice
2 tsp. lime cordial
Tonic water for topping up
• Garnish:
1 small cluster grapes

Shake all the ingredients, except the tonic water, together, with ice, in the shaker. Strain into the highball glass and top up with tonic water. Hang the cluster of grapes over the rim of the glass. Serve with a stirrer.

TARGA 911

Light, sweet drink for car drivers
• Highball/Collins glass

1½ ounces orange juice
1½ ounces passion-fruit juice
¾ ounce pineapple juice
¾ ounce lemon juice
¾ ounce nonalcoholic grenadine
• Garnish:
2 maraschino cherries

Mix the ingredients together, with ice cubes, in the glass. Spear the cherries on a toothpick and lay the garnish across the rim of the glass. Serve with a large stirrer.

RED SLIP

Sweet, fruity drink for a party
• Highball/Collins glass
• Shaker

1½ ounces strawberry syrup
1½ ounces grapefruit juice
Bitter grapefruit juice for topping up
• *Garnish:*
1 strawberry
1 sprig of mint

Shake all the ingredients, except the bitter grapefruit juice, together, with ice, in the shaker and strain into the highball glass over ice. Top up with bitter grapefruit juice. Spear the strawberry and the sprig of mint on a toothpick and lay the garnish across the rim of the glass. Serve with a stirrer.

AVALANCHE

Tangy, refreshing drink for hot days
• Highball/Collins glass

1 scoop lemon sorbet
Bitter lemon for topping up
• *Garnish:*
2 slices of lime

Put the lemon sorbet in the glass with crushed ice and top up with bitter lemon. Perch one slice of lime on the rim of the glass and add the other to the glass. Serve with a stirrer.

TROPICAL COOLER

Refreshing cooler for a Caribbean evening
• Highball/Collins glass
• Shaker

¾ ounce passion-fruit syrup
1½ ounces passion-fruit juice
¾ ounce lemon juice
Tropical bitter (exotic fruit-flavored carbonated drink) for topping up
• *Garnish:*
1 slice of star fruit
1 maraschino cherry

Shake all the ingredients, except the tropical bitter, together, with ice, in the shaker. Strain into the highball glass over crushed ice and top up with tropical bitter. Perch the slice of star fruit on the rim of the glass and fasten the cherry to it with a toothpick. Serve with a stirrer.

GRENADINA

Refreshing drink for the summer
• Highball/Collins glass

1 ounce nonalcoholic grenadine
¾ ounce lemon juice
Sparkling mineral water for topping up

Fill the glass one-quarter full with ice cubes. Pour the grenadine into the glass, then carefully pour the lemon juice on top, so they do not mix. Slowly top up with mineral water. Serve with a stirrer.

EXOTIC LEMON

Fruity, tangy drink for any occasion
• Highball/Collins glass

3½ ounces passion-fruit juice
1 kumquat, sliced
2 tsp. lemon juice
Bitter lemon for topping up

Mix the passion-fruit juice, kumquat slices, and lemon juice together in the highball glass with crushed ice. Top up with bitter lemon.

LEMON COOLER

Tangy, sour, refreshing cooler for the summer
• Highball/Collins glass
• Shaker

1½ ounces lemon juice
¾ ounce lime syrup
¾ ounce lime juice
Bitter lemon for topping up
• *Garnish:*
1 slice of lemon
2 maraschino cherries

Shake all the ingredients, except the bitter lemon, together, with ice, in the shaker. Strain into the highball glass over ice and top up with bitter lemon. Perch the slice of lemon on the rim of the glass. Fasten one maraschino cherry to it with a toothpick. Put the other cherry in the glass. Serve with a stirrer.

Nonalcoholic

ORANGE COOLER

Fruity, refreshing cooler for the summer
- Highball/Collins glass
- Shaker

1½ ounces orange juice
¾ ounce mandarin syrup
¾ ounce lemon juice
Bitter orange for topping up
- *Garnish:*
½ slice of orange
1 maraschino cherry

Shake all the ingredients, except the bitter orange, together, with ice, in the shaker and strain into the highball glass over crushed ice. Top up with bitter orange. Spear the slice of orange and the cherry on a toothpick and lay the garnish across the rim of the glass. Serve with a stirrer.

FLORIDA COCKTAIL

Fruity, sweet drink for any occasion
- Large cocktail glass
- Shaker

2 ounces pineapple juice
1 ounce lemon juice
2 tsp. nonalcoholic grenadine
1 dash Angostura bitters

Shake all the ingredients together well, with ice cubes, in the shaker, and strain into the glass.

KENYA

Fruity, sweet drink for any occasion
- Champagne glass
- Shaker

1½ ounces lemon juice
1½ ounces passion-fruit juice
¾ ounce pineapple syrup
2 tsp. banana syrup

Shake all the ingredients together, with ice cubes, in the shaker and strain into the champagne glass.

SUNBEAM

Fruity, long drink for a party
- Large stemmed glass
- Mixing glass

1 large grapefruit
1¾ ounces pineapple juice
1 ounce nonalcoholic grenadine
Bitter lemon for topping up
- *Garnish:*
2 maraschino cherries

Cut off a small lid from the top of the grapefruit and carefully squeeze the juice out of the grapefruit. Line the glass with a small, red napkin and put the grapefruit shell in the glass. Mix the grapefruit juice with the pineapple juice and grenadine in the mixing glass, pour into the grapefruit shell, and top up with bitter lemon. Spear the cherries on a toothpick and insert it into the grapefruit. Serve with a small straw.

MINT TONIC

Fruity, tangy drink for the summer
• Highball/Collins glass

4 peppermint leaves
2 tsp. sugar syrup
2 ounces lemon juice
1½ ounces peppermint syrup
Tonic water for topping up
• Garnish:
1 lemon peel spiral

Crush the mint leaves in the highball glass with the sugar syrup. Add a few ice cubes, the lemon juice, and peppermint syrup and stir well. Top up with the tonic water and stir again. Hang the peel spiral over the rim of the glass.

SHIRLEY TEMPLE

Fruity, tangy drink for any time of year
• Rocks glass

1½ ounces cherry juice
¾ ounce lemon juice
Ginger ale for topping up
• Garnish:
1 slice of lemon
2 maraschino cherries

Pour the juices into the glass over ice cubes, stir briefly, top up with ginger ale, and stir again. Perch the slice of lemon on the rim of the glass and fasten the cherries to it with a toothpick.

MARACAS

Fruity, sweet drink for a party
• Highball/Collins glass
• Shaker

1½ ounces pineapple juice
1½ ounces orange juice
1½ ounces grapefruit juice
¾ ounce passion-fruit syrup
¾ ounce lemon juice
• Garnish:
1 slice of star fruit

Shake all the ingredients together well, with ice cubes, in the shaker and strain into the highball glass. Perch the slice of star fruit on the rim of the glass.

GRAPEFRUIT LEMONADE

Fruity drink for any time of year
• Highball/Collins glass

2 ounces grapefruit juice
¾ ounce nonalcoholic grenadine
2 tsp. orange juice
Bitter grapefruit for topping up
• Garnish:
1 kumquat

Mix all the ingredients, except the bitter grapefruit, together, with ice cubes, in the glass. Top up with bitter grapefruit and stir briefly. Perch the kumquat on the rim of the glass.

Mint Tonic (left), Cherry Kiss (right)

TONIC FRESH

Fruity long drink for hot days
• Highball/Collins glass
• Shaker

2 ounces orange juice
1 ounce pineapple juice
¾ ounce lemon juice
¾ ounce raspberry syrup
Tonic water for topping up
• *Garnish:*
1 slice of orange

Shake the juices and syrup together, with ice cubes, in the shaker and strain into the highball glass. Top up with tonic water and stir briefly. Perch the slice of orange on the rim of the glass.

CHERRY KISS

Fruity, mild drink for any time of year
• Highball/Collins glass
• Shaker

3 ounces cherry juice
1¾ ounces pineapple juice
1 ounce lemon juice
¾ ounce cherry syrup
• *Garnish:*
¼ slice of pineapple
1 maraschino cherry

Shake all the ingredients together, with ice cubes, in the shaker and strain into the highball glass. Fasten the cherry to the piece of pineapple with a toothpick and perch the piece of pineapple on the rim of the glass.

PINEAPPLE MINT

Fruity, tangy drink for hot days
• Highball/Collins glass

4 ounces pineapple juice
2 ounces bitter lemon
2 dashes peppermint syrup
• Garnish:
¼ slice of pineapple

Carefully mix all the ingredients together, with ice cubes, in the highball glass. Perch the slice of pineapple on the rim of the glass.

GREEN DREAMS

Fruity, sweet drink for hot days
• Highball/Collins glass
• Shaker

2 ounces orange juice
2 ounces pineapple juice
1¾ ounces passion-fruit juice
¾ ounce peppermint syrup
• Garnish:
½ slice of pineapple

Shake all the ingredients together, with ice cubes, in the shaker and strain into the highball glass. Perch the slice of pineapple on the rim of the glass.

PUSSY FOOT

Fruity, tangy drink for a party
• Highball/Collins glass
• Shaker

1¾ ounces orange juice
1 ounce lemon juice
1 ounce pineapple juice
2 tsp. nonalcoholic grenadine
• Garnish:
½ slice of orange

Shake all the ingredients together, with ice cubes, in the shaker and strain into the highball glass. Spear the slice of orange on a toothpick and lay the garnish across the rim of the glass.

PRIMADONNA

Fruity, sweet drink for a party
• Highball/Collins glass
• Shaker

1½ ounces orange juice
1½ ounces grapefruit juice
1½ ounces passion-fruit juice
2 tsp. lemon juice
¾ ounce nonalcoholic grenadine
• Garnish:
1 slice of orange
1 slice of lemon

Shake all the ingredients together, with ice cubes, in the shaker and strain into the highball glass. Perch the slices of fruit on the rim of the glass.

PLANTER'S WONDER

Fruity, sweet drink for a party
• Highball/Collins glass
• Shaker

2 ounces orange juice
2 ounces pineapple juice
2 ounces passion-fruit juice
¾ ounce lemon juice
¾ ounce nonalcoholic grenadine
• Garnish:
1 slice of star fruit
1 slice of kiwi fruit
1 maraschino cherry

Shake all the ingredients together well, with ice cubes, in the shaker and strain into the highball glass over crushed ice. Spear the pieces of fruit on a toothpick and lay the garnish across the rim of the glass.

DOUBLE RAINBOW

Fruity, long drink for hot days
• Highball/Collins glass

4 ounces orange juice
¾ ounce lemon juice
2 tsp. nonalcoholic grenadine
Soda water for topping up
• Garnish:
1 slice of orange
1 slice of lemon

Mix the juices and grenadine in the highball glass, with ice cubes, and top up with soda water. Perch the slices of fruit on the rim of the glass.

MIAMI

Fruity, sweet drink for hot days
• Highball/Collins glass
• Shaker

5 ounces pineapple juice
2 tsp. lemon juice
2 tsp. sugar syrup
2 tsp. peppermint syrup
• Garnish:
½ slice of pineapple

Shake all the ingredients together well, with ice cubes, in the shaker and strain into the highball glass. Perch the slice of pineapple on the rim of the glass.

MENTHAPOL

Refreshing drink for hot days
• Highball/Collins glass

1½ ounces peppermint syrup
7 ounces sparkling mineral water for topping up
• Garnish:
1 sprig of mint

Pour the syrup and mineral water into the glass over plenty of ice and stir. Add the sprig of mint to the glass.

JAMAICA FRUIT

Fruity, sweet drink for a party
• Balloon-shaped wine glass
• Shaker

2 ounces orange juice
2 ounces pineapple juice
1 ounce passion-fruit juice
¾ ounce lemon juice
• Garnish:
½ slice of orange
1 maraschino cherry

Shake all the ingredients together, with ice cubes, in the shaker and strain into the balloon glass over ice cubes. Spear the slice of orange and the cherry on a toothpick and perch the fruit on the rim of the glass.

GOLDEN FOAM

Fruity, sweet drink for mornings or afternoons
• Highball/Collins glass
• Shaker

2¾ ounces carrot juice
1½ ounces pineapple juice
¾ ounce banana juice
• Garnish:
2 slices of carrot

Shake all the ingredients together well, with ice cubes, in the shaker and strain into the highball glass. Perch the slices of carrot on the rim of the glass.

RUBY ORANGE

Fruity, long drink for any occasion
• Highball/Collins glass

5½ ounces orange juice
2 tsp. lemon juice
2 tsp. nonalcoholic grenadine
• Extra:
1 wedge of lemon

Mix all the ingredients together, with ice cubes, in the highball glass. Add the wedge of lemon to the glass.

APRICOT MIX

Fruity, tangy drink for summer days
• Highball/Collins glass

3½ ounces orange juice
3½ ounces apricot juice
1½ ounces lemon juice
• Garnish:
1 slice of orange

Mix all the ingredients together, with ice cubes, in the highball glass. Perch the slice of orange on the rim of the glass.

Jamaica Fruit (left), Ruby Orange (middle), Apricot Mix (right)

EXOTIC ORANGE

Fruity, long drink for any occasion
• Highball/Collins glass

3½ ounces orange juice
3½ ounces passion-fruit juice
1 dash Angostura bitters
• Garnish:
1 slice of orange

Mix all the ingredients together, with
ice cubes, in the highball glass. Perch
the slice of orange on the rim of the
glass.

QUICKLY WAIKIKI

Fruity, sweet drink for a party
• Highball/Collins glass
• Shaker

5 ounces pineapple juice
¾ ounce lemon juice
2 tbsp. brown sugar
• Garnish:
½ slice of pineapple

Shake all the ingredients together, with
ice cubes, in the shaker and strain into
the highball glass. Perch the slice of
pineapple on the rim of the glass.

PASSION-FRUIT FREEZE

Fruity, mild drink for hot days
• Large champagne glass
• Shaker

2¾ ounces passion-fruit juice
2 tsp. lemon juice
2 tsp. raspberry syrup
Soda water for topping up
• Garnish:
1 maraschino cherry

Shake the fruit juices and syrup
together firmly, with ice cubes, in the
shaker and strain into the champagne
glass. Top up with soda water and stir
briefly. Perch the cherry on the rim of
the glass.

FRESH ORANGE

Fruity, tangy drink for any occasion
• Highball/Collins glass

2 ounces orange juice
¾ ounce lemon juice
¾ ounce pineapple juice
1½ ounces ginger ale
Soda water for topping up
• Garnish:
¼ slice of pineapple
1 piece of orange peel

Mix the fruit juices together well, with
ice cubes, in the highball glass. Top up
with ginger ale and soda water and stir
briefly. Perch the slice of pineapple and
the orange peel on the rim of the glass.

CAR DRIVE

Fruity, refreshing drink for any occasion
• Highball/Collins glass

1½ ounces pineapple juice

¾ ounce lemon juice

2 tsp. nonalcoholic grenadine

Ginger ale for topping up

• Garnish:

½ slice of pineapple

Pour the pineapple juice, lemon juice, and grenadine into the highball glass, over ice cubes. Stir and top up with ginger ale. Perch the slice of pineapple on the rim of the glass.

ARGENTINA

Fruity, sweet drink for a party
• Large highball/Collins glass
• Shaker

1¾ ounces pineapple juice

1¾ ounces apricot juice

1¾ ounces passion-fruit juice

1¾ ounces papaya juice

¾ ounce lemon juice

¾ ounce nonalcoholic grenadine

• Garnish:

¼ slice of pineapple

1 maraschino cherry

Shake the juices and grenadine together, with ice, in the shaker and strain into the highball glass over crushed ice. Spear the slice of pineapple and the cherry on a toothpick and lay the garnish across the rim of the glass.

GOLDEN GINGER ALE

Fruity, sweet drink for hot days
• Highball/Collins glass

1½ ounces orange juice

1½ ounces pineapple juice

Ginger ale for topping up

Mix the orange and pineapple juices together, with ice cubes, in the highball glass. Top up with ginger ale and stir.

SUMMER COOLER

Fruity, refreshing drink for hot days
• Highball/Collins glass

1½ ounces orange juice

1 dash Angostura bitters

Lemonade for topping up

• Garnish:

1 slice of lemon

Mix the orange juice and Angostura bitters together, with ice cubes, in the highball glass. Top up with lemonade and stir briefly. Perch the slice of lemon on the rim of the glass.

SUMMER DELIGHT

Fruity, sweet drink for hot days
• Highball/Collins glass

¾ ounce lime juice
¾ ounce raspberry syrup
Soda water for topping up
• Garnish:
4 raspberries
2 slices of lime

Mix the juice and syrup together, with ice cubes, in the highball glass. Top up with soda water and stir. Add the raspberries and perch the slice of lime on the rim of the glass.

ICE-CREAM SODA

Creamy drink for any occasion
• Large rocks glass

2 scoops flavored sorbet or ice cream, such as lemon and orange sorbet
Soda water for topping up

Put the sorbet or ice cream into the glass and top up with soda water. Serve with a spoon and a straw.

STRAWBERRY AND FRIENDS

Fruity, sweet drink for the summer
• Highball/Collins glass
• Mixing glass

1¾ ounces orange juice
1¾ ounces pineapple juice
1 ounce lemon juice
¾ ounce nonalcoholic grenadine
¾ ounce strawberry syrup
• Garnish:
2 strawberries

Mix all the ingredients together in the mixing glass and pour into the highball glass. Spear the strawberries on a toothpick and lay the garnish across the rim of the glass.

FRUIT CUP I

Fruity, tangy drink for a party
• Highball/Collins glass
• Shaker

2¾ ounces orange juice
2 ounces pineapple juice
2 ounces lime juice
¾ ounce lemon juice
¾ ounce nonalcoholic grenadine
• Garnish:
1 slice of orange
½ slice of lemon
3 maraschino cherries
1 pineapple segment

Shake all the ingredients together, with plenty of ice, in the shaker and strain into the highball glass. Perch the slice of orange on the rim of the glass and add the remaining fruit to the glass.

Nonalcoholic

FRUIT CUP II

Fruity, sweet drink for a party
• Highball/Collins glass
• Shaker

2¾ ounces passion-fruit juice
1½ ounces pineapple juice
1½ ounces lemon juice
¾ ounce orange juice
¾ ounce nonalcoholic grenadine
• Garnish:
½ slice of pineapple
1 maraschino cherry

Shake all the ingredients together, with ice cubes, in the shaker and strain into the highball glass. Spear the fruit on a toothpick and perch the fruit on the rim of the glass.

FRUIT CUP III

Fruity, mild drink for any time of year
• Highball/Collins glass
• Shaker

2¾ ounces orange juice
2¾ ounces pineapple juice
1½ ounces lemon juice
¾ ounce nonalcoholic grenadine
• Garnish:
1 slice of orange
1 maraschino cherry

Shake the ingredients together, with ice cubes, in the shaker and strain into the highball glass. Spear the slice of orange and the cherry on a toothpick and lay the garnish across the rim of the glass.

PINEAPPLE PEPPERMINT

Fruity, refreshing drink for any time of year
• Highball/Collins glass

4 ounces pineapple juice
2 dashes peppermint syrup
2 ounces bitter lemon
• Garnish:
1 sprig of mint

Mix the pineapple juice and peppermint syrup together, with ice cubes, in the highball glass. Top up with bitter lemon and stir. Add the sprig of mint to the glass.

ORANGE LEMONADE

Fruity, mild drink for any time of year
• Large rocks glass

1¾ ounces orange juice
¾ ounce lemon juice
¾ ounce sugar syrup
Soda water for topping up
• Garnish:
1 slice of orange

Mix the juices and the syrup together, with ice cubes, in the glass. Top up with soda water and stir briefly. Perch the slice of orange on the rim of the glass.

AMERICAN GLORY II

Fruity, sweet drink for any time of year
• Champagne flute

1 ounce orange juice
2 dashes sugar syrup
Lemonade for topping up
• *Garnish:*
1 slice of orange

Pour the orange juice and sugar syrup into the champagne flute over 2 ice cubes. Top up with lemonade and stir briefly. Perch the slice of orange on the rim of the glass.

REFRESHER

Fruity, sweet drink for any occasion
• Large rocks glass

1¾ ounces orange juice
¾ ounce nonalcoholic grenadine
Soda water for topping up
• *Garnish:*
1 slice of orange

Mix the orange juice and grenadine together, with ice cubes, in the glass. Top up with soda water and stir again. Perch the slice of orange on the rim of the glass.

EL DORADO II

Fruity, refreshing drink for a party
• Highball/Collins glass
• Shaker

1½ ounces guava juice

1½ ounces orange juice

1½ ounces passion-fruit juice

1½ ounces pineapple juice

Tonic water for topping up

• Garnish:

½ slice of pineapple

1 slice of orange

1 green maraschino cherry

Shake all the ingredients, except the tonic water, together, with ice cubes, in the shaker and strain into the highball glass. Top up with tonic water and stir briefly. Spear the fruit on a toothpick and perch the fruit on the rim of the glass.

STEFFI GRAF COCKTAIL

Fruity, sweet drink for any time of year
• Highball/Collins glass
• Mixing glass

1½ ounces pear juice

1½ ounces apricot juice

1½ ounces kiwi-fruit juice

1½ ounces orange juice

• Garnish:

1 slice of kiwi fruit

1 mini pear, peeled

1 slice of orange

Mix all the ingredients together, with ice cubes, in the mixing glass and strain into the highball glass. Spear the fruit on a toothpick and lay the garnish across the rim of the glass.

BALI-BOO

Fruity long drink for a party
- Highball/Collins glass
- Shaker

1½ ounces pineapple juice
1½ ounces passion-fruit juice
1½ ounces apricot juice
¾ ounce nonalcoholic blue curaçao
Bitter lemon for topping up
- *Garnish:*
½ slice of pineapple
1 maraschino cherry

Shake the juices and the curaçao together, with ice cubes, in the shaker and strain into the highball glass. Top up with bitter lemon and stir briefly. Spear the slice of pineapple and the cherry on a toothpick and add it to the glass.

BRUNSWICK COOLER

Tangy cooler for hot days
- Large rocks glass

¾ ounce lemon juice
¾ ounce sugar syrup
Ginger ale for topping up

Half fill the glass with ice cubes, pour the syrup and lemon juice into the glass, and stir well. Top up with ginger ale and briefly stir again.

PROOFLESS

Fruity, tangy drink for hot days
- Highball/Collins glass
- Shaker

3½ ounces lime juice
Tonic water for topping up
- *Garnish:*
1 slice of lime

Shake the lime juice, with ice cubes, in the shaker and strain into the highball glass. Top up with tonic water and stir briefly. Perch the slice of lime on the rim of the glass.

LEMON SQUASH

Fruity drink for hot days
- Large rocks glass

1 ounce lemon juice
2 tbsp. confectioners' sugar
Soda water for topping up
- *Garnish:*
1 slice of lemon

Half fill the glass with ice cubes. Mix the lemon juice and confectioners' sugar together in the glass, top up with soda water, and stir again. Perch the slice of lemon on the rim of the glass.

JAVA DREAM

Fruity, sweet drink for a party
• Highball/Collins glass
• Shaker

1½ ounces peach juice
1½ ounces banana juice
1½ ounces passion-fruit juice
¾ ounce nonalcoholic grenadine
Tonic water for topping up
• *Garnish:*
1 piece of peach
1 maraschino cherry

Shake the juices and the grenadine together, with ice cubes, in the shaker and strain into the highball glass. Top up with tonic water and stir briefly. Spear the fruit on a toothpick and lay the garnish across the rim of the glass.

SARATOGA COOLER

Fruity, mild drink for hot days
• Large rocks glass

¾ ounce nonalcoholic grenadine
¾ ounce lemon juice
Ginger ale for topping up

Half fill the glass with ice cubes and mix the grenadine and lemon juice together in it, stirring well. Top up with ginger ale and stir briefly again.

CHICAGO COOLER

Fruity, tangy cooler for hot days
• Large rocks glass

¾ ounce lemon juice
Ginger ale for topping up
Red grape juice for topping up

Half fill the glass with ice cubes. Pour the lemon juice into the glass and top up with half ginger ale and half grape juice. Stir briefly.

STRAWBERRY PLANT

Fruity, mild drink for a spring party
• Highball/Collins glass
• Shaker

2 ounces orange juice
2 ounces pineapple juice
1 ounce lemon juice
¾ ounce strawberry syrup
• *Garnish:*
1 strawberry

Shake all the ingredients together well in the shaker and strain into the highball glass. Perch the strawberry on the rim of the glass.

JUANA

Fruity, tangy drink for the summer
months
• Highball/Collins glass

2 ounces black-currant juice
¾ ounce lemon juice
¾ ounce orange juice
1 ounce apple juice
2 tsp. raspberry juice
Soda water for topping up
• *Garnish:*
1 slice of lemon
2 clusters of red currants

Mix the juices together in the highball
glass, top up with soda water, and stir
again. Perch the slice of lemon and one
of the clusters of red currants on the
rim of the glass. Add the other cluster to
the glass.

GRAPEFRUIT DREAM

Fruity, mild drink for any time of year
• Large rocks glass

1½ ounces grapefruit juice
¾ ounce nonalcoholic grenadine
Ginger ale for topping up

Mix the grapefruit juice and grenadine
together in the glass. Top up with ginger
ale and stir briefly.

BLUE BATAVIA

Fruity, mild drink for a party
• Highball/Collins glass
• Shaker

1 ounce pineapple juice
1 ounce pear juice
1 ounce passion-fruit juice
1 ounce apricot juice
2 tsp. lemon juice
2 tsp. nonalcoholic blue curaçao
Bitter lemon for topping up
• *Garnish:*
1 slice of lemon
1 maraschino cherry

Shake the juices and the curaçao
together, with ice cubes, in the shaker
and strain into the highball glass. Top
up with bitter lemon and stir briefly.
Perch the slice of lemon on the rim of
the glass and fasten the cherry to it with
a toothpick.

BERLIN

Fruity, long drink for every day
- Large brandy snifter
- Shaker

½ slice of pineapple, diced

2 slices of orange, chopped

2 tsp. lemon juice

1½ ounces pineapple juice

Apple juice for topping up

- *Garnish:*

1 slice of orange

Put the pieces of fruit in the balloon glass. Shake the lemon and pineapple juices together, with ice cubes, in the shaker and strain into the brandy snifter. Top up with apple juice and stir briefly. Perch the slice of orange on the rim of the glass.

FRUIT MIX

Fruity, long drink for hot days
- Highball/Collins glass
- Shaker

1½ ounces pineapple juice

1 ounce raspberry juice

¾ ounce orange juice

2 tsp. lemon juice

Soda water for topping up

- *Garnish:*

1 slice of lemon

1 slice of orange

Shake the juices together, with ice cubes, in the shaker and strain into the highball glass. Top up with soda water and stir briefly. Perch the slices of fruit on the rim of the glass.

PEPPERMINT TONIC

Refreshing long drink for hot days
- Highball/Collins glass

¾ ounce lemon juice

1 ounce peppermint syrup

Tonic water for topping up

- *Garnish:*

1 lemon peel spiral

Mix the lemon juice and the syrup together in the highball glass. Top up with tonic water and stir briefly. Hang the lemon peel spiral over the edge of the glass.

BORNEO GOLD

Fruity, long drink for the evening
• Highball/Collins glass

2 ounces apricot juice
1½ ounces banana juice
¾ ounce passion-fruit juice
Tonic water for topping up

Mix the fruit juices together, with ice cubes, in the highball glass. Top up with tonic water and stir briefly.

BELFAST COOLER

Fruity, tangy cooler for any occasion
• Large rocks glass

1¾ ounces lemon juice
Ginger ale for topping up

Half fill the glass with ice cubes, pour the lemon juice into the glass, top up with ginger ale, and stir briefly.

BICYCLE

Fruity, tangy drink for a party
• Highball/Collins glass

2 ounces mango juice
1½ ounces lemon juice
¾ ounce passion-fruit juice
2 tsp. nonalcoholic grenadine
Sparkling mineral water for topping up
• Garnish:
1 pineapple segment
1 maraschino cherry
1 sprig of lemon balm

Mix the juices and the grenadine together, with ice cubes, in the highball glass. Top up with mineral water and stir. Spear the slice of pineapple, the cherry, and lemon balm on a toothpick and lay the garnish across the rim of the glass.

BABOUIN

Fruity, long drink for a party
• Highball/Collins glass
• Shaker

1¾ ounces cherry juice
1½ ounces passion-fruit juice
1 ounce pineapple juice
¾ ounce lime juice
2 tsp. orange juice
• Extra:
¼ banana, peeled and sliced
A few pieces of pineapple
2 maraschino cherries

Shake all the ingredients together, with ice cubes, in the shaker and strain into the highball glass. Put the pieces of fruit in the glass. Serve with a spoon or long toothpick.

Babouin (left), Bicycle (right)

BORA-BORA

Fruity, sweet drink for a party
• Highball/Collins glass
• Shaker

3½ ounces pineapple juice
2 ounces passion-fruit juice
2 tsp. lemon juice
2 tsp. nonalcoholic grenadine
• Garnish:
½ slice of pineapple
1 maraschino cherry

Shake all the ingredients together, with ice cubes, in the shaker and strain into the highball glass. Perch the slice of pineapple on the rim of the glass and fasten the maraschino cherry to it with a toothpick.

PINEAPPLE FAREWELL

Fruity, sweet drink for hot days
• Large rocks glass

1½ ounces pineapple syrup
¾ ounce lemon juice
Soda water for topping up

Half fill the glass with ice cubes and mix the pineapple syrup and lemon juice together in the glass. Top up with soda water and stir.

SUNBREAKER

Fruity, long drink for any occasion
• Highball/Collins glass

2¾ ounces mango juice
¾ ounce lime cordial
Tonic water for topping up
• Garnish:
1 slice of orange
1 sprig of lemon balm

Mix the mango juice and lime cordial together, with ice cubes, in the highball glass. Top up with tonic water and stir. Perch the slice of orange and the sprig of lemon balm on the rim of the glass.

BIRD OF PARADISE

Fruity, sweet drink for a party
• Highball/Collins glass
• Shaker

2 ounces pineapple juice
2 ounces passion-fruit juice
2 ounces orange juice
2 tsp. lemon juice
2 tsp. nonalcoholic grenadine
• Garnish:
½ slice of pineapple
1 maraschino cherry

Shake the ingredients together, with ice cubes, in the shaker and strain into the highball glass. Perch the slice of pineapple on the rim of the glass and fasten the cherry to it with a toothpick.

Nonalcoholic

SUNRISE

Fruity, long drink for any occasion
• Highball/Collins glass
• Shaker

5 ounces orange juice
¾ ounce grapefruit juice
2 tsp. lemon juice
• Extra:
1 slice of orange
2 tsp. nonalcoholic grenadine

Shake all the ingredients together, with
ice cubes, in the shaker and strain into
the highball glass over ice cubes. Add
the slice of orange to the glass and pour
the grenadine over the slice of orange.

PEACH TREE

Fruity, mild drink for any time of year
• Highball/Collins glass
• Shaker

3½ ounces peach nectar
2 ounces orange juice
1 dash lemon juice
• Extra:
1 slice of orange
1 wedge of peach

Shake the ingredients together, with
ice, in the shaker and strain into the
highball glass. Add the fruit to the glass.

KIWI-KIWI

Fruity, long drink for hot days
• Highball/Collins glass

6 slices of kiwi fruit, peeled
¾ ounce raspberry syrup
2 tsp. lemon juice
Bitter lemon for topping up
• Garnish:
1 lime peel spiral

Put the slices of kiwi fruit into the
highball glass. Pour the syrup and juice
over them and top up with bitter
lemon. Hang the lime peel spiral over
the rim of the glass.

BOSTON COOLER

Sweet, fizzy drink for hot days
• Large rocks glass

1 lemon peel spiral
¾ ounce nonalcoholic grenadine
Ginger ale for topping up

Half fill the glass with ice cubes. Put the
lemon peel spiral in the glass and add
the grenadine. Top up with ginger ale
and stir well.

PEPPERMINT LEMONADE

Spicy, fresh drink for hot days
• Large rocks glass

¾ ounce peppermint syrup
¾ ounce lemon juice
Soda water for topping up

Mix the syrup and the lemon juice together, with ice cubes, in the glass. Top up with soda water and stir briefly.

MALAYSIAN DRINK

Fruity, long drink for a party
• Highball/Collins glass
• Mixing glass

2¾ ounces pineapple juice
1½ ounces grapefruit juice
¾ ounce nonalcoholic blue curaçao
Bitter lemon for topping up
• Garnish:
½ slice of pineapple

Mix the juices and the curaçao together, with ice cubes, in the mixing glass and strain into the highball glass. Top up with bitter lemon and stir briefly. Perch the slice of pineapple on the rim of the glass.

PEACHY

Fruity, fresh drink for the summer
• Balloon glass
• Shaker

4 ounces peach liqueur
2 ounces grapefruit juice
2 dashes lime juice
• Extra:
2 wedges of peach
2 slices of banana

Shake all the ingredients together, with ice, in the shaker. Fill the balloon glass one-third full with crushed ice and strain the drink into the glass. Add the fruit to the glass.

SWEET RAINBOW

Fruity, mild drink for any time of year
• Balloon glass
• Shaker

5 ounces orange juice
¾ ounce lemon juice
2 tsp. nonalcoholic grenadine
2 tsp. nonalcoholic blue curaçao
• Garnish:
1 slice of orange
1 slice of lemon

Shake the juices together, with ice, in the shaker and strain into the glass. Add ice to taste. Slowly pour first the grenadine, then the curaçao, over the drink. Perch the slices of citrus fruit on the rim of the glass.

Nonalcoholic

HAWAIIAN MIX

Fruity, mild drink for the hot months
- Large brandy snifter
- Shaker

2¾ ounces pineapple juice
1½ ounces orange juice
1 ounce grapefruit juice
¾ ounce lemon juice
1 ounce passion-fruit juice
• Extra:
Seasonal fruits, such as orange
segments, lemon wedges, slices of
pineapple, or slices of star fruit

Shake all the ingredients together
firmly, with ice, in the shaker and strain
into the brandy snifter filled one-third
full with crushed ice. Add the pieces of
fruit to the glass.

ORANGE TONIC

Fruity, mild drink for a party
- Highball/Collins glass
- Shaker

2 ounces orange juice
¾ ounce raspberry juice
¾ ounce nonalcoholic grenadine
Tonic water for topping up
• Garnish:
1 orange peel spiral

Shake the juices and the grenadine
together, with ice cubes, in the shaker
and strain into the highball glass. Top
up with tonic water and stir briefly.
Hang the orange peel spiral over the
rim of the glass.

LONG MISSISSIPPI

Very fruity drink for a party
- Large rocks glass

2¾ ounces black-currant juice
2¾ ounces orange juice
• Garnish:
1 slice of orange

Mix the ingredients together, with ice
cubes, in the glass. Perch the slice of
orange on the rim of the glass.

RED THING

Fruity, mild drink for hot days
- Highball/Collins glass
- Shaker

2 ounces orange juice
1½ ounces pineapple juice
¾ ounce lemon juice
2 tsp. nonalcoholic grenadine
• Garnish:
1 slice of orange
1 maraschino cherry

Shake all the ingredients together
firmly, with ice, in the shaker and strain
into the glass filled one-quarter full with
crushed ice. Perch the slice of orange
on the rim of the glass and fasten the
cherry to it with a toothpick.

APRICOT FIZZ

Fruity drink for the summer months
• Highball/Collins glass
• Shaker

2 ounces apricot juice
2 tsp. orange juice
2 tsp. lemon juice
Soda water for topping up

Shake the juices together firmly, with ice cubes, in the shaker and strain into the highball glass. Top up with soda water and stir briefly.

MELON

Refreshing drink for a party
• Highball/Collins glass

¼ ripe Galia or honeydew melon
¾ ounce nonalcoholic grenadine
Tonic water for topping up
• Garnish:
1 slice of star fruit

Using a melon baller, scoop out small balls of melon flesh and put them in the highball glass. Pour the grenadine over the melon balls, top up with tonic water, and stir briefly. Perch the slice of star fruit on the rim of the glass.

ANASTASIA

Fruity, mild drink for a party
• Large brandy snifter
• Shaker

2 slices of pineapple, diced
2 ounces pineapple juice
1½ ounces orange juice
1 ounce apple juice
¾ ounce lemon juice
Ginger ale for topping up
• Garnish:
1 maraschino cherry

Put the diced pineapple into the brandy snifter. Shake the juices together, with ice cubes, in the shaker and strain into the glass over the pineapple. Top up with ginger ale and stir briefly. Spear the cherry on a toothpick and lay the garnish across the rim of the glass.

APRICOFRUIT

Fruity, tangy drink for any time of year
• Highball/Collins glass
• Shaker

4 ounces apricot nectar
2¾ ounces grapefruit juice
2 tsp. lemon juice
• Garnish:
1 maraschino cherry

Shake all the ingredients together well, with ice, in the shaker and strain into the glass. Perch the cherry on the rim of the glass.

William Tell's Shot (left), Bahamas (right)

WILLIAM TELL'S SHOT

Fruity, tangy drink for any time of year
- Highball/Collins glass
- Shaker

3½ ounces apple juice

1¾ ounces grapefruit juice

¾ ounce lemon juice

2 tsp. nonalcoholic grenadine

2 dashes almond syrup

- *Garnish:*

1 mini apple or green maraschino cherry

Shake all the ingredients together, with ice cubes, in the shaker and strain into the highball glass. Top up with crushed ice. Spear the mini apple on a toothpick and lay the garnish across the rim of the glass.

BAHAMAS

Fruity, refreshing drink for any time of year
- Highball/Collins glass

5 ounces apple juice

¾ ounce lemon juice

2 tsp. nonalcoholic grenadine

- *Garnish:*

1 slice of star fruit

Mix all the ingredients together, with ice cubes, in the highball glass. Perch the slice of star fruit on the rim of the glass.

HAPPY MORNING

Fruity, sweet drink for any time of year
• Highball/Collins glass
• Shaker

4 ounces orange juice
2 ounces apricot nectar
2 tsp. lemon juice
2 tsp. nonalcoholic grenadine
• Garnish:
2 slices of orange

Shake all the ingredients together, with ice cubes, in the shaker and strain into the highball glass. Perch the slices of orange on the rim of the glass.

TWO GRAPES

Fruity, tangy drink for any time of year
• Highball/Collins glass
• Shaker

3½ ounces white grape juice
2 ounces grapefruit juice
¾ ounce orange juice
• Garnish:
2 grapes

Shake all the ingredients together, with ice, in the shaker and strain into the glass. Spear the grapes on a toothpick and lay the garnish across the rim of the glass.

FIVE KINDS

Fruity, refreshing drink for any time of year
• Large rocks glass
• Shaker

1¾ ounces orange juice
1¾ ounces grapefruit juice
¾ ounce pineapple juice
2 tsp. lemon juice
2 tsp. sugar syrup
• Garnish:
1 slice of orange
1 maraschino cherry

Shake all the ingredients together, with ice, in the shaker and strain into the glass. Perch the slice of orange on the rim of the glass and fasten the cherry to it with a toothpick.

RED APPLE

Fruity, fresh drink for any occasion
• Highball/Collins glass
• Mixing glass

2¾ ounces apple juice
1½ ounces red-currant juice
1½ ounces apricot nectar
• Garnish:
1 wedge of apple

Mix the ingredients together, with ice, in the mixing glass and strain into the highball glass over ice cubes. Perch the wedge of apple on the rim of the glass.

TENNIS DRINK

Fruity, mild drink for a party
• Highball/Collins glass
• Shaker

1½ ounces passion-fruit nectar
1½ ounces pineapple juice
¾ ounce lime juice
2 tsp. banana juice
¾ ounce light cream
• Garnish:
1 slice of orange
1 slice of lime

Shake all the ingredients together firmly, with ice, in the shaker and strain into the highball glass over ice cubes. Perch the slices of fruit on the rim of the glass.

PLANTER'S DREAM

Fruity, fresh drink for a party
• Highball/Collins glass
• Shaker

2¾ ounces orange juice
2¾ ounces pineapple juice
1½ ounces lemon juice
2 tsp. nonalcoholic grenadine
2 tsp. mango syrup
• Garnish:
2 slices of orange

Shake all the ingredients together firmly, with ice, in the shaker and strain into the highball glass. Top up with crushed ice. Perch the slices of orange on the rim of the glass.

MINT ORANGE

Tangy, fresh long drink for summer days
• Highball/Collins glass
• Shaker

¾ ounce peppermint syrup
2 tsp. lime juice
5½ ounces bitter orange
• Extra:
1 sprig of mint
1 wedge of lime

Shake the syrup and lime juice together well, with ice cubes, in the shaker and strain into the glass. Add ice to taste, top up with bitter orange, and stir briefly. Add the sprig of mint and the lime wedge to the glass.

PINEAPPLE DRINK

Fruity, tangy drink for the summer
• Highball/Collins glass

3½ ounces pineapple juice
2 tsp. lemon juice
3½ ounces bitter lemon
2 tsp. nonalcoholic grenadine
• Garnish:
½ slice of pineapple

Mix the pineapple and lemon juices together, with ice cubes, in the highball glass. Add the bitter lemon and stir briefly. Slowly float the grenadine on top of the drink. Perch the slice of pineapple on the rim of the glass.

ORANGE FREEZE

Fruity drink for hot days
• Balloon-shaped wine glass

¾ ounce orange juice
2 tsp. lime juice
Ginger ale for topping up
• Garnish:
1 kumquat

Put 3 tablespoons of crushed ice into
the glass with the orange juice and lime
juice. Stir, top up with ginger ale, and
stir again. Perch the kumquat on the
rim of the glass.

COLA FREEZE

Fruity, sweet drink for hot days
• Highball/Collins glass
• Shaker

1-2 scoops lemon sorbet
2 tsp. lemon syrup
Cola for topping up

Shake 2 tablespoons of crushed ice
with the sorbet and the syrup firmly in
the shaker, and strain into the highball
glass filled two-thirds full with crushed
ice. Top up with cola. Serve with a
stirrer.

PINEAPPLE FREEZE

Fruity, sweet drink for hot days
• Highball/Collins glass

2 ounces pineapple syrup
1 scoop pineapple sorbet
Soda water for topping up
• Garnish:
½ slice of pineapple

Pour the syrup into the highball glass
and fill the glass two-thirds full with
crushed ice. Add the pineapple sorbet
and top up with soda water. Perch the
slice of pineapple on the rim of the
glass. Serve with a spoon.

BERRY FREEZE

Fruity, mild drink for hot days
• Highball/Collins glass

1 ounce black-currant syrup
1 scoop black-currant sorbet
Soda water for topping up
• Garnish:
1 cluster red currants

Pour the syrup into the glass, fill the
glass two-thirds full with crushed ice,
and add the black-currant sorbet. Top
up with soda water. Perch the cluster of
red currants on the rim of the glass.
Serve with a long-handled spoon.

From left to right: Orange Freeze, Pineapple Freeze, Cola Freeze, Berry Freeze

TROPICAL HEAT

Fruity, sweet drink for any occasion
• Highball/Collins glass
• Mixing glass

1¾ ounces orange juice
1¾ ounces passion-fruit juice
1¾ ounces pineapple juice
2 tsp. lemon juice
2 tsp. nonalcoholic grenadine
• Garnish:
1 slice of star fruit

Mix all the ingredients together, with ice cubes, in the mixing glass and strain into the highball glass. Perch the slice of star fruit on the rim of the glass.

TROPICAL DREAM

Fruity, mild drink for a party
• Large champagne glass
• Shaker

2 ounces passion-fruit juice
2 ounces pineapple juice
2 tsp. lemon juice
2 tsp. nonalcoholic grenadine
• Garnish:
1 maraschino cherry

Shake all the ingredients together, with ice, in the shaker and strain into the champagne glass. Perch the cherry on the rim of the glass.

SEA WATER

Fruity drink for a summer party
• Highball/Collins glass
• Shaker

1½ ounces nonalcoholic blue curaçao
2 tsp. lemon juice
2 tsp. bitter lemon
¾ ounce ginger ale
Tonic water for topping up
• Extra:
1 tbsp. red currants, without stems
3 small slices of lime

Shake the curaçao and lemon juice together, with ice cubes, in the shaker and strain into the highball glass. Add the bitter lemon and ginger ale, top up with tonic water, and stir briefly. Add the red currants and 2 slices of lime to the glass. Perch the remaining slice of lime on the rim of the glass.

TROPICAL MAGIC II

Fruity, sweet drink for a party
• Highball/Collins glass
• Shaker

1½ ounces peach juice
1½ ounces grapefruit juice
1½ ounces banana juice
¾ ounce nonalcoholic grenadine
Tonic water for topping up

Shake the juices and the grenadine together, with ice cubes, in the shaker and strain into the highball glass. Top up with tonic water and stir briefly.

Nonalcoholic

GRANIZADO DE CASSIS

Fruity, mild drink for hot days
• Large rocks glass

¾ ounce black-currant cordial
2 tsp. orange juice
Soda water for topping up
• Garnish:
1 cluster of red currants

Mix the cordial and orange juice together in the glass and fill the glass three-quarters full with crushed ice. Top up with soda water and stir briefly. Hang the cluster of red currants over the rim of the glass.

GRANITO DI ARANCIA

Fruity, sweet drink for hot days
• Large brandy snifter

2 tsp. lemon juice
1 ounce orange syrup
Soda water for topping up
• Garnish:
1 sprig of lemon balm

Fill the brandy snifter two-thirds full with crushed ice and pour the juice and syrup over it. Top up with soda water and stir briefly. Perch the sprig of lemon balm on the rim of the glass.

GRANIZADO DE LIMON

Fruity, tangy, mild drink for hot days
• Large rocks glass

¾ ounce lime cordial
2 tsp. lime juice
Soda water for topping up
• Garnish:
1 lemon peel spiral

Mix the lime cordial and juice together in the glass and fill the glass three-quarters full with crushed ice. Top up with soda water and stir briefly. Hang the spiral of lemon peel over the rim of the glass.

GRANIZADO DE MENTA

Refreshing, tangy drink for a summer party
• Large rocks glass

¾ ounce lemon juice
2 tsp. peppermint syrup
Soda water for topping up
• Garnish:
A few fresh mint leaves

Mix the juice and syrup together in the glass and fill the glass three-quarters full with crushed ice. Top up with soda water, stir briefly, and add the mint leaves to the glass.

GRANITO DI LAMPONE

Fruity, mild drink for hot days
• Large brandy snifter

2 tsp. lemon juice
1 ounce raspberry syrup
Soda water for topping up
• Garnish:
1 slice of orange

Fill the brandy snifter two-thirds full with crushed ice and pour the juice and syrup over it. Top up with soda water and stir briefly. Perch the slice of orange on the rim of the glass.

GRANITO DI ASPERULA

Fruity, sweet long drink for hot days
• Highball/Collins glass

2 tsp. lime juice
1 ounce woodruff syrup
Soda water for topping up
• Garnish:
1 slice of orange

Fill the highball glass two-thirds full with crushed ice and pour the juice and syrup over it. Top up with soda water and stir briefly. Perch the slice of orange on the rim of the glass.

SHOOTING STAR

Fruity, refreshing long drink for a party
• Highball/Collins glass
• Shaker

2¾ ounces exotic fruit juice blend, such as passion fruit and mango juice
1¾ ounces pineapple juice
1 ounce orange juice
¾ ounce grapefruit juice
2 tsp. nonalcoholic grenadine
• Garnish:
½ slice of pineapple
½ slice of orange

Shake all the ingredients together, with ice, in the shaker and strain into the highball glass. Add crushed ice to taste. Perch the slices of fruit on the rim of the glass.

PINCASSO

Fruity, tangy drink for a party
• Highball/Collins glass
• Shaker

1¼ ounces red grape juice
1½ ounces grapefruit juice
¾ ounce lime juice
2 tsp. nonalcoholic grenadine
2 tsp. bitter lemon
Soda water for topping up
• Garnish:
1 sprig of lemon balm

Shake the juices and grenadine together, with ice cubes, in the shaker and strain into the highball glass. Add the bitter lemon, top up with soda water, and stir. Perch the sprig of lemon balm on the rim of the glass.

Nonalcoholic

Granito di Asperula (left), Dance with Me (right)

TAKE THIS

Refreshing, long drink for a party
• Highball/Collins glass

¾ ounce lemon juice
¾ ounce nonalcoholic grenadine
3½ ounces Sanbitter (Italian
nonalcoholic bitters)
• Extra:
½ slice of orange

Mix the juice and grenadine together
with plenty of ice cubes in the highball
glass. Top up with Sanbitter and stir
again. Add the slice of orange to the
glass.

DANCE WITH ME

Spicy, tangy drink for any time of year
• Highball/Collins glass

3½ ounces Sanbitter (Italian
nonalcoholic bitters)
2 tsp. lemon juice
3½ ounces bitter lemon
• Garnish:
1 lemon peel spiral

Mix the Sanbitter and lemon juice
together, with ice cubes, in the highball
glass. Add the bitter lemon and stir
carefully. Hang the lemon peel spiral
over the rim of the glass.

RED BUTLER

Fruity, tangy drink for hot days
• Highball/Collins glass

3½ ounces ruby orange nectar
3½ ounces Sanbitter (Italian nonalcoholic bitters)
• *Garnish:*
1 orange peel spiral

Slowly mix the ingredients together, with ice cubes, in the highball glass. Add the orange peel spiral to the glass.

SANTANA

Fruity, tangy drink for any time of year
• Highball/Collins glass

3½ ounces Sanbitter (Italian nonalcoholic bitters)
2 ounces orange juice
2 tsp. lemon juice
• *Garnish:*
1 slice of orange

Mix all the ingredients together, with ice cubes, in the highball glass. Perch the slice of orange on the rim of the glass.

BITTER AND SWEET

Spicy, refreshing drink for hot days
• Highball/Collins glass
• Shaker

¾ ounce lime cordial
2 tsp. nonalcoholic grenadine
3½ ounces Sanbitter (Italian nonalcoholic bitters)
• *Extra:*
1 wedge of lime

Shake the lime cordial and grenadine together firmly, with ice cubes, in the shaker. Fill the highball glass one-third full with crushed ice and strain the drink into the glass. Top up with the Sanbitter and stir briefly. Add the wedge of lime to the glass.

RED ROSES

Refreshing, bitter aperitif
• Large brandy snifter

3½ ounces nonalcoholic sparkling wine
3½ ounces Sanbitter or other nonalcoholic bitters
• *Garnish:*
1 red rosebud (not treated with chemicals)

Carefully mix the ingredients together, with ice cubes, in the brandy snifter. Perch the rose on the rim of the glass.

BITTER CASSIS

Fruity, bitter aperitif
• Highball/Collins glass

1½ ounces apple juice
1½ ounces black-currant nectar
3½ ounces Sanbitter or other
nonalcoholic bitters
• Garnish:
1 cluster of black currants

Mix the juice and nectar together, with
ice cubes, in the highball glass. Add the
Sanbitter and stir briefly. Hang the
cluster of black currants over the rim of
the glass.

BITTER CHERRIES

Fruity, bitter aperitif
• Highball/Collins glass

1½ ounces orange juice
1½ ounces cherry nectar
3½ ounces Sanbitter or other
nonalcoholic bitters
• Garnish:
1 slice of orange

Mix the juice and nectar together, with
ice cubes, in the highball glass. Top up
with Sanbitter and stir briefly. Perch the
slice of orange on the rim of the glass.

BITTER MINT

Spicy aperitif
• Highball/Collins glass
• Shaker

2 ounces grapefruit juice
1 ounce peppermint syrup
3½ ounces Sanbitter or other
nonalcoholic bitters
• Garnish:
1 sprig of mint

Shake the grapefruit juice and
peppermint syrup together firmly, with
ice, in the shaker and strain into the
highball glass. Add a few ice cubes, top
up with Sanbitter, and stir briefly. Add
the sprig of mint to the glass.

STEP

Spicy, bitter drink
• Highball/Collins glass
• Shaker

1½ ounces orange juice
¾ ounce grapefruit juice
¾ ounce lemon juice
2 tsp. nonalcoholic grenadine
3½ ounces Sanbitter or other
nonalcoholic bitters
• Garnish:
1 slice of orange
1 slice of lemon

Shake all the ingredients, except the
Sanbitter, together firmly, with ice
cubes, in the shaker and strain into the
highball glass. Add ice cubes to taste,
top up with Sanbitter, and stir. Spear
the slices of fruit on a toothpick and lay
the garnish across the rim of the glass.

PINK DUNE

Fruity, sweet drink for any time of year
• Highball/Collins glass
• Shaker

7 ounces pineapple juice
¾ ounce light cream
2 tsp. nonalcoholic grenadine
• Garnish:
½ slice of pineapple
1 maraschino cherry

Shake all the ingredients together, with ice cubes, in the shaker and strain into the highball glass. Top up with crushed ice. Spear the fruit on a long toothpick or skewer and add it to the glass.

PALERMO

Spicy, tangy drink for hot days
• Highball/Collins glass

1½ ounces orange juice
1½ ounces nonalcoholic vermouth,
such as Palermo vermouth
2 tsp. nonalcoholic grenadine
3½ ounces Sanbitter or other
nonalcoholic bitters
• Garnish:
1 slice of orange

Mix the orange juice, vermouth, and grenadine together, with ice cubes, in the highball glass. Top up with Sanbitter and stir briefly. Perch the slice of orange on the rim of the glass.

L'ARBRE DU CIEL

Fruity, sweet drink for a party
• Brandy snifter
• Shaker

1½ ounces coconut syrup

2 ounces pineapple juice

¾ ounce lemon juice

¼ tbsp. grated coconut

• Garnish:

¼ slice of pineapple

Shake all the ingredients together, with ice, in the shaker and pour into the brandy snifter. Perch the slice of pineapple on the rim of the glass.

ITALIAN COOLER

Spicy, refreshing drink for hot days
• Highball/Collins glass

1½ ounces nonalcoholic vermouth, such as Palermo vermouth

2 tsp. nonalcoholic grenadine

Soda water for topping up

• Garnish:

1 slice of lemon

Mix the vermouth and grenadine together well, with ice cubes, in the highball glass. Top up with soda water and stir again. Perch the slice of lemon on the rim of the glass.

MANDARIN CREAM

Fruity, sweet cream for a party
• Highball/Collins glass
• Shaker

2 ounces orange juice
1½ ounces mandarin syrup
1½ ounces light cream
1 dash nonalcoholic grenadine
1 egg yolk
• *Garnish:*
½ slice of orange
1 maraschino cherry

Shake all the ingredients together, with ice cubes, in the shaker and strain into the highball glass over ice cubes. Perch the slice of orange on the rim of the glass and fasten the cherry to it with a toothpick.

JONATHAN

Fruity, sweet drink for the afternoon
• Large rocks glass
• Shaker

3½ ounces black-currant juice
1¼ ounces orange juice
¾ ounce chocolate syrup

Shake all the ingredients together, with ice cubes, in the shaker and strain into the glass.

COCONUT BANANA

Sweet, fruity drink for a summer party
• Highball/Collins glass
• Shaker

2 ounces milk
¾ ounce light cream
¾ ounce cream of coconut
¾ ounce banana syrup
• *Garnish:*
1 slice of banana

Shake the ingredients together firmly, with ice, in the shaker and strain into the highball glass over crushed ice. Perch the slice of banana on the rim of the glass.

RED COCONUT

Sweet drink for a summer party
• Highball/Collins glass
• Shaker

1¾ ounces cream of coconut
1¾ ounces pineapple juice
¾ ounce strawberry syrup
2 tsp. light cream
• *Garnish:*
1 strawberry

Shake the ingredients together firmly, with ice, in the shaker and strain into the highball glass over crushed ice. Perch the strawberry on the rim of the glass.

BALI BEACH

Sweet, refreshing drink for a Caribbean party
- Highball/Collins glass
- Shaker

1½ ounces cream of coconut

1 ounce pineapple juice

Bitter lemon for topping up

- *Garnish:*

1 slice of lime

¼ slice of pineapple

1 maraschino cherry

Shake all the ingredients, except the bitter lemon, together firmly, with ice, in the shaker and strain into the highball glass over crushed ice. Top up with bitter lemon. Spear the fruit on a toothpick and lay the garnish across the rim of the glass. Serve with a stirrer.

LIME COLADA

Fruity, refreshing drink for a summer party
- Highball/Collins glass
- Shaker

2¾ ounces pineapple juice

1½ ounces lime juice

¾ ounce cream of coconut

2 tsp. nonalcoholic grenadine

- *Garnish:*

1 slice of lime

Shake all the ingredients together, with ice, in the shaker and strain into the highball glass. Top up with crushed ice. Perch the slice of lime on the rim of the glass.

COUPÉ 911

Sweet, long drink for a Caribbean party
- Highball/Collins glass
- Shaker

1½ ounces cream of coconut

2¾ ounces grapefruit juice

¾ ounce banana syrup

- *Garnish:*

1 slice of banana

Shake the ingredients together, with ice, in the shaker and strain into the highball glass over crushed ice. Spear the slice of banana on a toothpick and lay the garnish across the rim of the glass.

SWEET NOTHINGS

Fruity, sweet drink for a party
- Large brandy snifter
- Shaker

3½ ounces pineapple juice

1 ounce cream of coconut

1 ounce light cream

¾ ounce lemon juice

2 tsp. banana syrup

- *Garnish:*

2 slices of banana

2 maraschino cherries

Shake all the ingredients together firmly, with ice, in the shaker. Half fill the brandy snifter with crushed ice and strain the drink into the glass. Spear the slices of banana and the cherries on a toothpick and lay the garnish across the rim of the glass.

COCOMARA

Fruity, mild drink for hot days
• Highball/Collins glass
• Shaker

1½ ounces passion-fruit nectar
1½ ounces orange juice
1½ ounces grapefruit juice
¾ ounce cream of coconut
• *Garnish:*
1 slice of lime

Shake all the ingredients together, with ice, in the shaker and strain into the glass. Perch the slice of lime on the rim of the glass.

FRUIT COCO

Fruity, sweet drink for the summer months
• Highball/Collins glass
• Shaker

2¾ ounces orange juice
2¾ ounces pineapple juice
1½ ounces cream of coconut
2 tsp. lemon juice
• *Garnish:*
1 slice of orange
1 maraschino cherry

Shake all the ingredients together firmly, with ice, in the shaker. Fill the glass one-third full with crushed ice and strain the drink into the glass. Perch the slice of orange on the rim of the glass and fasten the cherry to the orange with a toothpick.

COCONUT KISS II

Fruity, sweet drink for a party
• Brandy snifter
• Shaker

1½ ounces pineapple juice
1½ ounces orange juice
2 tsp. lemon juice
1 ounce cream of coconut
1 ounce light cream
• *Garnish:*
½ slice of orange
1 slice of pineapple

Shake all the ingredients together firmly, with ice, in the shaker. Fill the glass one-third full with crushed ice and strain the drink into the glass. Spear the fruit on a long toothpick and add it to the glass.

COCONUT COCKTAIL

Sweet drink for a party
• Large champagne glass
• Shaker

1½ ounces pineapple juice
1½ ounces coconut milk
¾ ounce passion-fruit juice
2 tsp. lemon juice
2 tsp. nonalcoholic grenadine
1 tsp. cream of coconut

Shake all the ingredients together firmly, with ice cubes, in the shaker and strain into the champagne glass.

BANANAS

Fruity, sweet drink for any occasion
- Large champagne glass
- Shaker

2¾ ounces milk
¾ ounce cream of coconut
¾ ounce banana syrup
1 ounce light cream

Shake all the ingredients together, with ice cubes, in the shaker and strain into the champagne glass.

BONGO

Fruity drink for a party
- Highball/Collins glass
- Shaker

2½ ounces pineapple juice
1½ ounces mango juice
1½ ounces lemon juice
1 ounce orange juice
¾ ounce cream of coconut
- Garnish:
¼ slice of pineapple
1 maraschino cherry

Shake all the ingredients together, with ice cubes, in the shaker and strain into the highball glass. Spear the fruit on a toothpick and lay the garnish across the rim of the glass.

LUCKY DRIVER

Fruity, mild drink for the evening
- Highball/Collins glass
- Shaker

1¾ ounces orange juice
1¾ ounces grapefruit juice
1¾ ounces pineapple juice
¾ ounce lemon juice
¾ ounce cream of coconut
- Garnish:
1 slice of orange
1 slice of lemon

Shake all the ingredients together, with ice cubes, in the shaker and strain into the highball glass. Perch the slices of fruit on the rim of the glass.

HONOLULU STAR

Fruity, mild drink for a party
- Highball/Collins glass
- Shaker

1¾ ounces orange juice
1¾ ounces pineapple juice
1¾ ounces lime juice
¾ ounce cherry juice
¾ ounce cream of coconut
- Garnish:
1 orange peel spiral

Shake all the ingredients together, with ice cubes, in the shaker and strain into the highball glass. Hang the orange peel spiral over the rim of the glass.

GRAPEY

Fruity, tangy drink for a party
- Highball/Collins glass
- Shaker

3½ ounces grapefruit juice
1¾ ounces orange juice
1¾ ounces pineapple juice
¾ ounce lemon juice
¾ ounce cream of coconut
- *Garnish:*
1 orange peel spiral
¼ slice of pineapple

Shake all the ingredients together firmly, with ice cubes, in the shaker and strain into the highball glass. Hang the lemon peel over the rim of the glass and perch the slice of pineapple on the rim. Serve with a straw, if desired.

COCONUT ON VACATION

Fruity, sweet drink for the summer
- Highball glass
- Shaker

¾ ounce passion-fruit juice
¾ ounce peach juice
¾ ounce lemon juice
2 ounces cream of coconut
¾ ounce light cream
- *Garnish:*
½ peach

Shake all the ingredients together firmly, with plenty of ice, in the shaker and strain into the highball glass. Place the peach half over the mouth of the glass and insert a straw through the peach.

Nonalcoholic

CREAM OF COCONUT SODA

Fruity, sweet long drink for the summer months
- Highball/Collins glass
- Shaker

2 scoops coconut ice cream	
1½ ounces coconut milk	
1½ ounces pineapple juice	
1 tsp. cream of coconut	
2 dashes lemon juice	
Soda water for topping up	

Shake all the ingredients, except the soda water, together firmly in the shaker, and strain into the highball glass. Top up with soda water and stir briefly.

COCO EXOTIC

Fruity, sweet drink for a party
- Highball glass
- Shaker

1½ ounces mango juice	
¾ ounce peach juice	
2 tsp. passion-fruit juice	
1 ounce pineapple juice	
2 ounces cream of coconut	
2 tsp. cream	
Sparkling mineral water for topping up	
• *Garnish:*	
1 wedge of mango	

Shake all the ingredients, except the mineral water, together in the shaker and pour into the glass. Add mineral water to taste and stir. Perch the wedge of mango on the rim of the glass.

SUMMER SNOW

Fruity, sweet drink for a summer's evening
• Large rocks glass
• Shaker

1¾ ounces pineapple juice
2 tsp. lemon juice
1¾ ounces cream of coconut
1¾ ounces light cream
• *Garnish:*
1 tbsp. stiffly whipped cream
A little grated chocolate

Shake all the ingredients together firmly, with ice cubes, in the shaker and strain into the glass. Top the drink with whipped cream and sprinkle a little grated chocolate on top.

GOLDEN FLIP

Fruity, tangy drink for any occasion
• Rocks glass
• Shaker

1½ ounces lemon juice
2 tsp. ginger syrup
1 egg yolk
Soda water for topping up
• *Extra:*
Confectioners' sugar

Shake the lemon juice, syrup, and egg yolk together, with ice cubes, in the shaker and strain into the glass. Top up with soda water, stir briefly, and sprinkle a little icing sugar on top.

WHITE CITY

Fruity, sweet drink for any occasion
• Highball/Collins glass
• Shaker

1 ounce cream of coconut
1¾ ounces light cream
2 tsp. lemon juice
2¾ ounces pineapple juice
• *Garnish:*
1 tbsp. whipped cream

Shake all the ingredients together firmly, with ice cubes, in the shaker and strain into the highball glass. Garnish with whipped cream.

SIMPLY RED

Fruity, sweet long drink for any occasion
• Highball/Collins glass
• Shaker

4 ounces pineapple juice
¾ ounce lemon juice
¾ ounce cream of coconut
¾ ounce nonalcoholic grenadine
• *Garnish:*
¼ slice of pineapple

Shake all the ingredients together firmly, with ice cubes, in the shaker and strain into the highball glass. Perch the slice of pineapple on the rim of the glass.

MARTINIQUE II

Fruity, sweet drink for the evening
• Highball/Collins glass
• Shaker

¾ ounce cream of coconut
¾ ounce raspberry syrup
2¾ ounces pineapple juice
2 tsp. lemon juice
1½ ounces light cream
• Garnish:
½ slice of pineapple

Shake all the ingredients together firmly, with ice cubes, in the shaker. Fill the highball glass half full with crushed ice and strain the drink into it. Perch the slice of pineapple on the rim of the glass.

EXOTIC CUP

Fruity, sweet drink for a party
• Highball glass
• Shaker

1¾ ounces pineapple juice
1 ounce mango juice
¾ ounce passion-fruit juice
¾ ounce cream of coconut
2 tsp. lemon juice
2 tsp. nonalcoholic grenadine
Sparkling mineral water for topping up
• Garnish:
½ slice of pineapple
2 maraschino cherries

Shake all the ingredients, except the mineral water, together, with ice cubes, in the shaker and strain into the glass. Spear the fruit on a toothpick and lay the garnish across the rim of the glass.

QUEEN OF STRAWBERRIES

Fruity, sweet drink for a party
• Highball/Collins glass
• Shaker

2 ounces puréed strawberries
2 ounces pineapple juice
¾ ounce cream of coconut
¾ ounce light cream
• Garnish:
3 strawberries

Shake the ingredients together well, with ice cubes, in the shaker and strain into the highball glass. Finally, perch the strawberries on the rim of the glass.

TANGO GIRL

Fruity, sweet drink for a party
• Highball/Collins glass
• Shaker

1 ounce cream of coconut
2 ounces pineapple juice
2 ounces lemon juice
2 tsp. almond syrup
1 ounce light cream
• Garnish:
1 maraschino cherry

Shake all the ingredients together well, with ice cubes, in the shaker and strain into the highball glass. Perch the cherry on the rim of the glass.

COCO

Fruity, sweet drink for the evening
• Highball/Collins glass
• Shaker

1½ ounces pineapple juice
1½ ounces light cream
¾ ounce cream of coconut

Shake all the ingredients together well, with ice cubes, in the shaker. Fill the highball glass half full with crushed ice and strain the drink into the glass.

COCO CHERRY

Fruity, sweet long drink for hot days
• Highball/Collins glass
• Shaker

3 ounces cherry juice
2 tsp. pineapple juice
1¾ ounces cream of coconut
• Garnish:
¼ slice of pineapple

Shake all the ingredients together, with ice cubes, in the shaker and strain into the highball glass. Perch the slice of pineapple on the rim of the glass.

COCONUT SHELL

Fruity, sweet drink for a party
• 2 coconut shell halves
• Shaker

For 2 servings
2 coconuts
1¾ ounces banana juice
1 ounce cream of coconut
1 ounce cherry juice
1 ounce almond milk
1 ounce light cream
• Garnish:
2 maraschino cherries
½ banana, sliced

Cut the coconuts in half, reserving the milk. Cut out the flesh, chop finely, and reserve. Shake the coconut milk and the other ingredients together firmly, with ice cubes, in the shaker and strain into 2 of the coconut shells. Add the chopped coconut flesh, maraschino cherries, and sliced banana to the drinks. Serve with a spoon and straw.

Coco Cherry (left), Coconut Shell (right)

SPORTS FLIP

Fruity, sweet drink for any occasion
• Highball/Collins glass
• Shaker

2 ounces orange juice

1 ounce lemon juice

1 ounce passion-fruit juice

2 tsp. banana syrup

2 tsp. nonalcoholic grenadine

1 egg yolk

• Garnish:

1 slice of orange

Shake all the ingredients together firmly, with ice cubes, in the shaker and strain into the highball glass. Perch the slice of orange on the rim of the glass. Serve the drink with a straw.

BOSTON FLIP

Fruity, refreshing drink for hot days
• Rocks glass
• Shaker

1 ounce orange juice

2 tsp. raspberry syrup

2 tsp. peppermint syrup

1 egg yolk

2 dashes lemon juice

Soda water for topping up

• Extra:

Grated nutmeg

Shake all the ingredients, except the soda water, together, with ice cubes, in the shaker and strain into the glass. Top up with soda water, stir briefly, and sprinkle a little grated nutmeg on top.

ATHLETIC

Fruity, creamy drink for the afternoon
- Highball/Collins glass
- Shaker

2 ounces white grape juice
2 ounces light cream
¾ ounce lemon juice
1 tbsp. sugar
1 egg yolk
Soda water for topping up

Shake all the ingredients, except the soda water, together firmly, with ice cubes, in the shaker and strain into the highball glass. Top up with soda water and stir briefly.

GLASGOW FLIP

Fruity, sweet drink for any occasion
- Rocks glass
- Shaker

¾ ounce lemon juice
¾ ounce sugar syrup
1 egg
Ginger ale for topping up

Shake the lemon juice, syrup, and egg together, with ice, in the shaker and strain into the glass. Top up with ginger ale and stir.

ICE-CREAM FLIP

Sweet drink for summer days
- Rocks glass
- Shaker

1 scoop vanilla ice cream
¾ ounce vanilla syrup
1 egg
Soda water for topping up
- *Garnish:*
1 maraschino cherry

Shake the vanilla ice cream, vanilla syrup, and egg together in the shaker and pour into the glass. Top up with soda water and stir briefly. Perch the cherry on the rim of the glass.

GINGER ALE FLIP

Sweet drink for any occasion
- Champagne flute
- Shaker

3 tbsp. sugar syrup
1 egg yolk
Ginger ale for topping up

Shake the syrup and the egg together, with ice cubes, in the shaker and strain into the champagne flute. Top up with ginger ale and stir briefly.

Nonalcoholic

PINEAPPLE FLIP

Fruity, refreshing drink for any occasion
• Champagne flute
• Shaker

1 ounce pineapple juice
¾ ounce orange juice
1 egg yolk
Soda water for topping up

Shake the juices and the egg yolk together, with ice cubes, in the shaker and strain into the champagne flute. Top up with soda water and stir briefly.

BLUEBERRY MIX

Fruity, sweet drink for the summer
• Highball/Collins glass
• Shaker

2¾ ounces puréed blueberries
¾ ounce strawberry syrup
1½ ounces light cream
1½ ounces soda water

Shake the blueberry purée, strawberry syrup, and cream together, with ice cubes, in the shaker and pour into the highball glass. Add the soda water and stir briefly.

BITTER LEMON FLIP

Fruity, tangy drink for a party
• Highball/Collins glass
• Shaker

1 ounce lemon juice
¾ ounce grapefruit juice
2 tsp. nonalcoholic grenadine
2 tsp. light cream
1 tsp. sugar syrup
1 egg yolk
Bitter lemon for topping up
• Garnish:
1 slice of lemon

Shake all the ingredients, except the bitter lemon, together firmly, with ice cubes, in the shaker and strain into the highball glass. Top up with bitter lemon. Perch the slice of lemon on the rim of the glass.

BLUSHING VIRGIN

Fruity, sweet drink for the winter months
• Rocks glass

2 ruby oranges
2 scoops vanilla ice cream
4 ounces soda water

Peel one of the oranges, removing the peel in a continuous spiral. Squeeze the juice from both oranges. Put the ice cream into the glass, pour the orange juice over it, top up with soda water, and stir briefly. Hang the orange peel spiral over the rim of the glass.

BANANA SODA

Fruity, sweet drink for any time of year
• Highball/Collins glass

2 scoops vanilla ice cream
3½ ounces banana juice
2 tsp. lemon juice
Soda water for topping up

Mix the vanilla ice cream and the juices together in the highball glass. Top up with soda water and stir again.

SWEET SUSIE

Fruity, sweet drink for hot days
• Rocks glass

1 scoop vanilla ice cream
1 scoop pineapple ice cream
¾ ounce raspberry juice
Soda water for topping up
• Garnish:
A little whipped cream
2 strawberries

Put the ice creams and the raspberry juice in the glass, top up with soda water, and stir. Spoon whipped cream on top of the drink and add the strawberries. Serve with a spoon.

DRIVER

Fruity, mild drink for any time of year
• Highball/Collins glass
• Shaker

1¾ ounces passion-fruit juice
1½ ounces peach juice
1 ounce cream of coconut
¾ ounce lemon juice
Sparkling mineral water for topping up
• Garnish:
1 slice of kiwi fruit
1 maraschino cherry

Shake all the ingredients, except the mineral water, together, with ice cubes, in the shaker and strain into the highball glass. Top up with mineral water and stir. Perch the slice of kiwi fruit on the rim of the glass and fasten the cherry to the kiwi fruit with a toothpick.

STRAWBERRY SODA

Fruity, mild drink for the summer
• Rocks glass
• Shaker

1 scoop strawberry sorbet
¾ ounce lemon juice
¾ ounce strawberry syrup
Soda water for topping up

Shake the sorbet, lemon juice, and syrup together, with ice cubes, in the shaker and strain into the glass. Top up with soda water and stir briefly.

Banana Soda (back left), Driver (back right), Sweet Susie (front left), Strawberry Soda (front right)

THE MANDARIN

Creamy, sweet drink with milk for the afternoon
- Cocktail glass
- Shaker

¾ ounce mandarin syrup

¾ ounce milk

1¾ ounces light cream

Shake all the ingredients together, with ice cubes, in the shaker and strain into the glass.

PEACH MELBA DRINK

Fruity, sweet drink with milk for the summer months
- Highball/Collins glass
- Blender

1 tbsp. puréed raspberries

1 tsp. sugar

3½ ounces milk

1 tbsp. puréed peach

1 tbsp. light cream

1 scoop vanilla ice cream

- Garnish:

1 raspberry

Mix the raspberry purée and sugar together and put the mixture into the highball glass. Mix the milk, peach purée, cream, and vanilla ice cream together briefly in the blender and pour into the highball glass. Perch the raspberry on the rim of the glass.

PEAR AND CINNAMON MILK

Fruity, sweet drink with milk for every day
- Brandy snifter
- Blender

3½ ounces milk

1 tbsp. light cream

½ juicy pear, peeled and diced

1 tsp. sugar

½ tsp. vanilla-flavored sugar

1 tsp. lemon juice

½ tsp. ground cinnamon

- Garnish:

1 slice of apple

Mix all the ingredients together in the blender and pour into the balloon glass. Perch the slice of apple on the rim of the glass.

GRAPE EGGNOG

Fruity drink with milk for every occasion
- Highball/Collins glass
- Shaker

2¾ ounces red grape juice

2¾ ounces milk

2 tsp. sugar syrup

1 egg yolk

Shake all the ingredients together well, with ice cubes, in the shaker and strain into the highball glass.

ORANGE EGGNOG

Fruity, sweet eggnog for any time
of year
• Champagne glass
• Shaker

1½ ounces orange syrup
¾ ounce light cream
¾ ounce milk
1 egg

Shake all the ingredients together, with
ice cubes, in the shaker and strain into
the champagne glass.

BLUE ICE-CREAM SODA

Fruity, sweet drink with milk for hot
days
• Highball/Collins glass

2 scoops vanilla ice cream
1½ ounces milk
¾ ounce nonalcoholic blue curaçao
2 tsp. pineapple syrup
Soda water for topping up

Mix the ice cream, milk, curaçao, and
syrup together, with ice cubes, in the
highball glass. Top up with soda water
and stir briefly.

CHOCO MYSTERY

Creamy, sweet drink with milk for the
afternoon
• Large champagne glass
• Shaker

1½ ounces light cream
1½ ounces milk
¾ ounce cream of coconut
¾ ounce chocolate syrup
• Garnish:
Grated chocolate

Shake all the ingredients together
firmly, with ice cubes, in the shaker and
strain into the champagne glass.
Sprinkle a little grated chocolate on
top.

CHOCOLATE SHAKE

Sweet, long drink with milk for hot days
• Highball/Collins glass
• Shaker

2 scoops vanilla ice cream
3½ ounces milk
1 ounce chocolate syrup
• Garnish:
A little whipped cream
Grated chocolate

Shake all the ingredients together well
in the shaker and pour into the highball
glass. Garnish with a little whipped
cream and sprinkle grated chocolate
on top.

BLACKBERRY SHAKE

Fruity, sweet drink with milk for hot
summer days
• Rocks glass
• Blender

1 scoop vanilla ice cream
1¾ ounces blackberries
1 ounce blackberry syrup
2 tsp. lemon juice
Milk for topping up
• *Garnish:*
1 tbsp. stiffly whipped cream
*A little chocolate curls or chocolate
shavings*

Put the ice cream into the glass. Mix
the blackberries, syrup, and lemon
juice together in the blender, pour the
mixture over the ice cream, top up
with milk, and stir gently. Garnish the
drink with a little pile of whipped
cream and chocolate curls or shavings.

MINT ICE-CREAM SODA

Spicy, mild drink with milk for the
summer months
• Highball/Collins glass

3½ ounces milk
¾ ounce peppermint syrup
2 scoops vanilla ice cream
Soda water for topping up

Mix the milk, syrup and ice cream
together in the highball glass. Top up
with soda water and stir again.

ALMOND SHAKE

Sweet, spicy drink with milk for any
time of year
• Highball/Collins glass
• Shaker

5½ ounces milk
1½ ounces almond syrup
1 dash nonalcoholic grenadine
• *Garnish:*
Toasted, slivered almonds

Shake all the ingredients together, with
ice cubes, in the shaker and strain into
the highball glass over ice cubes.
Scatter a few toasted slivered almonds
on top of the drink.

HONEY FLIP

Fruity, mild drink for any occasion
• Highball/Collins glass
• Shaker

7 ounces milk
¾ ounce black-currant juice
1 tsp. honey
1 egg yolk
• *Garnish:*
1 cluster of black currants

Shake all the ingredients together
firmly, with ice cubes, in the shaker and
strain into the highball glass. Hang the
cluster of black currants over the rim of
the glass.

CANAAN

Spicy, sweet eggnog for any time of year
- Highball/Collins glass
- Shaker

5 ounces milk
1 egg
2 tsp. honey
- *Garnish:*
Ground cinnamon

Shake the milk, egg, and honey together well, with ice cubes, in the shaker and strain into the highball glass. Sprinkle a little ground cinnamon on top.

JOGGING

Sweet eggnog for the summertime
- Highball/Collins glass
- Shaker

1 scoop chocolate ice cream
3½ ounces milk
1 egg yolk
1 tsp. sugar
1 dash lemon juice
- *Garnish:*
Grated chocolate

Shake all the ingredients together well in the shaker and strain into the highball glass. Garnish with grated chocolate.

CHOCOLATE ORANGE

Fruity, sweet drink with milk for the summer
- Rocks glass

2 small scoops vanilla ice cream
¾ ounce chocolate syrup
¾ ounce orange syrup
Milk for topping up
2 tbsp. stiffly whipped cream
- *Garnish:*
¼ slice of orange
A little chocolate curls or chocolate shavings

Whisk the ice cream and syrups together in the glass, top up with milk, and stir again. Top the drink with whipped cream and garnish the cream with the slice of orange and the chocolate curls or shavings.

FLORIDA MILK

Fruity, mild drink with milk for any time of year
- Large cocktail glass
- Shaker

2 ounces milk
2 tsp. orange juice
2 tsp. lemon juice
2 tsp. nonalcoholic grenadine
2 tsp. light cream

Shake all the ingredients together firmly, with ice cubes, in the shaker and strain into the glass.

POLAR ORANGE

Fruity, sweet long drink for hot days
• Highball/Collins glass

2 scoops vanilla ice cream
1½ ounces milk
¾ ounce orange syrup
Soda water for topping up

Mix the ice cream, milk, and syrup
together, with ice cubes, in the highball
glass. Top up with soda water and stir
again.

PINEAPPLE MILK

Fruity, sweet drink with milk for every
day
• Highball glass
• Mixing glass

1 scoop pineapple ice cream
1½ ounces pineapple syrup
¾ ounce pineapple juice
2 tsp. lemon juice
Milk for topping up
• *Garnish:*
¼ slice of pineapple

Put the pineapple ice cream into the
glass. Mix the syrup and juices together
and pour the mixture over the ice
cream. Top up with milk, stir carefully,
and perch the slice of pineapple on the
rim of the glass.

BOSOM CARESSER

Fruity, refreshing eggnog for any time of year
• Rocks glass
• Shaker

1 ounce raspberry juice
1 egg
Cold milk for topping up

Shake the juice and the egg together in the shaker and pour into the glass. Top up with milk and stir briefly.

BILBERRY MILK

Fruity, sweet drink with milk for every day
• Large rocks glass

1¾ ounces bilberry or blueberry syrup
4 tsp. bilberries or blueberries
2 tsp. lemon juice
1 scoop vanilla ice cream
Milk for topping up

Mix all the ingredients, except the ice cream and milk, together in the glass. Add the ice cream, top up with milk, and stir the drink again carefully.

BLACKBERRY MILK

Fruity, sweet drink with milk for summer days
• Rocks glass

1 scoop vanilla ice cream
1 ounce blackberry syrup
Cold milk for topping up

Put the ice cream and syrup in the glass, top up with milk, and stir briefly.

CITRONELLA

Fruity, refreshing drink with buttermilk for the summer
• Highball/Collins glass
• Blender

1 scoop lemon ice cream
2 tsp. lemon juice
1 tsp. sugar
4½ ounces buttermilk
• Garnish:
1 slice of lemon
1 lemon peel spiral

Mix the ingredients together briefly in the blender and pour into the highball glass. Perch the slice of lemon on the rim of the glass and hang the lemon peel spiral over the rim.

SEA BUCKTHORN EGGNOG

Fruity eggnog for any time of year
• Highball/Collins glass
• Shaker

7 ounces milk
¾ ounce sea buckthorn syrup
1 egg yolk

Shake all the ingredients together firmly, with ice cubes, in the shaker and strain into the highball glass.

STRAWBERRY AND ORANGE SHAKE

Fruity, refreshing drink with buttermilk for every day
• Brandy snifter
• Blender

4½ ounces buttermilk
¾ ounce orange juice
1 tbsp. strawberry syrup
1 pinch grated orange peel
• Garnish:
1 slice of orange
½ strawberry

Mix the ingredients together briefly in the blender and pour into the brandy snifter. Perch the slice of orange and the strawberry on the rim of the glass.

Nonalcoholic

DREAM OF GRANADA

Creamy drink with buttermilk for any occasion
- Highball/Collins glass
- Mixing glass

7 ounces buttermilk

¾ ounce nonalcoholic grenadine

1 tbsp. cocoa powder

Mix all the ingredients together, with ice, in the mixing glass and pour into the highball glass.

CARIBBEAN MILKSHAKE

Fruity, sweet drink with buttermilk for the summer
- Highball/Collins glass
- Shaker

1¾ ounces banana juice

1¾ ounces pineapple juice

1¾ ounces buttermilk

¾ ounce nonalcoholic blue curaçao

• Extra:

Ground cinnamon

Shake all the ingredients together, with ice cubes, in the shaker, strain into the highball glass, and sprinkle a little ground cinnamon on top.

TROPICANA PINEAPPLE DRINK

Fruity, tangy drink with buttermilk for every day
- Highball/Collins glass
- Blender

4½ ounces buttermilk

½ cup diced canned pineapple rings

1 ounce grapefruit juice

1 tsp. grated chocolate

• Garnish:

½ slice of pineapple

Mix all the ingredients together in the blender and pour into the highball glass over ice cubes. Perch the slice of pineapple on the rim of the glass.

KIBA

Fruity, sweet drink with buttermilk for every day
- Highball/Collins glass
- Blender

3½ ounces buttermilk

1¾ ounces cherry juice

1¾ ounces banana juice

1 dash lemon juice

• Garnish:

Slices of banana

Mix all the ingredients together in the blender and pour into the highball glass. Spear the slices of banana on a toothpick and lay the garnish across the rim of the glass.

BANANA MIX

Fruity, creamy drink with buttermilk for every day
• Highball/Collins glass
• Blender

5 ounces buttermilk
½ banana, diced
Juice of ½ orange
1 tsp. sugar
½ tsp. vanilla-flavored sugar
• Garnish:
1 slice of orange

Mix all the ingredients together in the blender and pour into the highball glass. Perch the slice of orange on the rim of the glass.

TROPICAL SUN II

Fruity, tangy drink with buttermilk for every day
• Cocktail glass
• Blender

5½ ounces grapefruit juice
4½ ounces buttermilk
½ cup peeled and diced mango
1 tsp. sugar
• Garnish:
Sprig of mint

Mix all the ingredients together in the blender and pour into the glass. Perch the sprig of mint on the rim of the glass.

SONNY BOY

Fruity, creamy drink with yogurt for every day
• Small highball/Collins glass
• Blender

6½ tbsp. plain yogurt
2 tbsp. sea buckthorn juice (or syrup)
1 small egg yolk
1 tsp. fructose
Juice of 1 orange

Mix all the ingredients together in the blender and pour into the highball glass.

APRICOT-YOGURT DRINK

Fruity, fresh long drink with yogurt for summer days
• Highball/Collins glass
• Blender

½ cup plain yogurt
5 tbsp. puréed apricots
1 ounce orange juice
1 tsp. sugar
½ tsp. vanilla-flavored sugar
• Garnish:
1 slice of orange
1 sprig of lemon balm

Mix all the ingredients together in the blender and pour into the highball glass. Perch the slice of orange on the rim of the glass and fasten the sprig of lemon balm to the orange with a toothpick.

From left to right: Banana Mix, Tropical Sun, Sonny Boy, Apricot-Yogurt Drink

BLUEBERRY-YOGURT DRINK

Fruity, fresh drink with blueberries for the summer
- Highball/Collins glass
- Blender

½ cup plain yogurt
5 tbsp. puréed blueberries
½ tsp. vanilla-flavored sugar
A little grated lemon peel
- *Garnish:*
1 tbsp. whipped cream

Mix all the ingredients together in the blender and pour into the highball glass. Garnish with a dollop of whipped cream.

DRYAD

Fruity, sour drink with yogurt for the summer
- Champagne glass
- Blender

2½ ounces mixed fresh fruits of the forest, such as raspberries, blackberries, and blueberries
1 tbsp. unsweetened elderberry juice
2 tsp. raspberry syrup
5 tbsp. plain yogurt
- *Garnish:*
1 tbsp. whipped cream

Reserve a few blackberries. Mix all the ingredients together in the blender and pour into the champagne glass. Garnish with a rosette of cream and the reserved blackberries.

VANILLA-STRAWBERRY SHAKE

Fruity, sweet long drink with buttermilk for every day
- Highball/Collins glass
- Blender

2 small scoops strawberry ice cream
3½ ounces buttermilk
2 tbsp. light cream
2 tbsp. milk
1 tsp. vanilla-flavored sugar
- *Garnish:*
2 strawberry halves

Put the scoops of ice cream into the highball glass. Mix the remaining ingredients together in the blender and pour into the glass. Perch the strawberry halves on the rim of the glass.

MANDARIN SHAKE

Fruity, refreshing drink with yogurt for every day
- Highball/Collins glass
- Blender

3½ ounces mandarin segments
½ cup plain yogurt
2 tsp. lemon juice
1 tsp. sugar
- *Garnish:*
1 slice of lemon
1 mandarin segment

Mix all the ingredients together in the blender and pour into the highball glass. Spear the slice of lemon and the mandarin segment on a toothpick and lay the garnish across the rim of the glass.

WOODRUFF SHAKE

Fruity, sourish drink with buttermilk for the summer
• Highball/Collins glass
• Blender

1 scoop lemon sorbet
5 tbsp. buttermilk
1 tbsp. woodruff syrup
¼ sourish apple, peeled and diced
2 tsp. lime juice
1 tsp. light cream
• Garnish:
1 sprig lemon balm

Put the sorbet in the highball glass. Mix the remaining ingredients together in the blender and pour into the glass. Perch the sprig of lemon balm on the rim of the glass.

STRAWBERRY ICED COFFEE

Fruity, refreshing drink with coffee for hot days
• Rocks glass

1 scoop vanilla ice cream
1 scoop strawberry ice cream
½ cup cold, strong coffee
• Garnish:
A little stiffly whipped cream
¾ ounce strawberry syrup
2 small strawberries

Put the vanilla and strawberry ice creams in the glass and pour the coffee over it. Spoon whipped cream on top, pour the syrup over the cream, and garnish the cream with the strawberries.

COFFEE FLIP

Sweet drink for any time of year
• Rocks glass
• Shaker

1½ ounces cold, strong coffee
1 tsp. sugar syrup
1 egg
• Extra:
Grated nutmeg

Shake the coffee, syrup, and egg together in the shaker with ice cubes and strain into the glass. Sprinkle a little grated nutmeg on top.

ALMOND COFFEE

Creamy, long drink with coffee for hot days
• Sundae glass

2 scoops hazelnut ice cream
¾ ounce almond syrup
½ cup cold, strong coffee
• Garnish:
Stiffly whipped cream
Toasted, slivered almonds

Put the ice cream into the glass. Add the syrup and the coffee and stir briefly. Heap whipped cream on top and garnish with toasted, slivered almonds.

ORANGE ICED COFFEE

Fresh drink for hot days
• Sundae glass

2 scoops vanilla ice cream
½ cup cold, strong coffee
• Garnish:
Stiffly whipped cream
¾ ounce orange syrup
Grated chocolate

Put the vanilla ice cream in the glass and pour the coffee over it. Spoon the whipped cream on top and pour the syrup over. Garnish with a little grated chocolate.

MOCHA MIX

Refreshing drink with milk for the
summer months
- Highball glass
- Shaker

1 tsp. cold mocha coffee
½ cup milk
1 large scoop chocolate ice cream

Shake the mocha coffee and milk
together in the shaker and pour into
the highball glass. Add the ice cream
and stir briefly.

AZTEC FIRE

Creamy drink with coffee for summer
days
- Rocks glass

1 scoop vanilla ice cream
4 ounces cold coffee
1 pinch cocoa powder
• Garnish:
Ground cinnamon

Mix the ice cream, coffee, and cocoa
powder together in the glass. Sprinkle a
little cinnamon on top.

DUTCHMAN

Spicy, piquant pick-me-up
• Rocks glass
• Shaker

1¾ ounces carrot juice
1¾ ounces sauerkraut juice
Pinch of curry powder

Shake all the ingredients together firmly, with ice cubes, in the shaker and strain into the glass.

COUNTRY DREAM

Piquant, creamy drink for every day
• Large cocktail glass
• Shaker

1¾ ounces carrot juice
1½ ounces apple juice
1 tsp. crème fraîche

Shake all the ingredients together, with ice, in the shaker and strain into the glass.

BAVARIAN TOMATO

Spicy, piquant pick-me-up
• Highball/Collins glass
• Shaker

3½ ounces tomato juice
3½ ounces sauerkraut juice
1 tsp. ground caraway

Shake all the ingredients together, with ice, in the shaker and pour into the highball glass.

VIRGIN MARY

Heavily spiced pick-me-up
• Rocks glass

5¼ ounces tomato juice
Worcestershire sauce
Salt
Freshly ground black pepper
Hot-pepper sauce
½ stalk of celery

Pour the tomato juice into the glass, season heavily with the spices, and stir well. Add the celery to the glass.

PRAIRIE OYSTER

Spicy, piquant pick-me-up
• Cocktail glass
• Mixing glass

5 dashes Worcestershire sauce
1 tsp. olive oil
2 dashes hot-pepper sauce
Salt
Freshly ground black pepper
2 tbsp. tomato catsup
1 egg yolk
Sweet paprika

Put the Worcestershire sauce, then the oil, hot-pepper sauce, salt, pepper, and catsup into the glass. Put the whole egg yolk in the middle of the liquid and season with paprika. Do not stir!

TOMATO COCKTAIL

Well-seasoned pick-me-up to
counteract a hangover
• Highball/Collins glass
• Shaker

2¾ ounces tomato juice
1 egg yolk
Salt
Freshly ground black pepper
Hot-pepper sauce
Worcestershire sauce
Celery salt
1 dash lemon juice
1 dash tomato catsup
• Garnish:
Freshly ground black pepper
1 slice of lemon

Shake all the ingredients together, with
crushed ice, in the shaker and pour
into the highball glass. Sprinkle a little
pepper on top. Finally, perch the slice
of lemon on the rim of the glass.

CARLOTTA

Spicy, piquant drink for any occasion
• Rocks glass
• Mixing glass

1½ ounces celery juice
1½ ounces carrot juice
1½ ounces apple juice
1 dash lemon juice
1 tsp. chopped fresh parsley

Mix all the ingredients together in the
mixing glass and pour into the rocks
glass.

POWER JUICE

Spicy, piquant drink for mornings and
afternoons
• Rocks glass
• Mixing glass

3½ ounces beet juice
3½ ounces carrot juice
¾ ounce lemon juice
Freshly ground black pepper
• Garnish:
1 long, thin piece of cucumber

Mix the juices together in the mixing
glass, season to taste with a little
pepper, and pour into the glass over ice
cubes. Perch the piece of cucumber on
the rim of the glass.

JOGGER'S DRINK

Spicy, piquant drink with buttermilk for
every day
• Highball/Collins glass
• Blender

4½ ounces vegetable juice
3½ ounces buttermilk
Pinch grated fresh horseradish
1 dash lemon juice
Ground white pepper
Salt
• Garnish:
1 tsp. snipped fresh chives

Mix all the ingredients together well in
the blender and pour into the highball
glass. Sprinkle the snipped chives on
top.

TOMATO DRINK

Spicy, piquant pick-me-up
• Highball/Collins glass

3½ ounces tomato juice
5 tsp. celery salt
¾ ounce lemon juice
1 dash hot-pepper sauce
• Garnish:
Freshly ground black pepper
1 stalk of celery
1 cherry tomato

Mix the ingredients together in the highball glass and grind a little pepper over it. Put the stalk of celery in the glass and perch the cherry tomato on the rim of the glass.

VEGETABLE COCKTAIL

Spicy, piquant drink with buttermilk for every day
• Large cocktail glass
• Blender

1 ounce carrot juice
1 ounce celery juice
1 tsp. lemon juice
1 tsp. honey
3½ ounces buttermilk
Herb-flavored salt or salt and mixed herbs
Ground white pepper
• Garnish:
A few celery leaves

Mix all the ingredients together well in the blender and pour into the glass. Float the celery leaves on the drink.

TOMATO CUP

Piquant, creamy pick-me-up
• Cocktail glass
• Mixing glass

2 ounces tomato juice
1 tsp. crème fraîche
• Garnish:
A little fresh watercress

Mix the tomato juice and crème fraîche together, with ice cubes, in the mixing glass and strain into the cocktail glass. Garnish the drink with a little cress.

TOMATO PICANTE

Spicy, piquant drink with buttermilk for every day
• Large champagne glass
• Blender

3½ ounces tomato juice
1 tsp. lemon juice
1¾ ounces buttermilk
1-2 tbsp. Sangrita picante
Ground white pepper
Salt
• Garnish:
1 tbsp. sour cream
1 tsp. snipped fresh chives

Mix all the ingredients together well in the blender and pour into the champagne glass. Stir the sour cream and chives together and garnish the drink with a spoonful of the mixture.

COLD DUCK

CHAMPAGNE PUNCH

EXOTIC BOWL

Punches, bowls, and cups

MELON BOWL

ROSE CUP

GRAPE-GRAPPA PUNCH

WOODRUFF PUNCH

BERRY PUNCH

MANGO CUP

COLD DUCK I

Tangy, sour punch for summer evenings
• White wine glasses or punch glasses
• Punch bowl

Makes about 10 servings

2 lemon peel spirals

4 bottles white wine

2 bottles champagne or sparkling wine

Put the lemon peel spirals in the punch bowl. Pour the wine and champagne over them. Leave the lemon peels to infuse for a few minutes, then remove them.

CHAMPAGNE PUNCH I

Fruity, sweet punch as an aperitif
• Punch glasses or champagne flutes
• Punch bowl

Makes about 10 servings

2 lemons, sliced

2 oranges, sliced

1 pound green grapes, halved and seeded

Heaping ½ cup sugar

14 ounces bottled maraschino cherries, drained

7 tablespoons maraschino cherry juice (from the jar)

½ cup sherry

½ cup brandy

3 bottles champagne

Put the slices of lemon and orange and the grapes in the punch bowl together with the sugar, maraschino cherries, cherry juice, sherry, and brandy. Stir the ingredients, then refrigerate the punch for about 30 minutes. Add the champagne.

COLD DUCK II

Refreshing, light punch for any occasion
• White wine glasses
• Punch bowl

Makes about 10 servings

Grated peel of 1 lemon

2 bottles white wine

1 bottle champagne or sparkling wine

1 bottle low-sodium, sparkling mineral water

Put the lemon peel in the bowl, add the wine, cover the bowl, and refrigerate for 30 minutes to an hour. Remove the lemon peel and top up the punch with the champagne and mineral water. Stir carefully.

CHAMPAGNE PUNCH II

Very carbonated punch, suitable as an aperitif
• Punch glasses or champagne flutes
• Punch bowl

Makes about 10 servings

3 sprigs of mint

6 peaches, diced

2 ounces cognac

2¾ ounces peach- or orange-flavored liqueur

4 bottles champagne

Put the diced peach in the punch bowl. Roughly chop the mint and sprinkle it on top of the diced peach. Drizzle the brandy and liqueur over the diced peach and mint, cover, refrigerate, and leave to infuse for 1 to 2 hours. Stir and add the champagne.

Punches, Bowls, and Cups

Champagne Punch I

AMARENA CHERRY BOWL

Tangy, fruity punch for cozy evenings
• Punch glasses
• Punch bowl

Makes about 10 servings
2 large jars pitted Amarena or Morello cherries
2¾ ounces apricot brandy
2 bottles red wine
3 bottles sparkling wine or champagne

Drain the cherries, put them in the punch bowl, and drizzle the apricot brandy over them. Cover the punch, refrigerate it, and leave it to infuse for 30 minutes to an hour. Add the red wine, stir the punch, and top up with the sparkling wine or champagne.

ROSE CUP

Elegantly perfumed punch for festive occasions
• Punch glasses
• Punch bowl

Makes about 10 servings
8 fresh, scented yellow and red roses, in full bloom (untreated with chemicals)
2 bottles white wine
10 dashes rose water
2 bottles sparkling wine or champagne

Wash 6 of the roses, strip off the petals, and place them in a large bowl. Add the wine and rose water, cover, refrigerate, and leave to infuse for 4 to 5 hours. Strain the punch. Rinse the remaining 2 roses, strip off the petals, and place them in the punch bowl. Pour the punch mixture over the rose petals, stir briefly, and top up with sparkling wine or champagne.
Note: Use roses that you are absolutely certain have not been treated with insecticides or other chemicals.

OLD ENGLISH PUNCH

Alcoholic punch for winter evenings
• Punch glasses
• Punch bowl

Makes about 10 servings
2 bunches dried mint leaves
7 ounces whiskey
2 bottles white wine
2 bottles sparkling wine or champagne

Crumble the mint leaves a little, put them in a bowl, pour the whiskey over them, cover, and leave to infuse for about 15 minutes. Strain the punch into the punch bowl, top up with white wine, and refrigerate the punch for 2 hours longer. Stir the punch and top up with the sparkling wine or champagne.

Punches, Bowls, and Cups

STRAWBERRY CUP

Fruity, sparkling bowl for spring evenings
• Punch glasses
• Punch bowl

Makes about 10 servings
1½ pounds strawberries, hulled and quartered
3½ ounces strawberry-flavored liqueur
2 bottles white wine
2 bottles sparkling wine or champagne

Put the strawberries in the punch bowl, pour the liqueur over them, refrigerate, and leave to infuse for 30 minutes. Add the white wine, stir, and top up with sparkling wine or champagne.

APPLE-CALVADOS BOWL

Fruity punch for the evening
• Punch glasses
• Punch bowl

Makes about 10 servings
8 apples, peeled, cored, and sliced
Juice of 1 lemon
2 tbsp. sugar
3½ ounces Calvados
2 bottles white wine
1 bottle sparkling wine or champagne
1 bottle sparkling mineral water

Put the sliced apples in the punch bowl, drizzle the lemon juice over them, and sprinkle the sugar on top. Cover and refrigerate for 3 to 4 hours. Add the Calvados and white wine and stir. Top up with sparkling wine and mineral water.

WILLIAMS-CHRIST PUNCH

Fruity, sparkling punch for the evening
• Punch glasses
• Punch bowl

Makes about 10 servings
4 Williams pears, diced
1 ounce lemon juice
2 ounces Poire William
2 tbsp. sugar
2 bottles white wine
2 bottles sparkling wine or champagne

Put the diced pears in the punch bowl with the lemon juice, Poire William, and sugar. Stir carefully, cover, and refrigerate for 3 to 4 hours. Add the white wine, stir, and top up with sparkling wine or champagne.

GRAPE-GRAPPA PUNCH

Fruity punch for the evening
• Punch glasses
• Punch bowl

Makes about 10 servings
1½ pounds seedless green grapes, halved
3 tbsp. sugar
2 ounces grappa
Pared peel of ½ lemon, cut in a spiral
2 bottles white wine

Put all the ingredients, except the white wine, in the punch bowl and leave to infuse for about 2 hours. Top up with wine.

WOODRUFF PUNCH

Spicy punch for the merry month of
May
• Punch glasses
• Punch bowl

Makes about 10 servings

3 bunches fresh woodruff

1 orange, sliced

4 bottles dry white wine

1 bottle sparkling wine or
champagne

Rinse the woodruff, shake it dry, and
leave it to wilt overnight. Put one slice
of orange in the punch bowl and pour
2 bottles of white wine over it. Tie up
the bunches of woodruff and suspend
them in the bowl of white wine with
string; the stems should not touch the
wine, because the flavor is only
contained in the leaves. Cover the
punch and refrigerate it for about 30
minutes. Remove the woodruff, add
the remaining wine and the slices of
orange, stir, and top up the punch with
sparkling wine or champagne.

CIDER-CITRUS CUP

Refreshing punch for a party
• Punch glasses
• Punch bowl

Makes about 10 servings

2 oranges, sliced

3 limes, sliced

1 lemon, sliced

3 apples, diced

2 tbsp. lemon juice

1 bunch lemon balm or mint

5 bottles cider

Cut the slices of orange into quarters,
and cut the slices of lime and lemon in
half. Drizzle the lemon juice over the
slices of apple. Put all the fruit in the
punch bowl, place the sprigs of mint or
lemon balm on top, and pour the cider
over.

ICE BOWL

Fruity, light punch
• Punch glasses
• Punch bowl

Makes about 10 servings

2 oranges, sliced

2 lemons, sliced

2¾ ounces orange-flavored liqueur

2 bottles white wine

2 bottles red wine

2 bottles sparkling wine or
champagne

Cut the slices of orange in half and put
them in the punch bowl with the
lemon slices. Drizzle the liqueur over
the fruit and, depending on how soon
you intend to serve the punch, cover
and refrigerate for between 15 minutes
and 3 hours. Top up with wine and
champagne.

Punches, Bowls, and Cups

APRICOT-PORT PUNCH

Fruity, sparkling punch for a party
• Punch glasses
• Punch bowl

Makes about 10 servings

4½ pounds apricots, cut into quarters and stoned

¼ cup sugar

3½ ounces port

4 bottles white wine

Put the apricots in the punch bowl and sprinkle the sugar over them. Pour the port into the bowl, cover, and leave to infuse for 1 hour. Add the wine.

BERRY PUNCH

Tangy, fruity punch for any occasion
• Punch glasses
• Punch bowl

Makes about 10 servings

1 pound strawberries

½ pound raspberries

½ pound blackberries

2 tbsp. sugar

7 ounces cream sherry

3 bottles rosé wine

1 bottle sparkling wine or champagne

Rinse and prepare the berries. Put them in the punch bowl, sprinkle the sugar over them, cover, and refrigerate for about 20 minutes. Add the sherry, cover, and leave to infuse for 1 hour in the refrigerator. Stir the punch briefly, then top up with rosé wine and champagne or sparkling wine.

POMEGRANATE-PINEAPPLE BOWL

Tangy, fruity punch for any occasion
• Punch glasses
• Punch bowl

Makes about 10 servings

1 pineapple

2 ripe pomegranates

2 ounces orange-flavored liqueur

2 bottles white wine

1 bottle sparkling wine or champagne

1 bottle low-sodium, sparkling mineral water

Slice the pineapple, peel the slices, remove the tough core, and dice the slices. Make several cuts in the pomegranates from top to bottom, then peel them. If necessary remove the white skins from the seeds and collect any juice. Put the diced pineapple and pomegranate seeds in the punch bowl with the juice from the pomegranates. Drizzle the liqueur over, cover, and refrigerate for about 2 hours. Add 1 bottle of wine and leave to infuse for 1 hour longer. Add the remaining wine, stir, and top up with sparkling wine or champagne and mineral water.

PEACH CUP

Fruity punch for a summer party
• Punch glasses
• Punch bowl

Makes about 10 servings
8 ripe peaches, peeled and cut into
segments
3½ ounces cognac
Juice of 2 lemons
4 tbsp. sugar
2 bottles dry white wine
2 bottles dry sparkling wine or
champagne

If the peach segments are very big, cut
them in half and put them in the punch
bowl. Add the cognac, lemon juice,
and sugar, cover, and refrigerate for
about 2 hours. Add the white wine, stir
well, and top up the punch with the
sparkling wine or champagne.

MANGO PUNCH

Exotic, fruity punch for summer
evenings
• Punch glasses
• Punch bowl

Makes about 10 servings
3 ripe mangoes
3½ ounces apricot brandy
1¾ ounces dark rum
Juice of 2 oranges
Juice of 2 lemons
4 tbsp. sugar
2 bottles dry white wine
2 bottles dry sparkling wine or
champagne

Peel the mangoes and cut the flesh
away from the seed in thin segments.
Dice the mango flesh and put it in the
punch bowl with the apricot brandy,
rum, orange juice, lemon juice, and
sugar and refrigerate for 1 hour. Add
the white wine, stir well, and top up
with sparkling wine or champagne.

Punches, Bowls, and Cups

CHERIMOYA BOWL

Very fruity punch for the evening
• Punch glasses
• Punch bowl

Makes about 10 servings
2 ripe cherimoyas
½ pound strawberries, hulled and halved
4 green figs, quartered
2¼ ounces strawberry- or orange-flavored liqueur
¾ ounce lemon juice
2 bottles white wine
2 bottles sparkling wine or champagne

Cut the cherimoyas in half and remove the seeds. Carefully scoop out the flesh with a spoon and chop it finely. Put it in the punch bowl with the strawberries and figs. Pour the liqueur and lemon juice over the fruit, cover, and refrigerate for 2 hours. Add a bottle of white wine and refrigerate for 2 hours longer. Add the remaining white wine, stir, and top up with sparkling wine or champagne.

EXOTIC BOWL

Fruity, sparkling punch for a summer party
• Punch glasses
• Punch bowl

Makes about 10 servings
½ honeydew melon
6 dates, seeded and diced
4 ripe figs, peeled and diced
2 ounces cognac
3 kiwi fruit, peeled and sliced
3 bottles white wine
1 bottle sparkling wine or champagne

Remove the seeds from the melon and scoop out small balls from the flesh using a melon baller or teaspoon. Put the melon balls, dates, and figs in the punch bowl, drizzle the cognac over the fruit, cover, and refrigerate for 2 hours. Add the sliced kiwi fruit. Add ½ bottle of white wine and refrigerate the punch for 1 hour longer. Before serving add the remaining white wine, stir, and top up with sparkling wine or champagne.

MELON CUP

Refreshing punch for hot evenings
• Punch glasses
• Hollowed-out melon

Makes about 8 servings

1 large watermelon

2 ounces melon-flavored liqueur

1½ ounces brandy

2 tbsp. sugar

1 bottle dry white wine

1 bottle dry sparkling wine or champagne

Cut around the melon in a zigzag or Van Dyke pattern and remove the lid. Remove the seeds and scoop out small balls of flesh using a melon baller or teaspoon; the melon should be hollowed out well. Pour the liqueur, brandy, sugar, and white wine into the melon. Add the melon balls, stir, cover, and refrigerate for 2 hours. Add the sparkling wine or champagne before serving.

APPLE CUP

Fruity, sparkling punch
• Punch glasses
• Punch bowl

Makes about 10 servings

4 apples

1 lemon

3 tbsp. sugar

1 pinch ground cinnamon

3 bottles white wine

1 bottle sparkling wine or champagne

Peel, core, and finely chop the apples. Peel the lemon in a spiral and reserve the peel. Squeeze the juice from the lemon, put the chopped apple in the punch bowl, and immediately pour the lemon juice over the apple. Add the sugar, lemon peel, and cinnamon, pour 1 bottle of white wine over the fruit, cover, and refrigerate for 5 to 6 hours. Add the remaining white wine and champagne or sparkling wine.

CASSIS CUP

Fruity, sparkling bowl
• Punch glasses
• Punch bowl

Makes about 10 servings

10 ounces black currants

½ cup crème de cassis

2 bottles dry white wine

2 bottles dry sparkling wine or champagne

Rinse the berries and strip them from the stems. Put half the black currants in the punch bowl with the crème de cassis and 1 bottle of white wine, cover, and refrigerate for 3 hours. Strain the punch mixture and put the liquid in the punch bowl with the remaining black currants, white wine, and sparkling wine or champagne.

Punches, Bowls, and Cups

WILD STRAWBERRY PUNCH

Fruity, sparkling punch for a summer party
- Punch glasses
- Punch bowl

Makes about 10 servings

12 ounces wild strawberries

1 baby pineapple

2 bottles dry white wine

2 bottles dry pink sparkling wine or pink champagne

Wash and hull the strawberries. Slice the pineapple and peel the slices. Remove the plume and core and cut each pineapple slice into 8 pieces. Put the fruit in the punch bowl, pour the white wine over it, stir, cover, and refrigerate for 3 hours. Add the sparkling wine or champagne.

RED BURGUNDY PUNCH

Fruity, alcoholic punch for fall and winter evenings
- Punch glass or red wine glass
- Punch bowl

Makes about 10 servings

10 black currant leaves

1¾ ounces cognac

2 bottles full-bodied red wine

3 tbsp. sugar

2 bottles red sparkling wine or champagne

Put the black currant leaves in the punch bowl and pour the cognac over them. Cover the infusion and refrigerate it for 2 hours. If necessary, break up the sugar into smaller pieces. Add it to the infusion with the wine, then refrigerate the punch for another hour. Remove the black currant leaves before serving. Stir and top up with the sparkling wine or champagne.

RASPBERRY-LIME PUNCH

Tangy, fruity punch for a party
- Punch glasses
- Punch bowl

Makes about 10 servings

1 pound raspberries

1 lime, sliced

2 tbsp. sugar

2 bottles rosé wine

3 bottles sparkling wine or champagne

Wash and hull the raspberries. Cut the slices of lime in half and put them in the punch bowl with the raspberries. Sprinkle sugar over the fruit, cover, and refrigerate the infusion for 15 to 30 minutes. Add the rosé wine and champagne or sparkling wine.

SANGRIA I

Fruity, sweet punch for warm summer evenings
• Punch glasses
• Punch bowl

Makes about 10 servings

3 oranges, sliced

2 lemons, sliced

1 apple, peeled, cored, and sliced

4 peaches, skinned and diced

¼ cup sugar

1 cup plus 2 tbsp. orange juice

Juice of 1 lemon

2 cinnamon sticks

1½ ounces orange-flavored liqueur

2 ounces brandy

4 bottles red wine

½ cup low-sodium, mildly carbonated mineral water

Cut each slice of orange and lemon into 4 pieces and put them in the punch bowl with the sliced apple and diced peaches. Add the sugar, orange and lemon juices, cinnamon sticks, liqueur, and brandy. Stir slowly. Cover and refrigerate the infusion for 3 to 4 hours. Remove the cinnamon sticks, add the red wine, stir, and top up with mineral water.

SANGRIA II

Fruity, light punch
• Punch glasses
• Punch bowl

Makes about 10 servings

6 oranges, peeled and diced

Juice of 3 lemons

2¾ ounces rum or cognac

7 ounces Malaga wine or Madeira

½ cup sugar

3 bottles red wine

1½ bottles sparkling mineral water

Mix together the diced oranges, lemon juice, rum or cognac, Malaga or Madeira, and sugar in the punch bowl. Cover and refrigerate the infusion for 1 hour. Add the red wine and mineral water just before serving.

KUMQUAT PUNCH

Fruity, tangy punch for a party
• Punch glasses
• Punch bowl

Makes about 10 servings

10 kumquats, thinly sliced

5 tbsp. sugar

3½ ounces Cointreau

Juice of 2 lemons

2 bottles dry white wine

2 bottles dry sparkling wine

Put the sliced kumquats, sugar, Cointreau, and lemon juice in the punch bowl, cover, and refrigerate for 1 hour. Add the wine and refrigerate the infusion again for about 30 minutes. Top up with the sparkling wine or champagne.

Punches, Bowls, and Cups

Sangria I

MANDARIN-GRAPEFRUIT BOWL

Tangy, fruity punch for winter evenings
• Punch glasses
• Punch bowl

Makes about 10 servings
8 mandarins, segmented
6 pink grapefruits, segmented
1 lime, sliced
5 tbsp. sugar
2 ounces orange-flavored liqueur
1 ounce grenadine
2 bottles rosé wine
2 bottles sparkling wine or champagne

Put the fruit in the punch bowl with the sugar, orange liqueur, and grenadine. Mix carefully, cover, and refrigerate overnight. Just before serving, top up the punch, first with rosé wine, then with sparkling wine or champagne.

PINEAPPLE PUNCH I

Fruity, sparkling punch for a party
• Punch glasses
• Punch bowl

Makes about 10 servings
1 pineapple, peeled, cored, and diced
2 ounces blue curaçao
2½ bottles dry white wine
1 bottle sparkling wine or champagne

Put the diced pineapple in the punch bowl with the curaçao and 1 bottle of white wine, cover, and refrigerate the infusion for 3 to 4 hours. Add the remaining white wine, stir, and top up with sparkling wine or champagne.

BANANA-KIWI-FRUIT PUNCH

Fruity, sparkling punch
• Punch glasses
• Punch bowl

Makes about 10 servings
4 bananas, peeled and sliced
5 kiwi fruit, peeled and sliced
¾ ounce lemon juice
2 ounces kiwi-fruit-flavored liqueur
¾ ounce almond-flavored liqueur
3 bottles white wine
1 bottle sparkling wine or champagne

Put the sliced bananas and kiwi fruit in the punch bowl with the lemon juice, kiwi-fruit liqueur, and almond liqueur. Refrigerate for about 2 hours. Add the wine and champagne or sparkling wine.

KIWI FRUIT PUNCH

Fruity, refreshing bowl for any occasion
• Punch glasses
• Punch bowl

Makes about 10 servings
6 kiwi fruit
2 nectarines
¾ ounce light rum
1 bottle white wine
3 bottles bitter lemon

Peel the kiwi fruit, slice them thinly and, if necessary, cut each slice in half. Rinse the nectarines and cut the flesh away from the stone in thin segments; cut these in half. Put the fruit in the punch bowl, pour the rum over it, cover, and refrigerate the infusion for 1 hour. Add the wine and bitter lemon and stir.

Punches, Bowls, and Cups

Mandarin-Grapefruit Bowl (left), Banana-Kiwi Fruit Punch (right)

BANANA CUP I

Delicate, fruity punch for the evening
• Punch glasses
• Punch bowl

Makes about 10 servings
4 bananas
Juice of ½ lemon
1½ ounces green banana-flavored liqueur
1½ ounces light rum
3 tbsp. sugar
2 bottles dry white wine
2 bottles dry sparkling wine or champagne

Peel the bananas, slice them thinly, drizzle the lemon juice over them, and put them in the punch bowl. Add the banana liqueur, rum, sugar and 1 bottle of white wine. Cover and refrigerate the infusion for 1 hour. Add the remaining white wine and stir well. Top up the punch with sparkling wine or champagne.

BANANA CUP II

Fruity, sweet punch for a party
• Punch glasses
• Punch bowl

Makes about 10 servings
2¼ pounds bananas
Juice of 1 lemon
5 tbsp. sugar
1½ ounces light rum
¾ ounce maraschino or cherry-flavored liqueur
3 bottles white wine
2 bottles sparkling wine or champagne

Peel the bananas, slice them thinly, drizzle the lemon juice over them, and put them in the punch bowl. Add the sugar, rum, and liqueur and mix everything together. Add 1 bottle of white wine, cover, and refrigerate the infusion for 2 hours. Add the remaining white wine, stir, and add the sparkling wine or champagne.

APRICOT CUP

Fruity, refreshing punch for any occasion
• Punch glasses
• Punch bowl

Makes about 10 servings

2¾ pounds apricots
½ cup apricot- or peach-flavored liqueur
1½ ounces amaretto
5 tbsp. sugar
2 limes, sliced
2 bottles white wine
2 bottles sparkling wine or champagne

Blanch batches of the apricots in boiling water for about 1 minute, then refresh them in cold water and remove the skins. Cut the apricots in half, remove the stones, and thinly slice. Mix the apricot slices together with the liqueurs and the sugar in the punch bowl, cover, and refrigerate overnight. Cut each slice of lime in half and add them to the punch. Add the white wine, stir, and top up with sparkling wine or champagne.

ORANGE-CIDER PUNCH

Fruity, refreshing punch for any occasion
• Punch glasses
• Punch bowl

Makes about 10 servings

5 oranges, sliced
3½ ounces orange-flavored liqueur
2 cups orange juice
4 bottles cider

Cut each slice of orange into 4 pieces, put them in the punch bowl, and drizzle the liqueur over them. Cover and refrigerate the infusion for at least 2 hours, preferably overnight. Before serving, add the orange juice and cider.

FIG PUNCH

Fruity, sparkling cup for a summer evening
• Punch glasses
• Punch bowl

Makes about 10 servings

1¼ pounds ripe, green figs, quartered
2 tbsp. brown sugar
½ cup dark rum
1 bottle rosé wine
2 bottles sparkling wine or champagne
1 bottle sparkling mineral water

Put the quartered figs in the punch bowl and sprinkle the sugar over them. Pour the rum on top, cover, and leave everything to infuse for at least 5 hours, preferably overnight. Add the rosé wine, stir carefully, and slowly add the sparkling wine and mineral water.

Punches, Bowls, and Cups

BLACKBERRY CUP

Fruity, tangy cup
• Punch glasses
• Punch bowl

Makes about 10 servings
1 pound blackberries
1½ ounces orange-flavored liqueur
¾ ounce light rum
¼ cup sugar
3 bottles white wine
*1 bottle sparkling wine or
champagne*

Put rinsed blackberries in the punch
bowl with the liqueur and rum. Add
the sugar, mix everything carefully,
and refrigerate for about 1 hour. Add
1 bottle of white wine and cool the
infusion for 1 hour more. Add the
remaining white wine and top up with
sparkling wine or champagne before
serving.

CARIBBEAN PUNCH

Delicate, fruity punch for a party
• Punch glasses
• Punch bowl

Makes about 10 servings
4 star fruit, sliced
5 tbsp. sugar
2¾ ounces Grand Marnier
2¾ ounces dark rum
2 bottles dry white wine
2 bottles dry sparkling wine

Cut each slice of star fruit in half, put
them in the punch bowl, and sprinkle
the sugar over. Pour the Grand Marnier
and rum over the fruit, cover, refrigerate, and leave to infuse for about
2 hours. Add the white wine. Top up
with sparkling wine or champagne.

WHITE WINE PUNCH IN A PUMPKIN SHELL

Fruity, refreshing punch for any time of
year
• Punch glasses
• Large bowl

Makes about 10 servings
2 apples, thinly sliced
Juice of ½ lemon
7 ounces black grapes, halved
7 ounces green grapes, halved
1 lemon, sliced
½ cup dark rum
1 large pumpkin, hollowed out
4 bottles white wine

Cut each slice of apple into 4 pieces,
drizzle the lemon juice over them, and
put them in a bowl with the grapes and
sliced lemon. Pour the rum over the
fruit, cover, and refrigerate for at least
an hour. To serve, transfer the rum and
the fruit to the pumpkin shell, add the
wine, and stir.

PINEAPPLE PUNCH II

Fruity, nonalcoholic punch
• Punch glasses
• Punch bowl

Makes about 10 servings

1 pineapple, peeled and diced
3½ ounces pineapple syrup
3½ ounces lemon juice
3 bottles ginger ale
1 bottle sparkling mineral water

Put the diced pineapple, pineapple syrup, and lemon juice in the punch bowl, cover, and refrigerate for 1 hour. Stir and top up with ginger ale and mineral water.

FRUIT JUICE PUNCH

Fruity, sweet, nonalcoholic punch, suitable for a children's party
• Punch glasses
• Punch bowl

Makes about 10 servings

3 bananas, sliced
2 kiwi fruit, sliced and diced
2½ cups banana juice
2½ cups orange juice
2½ cups pineapple juice
7 ounces lemon juice
1 quart sparkling mineral water

Put the fruit and fruit juices in the punch bowl, cover, and refrigerate for 1 hour. Stir and add the mineral water.

LEMON PUNCH

Fruity, nonalcoholic punch
• Punch glasses
• Punch bowl

Makes about 10 servings

2 lemons
1 orange
4 cups pineapple juice
2 cups orange juice
3½ ounces lemon juice
3½ ounces sugar syrup
1 bottle sparkling mineral water
1 quart bitter lemon

Peel and slice the lemons and orange, then cut each slice into 4 pieces. Put the citrus peel, juices, and syrup in the punch bowl with the fruit, cover, and refrigerate for 1 hour. Remove the peel from the punch and add the mineral water and bitter lemon.

PEAR CUP

Fruity, nonalcoholic punch for any time of day
• Punch glasses
• Punch bowl

Makes about 10 servings

4 pears, peeled and diced
1½ ounces lemon juice
1 quart pear juice
1 bottle nonalcoholic wine
1 bottle nonalcoholic sparkling wine
1 bottle sparkling mineral water

Put the diced pears in the punch bowl with the lemon and pear juices, cover, and refrigerate for 30 minutes. Add the nonalcoholic wines, stir, and top up with mineral water.

Punches, Bowls, and Cups

Lemon Punch (left), Fruit Juice Punch (right)

TEA PUNCH I

Tangy, nonalcoholic punch for any time
of day
• Punch glasses
• Punch bowl

Makes about 10 servings
2 lemons, sliced
3 cups cold, strong black tea
Juice of 1 lemon
3½ ounces lime cordial
1 small bottle rum flavoring
3 bottles nonalcoholic sparkling wine

Cut the slices of lemon in half and put
them in the punch bowl with the tea,
lemon juice, lime cordial, and a little
rum flavoring, as desired. Cover and
refrigerate for 2 to 3 hours. Stir and top
up with the nonalcoholic wine.

FRUIT PUNCH I

Fruity, sweet, nonalcoholic punch for
any time of day
• Punch glasses
• Punch bowl

Makes about 10 servings
1 orange, sliced
2 sharp apples, cut into matchsticks
1 pear, cut into matchsticks
1 banana, peeled and sliced
1 quart orange juice
1 quart apple juice
2 cups pear juice
7 ounces banana juice
1 bottle sparkling mineral water

Cut each slice of orange into 4 pieces.
Put them in the punch bowl with the
remaining fruit and fruit juices, cover,
and refrigerate for 1 hour. Stir and add
the mineral water.

Punches, Bowls, and Cups

NONALCOHOLIC SANGRIA

Fruity, refreshing punch
- Punch glasses
- Punch bowl

Makes about 10 servings
4 oranges
1 lemon
6 nectarines, diced
Juice of 2 lemons
1 cup orange juice
2 quarts red grape juice

Remove the peel from one of the oranges in a spiral and reserve it. Remove the white pith and segment the orange. Thinly slice the remaining oranges and the lemon and cut each slice into 4 pieces. Put the orange peel spiral, orange segments, orange and lemon slices, and the diced nectarines in the punch bowl. Drizzle the lemon juice over them, cover, and refrigerate for about 20 minutes. Top up with the fruit juices.

KIWI FRUIT-BERRY PUNCH

Very fruity, nonalcoholic punch for any time of day
- Punch glasses
- Punch bowl

Makes about 10 servings
14 ounces strawberries, halved
½ pound raspberries
3 kiwi fruit, peeled and sliced
3½ ounces kiwi-fruit syrup
2 bottles nonalcoholic wine
1 bottle nonalcoholic sparkling wine
1 bottle sparkling mineral water

Put the fruit in the punch bowl, add the syrup and 1 bottle of nonalcoholic wine, cover, and refrigerate the infusion for 2 hours. Add the remaining wine, stir, and top up with mineral water.

KIWI FRUIT-STRAWBERRY PUNCH

Sparkling punch
- Punch glasses
- Punch bowl

Makes about 10 servings

10 kiwi fruit, peeled and sliced
1 pound strawberries, quartered
3 tbsp. sugar
2 ounces strawberry- or orange-flavored liqueur
2 bottles white wine
2 bottles sparkling wine or champagne

Put the sliced kiwi fruit and quartered strawberries in the punch bowl. Sprinkle the sugar over them, add the liqueur, cover, and refrigerate the infusion for 1 hour. Add the white wine, stir, and top up with sparkling wine or champagne.

CUCUMBER PUNCH

Tangy punch for the evening
- Punch glasses
- Punch bowl

Makes about 10 servings

½ cucumber, sliced
½ lemon, sliced
1 tbsp. sugar
2 bottles white wine
2 bottles sparkling wine or champagne

Put the cucumber slices in the punch bowl. Put half of the slices of lemon on top of the cucumber and sprinkle the sugar on top. Add 1 bottle of white wine, cover, and refrigerate the infusion for 3 to 4 hours. Strain, add the remaining white wine, stir, and top up with sparkling wine or champagne. Add the remaining lemon slices.

SPICED MELON PUNCH

Fruity, spicy punch for a summer party
- Punch glasses
- Punch bowl

Makes about 10 servings

2 honeydew melons
2 bunches fresh basil
2½ bottles German-style white wine, such as Gewürztraminer
1 bottle sparkling wine or champagne

Cut the melons in half, remove the seeds, scoop out balls of flesh with a melon baller or teaspoon, and put the melon balls in the punch bowl. Tie up a bunch of basil with string and place it on top of the melon balls. Add the white wine, cover, and refrigerate for at least 6 hours. Remove the basil. Roughly chop the remaining basil. Top up the punch with the sparkling wine or champagne and sprinkle the chopped basil on top.

NORDIC PUNCH

Hot Drinks

PHARISEE

TEA PUNCH

GINGER PUNCH

DECEMBER TEA

RUM PUNCH

SWEDEN PUNCH

FEUERZANGENBOWLE

CAFÉ PUCCI

SEAL GLÜHWEIN

NORDIC PUNCH

Aromatic, strong punch
- Heatproof punch glasses
- Large saucepan or stockpot

Makes about 10 servings

Grated peel of ¼ lemon

1 bottle full-bodied red wine, such as Burgundy

6 ounces port

½ cup strong, black tea

1¼ cups sugar

6 ounces cognac

Heat the lemon peel, wine, port, tea, and sugar together, stirring all the time. Do not let the mixture boil. If desired, the cognac can be warmed in advance and added to the punch just before serving.

BOSTON TEA PUNCH

Strong, spicy punch
- Heatproof punch glasses
- Large saucepan or stockpot

Makes about 12 servings

4 cups black tea

1 bottle dark rum

4½ ounces triple sec

Sugar to taste

12 thin slices of lemon

12 cloves

Heat the tea, rum, and triple sec together and add sugar to taste, stirring all the time, until the sugar dissolves. Do not bring to a boil. Warm the punch glasses and serve the punch in them. Spike each slice of lemon with a clove and add a slice of lemon to each glass of punch.

FEUERZANGENBOWLE

Fruity, alcoholic punch for winter celebrations
- Heatproof punch glasses
- Large saucepan and Feuerzangenbowle pan with sugar loaf tray

Makes about 14 servings

Juice of 2 oranges

Juice of 1 lemon

2 bottles red wine

1 cinnamon stick

6 cloves

1 sugar loaf

12 ounces dark rum (108 proof)

Heat the juices, red wine, and spices together in the large saucepan, but do not allow the punch to boil. Transfer the punch to the Feuerzangenbowle pan. Put the sugar loaf on the rest and suspend it over the pan. Baste the sugar loaf with a little rum and ignite it. Using a ladle, gradually pour more rum over the sugar loaf until it has completely melted. Stir the punch.

Feuerzangenbowle

CREAM PUNCH

Creamy, aromatic punch
- Heatproof punch glasses
- Large saucepan or stockpot

Makes about 10 servings

2 cloves

1 cinnamon stick

2 cups hot, black tea

¾ cup sugar

1 bottle red wine

Grated peel of 1 lemon

1 cup dark rum

Juice of 1 lemon

1 cup whipped cream

Heat the cloves, cinnamon stick, tea, sugar, red wine, and lemon peel together, stirring all the time, until the sugar dissolves. Do not let the mixture boil. Add the rum and lemon juice. Strain the punch through a strainer, pour into the glasses, and serve with a dollop of cream on top of each glass.

JAPANESE PUNCH

Aromatic, strong punch
- Heatproof punch glasses
- Large saucepan or stockpot

Makes about 8 servings

1 cup hot, green tea

½ cup sugar

Grated peel of 1 lemon

1 bottle Moselle wine

12 ounces arrak

Heat the tea, sugar, lemon peel, wine, and arrak together, stirring all the time, until the sugar dissolves. Do not let the mixture boil.

RUBY ORANGE PUNCH

Fruity punch
- Heatproof punch glasses
- Large saucepan or stockpot

Makes about 10 servings

1 cup sugar

Juice of 5 ruby oranges

Juice of 1 lemon

3 cups hot, black tea

2 cups dark rum

Dissolve the sugar in the orange and lemon juices, stirring all the time, and add the mixture to the tea. Add the rum and heat the punch, but do not let it boil.

SHERRY-TEA PUNCH

Alcoholic, aromatic punch
- Heatproof punch glasses
- Large saucepan or stockpot

Makes about 8 servings

½ cup sugar

2 cups hot, strong, black tea

2 cups sherry

1 cup arrak

Grated peel and juice of 1 lemon

Dissolve the sugar in the hot tea, stirring all the time. Add the sherry, arrak, and lemon peel and juice and heat through. Do not let the mixture boil.

Hot Drinks

SPANISH TEA PUNCH

Strong punch
- Heatproof punch glasses
- Large saucepan or stockpot

Makes about 10 servings

1 quart hot, black tea
2¾ ounces Grand Marnier
2¾ ounces Spanish brandy
1 cup dark rum
Sugar to taste

Heat the tea, Grand Marnier, brandy, and rum together. Do not let the mixture boil. Sweeten the punch to taste.

SHIP'S KOBOLD'S PUNCH

Aromatic, alcoholic punch
- Heatproof punch glasses
- Skillet and large saucepan

Makes about 10 servings

1 large knob of butter
¾ cup sugar
1 bottle port
14 ounces water
12 ounces arrak

Melt the butter in the skillet, add the sugar and cook, stirring, until it caramelizes. Leave to cool slightly, but it should not become completely cold. Heat the port, water, arrak, and caramel together, stirring all the time, until the caramel dissolves. Do not let the mixture boil.

GINGER PUNCH

Alcoholic, spicy punch
- Heatproof punch glasses
- Large saucepan or stockpot

Makes about 10 servings

1 piece of ginger root
1 cup water
Scant ½ cup sugar
2 cloves
1 bottle red wine
2 cups hot, strong, black tea
Juice of 1 lemon
7 ounces dark rum

Peel the ginger, dice it and add it to the water. Bring to a boil with the sugar and cloves and simmer for about 10 minutes, until a syrup forms. Mix the red wine, tea, and lemon juice together. Strain the ginger syrup through a strainer and add it to the punch with the rum. Check the sweetness and adjust if necessary.

SCANDINAVIAN PUNCH

Sweet, alcoholic punch
- Heatproof punch glasses
- Large saucepan or stockpot

Makes about 12 servings

3 cups water
1¼ cups sugar
1 quart arrak
3½ ounces white wine

Bring the water to a boil and dissolve the sugar in it, stirring all the time. Add the arrak and simmer over low heat, stirring constantly, until a syrup forms. Dilute the punch with the white wine before serving.

ICE-AGE PUNCH

Fruity, alcoholic punch
• Heatproof punch glasses
• Large saucepan or stockpot

Makes about 12 servings

1 orange

4 canned pineapple rings

Juice of 2 oranges

2 bottles red wine

½ cup arrak

½ cup dark rum

½ cup sugar

1 heaping teaspoon vanilla-flavored sugar

Remove the peel from the orange in a spiral. Carefully remove the pith from the orange and slice the flesh thinly. Drain the pineapple rings, reserving the juice, and finely chop. Heat the fruit with ½ cup of the pineapple juice and the remaining ingredients. Do not let the mixture boil. Pour the punch into the glasses and garnish the rim of each glass with a piece of orange peel spiral.

ORANGE PUNCH

Fruity, sweet punch
• Heatproof punch glasses
• Large saucepan or stockpot

Makes about 12 servings

1 quart water

1¼ cups sugar

2 cups white wine

1 cup brandy

1 cup light rum

3½ ounces maraschino

Juice of 2 lemons

Juice of 7 oranges

Bring the water to a boil with the sugar, stirring all the time, until the sugar dissolves. Add the remaining ingredients and heat through thoroughly, but do not let the punch boil.

SHERRY PUNCH

Aromatic punch
• Heatproof punch glasses
• Large saucepan or stockpot

Makes about 10 servings

1½ cups sherry

1½ cups arrak

¾ cup plus 2 tbsp. sugar

Grated peel of 1 lemon

3 cups water

Mix the sherry, arrak, and sugar together and leave to infuse for a short while. Add the water and heat the mixture, stirring all the time, until the sugar dissolves. Do not let the mixture boil.

Hot Drinks

PARISIAN PUNCH

Alcoholic, fruity punch
• Heatproof punch glasses
• Large saucepan or stockpot

Makes about 12 servings

1 quart hot, black tea

2 cups Armagnac

1 cup sugar

Juice of 5 oranges

Juice of 3 lemons

Heat all the ingredients together, stirring all the time, until the sugar dissolves. Do not let the mixture boil.

WINE PUNCH

Fruity punch
• Heatproof punch glasses
• Large saucepan or stockpot

Makes about 10 servings

1 bottle red wine

1 bottle white wine

Heaping 5 tbsp. sugar

1 orange, sliced

1 lemon, sliced

Juice of 1 orange

Juice of 1 lemon

4 cinnamon sticks

2 cloves

⅔ cup dark rum

Heat the wine and sugar together, stirring all the time, until the sugar dissolves. Do not let the mixture boil. Cut the slices of citrus fruit in half and add them to the wine with the fruit juices, cinnamon, and cloves. Heat the punch until it is just at boiling point, then stir in the rum.

JASMINE PUNCH

Aromatic, alcoholic punch
• Heatproof punch glasses
• Large saucepan or stockpot with heat-resistant handles

Makes about 12 servings

1 bottle cherry eau-de-vie

½ cup sugar

1 quart hot jasmine tea

24 maraschino cherries from a jar

Heat 1 cup of the cherry eau-de-vie with the sugar, stirring all the time, until the sugar dissolves. Ignite the alcohol mixture and extinguish the flames with the jasmine tea. Add the remaining cherry eau-de-vie and heat everything through, but do not let the mixture boil. Put 2 maraschino cherries in each punch glass and pour the hot punch over them. Ignite the punch and serve it with the flames still burning.

TEA PUNCH II

Strong punch
• Heatproof punch glasses
• Large saucepan or stockpot

Makes about 10 servings

1 quart hot, black tea

2 cups aquavit

Sugar to taste

Mix the tea and aquavit together and heat briefly, but do not let the mixture boil. Divide the sugar among the punch glasses (quantity to taste) and add the tea mixture.

FRUIT PUNCH II

Fruity, sparkling punch
• Heatproof punch glasses
• Large saucepan or stockpot

Makes about 8 servings

1 cup arrak

10 ounces fresh fruit, such as peaches, apples, pears, and oranges, peeled and diced

1 bottle white wine

1¾ ounces cognac

1 cup sparkling wine or champagne

Briefly heat the arrak and fruit together, stirring all the time, but do not let the mixture boil. Add the white wine and heat everything through again. Add the cognac and sparkling wine or champagne.

DUBLIN PUNCH

Very alcoholic punch
• Heatproof punch glasses
• Large saucepan or stockpot

Makes about 8 servings

2 cups water

3 cups Irish whiskey

¼ cup sugar

4½ tbsp. honey

Grated peel and juice of 1 lemon

½ cinnamon stick

Grated nutmeg

Heat the water until it is just at boiling point. Add all the remaining ingredients, except the nutmeg, and heat through, stirring all the time, but do not let the mixture boil. Remove the cinnamon stick and sprinkle a little grated nutmeg over the punch.

KING'S PUNCH I

Aromatic punch
• Heatproof punch glasses
• Large saucepan or stockpot with heat-resistant handles

Makes about 10 servings

2 cups hot, black tea

½ cup plus 2 tbsp. sugar

Heaping ½ cup packed brown sugar

2 cups white wine

1½ cups dark rum

Lemon juice

Heat the tea and sugar together, stirring all the time, until the sugar dissolves. Do not let the mixture boil. Add the white wine and rum and heat the punch through. Add a little lemon juice to taste and flambé the punch.

KING'S PUNCH II

Fruity, aromatic punch
• Heatproof punch glasses
• Large saucepan or stockpot

Makes about 12 servings

1 bottle white wine

2 cups water

½ cup plus 2 tbsp. sugar

Grated peel and juice of 2 oranges

Juice of 3 lemons

2 cups light rum

Mix all the ingredients together, except the rum. Cover the mixture and leave to infuse for 1 to 2 hours. Heat the punch through, but do not let it boil. Stir in the rum.

Hot Drinks

Fruit Punch (left), December Tea (right)

DECEMBER TEA

Fruity, sweet punch
• Heatproof punch glasses
• Large saucepan or stockpot

Makes about 10 servings

Scant 1 cup honey

1 quart hot, black tea

1¼ cups orange-flavored liqueur

Juice of 2 lemons

Juice of 2 oranges

1 tsp. ground cinnamon

1 cup whipped cream

Dissolve the honey in the tea, stirring all the time. Add the orange liqueur, lemon and orange juices, and cinnamon. Heat the punch, stirring all the time, but do not let it boil. Divide the punch among the glasses and top each glass with whipped cream.

GOOD NIGHT ALL PUNCH

Spicy punch
• Heatproof punch glasses
• Large saucepan or stockpot

Makes about 10 servings

5½ cups malt beer

4 tbsp. honey

2 tsp. preserved ginger syrup

Pinch ground white pepper

Pinch ground cloves

1 cinnamon stick

A day in advance, heat the beer, honey, and ginger syrup together, stirring all the time, but do not let the mixture boil. Put the spices in a cheesecloth bag, suspend it in the punch mixture, and leave to infuse overnight. Before serving, remove the bag of spices and reheat the punch.

EMPEROR PUNCH

Fruity, sweet punch
- Heatproof punch glasses
- Large saucepan or stockpot with heat-resistant handles

Makes about 8 servings
1 cup water
½ cup plus 2 tbsp. sugar
1 bottle dry white wine
¾ cup light or dark rum (108 proof)
Juice of 1 lemon

Heat the water and sugar together, stirring all the time. Add the wine and rum and heat through again, but do not let the mixture boil. Ignite the punch with a match and burn off the alcohol. Add the lemon juice to the punch and stir.

RUM PUNCH

Fruity, sweet punch
- Heatproof punch glasses
- Large saucepan or stockpot

Makes about 10 servings
1½ cups dark rum
1½ cups red wine
Juice of 3 lemons
1¾ cups plus 2 tbsp. sugar
1 bottle medium-dry white wine

Heat the rum, red wine, lemon juice, and sugar together, stirring all the time, until the sugar dissolves, but do not let the mixture boil. Stir in the white wine just before serving.

SWEDEN PUNCH

Aromatic punch
- Heatproof pottery mugs with handle
- Skillet and saucepan

Makes about 10 servings
4½ cups light red wine, such as pinot noir
2-2¾ ounces brandy
2 tsp. sugar
1 tsp. ground ginger
1 tsp. cardamom pods
10 cloves
- *Extra:*
1 cup chopped almonds
⅔ cup raisins

Heat all the ingredients together, but do not let the punch boil. Remove from the heat and leave to infuse for 2 to 3 hours. Heat through again and then strain. Put 1 teaspoon each of almonds and raisins in each mug and pour in the punch.

ST. PAUL'S PUNCH

Sweet, strong punch
- Heatproof punch glasses
- Large saucepan or stockpot

Makes about 8 servings
1 bottle Rhine wine
1½ cups Madeira
Heaping ¼ cup sugar
6 ounces brandy

Heat the wine, Madeira, and sugar together, stirring all the time, until the sugar dissolves, but do not let the mixture boil. Add the brandy and stir.

Sweden Punch

CHERRY PUNCH

Fruity punch
- Heatproof punch glasses
- Large saucepan or stockpot

Makes about 10 servings

14 ounces Amarena or Morello
cherries from a jar
4½ cups white wine
¾ cup sugar
½ cup light rum
1 tsp. ground cinnamon
3 cloves

Drain the cherries, reserving the juice.
Heat the cherries with ½ cup of the
cherry juice and the remaining
ingredients, stirring all the time, but do
not let the mixture boil. Remove the
cloves before serving.

CHAMPAGNE PUNCH

Aromatic, sparkling punch
- Heatproof punch glasses
- Large saucepan or stockpot

Makes about 8 servings

3½ ounces cognac
5 slices of lemon
Sugar to taste
1½ cups sparkling mineral water
1½ cups white wine
1½ cups sparkling wine or
champagne

Pour the cognac over the slices of
lemon and leave to marinate for a few
minutes. Dissolve a little sugar in the
mineral water and add to the lemon
mixture. Add the white wine and heat
everything together, but do not let the
punch boil. Add the sparkling wine or
champagne just before serving.

PUNCH DEMIDOFF

Sparkling, aromatic punch
- Heatproof punch glasses
- Large saucepan or stockpot

Makes about 8 servings

2 cups white wine
2 cups dry white wine
1 cup water
1 cup light rum
2 tbsp. sugar
Grated peel of 1 lemon
1 tsp. lemon juice
Sparkling wine or champagne to taste

Heat the wine, water, rum, sugar, and
lemon peel together, stirring all the
time, but do not let the mixture boil.
Add the lemon juice, check the punch
for sweetness, and adjust as necessary.
Add sparkling wine or champagne to
taste.

COFFEE-PORT PUNCH

Strong, aromatic punch
- Heatproof punch glasses
- Large saucepan or stockpot

Makes about 10 servings

2 cups strong, hot coffee
2 cups white port
2 cups dark rum
Sugar to taste

Heat the coffee, port, and rum
together, but do not let the mixture
boil. Gradually stir in sugar to taste,
stirring all the time, and continue
heating the punch until the sugar
dissolves.

Hot Drinks

PUNCH PERUSHIM

Aromatic, creamy punch
- Heatproof punch glass
- Saucepan

Serves 1

⅔ cup hot, black tea
2 tsp. sugar
2 tsp. dark rum
2 tbsp. light cream
A little whipped cream

Heat the tea, sugar, rum, and cream together, stirring all the time, but do not let the mixture boil. Pour the punch into the glass and top with whipped cream.

HAWAII PUNCH

Fruity, strong punch
- Heatproof punch glasses
- Skillet and large saucepan

Makes about 8 servings

1 large knob butter
¾ cup sugar
7 ounces canned pineapple chunks
1 bottle muscatel wine
1 cup hot, strong black tea
½ cup arrak
2½ ounces Madeira

Melt the butter in the skillet. Add the sugar and cook until it caramelizes and becomes golden brown. Leave the caramel to cool a little, but not set. Drain the pineapple chunks, retaining the juice. Heat the wine with the caramel, tea, arrak, 5 tablespoons of pineapple juice, and the pineapple chunks, stirring all the time. Do not let the mixture boil.

CHINA PUNCH

Aromatic, sweet punch
- Heatproof punch glasses
- Large saucepan or stockpot

Makes about 8 servings

Grated peel and juice of 1 orange
½ cup sugar
2½ ounces cherry eau-de-vie
2½ ounces arrak
2½ ounces lychee syrup
½ vanilla bean, split
2 cups hot, black tea
1 bottle white wine

Mix the orange juice, sugar, cherry eau-de-vie, arrak, lychee syrup, and vanilla bean together and leave to stand until the sugar dissolves. Heat the tea, wine, and orange peel together but do not let the mixture boil. Add the punch infusion and stir together. Strain the punch before serving.

AMERICAN PUNCH

Strong, aromatic punch
- Heatproof punch glass
- Saucepan

Serves 1

1½ ounces Madeira
¾ ounce dark rum
1 tsp. sugar
1 slice of lemon
1 clove
1 tea bag

Warm the punch glass. Heat the ingredients together and leave to infuse for about 5 minutes. Strain the punch into the warmed glass.

GRAPEFRUIT-ORANGE PUNCH

Fruity, aromatic punch
• Heatproof punch glasses
• Large saucepan or stockpot

Makes about 10 servings

1 bottle white wine

½ cup sugar

Juice of 3 oranges

Juice of 3 grapefruits

Juice of 1 lemon

2 cloves

1 cinnamon stick

1½ cups light rum

Combine all the ingredients, except the rum. Cover and leave to infuse for 30 minutes. Heat the punch, but do not let it boil. Stir in the rum. Remove the cloves and cinnamon stick before serving.

STRAWBERRY PUNCH

Very fruity, sweet punch
• Heatproof punch glasses
• Large saucepan or stockpot

Makes about 10 servings

1 pound fresh strawberries

5 cups water

1¼ cups sugar

1 cup light rum

Juice of 1 lemon

1 quart water

Rinse and hull the strawberries. Put them in ½ cup water, bring to a boil, and simmer for about 10 minutes. Add the sugar, rum, and light rum to the stewed fruit, cover, and leave to infuse for 2 to 3 hours. Add 1 quart water and heat the punch quickly to bring it almost to a boil, stirring all the time. Strain the punch and serve immediately.

Hot Drinks

PETERSBURG PUNCH

Fizzy, fruity punch
- Heatproof punch glasses
- Large saucepan or stockpot

Makes about 6 servings

1 bottle sparkling wine or champagne

1½ ounces cherry eau-de-vie

A little cognac

1¼ cups sugar

1 small, fresh pineapple, peeled and diced

Heat the sparkling wine or champagne, cherry eau-de-vie, cognac, and sugar to taste, together. Stir all the time until the sugar dissolves. Do not let the mixture boil. Add the pieces of pineapple and heat the punch through again briefly.

RUMGLÖGG

Strong, aromatic punch
- Heatproof punch glasses
- Large saucepan or stockpot

Makes about 10 servings

1 bottle red wine

1½ cups port

8 tbsp. sugar

8 cloves

1 piece of lemon peel

1 cinnamon stick

1½ cups dark rum

Heat all the ingredients, except the rum, together, stirring all the time, until the punch reaches boiling point. Turn down the heat, cover, and simmer over very low heat for about 15 minutes. Remove the spices and the lemon peel. Slowly warm the rum and add it to the punch. Serve hot.

SYLT GROG

Sour, fruity grog
- Heatproof punch glass
- Saucepan

Serves 1

3½ ounces water

1¾ ounces dark rum

1 tsp. honey

Juice of ½ lemon

Heat the water and add the rum, honey, and lemon juice. Stir well until the honey dissolves and pour into the glass.

BRANDY GROG

Fruity, alcoholic grog
- Heatproof punch glass
- Saucepan

Serves 1

1½ ounces brandy

2 tsp. sugar

Juice of ½ lemon

3½ ounces hot water

Heat the brandy, sugar, and lemon juice together, stirring all the time, until the sugar dissolves, but do not let boil. Add the water, stir, and transfer the grog to the glass.

HELIGOLAND GROG

Aromatic grog
- Heatproof punch glass
- Saucepan

Serves 1

2 ounces red wine

1½ ounces dark rum

1½ ounces water

Brown sugar, to taste

- *Garnish:*

1 slice of lemon

Heat the red wine, rum, and water together, but do not let boil. Put some sugar in the glass, add the grog, and perch the slice of lemon on the rim of the glass.

HOT BUTTERED RUM

Creamy grog
- Heatproof punch glass

Serves 1

2 sugar cubes

1¾ ounces dark rum

Boiling water for topping up

Butter

Put the sugar cubes in the glass, put a teaspoon or glass stirrer in the glass, add the rum and top up with boiling water. Dot the surface of the drink with butter and stir gently.

Hot Drinks

RUM GROG

Very powerful grog
• Heatproof punch glass

Serves 1

2 sugar cubes

Boiling water for topping up

1¾ ounces dark rum

Put the sugar cubes in the glass with a teaspoon or glass stirrer and fill the glass half full with boiling water. Stir to dissolve the sugar and add the rum.

KEITUM HOUSE GROG

Sweet, alcoholic grog
• Heatproof punch glass
• Saucepan

Serves 1

4 sugar cubes

1½ ounces hot water

1½ ounces dark rum

¾ ounce red wine

Pinch grated nutmeg

• Garnish:

1 slice of lemon

Mix the sugar and water together until the sugar dissolves. Add the rum and red wine and heat the mixture, but do not let it boil. Pour the grog into the glass, sprinkle a little nutmeg on top, and garnish the rim of the glass with the slice of lemon.

HOT HENRY

Aromatic grog
• Heatproof punch glasses
• Large saucepan

Makes about 4 servings

½ cup water

5½ tbsp. honey

6 cloves

6 black peppercorns

1 vanilla bean, split

½ nutmeg

1 cup vodka

Grated peel of ½ lemon

Heat the water and honey together, stirring all the time, until the honey dissolves. Crush the cloves and peppercorns, add them to the liquid together with the vanilla bean and nutmeg, and simmer the mixture for about 15 minutes. Add the vodka and lemon peel, cover the grog, and leave it to infuse for 5 minutes. Strain through a strainer and serve.

CANADA GROG

Sweet, aromatic grog
- Heatproof punch glass
- Saucepan

Serves 1

1½ ounces Canadian whisky

1 tbsp. maple syrup

Juice of ½ lemon

3½ ounces hot water

• Garnish:

½ slice of lemon

Mix the whiskey, maple syrup, and lemon juice together in the glass. Add the hot water and stir. Perch the slice of lemon on the rim of the glass.

SEAL GLÜHWEIN

Aromatic glühwein
- Heatproof punch glass
- Saucepan

Serves 1

1 tbsp. raisins

1½ ounces light rum

1¾ ounces white wine

1 tbsp. sugar

1 piece of lemon peel

Pinch of ground cinnamon

Put the raisins in the glass, pour the rum over them, and leave them to soak for a few minutes. Heat the white wine, sugar, lemon peel, and cinnamon together, but do not let the mixture boil. When heated, pour the mixture into the glass.

DUTCH GROG

Fruity, sweet grog
- Heatproof punch glasses
- Large saucepan or stockpot

Makes about 10 servings

3 cups arrak

1¼ cups sugar

Juice of 6 lemons

3 cups hot water

Heat the arrak, sugar, and lemon juice together, stirring all the time, but do not let the mixture boil. Add the water and warm the grog through again.

HOT LOCOMOTIVE

Sweet glühwein
- Heatproof punch glass
- Saucepan

Serves 1

1 egg yolk

1 tsp. honey

½ tsp. sugar

3½ ounces full-bodied red wine

2 dashes triple sec

Pinch of ground cinnamon

• Garnish:

1 piece of lemon peel

Mix the egg yolk, honey, and sugar together. Heat the wine, triple sec, and cinnamon together. Pour the hot liquid into the glass together with the egg yolk mixture. Garnish the rim of the glass with the slice of lemon.

Hot Drinks

NEGUS

Aromatic glühwein
- Heatproof punch glass
- Saucepan

Serves 1

3½ ounces port

1 tsp. sugar

1 piece of lemon peel

A little hot water

A little grated nutmeg

Heat the port, sugar, and lemon peel together. Do not let the mixture boil. Strain into the glass. Add a little hot water and sprinkle a pinch of grated nutmeg on top of the drink.

WHITE GLÜHWEIN

Aromatic glühwein
- Heatproof punch glasses
- Saucepan

Makes about 4 servings

1 bottle white wine

10 pieces of coarse sugar

1 clove

- *Garnish:*

4 slices of orange

Heat the wine, sugar, and clove together, but do not let the mixture boil. Strain it into the glasses. Perch a slice of orange on the rim of each glass.

RÜDESHEIM COFFEE

Aromatic specialty coffee
• Irish coffee glass

Serves 1

1½ ounces brandy
3 sugar cubes
Hot coffee for topping up
Whipped cream flavored with vanilla
2 tsp. grated chocolate

Warm the brandy and the glass. Put the sugar cubes and the warmed brandy in the glass. Ignite the brandy, burn off the alcohol, and extinguish the flames by adding the hot coffee, stirring all the time. Top the coffee with whipped cream and sprinkle grated chocolate on top.

IRISH COFFEE

Strong specialty coffee
• Irish coffee glass

Serves 1

1 tsp. brown sugar
1½ ounces Irish whiskey
1 cup hot coffee
Lightly whipped cream

Put the sugar in the glass, pour the whiskey over it, and heat the sugar mixture in the glass (special equipment is required to do this, including a spirit stove), but do not let it get too hot. Add the hot coffee and stir well. Float the cream on top of the coffee.

ITALIAN COFFEE

Spicy, almond-flavored specialty coffee
• Heatproof glass

Serves 1

1 ounce amaretto
1 cup hot coffee
Lightly whipped cream

Warm the amaretto in the glass, pour the hot coffee on top, and stir well. Float the cream on top of the coffee.

FRENCH COFFEE

Sweet, orange-flavored specialty coffee
• Heatproof glass

Serves 1

1 ounce Grand Marnier
1 cup hot coffee
Lightly whipped cream

Pour the Grand Marnier into the glass and warm it gently. Add the coffee and stir well. Float the cream on top of the coffee.

Rüdesheim Coffee

CAFÉ CHOCOLAT

Spicy specialty coffee
• Heatproof punch glass
• Saucepan

Serves 1

1 cup strong coffee
⅔ ounce semisweet chocolate
Pinch of ground cinnamon
Pinch of ground cardamom
2 tsp. brown sugar
¾ ounce white or brown crème de cacao
Whipped cream
Grated chocolate

Heat the coffee, but do not let it boil. Add chocolate, as desired, and stir until it melts. Add the cinnamon, cardamom, sugar, and cocoa liqueur and stir. Pour the drink into the glass, garnish with a rosette of cream, and sprinkle a little grated chocolate on top.

MEXICAN COFFEE

Very alcoholic specialty coffee
• Heatproof glass

Serves 1

1 tsp. brown sugar
¾ ounce dark rum
¾ ounce Kahlúa
1 cup hot coffee
Lightly whipped cream

Put the sugar in the glass, add the rum and liqueur, and warm everything gently (special equipment is required to do this, including a spirit stove). Add the coffee and stir well. Float the cream on top of the coffee.

PHARISEE

Aromatic specialty coffee
• Irish coffee glass

Serves 1

2 sugar cubes
1½ ounces dark rum
1 cup hot coffee
Lightly whipped cream

Warm the glass, put the sugar cubes and rum in it, top up with hot coffee, and stir. Float the cream on top of the coffee.

Hot Drinks

FRENCH MOCHA

Strong, aromatic grog
- Heatproof glass
- Small saucepan

Serves 1

1 ounce Armagnac

4 sugar cubes

1 tbsp. lemon juice

1 cup hot mocha-flavored coffee

Heat the Armagnac, sugar cubes, and lemon juice together, and pour into the glass. Add the mocha coffee.

CAFÉ PUCCI

Strong specialty coffee
- Heatproof punch glass

Serves 1

¾ ounce dark rum

¾ ounce amaretto

1 cup hot espresso coffee

A little brown sugar

Lightly whipped cream

Warm the rum and amaretto in the glass. Add the espresso and sugar to taste and stir. Float the cream on top of the coffee.

CAFÉ BRÛLOT

Spicy, aromatic specialty coffee
- Heatproof punch glass
- Saucepan

Serves 1

1½ ounces cognac

1 cup strong coffee

1 small piece of cinnamon stick

2 cloves

1 piece of orange peel

1 piece of lemon peel

Sugar to taste

Heat all the ingredients together, stirring all the time, but do not let the mixture boil. Strain it into the punch glass.

RED AND WHITE

Creamy, alcoholic hot drink
- Heatproof punch glass
- Saucepan

Serves 1

2 ounces milk

¾ ounce dark rum

¾ ounce light rum

¾ ounce cream

¾ ounce cherry-flavored liqueur

Heat the milk, both rums, and cream together, but do not let the mixture boil. Pour the mixture into the punch glass and slowly pour the cherry liqueur on top. Do not stir. Serve immediately.

GLOSSARY OF BAR AND COCKTAIL TERMINOLOGY

As in any other occupation, there is a vocabulary peculiar to professional bartenders. It is used internationally, but to lay people it is often almost incomprehensible. This glossary of technical jargon, therefore, is included to help enlighten you.

After-dinner drinks are drinks served after a meal, as the term implies. They are usually sweet and are intended to round off the meal.

Aperitifs are drinks served before the meal intended to stimulate the appetite. There are various basic types of aperitif: bitters, vermouth, wines, and sparkling wines, as well as cocktails or straight liquor mixed with soft drinks or water. Classic aperitif cocktails are the martini and Manhattan. It is important to remember aperitifs are served without straws and usually without ice cubes.

Bar spoons are used for measuring liquids and stirring.

Bowls, similar to punches, most frequently consist of wine, fruit, and champagne or sparkling wine. Take care to use only light wines with a natural effervescence, such as those similar to German wines from the Moselle. Never add ice cubes to the bowl or it will become diluted. Always add the sparkling wine or champagne (ice cold) just before serving, and do not stir the mixture, otherwise too much fizz will be released and the drink will taste flat. If you do not want the bowl to be too alcoholic, top it up with sparkling mineral water instead of a sparkling wine.

Brut is the name given to sparkling wines, especially champagne, which are very dry. Brut identifies the lowest level of sweetness and is even drier than "extra dry" on the label.
Built in the glass means that the drink is prepared in the glass in which it will be drunk.

Cobblers are long, chilled drinks that always contain fruit and usually have sparkling wine or soda added. A cobbler glass or champagne glass is filled one-third full with crushed ice, the alcoholic mixture is poured over it, and then the fruit is added. It is finally topped up with soda or sparkling wine. Cobblers should always be served with a bar spoon and straw.

Cocktails are short drinks, which consist of spirits, liqueurs, fruit, fruit juices, other flavorings, and fortified, sweet, or dessert wines. They are served ice cold, and drunk before or after meals, as well as for general enjoyment and stimulation at other times. Cocktails are stirred, shaken or mixed in the glass.

Champagne cocktails are drinks that are always topped up with champagne or sparkling wine.

Collinses are long drinks, which are mostly dry and are stirred in the glass. Collinses are usually served with a slice of lemon on the rim of the glass and with a straw. The classic version of this style of drink is a Tom Collins, a tall combination of gin, lemon juice, and sugar syrup with ice cubes. A John Collins is made with bourbon.

Coolers are thirst quenching, mild, sweet drinks, which, in addition to alcohol, almost always contain ginger ale. Serve them with a straw.

Crusta is the name given to the sugared rim on a glass.

Crustas are refreshing, long drinks which are served in glasses with a sugared rim. A straw should always be served with one of these popular after-dinner drinks.

Cups are similar to punches, but usually more alcoholic and not usually topped up with carbonated drinks.

Daisies are often very sweet and, therefore, were once thought of as exclusively for women. They are traditionally gin or whiskey based with a thin layer of a liqueur floated on the top. They are served with a straw and a bar spoon.

Dash is the smallest measurement when mixing drinks and cocktails.

Digestive is a drink consumed after a meal to assist digestion. Unflavored schnapps or eaux-de-vie are suitable as digestives, as are bitters and dry liqueurs, such as the caraway-flavored kümmel.

Dry applies to drinks such as champagne, dessert wines, and fortified wines, as well as spirits such as gin, which are differentiated according to the degree of sweetness. Other standard definitions for a drink's level of sweetness include "medium dry" (sweeter than dry) and "extra dry" (very dry).

Eggnogs, especially popular around Thanksgiving and Christmas, always contain milk and egg yolks and are served chilled or warm in a large rocks glass with a straw. They should not, however, be drunk by anyone who is ill, elderly, or pregnant, or by young children, because they contain raw eggs.

Fancy drinks are imaginative drinks that do not fit into any category of alcoholic mixed drink or cocktail and for which there are no basic recipes. The sole stipulation is that they should contain a maximum of 2 ounces alcohol and taste good.

Fixes are alcoholic, long drinks served in a rocks glass filled with finely crushed ice. They are popular aperitifs.

Fizzes are popular drinks. They contain fruit juice or another form of sweetener, alcohol, and plenty of soda water to give them their fizzy, bubbly texture. Serve them with a straw. Fizzes with egg whites are known as Silver Fizzes; those with egg yolks are Golden Fizzes; when a whole egg is included the drink is called a Royal Fizz; and when mixed with cream, a Cream Fizz.

Flips are long drinks, prepared in a shaker, which include egg yolks, sugar, and often a pinch of spice. They should not be shaken for too long, though, and they must be served immediately after preparation, otherwise they curdle and look unattractive. Flips, most popular in the last century, are usually served in special flip glasses or in champagne glasses with a straw.

Float means that before a drink is served, an ingredient is carefully poured on top of the drink. Thereafter, the drink should not be stirred.

Frappés, popular as an after-dinner drink, can be prepared from any spirit, but are most often made with a liqueur, such as green crème de menthe. Fill a champagne glass half full with crushed ice, add the

Glossary

spirit, stir quickly, and garnish with fruit, a straw, and a spoon. Ice-cream frappés are prepared in a blender.

Glühwein can be prepared using red or white wine, cider, or port. The customary flavorings and spices are lemon juice, sugar, cloves, and cinnamon. The wine is heated with the spices over low heat, but it should not be boiled. It is then strained into a heatproof punch or glühwein glass for serving.

Grog is a hot rum drink with sugar and boiling water. The tried and tested recipe states that sugar ought to be added, water is optional, and rum is a must, but the rum may be replaced by arrak, brandy, or whiskey.

Highballs are perfect thirst-quenchers from the long drinks family. They are served in tall, highball or Collins glasses with a few ice cubes, and often a long spiral of lemon peel and a straw. Many consist of a straight liquor and soft-drink mixer.

Juleps are refreshing, long drinks ideally prepared with fresh mint. If you can not obtain fresh mint, add 2 teaspoons of mint liqueur or mint cordial to the glass instead. Juleps are served with a straw and spoon.

Lemon twist is the name given to a small piece of lemon peel squeezed over a finished cocktail to flavor it with the essential oils or zest of the fruit.

Long drink is the classic name for all mixed drinks that consist of more than 5 ounces of liquid.

Milk shakes are popular nonalcoholic drinks.

Neat is the term for drinking a liquor straight, which means without a mixer, water, or ice.

On the rocks means the drink is served with ice cubes.

Pick-me-ups come under the category of fancy drinks. They are usually heavily seasoned and are popular as hangover cures. One of the best known is the Bloody Mary.

Pousse-cafés consist of a combination of various spirits and liqueurs of differing colors and weights. The liqueurs are poured into small, narrow, tulip-shaped glasses, one after the other, building up layers of color.

Puffs are mixtures of milk and spirits shaken in the shaker and topped up with soda. They are served in a large rocks glass or a double old-fashioned glass with a straw.

Punches may be hot or cold. A hot punch belongs to the hot drinks group and is prepared in a heatproof glass; a cold punch is mixed in the glass and then served with plenty of ice and fruit.

Rickeys are long drinks made of limes, sugar syrup, alcohol, and soda water.

Sangarees are slightly sweet, long drinks, which are either served cold in a highball glass or warm in a punch glass. In addition to alcohol, they always contain sugar, hot or cold water, and a trace of grated nutmeg.

Scaffas consist of syrup and several types of alcohol, and are an Italian variation on pousse-cafés.

Short drinks generally consist of at least 23/4 ounces of liquid, but less than 5 ounces.

Shrubs are similar to bowls or punches. Traditionally a shrub included spirits, fortified wines, fruit, and sugar, but today they are just as likely to be nonalcoholic. The ingredients are combined in a punch bowl and left to infuse in the refrigerator for five days. Soda water is added just before the shrub is served in punch glasses.

Slings are long drinks similar to punch that are prepared warm or cold. The main ingredients are lemon or lime juice, grenadine or sugar syrup, as well as alcohol such as brandy, arrak, or gin.

Smashes are similar to juleps, but prepared in the shaker.

Sodas are refreshing, long drinks, which mostly consist of spirits such as gin, whiskey, or brandy, as well as vermouth or Cynar. To make,

Glossary

put 2 or 3 ice cubes in a glass, squeeze the peel of a lemon or orange over them, add the desired alcohol, and top up with cold soda water. Sours are prepared in a similar way to fizzes, but only get a shot of soda at most, rather than being topped up with it.

Squeeze the peel, in terms of drinks, means squeezing a piece of citrus peel over a drink so the essential oils, or zest, from the peel fall into the drink, giving it a particular flavor.

Swizzles are tropical long drinks. Fill a tall glass with crushed ice; add lime juice, sugar syrup, rum, and a dash of bitters and stir with a long stirrer (called a swizzle stick) until the glass frosts over and a little foam appears on top of the drink. Serve with a straw.

Toddies are close relatives of slings and like them may be served cold or warm. Cold toddies are served in a rocks glass and hot toddies in a heatproof punch glass. You do not need as much liquid to top them up as you do for slings. For this reason toddies are also more alcoholic. Tonics are particularly dry, refreshing, long drinks made by topping up a straight liquor over ice with tonic water. Gin and tonic is one such drink that is very popular.

Tropicanas are refreshing, sweet, long drinks, usually made from tropical fruit juice and rum. If they are prepared with coconut milk, they are also called coladas. The imaginative garnish is important. Twists are short drinks. They consist of fruit syrup or nectar, fruit juice, liqueur, and the spirit of your choice. All these ingredients are stirred in a mixing glass, then served over crushed ice in a champagne glass.

Zooms are sweet, very nutritious drinks that are filling enough to be a small snack. They consist of eggs, honey, cream, alcohol, and ice cubes, and are usually shaken. They should not be drunk by the elderly, anyone who is ill or pregnant, or by young children.

WHICH DRINK FOR WHICH OCCASION?

Below you will find suggestions for drinks suitable for specific occasions.

After meals

Brandy Zoom   62
Cherry Cream   380
Drugstore   310
Empire   160
Festival   266
French Connection I   59
Golden Nail   85
Green Dragon   67
Greenwich   300
Helvetia   381
Hoarfrost I   158
Red Russian   122
Ridley   324
Rum Alexander Cocktail   199
Stinger   56
Time Bomb   378
Toronto   81
Victoria   264
Zoom   56

Afternoons

Alexandra Cocktail   170
B and B   56
Brandy Eggnog   70
Brandy Flip   59
Fluffy F   268
Gospodin   116
Grace of Monaco   328
King Alfonso   271
Orange Flip   159
Top of the Hill   344
White Cap   134

Aperitifs

Adonis   344
Berlenga   353
Boston   296
Campari and Lemon   314
Dry Manhattan   74
Dry Martini   148
Ecstasy   56
Fernando II   378
Gordon's   354
Green Sea   116

Jack Rose   296
Lady Be Good   62
Little Devil   204
New Yorker   80
Robson   200
Shakerato   310
Sidecar   56
Spotlight   247
Star Cocktail   302
Sweet Martini   148
Temptation   368
Trocadero   344
Vodka Special   122

For a Caribbean theme party

Cachaça-based drinks   361-366
Rum-based drinks   197-238

For a children's party

Blackberry Milk   460
Canaan   457
Chocolate Shake   455
Golden Foam   408
Jamaica Fruit   408
Jonathan   440
Kenya   403
Maracas   404
Pear and Cinnamon Milk   454
Pineapple Cocktail   397
Queen of Strawberries   447
Steffi Graf Cocktail   415
Summer Delight   412
Vanilla-strawberry Shake   464

For a cocktail reception

Balla Balla   151
Bucks Fizz   240
Champenois   242
Corsair   389
Exterminator   155
Happy Birthday   163
Lady Di   156
Lila Crystal   244
Monte Carlo Imperial   177
Net Roller   155
Red Moon   59
Tarantella   118
Theater   154

Index

INDEX OF RECIPES BY TYPE OF DRINK

Index

Index

Index

Slings

Sours

Sparkling wine/champagne cocktails

Index

Specialty coffees (hot)

Drinks not listed in this index of recipes are fancy drinks which do not fall within any of the specified categories. These are mostly long drinks.

INDEX OF RECIPES BY STYLE

This index lists all cold drinks and bowls. Hot drinks are not listed here because they represent a category on their own.

Index

Index

Dry

Effervescent

Fruity

Index

Mild

Refreshing

Index

Index

Index

543

Sweet and sour

Index

ALPHABETICAL INDEX
(RECIPES AND INGREDIENTS)

Index

Index

Index

Index

Index

Index

Index

AWARD-WINNING DRINKS AND THEIR CREATORS